SpringerWienNewYork

European Community Studies Association of Austria
(ECSA Austria) Publication Series

Volume 11

Schriftenreihe der
Österreichischen Gesellschaft für Europaforschung
(ECSA Austria)

SpringerWienNewYork

Stefan Griller
Jacques Ziller (eds.)

The Lisbon Treaty

EU Constitutionalism without
a Constitutional Treaty?

SpringerWienNewYork

Univ.-Prof. Dr. Stefan Griller
Research Institute for European Affairs,
Vienna University of Economics and Business Administration, Austria

Univ.-Prof. Dr. Jacques Ziller
Dipartimento „Libero Lenti", Sezione di Studi Politico Giuridici
Università di Pavia, Italy

Financial support was given by *Bundesministerium für
Wissenschaft und Forschung,* Wien,
and the
European Commission, DG Education and Culture, Brussels

SpringerWienNewYork is a part of Springer Science + Business Media
springer.com

Typesetting: Camera ready by editors
Printing: Ferdinand Berger & Söhne Gesellschaft m.b.H., 3580 Horn, Austria

Printed on acid-free and chlorine-free bleached paper
SPIN: 12278053

Library of Congress Control Number: 2008933214

ISSN 1610-384X

ISBN 978-3-211-09428-0 SpringerWienNewYork

Giuliano Amato

Preface

Immediately after the rejection of the Constitutional Treaty in France and in the Netherlands, I was tempted not to comply with a contract according to which I was expected to write on the European Constitution within a very close deadline. "What is the sense of it now?" I tried to argue. "I cannot be obliged by a contract without an object".

I was wrong at that time and we would be equally wrong now, should we read the Irish vote on the Lisbon Treaty and the Lisbon Treaty itself as the dead end for European constitutionalism. Let us never forget that the text rejected in May 2005 was not the founding act of such constitutionalism. To the contrary, it was nothing more than a remarkable passage in a long history of constitutional developments that have been occurring since the early years of the European Community. All of us know that the Court of Justice spoke of a European constitutional order already in 1964, when the primacy of Community law was asserted in the areas conferred from the States to the European jurisdiction. We also know that in the previous year the Court had read in the Treaty the justiciable right of any European citizen to challenge her own national State for omitted or distorted compliance with European rules. Legal scholars were consequently bound to conclude that a Treaty giving ground not just to mutual obligations among the undersigning States but also to individual rights directly stemming from its clauses was a very peculiar Treaty, hybridised by constitutional genes.

The process of hybridisation continued in the following years: the direct election of the European Parliament, the consequent transformation of its role in the legislative process (not only its advisory role *vis-à-vis* the Council of Ministers but increasingly its legislative role in the co-decision procedure), the Commission as the Executive responsible towards the Parliament and subject to a vote of confidence, and finally the adoption of a Charter of Rights, based on the Treaty and on the common constitutional traditions of the Member States. These are just the main developments due to the long march of the constitutional genes throughout our common European architecture.

Despite such developments, the architecture has never become entirely constitutional. Not only have the *Herren* of the Treaty retained their power to ratify some of the main common decisions, but, most significantly, all the new missions to be pursued in common on the basis of the Maastricht Treaty were bestowed upon intergovernmental co-operation, and not upon the Community method. Since Maastricht, we have had two Europes running on parallel tracks, sometimes connected to each other, but basically separate. The distinction between European Union and European Community is the clearest (and most confusing) evidence of such ambivalence.

If it is true that *"nomina sunt substantia rerum"*, you would have expected the Constitution to do away with it. But it did not. To be sure, it did enhance the rate of constitutionalism by adding constitutional symbols and by several other far more substantive innovations (merging the Union and the Community was one of them). But it has also maintained most of the procedures of the intergovernmental Europe and the ratifying role of the States, when such elements were already embedded.

The limits of the innovations introduced by the Constitution disappointed the most fervent supporters of the "ever closer integration". Assuming, as I do assume, that the Lisbon Treaty will eventually be ratified, why then, should it be seen as the end of European constitutionalism? Its name is not Constitution and the clauses on the constitutional symbols have been deleted, but the bulk of the substantive changes enhancing the rate of constitutionalism remain. If one looks back at the long history of our incremental constitutional developments, no reason can be found to deny that this history would continue.

The impact of the downgrading of the Constitution might be another one. The fall of the name and of the symbols, accompanied by the protocols and declarations by which our Member States assert and re-assert their existing sovereign prerogatives, is the unequivocal expression of a mood not precisely in favour of bold steps towards further integration. It is not necessarily a generalized mood. It more likely reflects the price the majority (and Ireland was an active component of it) had to pay to a very rigid eurosceptic minority. In any case, the foreseeable impact is a slowing down in the implementation of the clauses of the Treaty which offer the Member States the opportunity to go beyond the existing levels of integration, such as crossing *passerelles* that lead from unanimity to majority voting.

However, such clauses are there, and, if and when the Treaty will be ratified they will be ready to be used whenever the Member States decide to take advantage of the opportunity they offer to them. Nobody can predict when, but the mood of the States depends on variables that at least in some cases may rapidly change and consequently isolate the most stubborn ones. What has happened in Poland after the electoral victory of the Civic Platform is very instructive. Furthermore, other clauses rescued by the Lisbon Treaty may be activated in spite of the reluctant Member States and may produce far-reaching effects in terms of constitutional innovation. Let me take two examples.

The first example refers to individual rights and the limits the Union meets in regulating them. The principle expressed by the Court of Justice before the proclamation of the Charter in 2000 was that the Union cannot violate the rights protected at the European level (nor can the Member States do it, when implementing Union law), but it has no power to *promote* them, the only exception being anti-discriminatory measures based on article 13 of the EC Treaty. The Charter does not intend to change that principle, as one of its final clauses explicitly states that the Charter is not aimed at widening the competencies of the Union, and on this assumption the Member States have accepted to give it legal force with the Lisbon Treaty.

But look at the Area of Freedom, Security and Justice. Look at new articles 62 and 63, which respectively provide for the ordinary legislative procedure (which means co-decision and majority voting) to set a uniform status of asylum for national of third countries, valid throughout the Union, and the rights of third-countries nationals residing legally in a Member State. Look also at new article 69A, para. 2, which offers a legal basis for a directive (to be adopted, again, by the ordinary legislative procedure) establishing minimum rules concerning the rights of individuals in criminal procedure and concerning the rights of victims of crime. These clauses confer to the Union a legislative competence that goes beyond the pre-existing obligation not to violate human rights when regulating sectors under its jurisdiction. The promotion of human rights is necessarily included in such competence. Nor is the notion of 'minimum rules' inconsistent with the promotion of rights. To the contrary, minimum rules have substance and meaning as long as they enhance the pre-existing standards in those Member States with the lowest ones. A gate to the future has thus been opened.

The second example goes to the heart of the European ambivalence, and to the future of the co-existing Europes (the communitarian and the intergovernmental ones). Despite the merging of the European Union and the European Community into one legal entity, most of the previously intergovernmental missions – as already noted – remain intergovernmental in terms of responsibilities and procedures. Only in the Area of Freedom, Security and Justice has the already ongoing process of transferring some competencies from the co-operative method to the communitarian one been continued. In other areas, the Constitution and subsequently the Lisbon Treaty have preserved the distinction between the two methods, but they have also built bridges between them, for the sake of better delivery. The most symbolic one is the double hatted High Representative, who will exercise the joint (but still separate) responsibilities of the Common Foreign and Security Policy of the Council and of the External Relations of the Commission, with the support, however, of a single diplomatic service (a very elaborate bridge…). All of us know that these bridges are not the same as the real ones, for they not only connect the two sides of the gap but may also reduce the distance between them. Will it happen in the foreseeable future? In the case of the double hatted High Representative, this development is entirely in the hands of the Member States and the declarations and protocols accompanying the Lisbon Treaty make it quite unlikely, at least at the moment. It is not so in the crucial area of the relationship between the Council and the Parliament, where the gap between the two Europes generates an increasingly unsustainable vacuum of democratic responsibility.

The Council of Ministers in its several formations, and still more so the European Council, have the formal task to define policies (*Richtlinien*, we would call them in German), both in the intergovernmental sectors and in the communitarian ones, which are European in nature. To whom do they respond for defining and pursuing such policies? National Governments have always argued that the Council is formed by national Ministers, or Prime Ministers, who respond to their national Parliaments and have nothing to do with the European Parliament. But national Parliaments politically and institutionally devote their attention to safeguarding their national interests at the European level, not to the European quality of the policies adopted at that level. There is a European Parliament here, but the European Parliament is limited to scrutinising the proposals and the activities of the Commission. If you look at this matter in constitutional terms, you conclude that in the Union we have not one, but two Executives, one with a capital E and another one with a small e, and the European Parliament has a political relationship with the latter, not with the former.

Now, if we carefully read the Lisbon Treaty, we find clauses designing the first arches for bridging this vacuum. In the areas where the open method of co-ordination applies, "the European Parliament will be kept fully informed". In the area of Foreign and Security policy, whatever the European Council and the double hatted High Representative do, they have to report to the European Parliament. In the area of police co-operation, regulations adopted by co-decision "shall lay down procedures for scrutiny of Europol's activities by the European Parliament, together with national Parliaments". Finally, the President of the European Council "shall present a report to the European Parliament after each of the meetings of the European Council".

That is not a fully fledged political responsibility of the Councils before the European Parliament, but the wall behind which national Governments have protected their intergovernmental activities is falling down. The long history of our national parliaments tells us how political responsibility may grow out of initially limited and narrow prerogatives. Whether this growth will occur in the case of the European Parliament is an open and intriguing question.

Along the same lines, a second and no less intriguing question is open. If the European Parliament should succeed in extending its political scrutiny upon both the existing Executives, for how long would those Executives remain separate? This question too finds a fragment of an answer in the Treaty. When the proposal was advanced in the Convention to merge the Presidency of the European Council and the Presidency of the Commission into a single figure, quite predictably it was rejected. But something of it has remained: while the two positions were initially defined as incompatible with each other, according to the final text and to the Lisbon Treaty, the President of the Council "shall not hold a national office". No other incompatibilities are set forth.

Nobody is so naïve as to expect future developments to depend on written clauses rather than on those who will use them. However, written clauses give such developments the necessary underpinnings, pointing in some directions and excluding other ones. The

Treaty of Lisbon does not shut the door to a future of enduring
European constitutionalism. To the contrary, it paves the way for it.
This volume is a valuable map illustrating the routes to be followed
by those who want European constitutionalism to continue. I
warmly recommend it to the Irish electors, who have always been
and remain sincere supporters of a better Europe.

Preface by the editors

It was during the German Council Presidency in 2007 that ECSA Austria decided to organise an international conference on the EU's constitutional developments irrespective of an eventual outcome of the ongoing political debates. When the draft treaty finally saw the light as "Lisbon Treaty", it was decided to join forces with the Law Department of the European University Institute and with its Robert Schuman-Centre for Advanced Studies in Florence.

Consequently, on April 11 and 12, 2008, when spring was supposed to be in full blow in Tuscany and the Irish referendum was still quite far ahead, a conference was held in Florence to discuss the changes of the European Union's constitutional framework that were to be expected, should the Lisbon Treaty enter into force. Special strain was laid on the envisaged reforms in the fields of institutions, fundamental rights, democracy, external relations, justice and home affairs, and economic and monetary policy. All this was addressed against the background of the general debate on the constitutional developments in Europe. The book at hand includes the revised version of the papers presented during these two days in Florence. In addition, *Giuliano Amato*, who had to cancel his participation in the conference due to the Italian elections on 13 April agreed to write a preface. We appreciate that very much!

During the printing process, the Irish referendum on June 12, 2008, produced a negative result. Whatever the final consequences of this rejection will be in a more or less distant future, we decided to go ahead with publishing this book without delay: First, it is still unclear whether or not the Lisbon Treaty, or a revised version of it, eventually might enter into force, and second (and perhaps more important, at least from an academic point of view) this uncertainty does not reduntantise a thorough debate of this stage of the constitutional project which has been occupying the political and also the academic agenda in Europe for almost a decade, first in the shape of the Treaty establishing a Constitutional Treaty for Europe, and later in the version of the Lisbon Treaty. Only *Giuliano Amato*'s preface and *Jacques Ziller*'s contribution on the process of ratification were modified in order to take these most recent developments into account.

We would like to thank all supporters of the conference and the publication of this book: In financial terms, these are in the first line the European Commission, Directorate General for Education and Culture, and the Austrian Federal Ministry for Science and Research. Without their support, it would have been impossible even to think of a reunion like that in Florence or to produce this book. Special thanks go the hosts of the conference in Florence, the Law Department of the European University Institute and the Robert Schuman Centre for Advanced Studies, RSCAS. The RSCAS's conference centre provided for a perfect organisation as well as an inspiring atmosphere, both of which contributed largely to the outcome of the meeting, and thereby to the quality of the book at hand.

Vienna and Pavia, August 2008

Stefan Griller   Jacques Ziller

Table of Contents

Abbreviations

ACAS: Advisory, Conciliation and Arbitration Service
ACP: African, Caribbean and Pacific Countries
ADB: African Development Bank
AETR: *Accord relativ au travail des équipages des véhicules effectuant des transports internationaux effectuant par route* (European Agreement concerning the Work of Crews of Vehicles Engaged in International Road Transport)
AFSJ: Area of Freedom, Security and Justice
Art.: Article
AT: Accession Treaty

BEPG: Broad Economic Policy Guidelines
BIS: Bank of International Settlements

CCP: Common Commercial Policy
cf.: confer
CFI: Court of First Instance (of the European Court of Justice)
CFSP: Common Foreign and Security Policy
CHR: Charter of Human Rights
Coreper: Committee of Permanent Representatives
CSDP: Common Security and Defence Policy
CT: Constitutional Treaty

DG: Director General
DGE: Council of the EU, Directorate-General E – External Economic Relations, Politico-Military Affairs
DTC: *Declaración de Tribunal Constitucional* (Declaration of the Spanish Constitutional Court)
DWP: Department of Work and Pensions

e.g.: *exempli gratia*
EBRD: European Bank for Reconstruction and Development
EC: European Community/ies
ECB: European Central Bank
ECHO: European Commission Humanitarian Aid department
ECHR: European Convention for the Protection of Human Rights and Fundamental Freedoms; European Court of Human Rights

ECJ: European Court of Justice
ECR: European Court Report
ECSC: European Coal and Steal Community
ed(s).: Editor(s)
EEA: European Economic Area
EEAS: European External Action Service
EEC: European Economic Community
EFTA: European Free Trade Area
EIB: European Investment Bank
EMS: European Monetary System
EMU: Economic and Monetary Union
EP: European Parliament
ESCB: European System of Central Banks
esp.: especially
et al.: *et alii*
et seq.: *et sequentis*
EU: European Union
EUI: European University Institute, Florence

FAC: Foreign Affairs Council
FAO: Food and Agriculture Organization of the United Nations
FDI: Foreign Direct Investment
fn: Footnote
FOC: Flag of Convenience
FSU: Finnish Seaman's Union

GAC: General Affairs Council
GAERC: General Affairs and External Relations Council
GATS: General Agreement on Trade in Services
GATT: General Agreement on Tariffs and Trade
GMO: Genetically Modified Organism

HL: House of Lords

i.e.: *id est*
Ibid: *Ibidem*
IBRD: International Bank for Reconstruction and Development
IGC: Intergorvernmental Conference
IIA: Interinstitutional Agreement
ILO: International Labour Organization
IMF: International Monetary Fund

ITF: International Transport Workers' Federation

JHA: Justice and Home Affairs

litt.: *littera*
LT: Lisbon Treaty

MEP: Member of the European Parliament
MS: Member State(s)

NAFTA: North American Free Trade Agreement
NATO: North Atlantic Treaty Organisation
NCB(s): National Central Bank(s)
NGO: Non Governmental Organisation
No: Number

OECD: Organisation for Economic Co-operation and Development
OJ: Official Journal of the European Union
OLAF: *Office Européen de lutte anti-fraude* (European Antifraud
    Office)
OMC: Open Method of Co-ordination
OSCE: Organization for Security and Co-operation in Europe

para: Paragraph
PRAC: *Procédure de réglementation avec contrôle* (regulatory
    procedure with scrutiny) (according to Decision 2006/512/EC)
PSC: Political and Security Committee

QMV: Qualified Majority Voting

REACH: European Community Regulation on chemicals and their
    safe use (EC 1907/2006)
RELEX: External Relations

SAR: Special Administrative Region (of Hong Kong)
SGP: Stability- and Growth-Pact

TEAEC: Treaty establishing the European Atomic Energy
    Community
TEC: Treaty establishing the European Community

TEU: Treaty on European Union (before the amendments by the
    Lisbon-Treaty)
TEU-L: Treaty on European Union as amended by the Lisbon
    Treaty
TFEU: Treaty on the Functioning of the European Union
TRIMS: Trade-Related Investment Measures
TRIPS: Trade Related Aspects of Intellectual Property Rights
TULR(C)A: Trade Union Labour Relations (Consolidation) Act

UK: United Kingdom of Great Britain and Northern Ireland
UN: United Nations Organization
UNESCO: United Nations Educational, Scientific and Cultural
    Organization
UPOV: *Union internationale pour la protection des obtentions
    végétales* (International Union for the Protection of New
    Varieties of Plants)
US(A): United States of America

Vol.: Volume

WHO: World Health Organization
WTO: World Trade Organization

José Maria Beneyto

From Nice to the Constitutional Treaty: Eight Theses on the (Future) Constitutionalisation of Europe

I. A Constitutional Moment

Who now remembers Europe's Constitutional Treaty? There was however a relatively easy road from Nice to the Laeken Declaration and then to the work of the Convention and the drafting of the first document in the history of European integration risking the "Constitution" banner on its front page, even if it finally had to be modestly renamed as a "Treaty establishing a Constitution for Europe". Compared to the draft Constitution prepared by the European Parliament in the follow-up to the Maastricht Treaty, whose promoters were quickly branded as old fashioned federalists, the momentum surrounding the elaboration of the Constitutional Treaty was a happy one. The discussion about a Constitution for Europe and the debate on the future of Europe became a significant political issue and it was even made – by *Jürgen Habermas*, particularly – intellectually fashionable. It seemed suddenly as if the destiny of the European continent – the big question marks about Europe's identity, its specific response to the challenges posed by globalisation, the defence of its values and the promotion of its ideas of citizenship and mixed economies – had to be necessarily linked to the fate of the final results of the Convention.

There was indeed a 'Constitutional Moment'.[1] Although *Valéry Giscard d'Estaing*, the president of the Convention itself, had dubbed it the European Philadelphia, the Convention certainly lacked some essential elements in order for it to be officially considered a constitutional convention; above all, the lack of enthusiasm of some member states' Governments with the process and, as time would demonstrate, also a perceived strangeness by European citizens. Nevertheless, with the hindsight of later years, this constitutional moment signals a certain higher level of constitutional audacity, in a sense a departure from the well-trodden paths of Community history. Issues such as human rights, European values, the "European social model", the characteristic interaction of the European construct between unity and diversity in its relations with member states, the question of the democratic deficit, the role of Europe in the world, or the "*telos*" ("*finalité*") of the Union, were brought for the first time openly to the fore, together with more technical matters – a renewed institutional structure, a clarification of the division of competences between Brussels and the national

---

[1]   *Weiler* (2002).

capitals, the inclusion of the Charter of Fundamental Rights with binding validity, the recognition of a single legal personality for the Union and the dismantling of the 'pillars' approach, the comprehensive extension of the Community method to justice and home affairs, the establishment of a larger institutional capacity in foreign policy and defence, etc. – all topics which had been at the heart of the Laeken Declaration.

The idea of a Constitution regained its progressive-integrationist connotation. There was no final result as to which should be the final picture of the integration process – rather, the process of integration / constitutionalisation itself was redefined as the main goal of European unity – but the emphasis in the two Preambles (to the Constitutional Treaty itself and to the Second Part, containing the Charter of Fundamental Rights), as well as in the introductory articles of the text, on civic-republican values, and on the moralistic self-elevation of the Union to an organisation promoting human rights, the rule of law and democratisation in the world, reaffirmed to what extent enlargement had helped in the last fifteen years to shape the new role of the European Union in terms of a vast project for expanding democracy, respect for fundamental rights and economic stability towards the outer concentric circles of an ever increasing number of countries.

Thus, the significant further step in the dynamic of constitutionalisation of the Union which the Constitutional Treaty implied appeared explicitly tied up with what sometimes has been called "Europeanisation", or in other words, the extension of the positive results of European integration towards the Balkans, the former Soviet republics and the South Mediterranean countries, as well as to other parts of the world thanks to the complex array of external agreements put in place.

The second consequence of the turn to constitutionalism was a strengthened foundation of the legitimacy of the Union upon two clearly defined elements, its citizens and its member states, a notion of 'double legitimacy' which has not however been retained by the Lisbon Treaty. Together with the possibility of participation in the legislative process granted to national parliaments through the early warning mechanism and the introduction of a somewhat limited citizens' initiative to advance legislative proposals, the recognition of the primacy of European law over the national legal orders and the constitutionalisation of the symbols (flag, anthem, Europe Day) would undoubtedly have reinforced European citizenship and would have helped to reduce the perceived democratic shortcomings of the Union.

The fact that the symbols and the formal enshrining of primacy were among the trade-offs demanded by a not-insignificant number of member states' Governments in exchange for the acceptance of the Reform Treaty certainly has to be seen as a minus in the overall evaluation of the final outcome of the process initially launched through the famous *Joschka Fischer*'s speech at Humboldt University in Berlin on the occasion of the commemoration of the fiftieth anniversary of the *Schuman* Declaration in the year 2000.

However, if an assessment of the nearly ten years of constitutional debate is required, the evidence that much of what had been achieved by the Convention remains in the final Lisbon Treaty (once it is ratified by all member states) clearly demonstrates that the constitutional moment was certainly productive. The enforcement of the Charter of Fundamental Rights, the recognition of the single legal personality of the Union, with the parallel overcoming of the different treaties' and pillars' structure, and – last but by no means least – the establishment of the European Council as an institution of the Union, are to be considered as among the most relevant achievements of the process.

Finally, once the constitutional fatigue prompted by the intricate details of the elaboration and adoption of the new Treaty has been overcome, quite a number of the new issues, initiatives and proposals which were discussed in the context of the Convention and the subsequent IGCs – and which were not included in the final Lisbon text – will most likely reappear in the future. And there may well come a time in which one of the most salient obstacles to a successful constitutionalisation of the European Union, namely the reluctance to take the step towards majority voting in the ratification of any Treaty reform, is finally superseded.

II. The reshuffling of the institutional balance of power

Compared to the Nice Treaty, the Constitutional Treaty implied a significant shift in the functional division of powers of the Union.

At the centre of the renewed institutional structure emerged the European Council, with its stable presidency and robust political and legal powers. The European Council became another institution of the Union, whose competences are aimed at its strategic leadership and external representation. Consequently, no legislative function was attributed to it. However, for the first time, the European

Council was able, according to the provisions of the Constitutional Treaty (and now also of the Lisbon Treaty), to adopt decisions which, when taking legal effect against third persons, may be controlled by the Court of Justice. Together with the already existing possibility of legal scrutiny by the Court of the procedural rules of the European Council, the formalisation of the workings and the decision-making of this formerly exclusively political body marks significant progress towards constitutionalisation and indicates that the Heads of Government attach an increasing importance to assuring control over the decisional process of the Union.

The European Council appears now at the apex of the institutional hierarchy, taking decisions by qualified majority voting on the appointment of its own President and the Ministry of Foreign Affairs, on the establishment of the number and competences of the different Council formations, on the appointment of the President of the Commission before ratification by the European Parliament, and on the decision on the number of members of the Commission and the rotation system to be followed for their nomination after 2014.

The formal recognition of the central role of the European Council in the institutional architecture of the Union is reinforced by its 'supra-constitutional' control of member states through the procedure on severe violation of common values (Article I-59 in the Constitutional Treaty, again Article 7 in the Lisbon Treaty). Although neither the Constitutional Treaty nor the Lisbon Treaty introduced new changes in a provision which had been initially inserted in the EU Treaty in Maastricht, and later reviewed – as a consequence of the experience gained through the Austrian case – in Amsterdam, the reinforced competences of the European Council, accompanied by its watchdog function on the orthodox application of 'the European values' by member states, shows the transformation of the European Council from a purely political and diplomatic body, whose original inspiration was to serve as a meeting opportunity for the Heads of Government and as a source of overall strategic impulse, to a crucial decision-making body, whose political responsibility *vis-à-vis* the citizens of the Union and the other institutions – formally restricted to a report by its President to the European Parliament at the conclusion of his / her mandate – will certainly require further development in the future.

Another relevant institutional novelty of the Constitutional Treaty was the creation of a President (or Chair) of the European Council for a period of two and a half years, who may be re-appointed for another similar period, replacing the system of rotating pre-sidencies every six months, which is generally perceived as noto-riously inefficient.

The main function of the President will be to drive forward the work of the European Council, ensuring better preparation and con-tinuity, and to favour cohesion and consensus among its members, but the President will also provide the external representation of the Union in foreign affairs and defence.

The figure of the President was already conceived in the Con-stitutional Treaty as inherently ambiguous. The door was left open for either an activist President with real powers – who in such case will have to cope with complex interaction with the other members of the European Council (acting Heads of Government, unlike him or her) as well as with the High Representative and the President of the Commission – or, alternatively, for a 'Chair' with exclusively formal capacities.

As to the institutional triangle formed by the Council of Minis-ters, the European Commission and the European Parliament, the establishment of qualified majority voting within the Council as the general rule and of the co-decision procedure between Parliament and Council as the ordinary legislative procedure, together with the substantial expansion of the policy areas subject to co-decision and qualified majority voting, meant a substantial improvement in terms of more efficiency and transparency of EU legislation.

The strengthening of participation by the Parliament in the legislative procedure was accompanied by a useful clarification of the internal hierarchy of norms, whereby the Commission saw its role as the main executive body of the Union reinforced.

The Constitutional Treaty also foresaw the emergence of two new players, whose efficiency within the implicit inter-institutional arrangements governing the Union will however need to be tested in the not too distant future.

The first innovation regards the flamboyant figure of a Minis-ter for Foreign Affairs (renamed, in the Lisbon Treaty, the High Re-presentative of the Union for Foreign Affairs and Security Policy), who, bestowed with a rather ambivalent 'double hat' function in his / her capacity as both Vice-President of the Commission and per-manent President of the Foreign Affairs Council, raises a number of questions as to the proper institutional setting and the ultimate ef-fects of the presence of this figure within two institutions whose tra-ditional nature relates, respectively, to an intergovernmental origin in the case of the Council, and to the most characteristic representation of the supranational interest in the case of the Commission.

Assisted by the newly created Diplomatic Service of the Union and able therefore to determine the strategic goals of the Union in foreign policy (and eventually also in the security and defence areas), should the High Representative in addition be able to employ the human, technical and financial resources of the Commission in trade, commercial policy and humanitarian aid and development, in real life this complex figure may well face significant difficulties in day-to-day interaction, not only with the other members of the Commission (taking into account, in particular, the external dimensions of most Community policies) and its President, but also with the President of the European Council (responsible of the external representation of the Union "without prejudice to the competences of the High Representative", according to Article I-22 of the Constitutional Treaty, now Article 15 of the Lisbon Treaty), as well as with the individual Foreign Affairs Ministers of the member states.

The second innovation regards the new method of participation of national parliaments in the legislative process through the 'early warning' system, which, according to the language of the Constitutional Treaty, allowed two thirds of national legislatures to oppose a legislative proposal of the Commission based on subsidiarity objections. Although the negative vote of these national legislatures will not prevent the Commission from going ahead with the proposal, the system is based on the assumption that the political pressure exercised by a number of national parliaments over the Commission in a particular case would compel it to follow the position expressed by them. National legislatures were also granted the possibility, in case of conflict, of recourse to the European Court of Justice.

The politically most sensitive issue and the one which also obtained the widest media attention was undoubtedly the new voting system within the Council of Ministers. Here, whereas the Convention had proposed a relatively simple double majority mechanism, based on the vote of 50% of member states and 60% of the aggregated population, thus significantly departing from the three-tier system which had been negotiated with great difficulty in Nice, the Constitutional Treaty finally adopted a scheme, which was supposed to enter into force in 2009, that foresaw a majority of 55% of the member states, provided theses countries represented 65% of the total EU population.

The Constitutional Treaty also introduced a number of voting safeguards, particularly for those sensitive areas (such as foreign and security policy or some aspects of economic policy) where the legislative proposal does not originate at the initiative of the Commission.

The new voting provisions devised by the Convention and later modified by the IGC effectively signalled one of the most important changes in relation to Nice and to the philosophy that traditionally lay behind the Council voting system, which since the Treaty of Rome had relied heavily on specific features of the member states, the size of the population being just one important element among others for determining the number of votes of each member state in the Council of Ministers. After the Convention, more weight was given to the population, based on the assumption that stronger proportionality in relation to the population also meant more democracy, thus somewhat diffusing the state-based nature of the Council.

Similarly important was the decision to streamline the working of the Council formations, establishing a clear distinction between the General Affairs Council and the Foreign Affairs Council (which should be presided over by the Minister for Foreign Affairs) and creating for the other Council formations a system of rotation according to which teams of three member states would assume the presidency of the various Council configurations for periods of eighteen months.

The Constitutional Treaty also introduced into the Treaty the distinction between legislative and executive functions of the Council, which had been decided by the Heads of Government at the meeting of the European Council in Seville, and it confirmed that meetings in which the Council deliberates and votes on legislative proposals would be open to the public. Somewhat surprisingly, these innovations of the Constitutional Treaty, aimed at improving the functioning of the Council, were not elevated to the level of primary law by the Lisbon Treaty.

As to the Court of Justice, neither the Convention nor later the IGCs were willing to discuss the larger reforms that a number of qualified observers and the Court itself had suggested were required. Thanks to the Constitutional Treaty, a clear reduction of the policy areas which continue to fall outside of the jurisdiction of the Court (now basically limited to foreign affairs and defence) was attained, and the jurisdiction of the Court for the delimitation of competences and fundamental rights cases was confirmed. But the annulment action for individuals before the Court, although made slightly more flexible, was not extended, and other very relevant issues, such as the internal organisation of the Court, formed now by 27 judges, or the link with national courts, were not substantiated.

Significantly enough, the Commission did not attract much attention during the Convention. As will be recalled, the Commission made some attempts to stage a parallel scenario (the "Penelope" initiative), openly hinting at its uneasiness with the constitutional text as it was being negotiated by the different parties.

In the end, the Constitutional Treaty did include some minor modifications concerning the European Commission. Apart from the reduction of the size of its members (which was supposed to be put in place after 2009), the Treaty provided a clarification concerning the nomination of the President of the Commission, for which formal consideration must now be made of the results of the elections to the European Parliament. More powers were also given to the President, allowing him or her to dismiss individual Commissioners and to nominate Vice-Presidents without the prior acceptance of the Commission's *Collège*.

There remain few doubts that after the Constitutional Treaty (and also the Lisbon Treaty), simplification – one of the main objectives of the Laeken Declaration – has now become a misnomer.

In fact, the renewed institutional design leaves open quite a number of different options as to its future. It has still to be proven that the European Council will be able to fulfil the strategic and political functions assigned to it, particularly considering the likely difficulties in the day-to-day relations among the President of the European Council, the High Representative and the President of the Commission – not to forget the interactions with their national counterparts, the Heads of Government and, in some cases, also the national Ministers, especially the Foreign Affairs Ministers.

The management of the dualist nature of the High Representative will require a high degree of diplomatic and political acumen, while its ambivalent characteristics also raise a number of questions as to the future development of the EU system. Taking into consideration a possible – conceivably quite distant – convergence in the future of the functions of the two Presidents (of the Commission and of the European Council), the consequence of a progressive shifting of the executive functions that are today in the hands of the Commission in the direction of the European Council may well be a model implicit in the Constitutional Treaty and for which the complex figure of the High Representative (if successful) might serve as a precursor.

Does this necessarily mean that among the consequences of the institutional architecture delineated by the Constitutional Treaty a reinforcement of the tendency towards stronger intergovernmental features of the EU is unavoidable?

Nothing is actually yet written in stone. The strengthening of the position of the European Council may actually imply a para-doxical (dialectical) result: it will most likely have a downgrading effect on the current position of the Commission, but it will also probably advance a certain 'federalisation' of the European Council (and of its members, the Heads of the national Governments).

In theory, the system could evolve in the direction of more convergence between the supranational and the intergovernmental institutions of the Union, or it could definitively degrade the Com-mission to a role of qualified Secretariat of the Council / European Council. However, it is likely that, as so often in previous periods in the history of European integration, the EU may not develop along unidirectional lines (either intergovernmental or supranational), but rather by creating its own specific model whereby sovereign states are further 'integrated' while at the same time they reassert them-selves as crucial actors of the integration process.

Within this latter scenario, the experiment with the ambiva-lence of the High Representative may well play a quite interesting anticipatory role, in the same way as the programme of decentral-isation of competition policy in favour of the national antitrust au-thorities in recent years – to take just one example from a very dif-ferent area, but with parallel results – has proven to be the best way to bind national administrations with a dense network of daily inte-gration under the reinforced authority of the Commission.

III. The lack of a global strategy in Foreign Affairs and Security, if not resolved, may impair the new, important institutional innovations introduced in this area, whose efficiency remains to be tested

The time of the Convention coincided with one of the most difficult crises in transatlantic relations since the end of World War II. The aftermath of the Iraq conundrum has however strengthened the need for the US to act together with the Europeans. *Vis-à-vis* other coun-tries, the EU provides international legitimacy, but the moralistic aspirations of the Union are not matched by its strategic prowess and operational capacities, which are well below the expectations that the Union has raised and the responsibilities in the international arena that it is expected to effectively assume.

As an essential component of the principles and common objectives of the EU, the Constitutional Treaty emphasised the commitment of the Union to international norms, to the development of International Law, and in particular to the respect of the principles enunciated in the Charter of the UN (Arts. I-3 and I-8 of the Constitutional Treaty, now Art. 3.5 of the Lisbon Treaty. There was also a redefinition of the goals of the Union from the perspective of the objectives pursued by the UN and which today form a specific body of UN doctrine (and parlance): peace, security, sustainable development, mutual respect among peoples, just and free commerce, the eradication of poverty, and protection of human rights (especially the rights of children).

Although the Lisbon Treaty reduced the rhetorical grandeur which had prevailed among the members of the Convention at the time of drafting these introductory articles, and labelled the international commitments of the Union as "a contribution" – rather than trying to overburden the Union with the role of protagonist in the protection and promotion of international law – there persists an identifiable imbalance between the ambitious objectives set for the Union, the new institutional arrangements in Foreign Affairs and Security, and the absence of clear strategic positions which would be effectively followed by all member states in their foreign relations.

It is clear, however, that the Constitutional Treaty was able to advance quite substantially in the clarification and precision of the legal framework, particularly in the area of defence. Besides the above-mentioned institutional innovations of the Diplomatic Service and the High Representative, as well as the important achievement of a single legal personality for the Union, the Constitutional Treaty foresaw a category of acts of the Council itself and of the European Council in this area with the name of "decisions", which replaced the old typology of common strategies, common positions, joint actions and decisions. There was also the formalisation within the Treaty of the Neighbourhood Policy as a new policy instrument, which was granted its own legal basis, in parallel to the other existing categories of external agreements, and the Union also obtained a specific competence in humanitarian aid. However, as already mentioned, no progress was made as to submission of the decisions (which are not legislative acts) adopted in foreign affairs and security to the scrutiny of the Court of Justice.

The most significant changes as compared to the Nice Treaty were introduced in the defence area. The Constitutional Treaty broadened the scope of the – so far mostly successful, but still very limited – Petersberg missions, refining its goals and recourse to civil and military resources, and including the fight against international terrorism as an overall objective of these missions. The final objective of a "common defence" as the end result of an incremental common policy in security and defence, which should then be decided unanimously by the European Council, was for the first time legally enshrined in the Treaty.

The Convention was particularly concerned with laying the foundations for extending the civil and military operational capacities offered by member states to the Union. Following the broader consensus attained within the group of Convention members participating in the deliberations on the Defence chapter, the Constitutional Treaty expressed the formal commitment of the member states to subsequently improve the military capacities of the Union. As the main instrument for the setting of the required capacities, to promote harmonisation of industrial defence policies, propose multilateral projects and favour technological research, the former protocol on the European Defence Agency was included in the Treaty and the functions of this body were more precisely defined.

Another relevant innovation of the Convention was the creation of a specific form of enhanced co-operation among a limited number of member states in defence, which received the name of "permanent structured co-operation", basically open to all other member states, subject to the fulfilment of certain conditions. Those member states willing to subscribe to more binding commitments with respect to further military capacities for specific missions were supposed to establish among themselves a permanent structured co-operation.

The Treaty also formalised the solidarity clause – adopted by the Council in the aftermath of the Madrid and London terrorist attacks – whereby member states obliged themselves to supply assistance and help to any other member state suffering armed aggression in its territory, and this "in conformity with Article 51 of the UN Charter", as well as with other security obligations of member states, including NATO.

The future will show whether the new institutional mechanisms of the Constitutional Treaty, together with the instruments laid down for enhancing the military and civil operational capacity of the Union, will be sufficient to underpin the ambition of the Union to act as an efficient and responsible global player. As the Convention made clear, posited in an international scenario in which China, India, Russia, Brazil and other large countries are assertively seeking a new global assignment of functions world-wide, the capacity of the Union to act coherently and purposefully on the international stage will be crucial for the development of European constitutionalism in the years to come.

IV. If the direct consequence of the terrorist attacks in New York, Madrid and London was a substantial communitarisation of matters relating to the Area of Freedom, Security and Justice, this may well have been achieved to the detriment of the further development of other policy areas

Even if the *securitization* of the policy debate was not as acute in Europe as it was in the US, it nevertheless left behind a clear imprint on the Constitutional Treaty, to the prejudice of the two other dimensions – freedom and justice. However, the perceived demand for security on the part of European citizens made it possible for all the remnants from Nice within the third pillar to be brought under the umbrella of the Community method.

The Area of Freedom, Security and Justice received more clearly defined objectives, it was recognised as a space of shared competence between member states and the Union institutions, and it was subjected to the Court's jurisdiction. The policies concerning border controls, asylum and immigration were given more precise lines of action; thus, border controls were defined as aiming at the establishment of an integrated system for management of the external borders of the Union, the goal of a common European asylum system was neatly outlined, and the basic tenets of a common immigration policy were determined. While the principle of burden-sharing among member states for the reception of refugees and displaced persons in the case of massive population fluxes was tentatively accepted as part of the common asylum policy, there was however no recognition of a Union competence in relation to national immigration quotas. Nor was any provision included which would permit the harmonisation of national legislation in this area.

As regards judicial co-operation in civil matters, the Constitutional Treaty did not introduce significant innovations when compared to Nice. It made explicit the possibility of adopting measures for the approximation of national legislation and it slightly expanded the list of – *numerus apertus* – matters which may be the object of the Union competence in this field.

In the areas of judicial and police co-operation in criminal matters, the main achievement of the Constitutional Treaty was to generalise the community method. This effectively means that the Council will now decide – with certain limitations – by qualified majority voting (including such relevant subjects as the harmonisation of criminal procedures and the approximation of national legislation on crimes), the Parliament will be fully involved through the ordinary legislative procedure (co-decision), and the right to propose legislation goes back to the Commission, limiting the possibility of member states initiating legislation to a joint proposal by a minimum of a quarter of member states (currently, seven countries). Qualified majority voting was also foreseen for the development of Eurojust and Europol, while unanimity continues to be the rule for the decision to establish a European Prosecutor. Nor did the Convention make any progress in the much discussed alleged need for adopting a European Civil Code, or at least a European Civil Code on Contracts.[2]

The redirection of nearly all of the old justice and home affairs pillar within the first pillar was a remarkable constitutional achievement of the Convention and the Constitutional Treaty, which has also been confirmed by the Lisbon Treaty. It remains to be seen whether the implementation of the new provisions in this field may have spill-over effects on other areas, such as Foreign Affairs and Security, taking into account the lesser degree of division between external and internal security that the fight against terrorism has brought with it.

---

[2]   A detailed comparison between the Constitutional Treaty and the Nice Treaty is provided by the published research conducted by the Instituto de Estudios Europeos, Universidad CEU San Pablo and directed by *Méndez de Vigo* (2007).

V. The Convention debates showed quite remarkable differences among member states with regard to their views on economic governance and on the social dimension of Union policies, making these two areas in which no significant innovation was introduced in the Constitutional Treaty

The Convention work took place in a period of relative stable economic and financial conditions. However the lack of consensus of member states on the level of economic co-ordination and on progress towards economic union, and particularly the stark differences in perspectives on social policy, confirms these two policy areas as especially resistant to further constitutionalisation.

To be sure, there has so far been only very limited discussion on what should be the appropriate level of constitutionalisation of monetary and economic union. The provisions within national constitutions dealing with economic and monetary governance are usually quite sparse. However, given the multileveled constitutional structure of the Union, there are sufficient arguments to support the need for a formalisation at the constitutional level of the basic norms regulating the economic-monetary architecture of the Union.

No proposal representing any significant change in the co-ordination of economic policies and on the internal market emerged from the discussions within the Convention. The Constitutional Treaty (and also the Lisbon Treaty) saw some enhancement of the Commission's role in the decision-making leading to the adoption of broad economic policy guidelines and on the procedure on excessive deficits. There was also a general Declaration on the Stability and Growth Pact attached to the Treaty. But some of the most obvious issues, such as the confusion surrounding the external representation of the Economic and Monetary Union (with competences now divided between the Commission, the Council and the European Central Bank) were not tackled at all. Further, no formalisation or further development of the Eurogroup, which would be consistent with the real situation where the most important decisions concerning Economic and Monetary Union are being taken within this informal body, was put forward.

Many other issues, which have regularly been targeted as the main objectives for a more ambitious reform of EMU, were also not dealt with by the Convention. This applies particularly to the discussion on the establishment of EU sector regulators, in such areas as finance, telecommunications, energy or even competition. Nor did the Convention address one of the foremost menaces to the consolidation of the internal market, namely the different degrees of market liberalisation within member states and the (sometimes aggressive) responses given by national governments to individual attempts to advance transnational corporate integration.

The Convention and the Constitutional Treaty were equally silent regarding the economic and financial consequences of globalisation for the Economic and Monetary Union, and particularly regarding the effects of the emergence of new economic powers and their challenge to the international economic-monetary regime created after World War II. There was no foresight at all in laying down a regulatory framework at the EU level for such new phenomena, for instance, as the massive investments coming from sovereign funds and their repercussions on the free trade principles of the internal market.

If these topics were consciously neglected, others which would have also required the attention of the Convention, like the much debated question of the quality of legislation, were simply not on the agenda. The Constitutional Treaty did however score quite highly on competition policy, compared to the somewhat despairing results of the Lisbon Treaty.

VI. The Constitutional Treaty did not take a position on the issue of increased complexity and difficulties of internal management of the European Union, but it removed important obstacles to the functioning of enhanced co-operation

The general provisions of the Constitutional Treaty on enhanced co-operation were basically equivalent to the Nice provisions. The only significant change was the amendment of the minimum number of participating member states, which was modified from eight to one third.

Another significant innovation was the extension of enhanced co-operation to the Common Foreign and Security Policy, and no longer only for the implementation of a joint action or a common position.

Establishing enhanced co-operation in foreign affairs and security requires as a pre-condition a unanimous decision by the Council. However, member states participating in a specific enhanced co-operation may decide to act within the framework of the enhanced co-operation based on qualified majority voting, although this provision is not applicable to defence or military matters.

Again, enhanced co-operation poses a significant challenge to the further constitutionalisation of the Union. This is particularly so if the areas of development of closer co-operation among member states are, as may be expected: defence where as previously stated specific provisions for "permanent structured co-operation" were foreseen in the Constitutional Treaty; and the creation of a core of countries in relation to the Common Foreign Policy and Security.

VII. The Constitutional Treaty failed to address new concerns of citizens and to legislate for the future in increasingly relevant areas

It is likely that for some segments of the EU population the discussions of the Convention taking place in the European Parliament in Brussels and the successive texts of the Constitutional and the Lisbon Treaties remained quite distant and abstruse. A certain constitutional exhaustion may also have been perceived by the time of the second IGC and the difficulties for member state Governments to ratify the constitutional document. A more visible role for Europe in the global agenda may also have emerged more clearly from the debates of the Convention. The Lisbon Treaty attempted to cope with these shortcomings by extending Union competence to new policies, such as climate change, and by articulating more precise objectives in energy policy and energy supply. However, there was no advancement in other fields, also of explicit interest to citizens, such as social policy or the Neighbourhood Policy, particularly in the latter's relation to the open question of the limits of Europe.

VIII. The Constitutional Treaty did achieve significant improvements in the democratisation of the Union, but it did not substantially overcome the perceived lack of closeness to citizens

Does the final result of the attempted constitutionalisation amount to more transparency and efficiency, more simplification and flexibility, more closeness of the European project to European citizens? In other words, at the end of nearly ten years of European constitutionalism, have the initial goals of the Laeken Declaration been achieved?

The answers to these questions will certainly differ. Probably the most positive responses will relate to the advancement of more efficient – and possibly also more flexible – institutional arrangements. Much has been achieved in terms of setting the stage for a streamlining of the activities of the Union and the functioning of its bodies. However, as previously mentioned, this alleged efficiency remains to be proven, and the final balance of the other objectives pursued – simplification and a closer proximity to citizens – seems to have obtained a less positive score.

What should be said about further democratisation? The new instruments – the popular legislative initiative, participation of national parliaments through the early warning mechanism, new provisions on subsidiarity with a better access of the regions to the Court, and new provisions concerning democracy in the Union – have to be tested, but they signal a clear attempt to promote democratic principles. Some of them, like the popular legislative initiative, have been very carefully (maybe too carefully) limited. Other positive means of fostering a closer proximity to citizens – such as symbols – were adopted by the Constitutional Treaty, but they fell by the wayside as pre-conditions for the *de-constitutionalisation* of the Lisbon Treaty.

The non-modification of the ratification and the revision method proved in the end to be one of the most significant weaknesses of the Constitutional Treaty. What has been retained is the simplified revision procedure of the two *'passerelle'* or bridging clauses, for the transition under certain conditions to qualified majority voting and for the transition to the ordinary legislative procedure, which can only metaphorically be referred to as 'revision' procedures.

As to ratification, a public debate on the Constitutional Treaty did take place, especially in those countries where the Treaty had to be ratified by popular vote. The referenda proved however to be a very ambivalent instrument in order to detect public opinion and allow the public to express their views on European affairs. As often stated, the two negative referenda in France and in the Netherlands became entangled with a number of many other different issues, at which conjuncture a protest vote crystallised, which was not necessarily directed against the Treaty. The negative results in France and in the Netherlands have tainted referenda with a negative connotation. They are now being perceived – rightly or wrongly – as very risky exercises and not as an inherently genuine expression of popular sentiment on European questions.

Certainly, the European Constitution cannot be the magic solution to all of Europe's problems, but the experiment in European constitutionalism over the last nine years is of significant value. The Constitutional Moment was an attempt to make a more democratic, transparent, efficient and 'close to the citizen' European Union; the results will now have to be tested through the application and implementation of the Lisbon Treaty. European constitutionalism, for its part – like the integration process itself – continues to be an ongoing project.

References

Iñigo Méndez de Vigo (dir.) (2007): ¿Qué fué de la Constitución Europea? El Tratado de Lisboa: Un camino hacia el futuro. With a foreword by *Marcelino Oreja Aguirre.*, Madrid (Planeta) 2007.

Joseph H. Weiler (2002), A Constitution for Europe? Some Hard Choices, in: Journal of Common Market Studies 40 (2002), No. 4, 563-580.

Stefan Griller

Is this a Constitution?
Remarks on a Contested Concept

I. The Rhetoric of the European Council

In its mandate of June 2007, the European Council asked the IGC to draw up a 'Reform Treaty' "with a view to enhancing the efficiency and democratic legitimacy of the enlarged Union, as well as the coherence of its external action". It continued: "The constitutional concept, which consisted in repealing all existing Treaties and replacing them by a single text called 'Constitution', is abandoned".[1]

---

1   Presidency Conclusions, 21/22 June 2007, 11177/07, Annex I, 15.

    At the time of writing, the text of the Draft Lisbon Treaty which is the outcome of this mandate can be found in OJ No 2007/C 306/1; a

The astonishing contention in this phrase is that is equates the 'constitutional concept' with the creation of a single text named 'Constitution'. To put it bluntly, this is a caricature of every constitutional concept including the one at EU level, if we agree that calling a text a 'Constitution' must have something to do with its contents, not only with its name and uniformity of the text. In other words, it has much more to do with what the European Council spelt out as the agenda of the ICG in the sentence on efficiency, democratic legitimacy, and coherence of external action. The impression is that denying the constitutional character of the enterprise is downplaying the weight of the envisaged reforms.

The purpose of the 'repealing-phrase' in the Presidency Conclusions clearly is, as has already been pointed out,[2] non-analytical. Instead, it serves the political effort to find a convincing reason for avoiding dangerous referenda on the new Treaty. The argument runs as follows: these referenda were needed because of the 'constitutional concept' of the Draft Treaty establishing a Constitution for Europe. Avoiding this concept makes future referenda unnecessary.

However, this is not convincing. It is certainly not correct to reduce the constitutional concept – and thereby implicitly also the reasons for the national referenda – of the Draft Treaty on the Constitution for Europe to the creation of a single text called 'Constitution'. To a certain extent this flaw is acknowledged also by the European Council in the same document, a few lines later, when it is stressed that the Treaty on European Union (TEU-L) and the Treaty on the Functioning of the European Union (TFEU) "will not have a constitutional character". Here, it is not only confirmed that the term 'Constitution' should not be used. It is also announced that the 'Union Minister for Foreign Affairs' will be called 'High Representative of the Union for Foreign Affairs and Security Policy'; that the denominations 'law' and 'framework law' will be abandoned, the existing denominations 'regulations', 'directives'

---

consolidated version of the Treaty on European Union (TEU-L) as amended and the Treaty on the Functioning of the European Union (TFEU) was published by the Council only in April 2008, 6655/08, 15 April 2008. The Draft Treaty Establishing a Constitution for Europe, the constitutional concept of which should be "abandoned", is to be found in the OJ No 2004/C 310/1.

2   *Ziller* (2007), 115 *et seq.*

and 'decisions' being retained; that there will be no Article mentioning the symbols of the EU such as the flag, the anthem or the motto; and that the Article on the primacy of EU law should not be retained, and the IGC should instead adopt a Declaration recalling the existing case law of the EU Court of Justice. Even if, also in this passage, there is a certain thrust on terminology, it is clear that these are substantive issues, and it is equally clear that the effort is to avoid, as far as possible, the similarities to aspects of constitutionality we are very familiar with at the Member States' level. In other words: several parallels to the characteristics of a statal constitution should be avoided. The deletion of the symbols and the express spelling out of the primacy rule clearly go beyond terminological modifications.

Consequently, the first conclusion is: the suggestion offered by the European Council, that the reform Treaty (Lisbon Treaty) is, contrasting to the Draft Constitutional Treaty of 2004, no Constitution for the simple reason that it would not create a single text named "Constitution" is not convincing. Having said this inevitably raises the question of the concept of a "Constitution" and confront it with the contents of the treaties as they stand today and of the Lisbon Treaty.

II. The Draft 'Constitutional Treaty' of 2004 – a Misnomer?

An alternative evaluation of the developments from the Constitutional Treaty to the Lisbon Treaty could be called the 'classical' stance on constitutionalism: namely that an international treaty is to be strictly discerned from a 'Constitution' and that even the Draft Constitutional Treaty of 2004 in substance is an international treaty. Consequently, calling this Treaty a 'Constitution' had been a misnomer at the outset. Even in the title of the Draft Treaty itself this becomes obvious by the fact that it is still, by explicit self reference, both a Constitution *and* a Treaty.

The borderline between a treaty under international law and a Constitution would only be transgressed if future amendments would no longer be a prerogative of the Member States as the masters of the treaties, but a competence of the Union organs. Thus, the Treaty would only have 'established' a Constitution if future amendments could be enacted by the Union itself. However, this would not have been the case: also under the Constitutional Treaty, the ratification of proposed amendments by all Member States in accordance with their respective constitutional requirements would have remained mandatory.[3] Also, and as a consequence, no *Kompetenz-Kompetenz* – the right of the Union to define its own competences – would have been included in this text.[4] The Union should not be transformed into a State.[5] Removing the name 'Constitution' from such a text consequently appears as a sort of rectification. Such rectification would probably not provide good reasons for avoiding referenda. But it would nevertheless clarify the limited constitutional impact both of the Constitutional Treaty and the Treaty of Lisbon. Both of them would be devoid of any constitutional character.

Some commentators obviously tend to look at the Draft Constitutional Treaty this way.[6] Arguably this is also the position taken by the French *Conseil Constitutionnel*[7] when it scrutinised the draft Treaty in 2004.

Frequently, the rationale behind such reasoning is that the term 'Constitution' should be reserved for the legal fundament of States and be avoided for international treaties. This is often combined with the proposition that a 'constitutional moment', that is the creation of a new State, or the loss of sovereignty, would be reached only if the capacity to define its own competences (*Kompetenz-Kompetenz*) would be shifted to the 'common organs' of a community of States, which is closely related to the amendment mechanism. Conversely, this would immunise most substantive changes of a common legal fundament from the label 'Constitution', as long as the amendment mechanism follows the traditional pattern of international treaties.

Indisputably, the argument is valid insofar as also the Lisbon Treaty is a Treaty under international law, and also future amendments of the TEU-L, the TFEU, and the Treaty establishing the European Atomic Energy Community (TEAEC) can only be changed by consent of all Member States. This is not only true with regard to the ordinary but also regarding the newly introduced

---

3   Articles IV-443-445 Draft Constitutional Treaty.

4   Article I-11(1) Draft Constitutional Treaty.

5   All of these points are rightly stressed e.g. in *Piris* (2006), 131 and 186.

6   Compare e.g. *Triantafyllou* (2007), 242 *et seq.*

7   Decision n. 2004-505, 19 novembre 2004, §§ 9 and 10.

simplified revision procedure.[8] Furthermore, there is certainly also no transfer of *Kompetenz-Kompetenz*. Quite the contrary: What is now called the 'principle of conferral' is designed to ensure that "the Union shall act only within the limits of the competences conferred upon it by the Member States in the Treaties to attain the objectives set out therein. Competences not conferred upon the Union in the Treaties remain with the Member States."[9] Consequently the contention could be that due to those most relevant features both the Lisbon Treaty and the Draft Constitutional Treaty do not give rise to call them a 'Constitution'.

Nevertheless, and in order to make things short: both contentions are not convincing. Regarding terminology, it is well known that the term 'Constitution' in practice is not reserved for States.[10] On the contrary, it often captures the basic legal fundaments of an international organisation, even if it is beyond any doubt that this is a 'Treaty' under international law.[11] In general, what is covered by this notion is the founding treaty leading to the establishment of an organisation, including its legal personality, as well as amendment and termination procedures. Furthermore, legal theorists often refer to the 'constitutions' of confederations.[12] Moreover, several founding instruments of traditional international organisations are expressly titled as 'constitution'. This is so in the case of UNESCO,

---

8   Article 48 TEU-L. The *'passerelle'* in Article 48(7) TEU-L might be seen differently, allowing for the introduction of qualified majority voting in the Council by unanimous decision of the European Council. However, this is a very limited power. Making use of it would more be a measure implementing that Article than amending the Treaty. Also, it is not really new: a similar *'passerelle'* already exists today in Article 42 of the pre-Lisbon TEU.

The Draft Constitutional Treaty contained the very same provisions in Articles IV-443-445.

The simplified amendment procedures in Article 48(6) and (7) TEU-L are not available for the TEAEC.

9   Article 5(2) TEU-L.

10 For a comprehensive discussion of the detachment of "Constitution" and "State": *Peters* (2001), 93 *et seq.*

11 See *Schermers / Blokker* (2003) § 1146.

12 Compare *Kelsen* (1949), 319: "[t]he constitution of the central community which is at the same time the constitution of the total community, the confederacy ....".

the WHO, the ILO and the FAO. However, it should be clear that this is only a matter of terminology, while the substantive issue of transforming an international community to a State is thereby not addressed.

One could feel tempted to stop here and put the issue aside by simply pointing to the fact that the ECJ addressed the TEC as the basic 'constitutional charter' of the Community.[13] However, obviously the ECJ referred to something more substantial than just the founding instrument as such. It emphasised that the EC "is a Community based on the rule of law, inasmuch as neither its Member States nor its institutions can avoid a review of the question whether the measures adopted by them are in conformity with the basic constitutional charter, the Treaty".[14] And it is not by chance that the Court stressed the common features of the Community and the Member States which begs the question to what extent the 'Constitution' of the EU resembles that of States and qualifies the Union itself as something similar to a State?

Connected and more complex is the issue of *Kompetenz-Kompetenz*.[15] It shall suffice to point out that the critical yardstick under international law for the delimitation of States is self determination, not centralisation. Thus transferring the right to amendments to common organs is certainly a very important feature. However, decentralised amendment procedures giving a decisive say to the members of the community (like in the EU) do not necessarily entail that the respective community is *not* a State. A number of federal States such as the US, but also Germany and Switzerland retain a decisive influence to their component States when it comes to amendments of the constitution. Conversely, rules allowing for the amendment of Treaties by a majority of ratifications of the Member States or even by a decision of an organ of the organisation are quite common and far from automatically transforming the organisation into a State.[16] Thus, not transferring the *Kompetenz-Kompetenz* to the 'central level' is no guarantee that the Union would not turn into a State.

---

13   Case 294/83, *Les Verts*, 1986 ECR, 1339, para. 23. See also Opinion
     1/91, *EEA I*, 1991 ECR, I-6079, para. 21.

14   Case 294/83, *Les Verts*, 1986 ECR, 1339, para. 23.

15   See, most notably *Lerche* (1995).

16   *Schermers / Blokker* (2003) § 1173 *et seq.*

To put it differently: Transferring the *Kompetenz-Kompetenz* to the Union would probably create a new State – as soon as the clause it is filled with life and used for a substantive array of areas. But reserving a decisive say to the Member States might not be a guarantee against the creation of a State; what might emerge is a decentralised State where the component States might nevertheless be qualified as organs of the new entity. This is far from being grey theory in a Union which already today on the grounds of transferred powers and without *Kompetenz-Kompetenz* impacts on almost every national competence. So why should it need *Kompetenz-Kompetenz*? Furthermore, majority decision taking on amendments is not at all an unambiguous criterion for a distinction. So even if the term 'Constitution' would be reserved for States we are still not on safe grounds for avoiding it with regard to the EU.

Consequently, neither the qualification of the EU as based on an international Treaty both on the grounds of the Constitutional Treaty and the Lisbon Treaty, nor the ratification requirement for amendments provide a good reason for avoiding or discarding the term 'Constitution'.[17] Moreover, it is at that point not clear what it means to address the current and the future Treaties as 'Constitution' This invites for some basic reflections on constitutional concepts.

III. Thin and Thick Concepts of a Constitution

Let us begin with some fundamental issues of constitutions and constitutionalism, irrespective of whether or not we are dealing with States, International Organisations, or International Law.

A legal norm may be defined as the meaning of an act of will posited from man and aiming at the behaviour of man. This is the starting point of a positivist concept. A legal order may thus be conceived as a system of norms which is effective and can, to that end, principally be enforced by coercion.[18]

---

17   Similarly *Ziller* (2005), 35.

18   *Kelsen* (1967), 4 *et seq*. It shall be stressed that relying on this starting point does not necessarily include, and in fact does not include in the case of this author, accordance with other features of *Kelsen*ianism; especially not with the contention that a basic norm (*Grundnorm*) is an epistemological necessity in the *Kant*ian sense, and also not that only enforceable norms can be considered as norms (which creates difficulties for permissions and authorisations).

To determine whether any specific norm is part of a legal system – valid or binding law in a given situation – it is essential to identify what is commonly called a 'rule of recognition'. This is a rule authorising the enactment of the norm in question. The identification of such authorisation may lead to a chain of such rules of recognition. In principle such a chain might be infinite, in other words: it is not self explaining which ultimate rule of recognition should be accepted as binding. But the answer is essential in order to determine which norms govern which situations, or whether we are dealing with morals, wishful thinking, the command of gangsters, or an attempt of a revolution. Many answers are given. Some claim that justice is the ultimate yardstick and at the same time the decisive authorisation rule;[19] a variation of this might be the 'we the people rule'.[20] Others say that there it is an epistemic necessity to postulate a basic norm, even if this should be fictitious.[21] This is connected to the proposal to only assume such a basic norm with regard to effective legal systems while the content of those rules might be irrelevant. However, such a basic norm might be superfluous. It might be sufficient to qualify every effective system of norms as a legal order.[22]

On the grounds of such a definition of a legal order a second step might be to identify the *constitution* of that order. Not every norm within the system deserves to be qualified as constitutional. More than one concept is conceivable,[23] and in fact many different proposals are made, to a certain extent reflecting the differences in the underlying conceptions of law. While any positivist approach would avoid prescriptive elements aiming at specific contents, this is different especially with the concept of European Enlightenment and related conceptions. The latter would introduce rights based 'justice' as an essential feature of a constitution.

---

19   E.g. *Alexy* (2002).

20   In essence this means that only democratically legitimate legal systems can be qualified as 'law'.

21   *Kelsen* (1967), 198 *et seq*.

22   *Hart* (1994). A legal system consequently might be qualified as (extremely) unjust – like e.g. that of the "Third Reich" – but nevertheless it would constitute law, as long as it is effectively enforced.

23   Compare only *Craig* (2001), 126 *et seq*; *Gray* (1979), 191 *et seq*.

Only some, however important types shall be introduced. One might distinguish 'thin' and 'thick' concepts of constitutions and constitutionalism depending on the properties required to call a set of rules a 'Constitution' or a legal system 'constitutional':

- The *minimalist concept* which one might also call *formal or positivist*:[24] 'Constitution' in a *material sense* is the positive norm or norms which regulate the creation of general legal norms (legislation). This might be a written or unwritten constitution brought about by custom. It necessarily includes the determination of the organs authorised to create general legal norms. A "constitution" in the *formal sense*, by contrast, is the set of norms in the legal system which is more stable in terms of alteration procedures than the (subordinate) rest of the legal order. The core purpose of these rules is to entrench the Constitution in the material sense. The formal constitution could also include other rules, e.g. fundamental rights limiting the powers of the legislator, the rule of law, democracy, separation of powers etc. However, none of these would be a constitutive element of a 'Constitution'. In principle, such a concept can be applied to State law and also to International law as a legal order.[25]

- The *concept of European Enlightenment*,[26] coined in Article 16 of the French declaration of the rights of men and of the citizen (1789): "Any society in which the guarantee of rights is not secured, and in which the separation of powers is not determined, has no constitution at all."[27] According to this approach, which

---

24 E.g. *Kelsen* (1967), 221 *et seq*; see also *Hart* (1994), 71 *et seq*.

25 Regarding the latter compare *Verdross* (1926). It might be seen as a variation to address the UN-Charter as the constitution of international community: *Fassbender* (1998).

26 E.g. *Ziller* (2005), 2 *et seq*.

   Some reservation regarding the authorship as expressed in the term "European" is appropriate, though: *Lafayette* drew in his proposals mainly from the bills of rights of the individual North American States which themselves cannot simply be traced back to the well known English sources, the latter lacking higher rank and enforceable individual rights; compare *Jellinek* (1901), 13 *et seq*, 43 *et seq*.

27 "Toute société, dans laquelle la garantie des droits n'est pas assurée, ni la séparation des pouvoirs déterminée, n'a point de constitution".

is of course very much related to statal systems, the Constitution has to fulfil three essential functions: the recognition of the rights of citizens; the organisation of the relations between the government and the governed; the establishment of a system of checks and balances among the branches of the government, especially between the legislative and the executive branches.

There are many variations to this concept, some of them detailing the approach further.[28] Summing up in sober language one might coin the core subject of a Constitution – and omitting certain controversies – in defining and authorising certain organs to enact (and to enforce) law which is directly binding on the citizens, to define the law making procedures, and to establish limits to the powers of the authorised organs, especially limits flowing from rights of citizens and requirements of checks and balances.

The analytical framework of a constitution in the material and in the formal sense can be combined with such an approach. This 'thicker' concept of a constitution relates mainly to the constitution in the material sense which usually would be entrenched (but not necessarily so).

Jellinek (1901), 40 *et seq* points to the Bills of Rights of New Hampshire and of Massachusetts as models for Article 16. The latter, however, is much shorter and clearer in language (as are many of the French stipulations).

28   Compare only *Craig* (2001), 126 *et seq*, and *Pernice* (2001), 158, *Streinz / Ohler / Herrmann* (2008), 8 *et seq*, with further references.

What is deliberately not included in the above concepts is the contention that a 'true' constitution must contribute to the shaping of collective identity. This may be desirable for a 'good' constitution. This author holds that such ambition should be kept apart from the conceptual debate. Even more problematic is the stance – emphatically voiced not the least in the German debate – that the 'relative homogeneity' of a polity (a people, a nation) might be an indispensable *prerequisite* for the existence and / or the establishment of a constitution. On the author's view on these issues compare *Griller* (2005), 237 *et seq*, 243 *et seq*.

- The *optimisation concept* or *international constitutionalism:*[29] more or less well defined notions of national constitutions such as the rule of law, checks and balances, human rights protection, and democracy, are being developed, detected, and/or advocated for mostly with regard to international law. Striving for the realisation of such concepts can be addressed as 'constitutionalism'.[30] In the context of the development of the international legal order such development is seen as a chance to compensate for the deficiencies resulting from 'globalisation' and/or the transfer of powers from national constitutional systems to international organisations and bodies. As a consequence it might be justifiable to talk about constitutional principles originally derived from national law which are equally to be found and optimised in (mainly) international law (EU law, WTO law, or the international legal order as such). Consequently it would be justified to isolate 'constitutional elements' in that development, and / or to develop a scale of more or less 'constitutional' systems or subsystems of law.

There is no categorical difference to the concept of the Enlightenment. Optimisation can also be pursued within the latter. However, the focus is different in that this had been developed for nation states while what is here called international constitutionalism is mainly targeted at international law or subsystems of international law.

It is conceivable that constitutions as sketched out above do also exist within subsystems of legal orders. This may be so even on the grounds that such a subsystem may be seen as a delegated legal order, not as a legal order of its own. In this sense there can be constitutions of component states of federal states as well as constitutions of international organisations like those mentioned,[31] but also of organisations without an explicit self reference of that kind

---

29 Compare for the following *Peters* (2006). It is not that *Peters* would advocate the concept sketched out in the above text which is very much a simplification. But she excellently coins the most important "ingredients" as emerged during the last decades. Compare also *Schorkopf* (2007), 187 *et seq.*, esp. 197 *et seq.*; *de Wet* (2006).

30 *Peters* (2006), 582 *et seq.*, 599 *et seq.*; but compare also *Craig* (2001), 127 *et seq.*; *Weiler* (1999), 221 *et seq.*

31 Compare in the above text after fn 12.

like the WTO.[32] This is important with regard to the EU insofar as it is consequently conceivable that the Union has a constitution not only on the grounds of the prevailing view developed by the ECJ that it constitutes an "independent source of law",[33] but also on the grounds of the earlier contention differing slightly but importantly in that "...the Community constitutes a new legal order *of international law*".[34]

IV. Interim Conclusions and Remarks

A. Yes, It's a Constitution

If we agree that sets of norms fulfilling the criteria presented above should be captured by the notion of a 'Constitution', the result is obvious: the EU already today has a Constitution, it would have had one under the Treaty establishing a Constitution for Europe, and it would have a Constitution on the basis of the Lisbon Treaty. This is true not only on the grounds of the 'thin' positivist concept but also on the grounds of the 'thicker' concept of European Enlightenment and international constitutionalism.

The Treaties as they currently stand define legislative organs – mainly the Council or the Council together with the European Parliament, and the Commission having the monopoly of initiative whenever the 'Community Method' applies. Sources of primary and secondary law are binding not only upon the Member States but also on citizens, as far as direct application is foreseen. Limits of legislation result, amongst others, from fundamental rights as guaranteed by the ECJ which is relying on the common constitutional traditions of the Member States and draws from the European Convention for the Protection of Human Rights and Fundamental Freedoms (ECHR).[35] Separation of powers is foreseen not only vertically – through the division of competences between the EU and the Member States – but also horizontally between the institutions and

---

32   For the respective dispute see only *Dunoff* (2006); *Simma / Pulkowski* (2006); *Trachtmann* (2006).

33   Case 6/64, *Costa v ENEL*, 1964 ECR, 585, 593 f; Case 11/70, *Internationale Handelsgesellschaft*, 1970 ECR, 1125, para. 3.

34   Case 26/62, *van Gend en Loos*, 1963 ECR, 1, 12 (emphasis added).

35   Article 6 TEU-L.

organs of the EU – mainly through what is called the 'institutional balance'.[36]

Consequently, and even against the background of substantially differing concepts of constitution and constitutionalism, it can safely be said, even claiming that this is the prevailing view today: "The 'constitutional law' of the European Communities consists of all the rules of Community law relating to the general objectives, the allocation of competences and the way in which the legislative, executive and judicial functions are performed within the Community... the constitutional law of the *European Union* extends the analysis to cover the areas in which the Union does not act as the Community".[37]

The Union and the European Community will be merged by the Treaty of Lisbon. This makes things clearer but does not change the substance of the 'constitutional issue'. Furthermore, in all of the above mentioned fields the Lisbon Treaty, once ratified, entails minor or major changes if compared to the status quo.[38] They relate mainly to the protection of individual rights (through making the Charter of Fundamental Rights binding law), democratic aspects of law making both regarding the procedures and the organs involved, and the separation of powers (both vertically and horizontally). This means that the Constitution of the EU will be changed considerably by the Lisbon Treaty. But it does not mean that there is no Constitution.

B. Disclaimers

It might be worth reflecting that, as a matter of principle, specifying the contents of a definition as an element of scientific ambition is a matter of utility rather than truth. If we find it fruitful to conceptualise the term 'Constitution' as proposed, there is no strong argument against addressing both the Constitutional Treaty and the Lisbon Treaty as constitutions, to be more precise: as a draft for the replacement of and a draft for an amendment to the actual constitution respectively. We could also discuss whether the explicit self

---

36 Compare only *Lenaerts / Verhoeven* (2002); *Jacqué* (2004).

37 *Lenaerts / van Nuffel* (2005) para. 1-020, with further references. Compare also not only the title of the book but also the arguments in *Weiler* (1999), esp. 3-101, and 221-237.

38 The substance of these changes is addressed in other contributions to this volume.

reference or 'explicit' avoidance meets the usual delimitations of scientific language. Even if this would not be the case, the title 'Constitution' would not simply be wrong, but would probably change the use of the term in what we might call a legal '*Sprachspiel*', a language-game in the sense of *Wittgenstein*. Also avoiding such denomination is a meaningful 'move' within that game involving academics, politicians and citizens, not the least also organs of Member States and of the EU. As already mentioned, an important component of that 'move' in the Lisbon Treaty is to avoid similarities to constitutions of nation states.

However, several things should be kept apart from such analysis: first there is the issue of the eventual transformation of the Union into a state. By accepting that the Treaties do fulfil the mentioned functions of all of the presented constitutional concepts we acknowledge the state-like appearance of the Union. This neither implies that the Union actually is a State nor that it should become one. Admittedly, there is a point in assuming that it was the suspicion or fear that using the term 'Constitution' would entail or at least promote the future creation of a European State which triggered the opposition against such terminology. And it is to be conceded, even, that using the same term as for the legal fundaments of states for an entity which comes near a State in terms of its legal functions might indeed induce such development. On these grounds there might even be a point in assuming that concerns of this type influenced the negative outcome of the referenda in the Netherlands and in France on the Constitutional Treaty. In turn it might be 'rational' to avoid the term in the Lisbon Treaty. However, avoiding the term does neither mean that, legally speaking, the Treaty should not be qualified as a 'Constitution' nor that this would eliminate the substantive reasons for the negative referenda outcomes.

Second, regarding the debate on constitutionalism in general, calling the existing and the future amended Treaties a Constitution does not include a specific evaluation of its contents, neither a negative nor a positive one. It goes without saying that everywhere in the world we can observe deficient constitutions, or at least constitutions with a potential to be improved. By calling the Treaties a Constitution and the Lisbon Treaty an important constitutional amendment we do not necessarily imply that they establish sufficient limits to power, an optimal expression of the European polity, or that the guarantees for a system of deliberation (democracy) at

European level would be satisfactory.[39] We are simply saying that this is the fundament of the normative order of the EU which regulates law making and also addresses these issues.

V. A Step toward European Statehood?

A. Introductory Remarks

We have already seen that avoiding any 'constitutional language' in the Lisbon Treaty serves the purpose of avoiding similarities to constitutions of nation states. What should be discouraged is any suggestion that concluding this new 'Treaty' could be the next or even the decisive step to European statehood. This begs the question why this should be of importance at all and to what extent this move can be successful, in other words: what are the remaining differences between the EU and a state, and would the Lisbon Treaty change this significantly, or would the Constitutional Treaty have changed it?

In contemporary academic contributions such debate is widely avoided;[40] rather the concentration is on elaborating on the specific, 'sui-generis' features[41] of the Union and the European Communities respectively in a 'post-national' or 'post-Westphalian' world. Debates on statehood appear to be outdated or beside the point with regard to a development which arguably from the beginning aimed at overcoming the traps of nationalism, historically being a close ally of statehood.

The Lisbon Treaty and the preceding controversies on the Draft Constitutional Treaty however make apparent that the issue has not simply "gone away" by avoiding it. This is less surprising if the broader picture of international law is taken into account.

At stake is the consequence of an entity being qualified as a 'sovereign' state under international law (even with restricted competences), or as something different, be it a 'state' within a federa-

---

39   To mention some of the most popular elements of constitutionalism: compare *Poiares Maduro* (2005), 333.

40   But compare e.g. *von Bogdandy* (1999), *Dashwood* (1998), *Mancini* (1998) and *Weiler* (1998).

41   Such as 'Multilevel Constitutionalism' (*Pernice* (1999)), 'Supranational Federalism' (*von Bogdandy* (1999)), or 'European Commonwealth' (*MacCormick* (1999)), to name but a few of the many well argued proposals.

tion, or be it a component of an international organisation depriving it of its legal capacity under international law.[42] If we agree that one of the most salient features for a 'sovereign' state is the existence or the non-existence of legal personality *under international law* with all its repercussions – e.g. the ability to enter into international agreements, including membership rights in international organisations, liability under international law for wrong doing, exclusive jurisdiction, the protection flowing from the prohibition of the use of force and the right of non-intervention –, it becomes abundantly clear that the point is of vital importance for the Member States of the Union, and still remains to be even against the background of the obligations resulting from EU membership.[43] Retaining the status of 'sovereign' States makes sure that the bundle of legal rights and obligations under international law are still available, in contrast to entities not being sovereign in this sense. Legal certainty not only for EU Member States but also for all other States in the world is thus preserved. This is the more the case as long as the Union itself is not in the legal condition taking over as a *fully fledged*, 'sovereign' member of the international community.[44] And this arguably is not the case until the Union itself will either become a State or alternatively an international organisation acquiring, under the acceptance of the international community and the Member States, the whole 'bundle' of sovereign rights from its members. For, international law does not offer a third alternative to confederations – international organisations being captured by that notion – and (federal) states.[45] Summing up, the difference between

---

42 Compare for the following e.g. and especially *Oeter* (2002), 275 *et seq*, and 283 *et seq*, with further references; *Brownlie* (2003), 287. But compare already also *Kelsen / Tucker* (1966), 259.

It shall be stressed that this is by no means denying the merits of the contemporary debate as well as the important changes sovereignty has undergone in recent decades: compare e.g. *Walker* (2003).

43 Very clearly addressed e.g. in the speech by *Jacques Chirac* to the German *Bundestag*, 27 June 2000 (LE MONDE, 28 June 2000, 16) stressing that neither the French nor the Germans envisage the creation of a European Super State "qui se substituerait à nos Etats-nation et marquerait la fin de leur existence comme *acteurs de la vie internationale*".

44 *Giegerich* (2003), 730 *et seq*.

45 In the same vein *Leben* (2000), esp. 110 *et seq*.

being a state *directly* subordinate to international law and a component of a larger community replacing it in general involves the issue
of 'international presence', international responsibility, and protection by international law. Coined in an abbreviation, sovereignty
continues to be the decisive aspect of an entity forming a full member of the international community or not.[46]

This remains so irrespective of the multitude of obligations
which arguably transformed EU Member States to sovereign States
with restricted competences. The *internal structure* of the EU with
its undeniable specificities should not be confounded with the relevance of statehood *vis-à-vis* the rest of the world. Arguably this is
an important aspect of the background to the changes from the
Draft Constitutional Treaty to the Lisbon Treaty.

B. Elements of Statehood

According to the 'Three-Elements-Doctrine' the essential elements
of a State are State territory, State people, and State power.[47] With
regard to the EU[48] it is claimed that it lacks all elements but especially the third one, since the power to use force is still monopolised
by the Member States. It is argued in particular that military and
police affairs, as well as the enforcement of European law in general, remain within the national sphere, and that the Union lacks
also *Kompetenz-Kompetenz*.[49]

These observations are all true. However, they are not really
convincing when it comes to the delimitation of confederations or
Unions of States under international law and States.[50]

---

46 To the same end *Oeter* (2002), 285.

47 Pathbreaking *Jellinek* (1914), 394 *et seq*. This is still relevant today
    under international law: compare *Brownlie* (2003), 70 *et seq*; *Cassese*
    (2003), 71 *et seq*.

48 The discussion in the text is dependent neither on the legal personal-
    ity of the EU nor on a specific characterisation of the relationship
    between the EU and the Communities. Thus it of relevance both for
    the status quo ante before and after the Lisbon Treaty.

49 Compare e.g. *Everling* (1993), 941 *et seq*; *Oppermann* (1994), 91;
    Piris (2006), 192 *et seq*.

50 The argument shall only be sketched out briefly here. For a full de-
    bate compare *Griller et al.* (2000), 65 *et seq*; *Griller* (2005), 220 *et
    seq*.

As for the territorial scope of Union law, it has to be said that international law requires a definition of state territory for the sake of delimiting governmental powers.[51] There is no reason why such delimitation cannot be accomplished by referring to the territories of the Member States. As for the definition of a 'state people', it is, under international law, somewhat synonymous with that of population. In other words, the people of a state need not form a nation (or a 'homogeneous people') and it may occur that several nations are gathered in one state or that one nation can be spread over or divided into several states[52] – to mention only the well known examples of Switzerland, Belgium, Canada, South Africa or India.[53]

The most salient issue certainly is that of State power. Suffice it to say that already today the regulatory powers of the Union and the Communities do not lag far behind those of central authorities in a loosely integrated federal state. Despite acknowledged limits in several fields including foreign affairs, the EU clearly has a 'state-like' appearance in terms of powers. As a general impression, this view is acknowledged even by writers fiercely opposed to the concept of European statehood *per se*.[54]

It is relatively undisputed that Community competences nowadays impinge on nearly every field of national law-making. It is only of secondary concern that the exact degree of this intrusion into the core of national sovereignty (in the sense of political independence) is difficult to estimate. Moreover, this calculation varies from state to state, depending on the division of powers between legislative and executive institutions at the national level.[55]

---

51   E.g. *Brownlie* (2003), 71.

52   See *Doehring* (1987), 425: "For the definition of State population, homogeneity regarding ethnic, cultural, religious, racial or other criteria is not decisive. A multinational State can be a State under international law, and the criteria mentioned above are only relevant when defining the nation as a bearer of the right of self-determination." Compare also *Cassese* (2003), 73.

53   For a discussion of these examples, see *Mancini* (1998).

54   E.g. *Isensee* (1995), 572 *et seq.*

55   The legislative organs, *i.e.* parliaments, in Member States like Great Britain and France with a traditionally strong executive may be less affected than those in states like Germany or Austria, where thorough determination of each act of the executive by the legislature is mandatory under constitutional provisions.

In essence, the powers of the Union and the Communities encompass what is necessary for a federal state; in terms of competences maybe still a rather weak federal state, yes, but nevertheless a federal state in the sense that both central and component entities enact laws directly binding for the citizens within defined fields of activity, that there is participation of the component entities in the law making of the central entity, and that there is a mechanism of judicial settlement of disputes in cases of conflicts between them.[56]

The most forceful objection against the view that foreign affairs, military matters, other specified fields, or law enforcement in general have to be centralised in order to transform a community of states into a federal state is that the essential element of the notion of state power, at least in international law, is *not* to secure a certain element of centralisation *within* a polity but to secure – in addition to validity and efficacy – independence from outside powers. State power under international law is a decisive criterion when ascertaining self-governance,[57] but not when ascertaining the specific degree of centralisation within a state.[58] It has already been contended that the same is true for the well known debate on *Kompetenz-Kompetenz*.[59]

This is not to say that the issue of centralisation is completely irrelevant. But it is submitted that there are no good reasons to define, in terms of specific fields of activity, sort of *à priori* competences the centralisation of which would be indispensable. As far as the necessary degree of centralisation, in general terms of 'regulatory output', is concerned, neither international law nor theory provide for a precise dividing line. Instead, "there is a smooth transition from loose cooperation between states to structured cooperation within an international organization, just as there is a smooth

---

56 See e.g. *Lenaerts* (1990); *Weiler* (2000), 239.

57 Meaning the ability to form a will of its own, not the absence of obligations. Compare *Doehring* (1987), 426.

58 Compare the thorough study by *Kunz* (1929), 660, who stresses that the division of competences in the field of foreign affairs is a mere question of positive law for the federal state and that under international law, the centralisation of competences does not constitute a decisive difference between a confederation and a federal state.

59 Compare in the above text near fn 15.

transition between some international organizations and sovereign states".[60]

Therefore, the conclusion is that the existing relationship between the Union (and the Communities) and its Member States does not decide the statehood of the Union conclusively.

C. The Lack of Will to Found a European State

Why, then, is the Union not perceived as a state, if the existing powers might actually be sufficiently comprehensive, if a European territory and a European population can be identified, that is to say, if the structural state of affairs is sufficient?

The contention is that the reason is simply the absence of will, on the part of the Member States and the institutions of the Union, to found a European State,[61] and the absence of corresponding acts recognising the Union's statehood on the part of the international community. This lack of will is reinforced by the Lisbon Treaty given the very absence of provisions aiming at an alteration of the current situation. However, this would have been only marginally different if the Draft Constitutional Treaty would have entered into force, as shall be shown.

The Member States of the Union are not yet prepared to change the legal quality of their relations to state law, which would be the primary implication of the foundation of a European state.[62] If the above quoted contention of the "smooth transition between some international organisations and sovereign states" is true this implies that the triad of state power, state people and state territory under international law allows for some discretion. In general, decisions on classification for entities within the zone of uncertainty

---

60   *Schermers / Blokker* (2003), § 31.

61   This is rightly stressed, as a sort of bottom line, e.g. in *Piris* (2006), 194: "In the end, the strongest argument of all against the idea of the EU being a State or becoming a State, is that the Member States simply do not want that".

62   It should at the same time be noted that this would *not* imply the loss of the capacity of the Member States to act in the international sphere, especially the right to conclude treaties. Compare in this respect – the disputed issue being whether, in a case where members of a federation are empowered to conclude treaties with third parties, these members are to be classified as partial subjects of international law or only as components of a decentralised state – *Kunz* (1929), 130, 660 *et seq.*, 678 *et seq.*; *Verdross* (1926), 125 (but see also 123).

rest with the international community. The Union, having tran-
scended the traditional limits of confederations (including international organisations), but still not equipped with the full range of
the *usual* and *traditional* insignia of a state, seems to have a choice.
To date, it has avoided choosing statehood, with the international
community accepting this *status quo*.

In fact, according to the prevailing view, international law itself provides the basis for such a situation.[63] While the general principle is that a polity clearly fulfilling all three criteria of statehood
should be classified as a state, even if it would deny being one,[64]
there are specificities to be observed for non-typical 'borderline
cases'. Uncertainties in the application of the traditional 'three elements' theory are inevitable and well known in practice.[65] It is possible that an entity can be recognised as a new state without or before fulfilling all of the criteria. And it is equally possible that a
polity that *does* fulfil all of the criteria might not be recognised in
international terms. This is relevant also for the EU which might be
a specific 'borderline case' with ever more competences being
transferred from the Member States. Where a clear cut decision is
not possible, it seems only natural that the international community
would respect the will of the entity in question.[66] As long as there is
no expression of will to form a new state, there is no reason to treat
this special community as if it had reached such a decision. The
situation would be more difficult if there was international pressure
on the entity to act as a state in the international sphere.[67] But as

---

63   For closer analysis compare *Brownlie* (2003), 86 *et seq*, *Cassese*
     (2003), 74; *Crawford* (2006), 17 *et seq* (on the EU 495 *et seq.*).

64   Compare *Doehring* (1987), 423.

65   Recent examples are offered by the recognition of Croatia, Slovenia,
     Bosnia-Herzegovina, and Kosovo by (parts of) the international
     community.

66   Some scholars argue that a state population under international law
     only exists if the overwhelming part of the population is willing to
     form a particular state. *Doehring* (1987), 424 writes: "[a] population
     whose majority refuses to be assembled as a State population does
     not correspond to the requirements for identifying a State in interna-
     tional law".

67   Such a pressure might at least partly develop in the framework of the
     participatory rights of the EU and the Member States respectively, in
     international organisations such as the WTO, the IMF, etc. It might

long as this is not the case, ultimately, even a highly integrated international organisation such as the European Union together with its members has the final say.

Needless to say, the fact that the Union and its Member States have so far chosen to refrain from the expression of such will or intention is not merely casual. In truth, most of the EU Member States simply prefer to uphold the idea that the Union is a community based on international law,[68] leaving untouched their own legal quality as states under international law. Furthermore, most of the Member States would be prevented by their national constitutional systems from assenting to such a step. Constitutional amendments, in some cases including a referendum, would be the constitutional prerequisite to the foundation of a European state.[69] Nothing indicates that this is about to change in the near or even in the far future.

D. Changes Made by the Lisbon Treaty –
Compared to the Draft Constitutional Treaty

1. Traces of Statehood

If one scrutinises both the Draft Treaty establishing a Constitution for Europe and the Lisbon Treaty for reinforcing or developing further the already existing 'traces of statehood' in terms of centralisation and structural insignia of statehood, ambivalent strands may be detected.[70]

---

be looked at as an advantage for the EU to dispose of the voting rights of all of its members, given that federally structured states are quite naturally treated as one state.

68   In 'academic language' this can be expressed like in *de Witte* (1999), 210: "The principles of direct effect and supremacy, as presently formulated and accepted, continue to confirm the nature of EC law as that of a branch of international law, albeit a branch with some unusual, quasi-federal, blossoms."

69   Compare e.g. the contributions in *Kellermann / de Zwaan / Czuczai* (2001). In some Member States, especially in Germany, it is even (but not yet convincingly) argued that the constitution would completely impede such an amendment – see e.g. *Isensee* (1995), 575 *et seq.*

70   It was already mentioned above that similarities to national constitutions should be avoided: the 'Union Minister for Foreign Affairs' was renamed the 'High Representative of the Union for Foreign Af-

What is continued – respectively would have been continued under the Constitutional Treaty – is the transfer of powers to the European Union. Specifically remarkable in this respect are the new provisions regarding the area of freedom, security and justice including not only the current powers from today's first and third pillar but including new ones.[71] Respective primary and secondary legislation consequently comes under the supranational features of direct effect and primacy. Another example which can hardly be overestimated is the reform of the Common Commercial Policy. The Constitution expands its scope to the conclusion of agreements relating to services, the commercial aspects of intellectual property and foreign direct investment.[72] Contrasting to the present situation under the Nice Treaty, this is an *exclusive* competence in its entirety. Among others, nearly the whole range of WTO-subjects would come under the new *exclusive* competence.[73] As a consequence, the Member States lose their right to conclude international agreements in these fields. Their ability to act in international fora is thereby considerably diminished.

The far reaching general clauses granting political discretion in expanding the scope of Union law by secondary legislation did not disappear, but were only marginally adjusted. In order *to achieve the establishment and functioning of the internal market*, the EU may still "adopt the measures for the approximation" of Member

---

fairs and Security Policy'; 'law' and 'framework law' does not appear in the text, the existing denominations 'regulations', 'directives' and 'decisions' being retained; and the symbols of the EU such as the flag, the anthem or the motto were deleted from the text. These changes will not be addressed in more detail as is contended that they have no bearing on the issue in their own right. This could be different in the context of more powerful arguments. However, such arguments seem to be missing as will be shown.

71   Title V TFEU; Part III, Title III, Chapter IV of the Constitutional Treaty.

72   Article 207 TFEU; Article III-315 of the Constitutional Treaty.

73   This might be different only regarding international agreements in the field of transport. Arguably, Article 207(5) TFEU [Article III-315(5) of the Constitutional Treaty] would create a shared competence in this field. Thus, there would still be the option to conclude (WTO-) agreements in this field as mixed agreements.

States' legislation.[74] It remains also possible to decide on the *'necessary' action* in cases where the Constitution has not provided the "necessary powers"[75] – under the new but insignificant condition that the action has to be "within the framework of the policies defined in the Treaties".

The clearer categorisation of the competencies[76] in exclusive, shared, and supporting, co-ordinating and supplementing competencies – while leaving the category open especially with regard to common foreign and security policy – does not reduce the far reaching scope of powers as transferred by the Lisbon Treaty.

Taken altogether, deliberate conferral by the Member States is being continued and deepened. A major and ever growing part of the applicable law in the Member States would be Union law or national law determined by Union law.

As a kind of counterpoise to that, the Lisbon Treaty stresses the persistent importance of the Member States and their competencies. The respect of the Union not only for the equality of the Member States but also for their national identities is expressly stipulated.[77] The Treaties protect their "fundamental structures, political and constitutional, inclusive of regional and local self-government", and call upon the Union to respect "their essential State functions, including ensuring the territorial integrity of the State …". Also, revamping the competencies certainly not only aims at clarification but includes markedly conservatory elements designed to preserve the statal character of the Member States.[78] This happens by upholding the so-called principles of conferral, subsidiarity and proportionality. Furthermore, the backside of the coin is expressly spelt out as well: "Competences not conferred upon the Union in the Treaties remain with the Member States."[79] It is

---

74 Article 114 TFEU; with slightly different wording Article III-172 of the Constitutional Treaty.

75 Article 352 TFEU; with slightly different wording Article I-18 of the Constitutional Treaty.

76 Article 2 TFEU; Article I-12 of the Constitutional Treaty.

77 Article 4 TEU-L; Article I-5 of the Constitutional Treaty.

78 In parts, this is a continuation of similar efforts starting with the Maastricht Treaty at the latest; compare *Dashwood* (1998), 201 *et seq.*

79 Article 5(2) TEU-L; Article I-11 of the Constitutional Treaty (with slightly different wording).

thereby reinforced that the conferral of competencies by the Member States is a condition for a corresponding power of the Union meaning that it is not in the Union's discretion to determine its own competencies (*Kompetenz-Kompetenz*).

Another important feature, as already mentioned previously, is the provisions relating to the legal foundation of the Union including amendment procedures. First, we are dealing with a *Treaty* concluded by the Member States and open to all "European States".[80] As far as the conclusion and the possible termination of the Treaties are concerned, the citizens are represented by their States.[81]

Second, the TEU-L differentiates between ordinary and simplified revision procedures. Ordinary revisions[82] can be initiated by any Member State, the European Parliament or the Commission. The European Council consequently convenes a Convention similar to the one which drafted the Constitutional Treaty, composed of representatives of the national Parliaments, of the Heads of State or Government of the Member States, of the European Parliament and of the Commission. The Convention can adopt by consensus a recommendation for amendments to an intergovernmental conference. Only minor changes can be submitted – by skipping the Convention procedure – directly to such a conference by the European Council and with the consent of the European Parliament. Changes accorded by the intergovernmental conference enter into force only after being ratified by all Member States in accordance with their respective constitutional requirements. Simplified revisions are twofold. The first alternative[83] concerns the so-called *Passerelle*: it authorises the Council to introduce qualified majority voting or the ordinary legislative procedure in those cases where the TFEU or

---

80 Article 49 TEU-L; Article I-1 of the Constitutional Treaty.

81 In its language – however not regarding the substance of enactment and amendments – the Constitutional Treaty went a step further. It stated that the establishment of the Union would not only reflect the will of the States of Europe but also the will of the citizens of Europe: Article I-1 of the Constitutional Treaty; compare also the preamble (last recital) saying that the members of the European Convention prepared the draft of the Constitution "on behalf of the citizens and the States of Europe" which was equally discarded from the Lisbon version.

82 Article 48 TEU-L; Article IV-443 of the Constitutional Treaty.

83 Article 48(7) TEU-L; Article IV-444 of the Constitutional Treaty.

Title V of the TEU-L stipulates unanimity or a special legislative procedure. The second alternative[84] concerns internal Union policies and action. It allows for revising all or part of the provisions on internal policies and action by unanimous European decision to be taken by the European Council. However, such a decision needs the approval by the Member States in accordance with their respective constitutional requirements, and it must not increase the competencies of the Union. Thus, also the simplified procedure foresees the co-operation of institutions of the Union and of the Member States as a prerequisite of alterations.

Of central importance with regard to the subject of statehood is the new clause providing for voluntary withdrawal from the Union, basically simply by notification and the subsequent lapse of a two years period.[85] Certainly it would be unusual (but not inconceivable) to include such a clause in the constitution of a federal State. And it had been disputed whether unilateral withdrawal from the EU would be legal.

Taken altogether these alterations would not produce a qualitative leap compared to the situation as it stands today. It goes without saying that there would still be no clear cut limitation for the competencies of the EU, and no corresponding guarantee of national 'sovereignty' for the Member States. There would be a continuation with the development of the last decades, namely the transfer of competencies to the European level resulting in a substantial restriction of the Member States' ability to take policy decisions on their own; this capacity would be continued to be shifted gradually to the EU. In a counterbalancing effort, however, the new Treaty is eager to avoid the impression that the Member States' status is substantially diminished, by stressing the respect for their identities including the essential State functions. The fragile balance between preserving the statal quality of the Member States and strengthening the capacity of the EU would continue to exist. Consequently, the unified EU would still remain in the undecided state of suspense, in a material sense, between a confederation and a federation. The formal status of State sovereignty would not be wiped out on the side of the Member States, and it would not be transferred to the EU.

---

84   Article 48(6) TEU-L; Article IV-445 of the Constitutional Treaty.

85   Article 50 TEU-L; Article I-60 of the Constitutional Treaty.

2. Primacy

There is a difference between the Draft Constitutional Treaty and the Lisbon Treaty regarding the so called "primacy clause". The Constitution for the first time would have included an explicit primacy clause for the law adopted by the institutions of the union, thereby coining the respective jurisprudence of the ECJ: "The Constitution and law adopted by the institutions of the Union in exercising competences conferred on it shall have primacy over the law of the Member States."[86]

The Lisbon Treaty, by contrast and as already mentioned, suppresses this clause. What is included instead is a declaration (No 17) to the Treaties "concerning primacy". It recalls "that, in accordance with well settled case law of the Court of Justice of the European Union, the Treaties and the law adopted by the Union on the basis of the Treaties have primacy over the law of Member States, under the conditions laid down by the said case law." The Intergovernmental Conference also decided to attach as an Annex to the Final Act an Opinion of the Council Legal Service. In its core part, this opinion reads as follows: "The fact that the principle of primacy will not be included in the future treaty shall not in any way change the existence of the principle and the existing case-law of the Court of Justice".

Is this difference between the Constitutional Treaty and the Lisbon Treaty significant?

First, the primacy clause would have made the previous jurisprudence explicit without significantly changing it.[87] Thus, conflict-

---

86   Article I-6 of the Constitutional Treaty. See also Declaration no. 1 to the Constitutional Treaty: "The conference notes that Article I-6 reflects existing case-law of the Court of Justice of the European Communities and of the Court of First Instance".

87   *Piris* (2006), 82 *et seq.* Compare also *de Witte* (2007), §§ 12 *et seq*; *Eriksen / Fossum / Kumm / Menéndez* (2005), 20 *et seq.*; *Streinz / Ohler / Herrmann* (2008), 88.

    This view was also taken by the French Conseil Constitutionnel in its Decision n. 2004-505, 19 novembre 2004, §§ 9 ff. It stressed, among others, that the reach of the primacy principle would not have been extended, and that Article I-5 of the Constitution included the guarantee for "national identities" including the "fundamental structures, political and constitutional". Similarly is the Decision of the Spanish Constitutional Court, DTC 1/2004, de 13 de diciembre de 2004.

ing Member States' law would have been superseded by directly
applicable Union law. In substance, this would have been a continuation with the current situation. This would not have entirely
excluded the reservation of certain Member States' constitutional
Courts on their own prerogative for the protection of core features
of their national constitutions such as fundamental rights protection
or retained national competencies. It could have been argued that
primacy was only granted if the Union was exercising conferred
competences which could still have been scrutinised by national
courts.

Second, it has to be noted that under the Constitutional Treaty
it might have been possible to advocate primacy not only with regard to former "third pillar" law but also regarding European decisions in the framework of the CFSP including International Agreements in the field of CFSP.[88] This seems to be difficult under the
Lisbon Treaty which stresses strongly that CFSP "is subject to specific rules and procedures",[89] thereby arguably preserving the current intergovernmental character of this policy more than the Constitutional Treaty would have done.

All this indicates that the Constitutional Treaty would not have
changed the substance of the primacy rule. Yet it was put forward
that the new primacy rule would change the legal quality of the
relation between the Union and the Member States. Codifying the
principle of supremacy in the Constitution would, as was contended, go far beyond the case law of the ECJ and thus produce a
qualitative change.[90] By accepting the Constitutional Treaty, the
Member States would accept primacy of EU law over the *entire*
corpus of national law. Reservations with respect to the core of
national constitutional law, like in the Maastricht-judgement of the
German Constitutional Court, would no longer be possible. Such
national reservations could no longer be upheld on the grounds of
the new Treaty. The guarantee for the national identity of the Member States[91] would only exist at EU level. Its observation would be
exclusively a question of Union law making the ECJ the last arbiter
in the matter.

---

88   *De Witte* (2007), § 10 *et seq.*

89   Article 24(1) TEU-L.

90   *Öhlinger* (2005), 691 *et seq; Öhlinger* (2007), 350 *et seq.*

91   Article I-5(1) of the Constitutional Treaty.

However, it is not easy to infer such far-reaching consequences from the codification of the supremacy principle given the limitations resulting both from the clause "in exercising competences conferred on it" and the guarantees for the national identity. These clauses could have been the anchor for the Member States' courts to limit any encroachments on national 'sovereignty'. Regarding fundamental rights protection, it has furthermore to be borne in mind that the Draft Constitution did not only expressly secure the level of protection as recognised by Union law, international law and international agreements but also "by the Member States' constitutions".[92] This could even encourage Member States' reservations against the notion of unconditional supremacy of community law over national law, and is certainly not strengthening the ECJ's jurisprudence in this respect.[93]

Moreover, future amendments to the Constitution would have been subject to national ratification and judicial control regarding their constitutionality. Of course, the threat of an open conflict between the ECJ and national courts insisting on their power to preserve national sovereignty would not have been eliminated. Rather the 'co-operation' between the ECJ and national courts in the enforcement of the respective constitutions would have continued.

If it is agreed that the Constitutional Treaty would not have changed much in this respect it is difficult to argue that the Lisbon Treaty will, given its comparative silence on the issue.[94] There is neither a good reason to hold that primacy should be discarded nor that it should be extended compared to the Status Quo or the Constitutional Treaty. The latter stance could be considered given that Declaration No 17 is unconditional and does not mention the competences of the Union. However, the limits of the Union's powers to conferred competences cannot really be challenged.[95] It is not difficult for a Member State court to invoke this restriction quite similarly as it has happened in the past.

---

92   Article II-113 of the Constitutional Treaty. This is now included in Article 53 of the Charter of Fundamental Rights.

93   For a discussion of this controversial provision see *Griller* (2002); for a different view compare e.g. *Rengeling / Szczekalla* (2004), esp. para. 495.

94   In the same vein *Ziller* (2007), 139 *et seq.*

95   Article 4(1)(2) and Article 5(1)(2) TEU-L.

Taken altogether there seems to be little textual or contextual support for the contention that the Primacy Clause in the Constitutional Treaty would have brought a decisive step into the direction of Statehood of the European Union. The lack of such a clause in the revised Treaties does not create a big difference either.

VI. Conclusions

The alleged abandonment of the 'constitutional concept' in the Lisbon Treaty as compared to the Draft Constitutional Treaty reanimates the dispute on whether the Union does already have a constitution, or should have one in the future. The answer offered here is that, yes, the Union has a constitution, and in a double sense: First in the sense that every international organisation has a constitution. Second and more important in the sense that the current Treaties already fulfil the functions traditionally ascribed to constitutions *of states* both in a 'thin' positivist understanding but also in a 'thick' understanding reflecting the achievements of European Enlightenment.

The Lisbon Treaty to a certain extent reinforces this development by bringing additional competences under what used to be called the 'Community method' of supranational law making, most notably in the 'Area of Freedom, Security and Justice', and in the Common Commercial Policy. In addition, the Treaty fosters and develops further essential constitutional elements such as democratic law making (majority decisions in the Council with the European Parliament acting as a true co-legislator) and limits to the legislator as included in Fundamental Rights of the citizens. It also enhances legal consistence by merging the European Union and the European Community into one single legal personality. Taken altogether, the Lisbon Treaty is yet another important stage in the constitutional development of the European Union.

That the Union still is no state and assumedly will not turn into a state in the years to come is not, as is sometimes argued, due to a lack of power, state people, or territory. By contrast, already today in terms of powers the Union has reached a degree of centralisation which would be sufficient. The reason is simply the lack of a founding will on the side of the Member States. The Constitutional Treaty would not have changed that. The Lisbon Treaty will not either.

References

Robert Alexy (2002), The Argument from Injustice, Oxford (Clarendon Press) 2002.

Armin von Bogdandy (1999), Supranationaler Föderalismus als Wirklichkeit und Idee einer neuen Herrschaftsform, Baden-Baden (Nomos) 1999.

Ian Brownlie (2003), Principles of Public International Law, Oxford (Oxford University Press) [6]2003.

Antonio Cassese (2003), International Law, Oxford [2]2003.

Paul Craig (2001), Constitutions, Constitutionalism, and the European Union, in: European Law Journal 7 (2001), 125-150.

James Crawford (2006), The Creation of States in International Law, Oxford (Clarendon Press) [2]2006.

Alan Dashwood (1998), States in the European Union, in: European Law Review 23 (1998), 201-216.

Karl Doehring (1987), State, in: *Rudolf Bernhardt* (ed.), Encyclopedia of Public International Law, instalment 10, Amsterdam (North Holland) 1987, 423-428.

Jeffrey L. Dunoff (2006), Constitutional Conceits: The WTO's 'Constitution' and the Discipline of International Law, in: European Journal of International Law 17 (2006), 647-675.

Erik O. Eriksen / John E. Fossum / Matthias Kumm / Agustin J. Menéndez (2005), The European Constitution: the Rubicon crossed?, ARENA, Oslo 2005.

Ulrich Everling (1993), Überlegungen zur Struktur der Europäischen Union und zum neuen Europa-Artikel des Grundgesetzes, in: Deutsches Verwaltungsblatt 108 (1993), 936-947.

Bardo Fassbender (1998), The United Nations Charter as Constitution of the International Community, Columbia Journal of Transnational Law 36 (1998), 529-619.

Thomas Giegerich (2003), Europäische Verfassung und deutsche Verfassung im transnationalen Konstitutionalisierungsprozeß: Wechselseitige Rezeption, konstitutionelle Evolution und föderale Verflechtung (= Beiträge zum ausländischen öffentlichen Recht und Völkerrecht, Vol. 157), Berlin (Springer) 2003.

Thomas C. Grey (1979), Constitutionalism: An Analytic Framework, in: *J. Ronald Pennock / John William Chapman* (eds.), Constitutionalism, New York (New York University Press) 1979, 189-209.

Stefan Griller (2002), Primacy of Community Law: a Hidden Agenda of the Charter of Fundamental Rights, in *Dimitri Melissas / Ingolf Pernice* (eds.), Perspectives of the Nice Treaty and the Intergovernmental Conference in 2004, Baden-Baden (Nomos) (2002), 47-61.

Stefan Griller (2005), Die Europäische Union. Ein staatsrechtliches Monstrum?, in: *Gunnar Folke Schuppert / Ingolf Pernice / Ulrich Haltern* (eds.), Europawissenschaft, Baden-Baden (Nomos) 2005, 201-272.

Stefan Griller / Dimitris Droutsas / Gerda Falkner / Katrin Forgó / Michael Nentwich (2000), The Treaty of Amsterdam. Facts, Analysis, Prospects, Vienna (Springer) 2000.

H. L. A. Hart (1994), The Concept of Law, Oxford (Oxford University Press) [2]1994.

Josef Isensee (1995), Integrationsziel Europastaat?, in *Olle Due / Marcus. Lutter / Jürgen Schwarze* (eds.), Festschrift für Ulrich Everling, Vol. 1, Baden-Baden (Nomos) 1995, 567-592.

Jean-Paul Jacqué (2004), The Principle of Institutional Balance, in: Common Market Law Review 41 (2004), 383-391.

Georg Jellinek (1901), The Declaration Of The Rights Of Man And Of Citizens: A Contribution To Modern Constitutional History, New York (Henry Holt and Company) 1901.

Georg Jellinek (1914), Allgemeine Staatslehre, Berlin (Häring) [3]1914.

Alfred E. Kellermann / Jaap W. Zwaan / Jenö Czuczai (eds.) (2001), EU Enlargement – The Constitutional Impact at EU and National Level, The Hague (T. M. C. Asser Press) 2001.

Hans Kelsen (1949), General Theory of Law and State, Cambridge/MA (Harvard University Press) 1949.

Hans Kelsen (1967), Reine Rechtslehre, Vienna (Deuticke) [2]1960 [English version cited: Pure Theory of Law, translated by *Max Knight*, Berkeley/Los Angeles (University of California Press) 1967].

Hans Kelsen / Robert W. Tucker, Principles of International Law, New York (Holt, Rinehart and Winston) 1966.

Josef L. Kunz (1929), Die Staatenverbindungen, Stuttgart (W. Kohlhammer) 1929.

Charles Leben (2000), A Federation of Nation States or a Federal State?, in: *Christian Joerges / Yves Mény / Joseph H. Weiler* (eds.), What Kind of Constitution for What Kind of Polity? Responses to Joschka Fischer, San Domenico (Robert Schuman Centre) 2000, 99-111.

Koen Lenaerts (1990), Constitutionalism and the Many Faces of Federalism, in: The American Journal of Comparative Law 38 (1990), 205-263.

Koen Lenaerts / Piet van Nuffel (2005), Constitutional Law of the European Union, London (Sweet&Maxwell) [2]2005.

Koen Lenaerts / Amaryllis Verhoeven (2002), Institutional Balance as a Guarantee for Democracy in EU Governance, in *Christian Joerges / Renaud Dehousse* (eds.), Good Governance in Europe's Integrated Market, Oxford (Oxford University Press) 2002), 35-88.

Peter Lerche (1995), "Kompetenz-Kompetenz" und das Maastricht-Urteil des Bundesverfassungsgerichts, in: *Jörn Ipsen et al.* (Hrsg.), Verfassungsrecht im Wandel, Festschrift zum 180jährigen Bestehen des Heymanns Verlags, Cologne (Heymann). 1995, 409.

Neil MacCormick (1999), Questioning Sovereignty. Law, State and Nation in the European Commonwealth, Oxford (Oxford University Press) 1999.

Miguel Poiares Maduro (2005), The importance of being called a constitution: constitutional authority and the authority of constitutionalism, in: International Journal of constitutional law 3 (2005), 332-356.

G. Federico Mancini (1998), Europe: The Case for Statehood, in: European Law Journal 4 (1998), No. 1, 29-42.

Theo Öhlinger (2005), Der Vorrang des Unionsrechts im Lichte des Verfassungsvertrags, in: *Jürgen Bröhmer / Roland Bieber / Christian Calliess / Christine Langenfeld / Stefan Weber / Joachim Wolf* (eds.), Internationale Gemeinschaft und Menschenrechte, Festschrift für Georg Ress zum 70. Geburtstag, Cologne (Heymanns) (2005), 685-698.

Theo Öhlinger (2007), Die Ratifikation des Verfassungsvertrages in Österreich – Anmerkungen zum konstitutionellen Gehalt des Verfassungsvertrages, in: *Waldemar Hummer / Walter Obwexer* (eds.), Der Vertrag über eine Verfassung für Europa, Baden-Baden (Nomos) 2007, 343-358.

Stefan Oeter (2002), Souveränität – ein überholtes Konzept?, in: *Hans-Joachim Cremer / Thomas Giegerich / Dagmar Richter / Andreas Zimmermann* (eds.), Tradition und Weltoffenheit des Rechts. Festschrift für Helmut Steinberger, Berlin (Springer) (2002), 259-290.

Thomas Oppermann (1994), Zur Eigenart der Europäischen Union, in: *Peter Hommelhoff / Paul Kirchhof* (eds.), Der Staatenverbund der Europäischen Union, Heidelberg (Müller) 1994, 87-98.

Ingolf Pernice (1999), Multilevel Constitutionalism and the Treaty of Amsterdam: European Constitution-Making Revisited, in: Common Market Law Review 36 (1999), 703-750.

Ingolf Pernice (2001), Europäisches und nationales Verfassungsrecht, Veröffentlichungen der Vereinigung der deutschen Staatsrechtslehrer 60 (2001), 148-193.

Anne Peters (2001), Elemente einer Theorie der Verfassung Europas, Berlin (Duncker & Humblot) 2001.

Anne Peters (2006), Compensatory Constitutionalism: The Function and Potential of Fundamental International Norms and Structures, in: Leiden Journal of International Law, 19 (2006), 579-610.

Jean-Claude Piris (1999), Does the European Union have a Constitution? Does it need one?, in: European Law Review 24 1999, 557-585.

Jean-Claude Piris (2006), The Constitution for Europe: A Legal Analysis, Cambridge (Cambridge University Press) 2006.

Hans-Werner Rengeling / Peter Szczekalla, Grundrechte in der Europäischen Union. Charta der Grundrechte und Allgemeine Rechtsgrundsätze, Cologne (Heymann) 2004.

Henry G. Schermers / Niels M. Blokker, International Institutional Law, Boston / Leiden (Martinus Nijhoff Publishers) [4]2003.

Frank Schorkopf (2007), Grundgesetz und Überstaatlichkeit, Tübingen (Mohr Siebeck) 2007.

Bruno Simma / Dirk Pulkowski (2006), Of Planets and the Universe: Self-contained Regimes in International Law, in: European Journal of International Law 17 (2006), 483-529.

Rudolf Streinz / Christoph Ohler / Christoph Herrmann (2008), Der Vertrag von Lissabon zur Reform der EU, München (C.H. Beck) ²2008.

Joel P. Trachtman (2006), The Constitutions of the WTO, in: European Journal of International Law 17 (2006), 623-646.

Dimitris Triantafyllou, Les procedures d'adoption et de revision du traité constitutionnel, in: *Giulio Amato / Hervé Bribosia / Bruno de Witte* (eds.), Genesis and Destiny of the European Constitution, Brussels (Bruylant) 2007, 223-245.

Alfred Verdross, Die Verfassung der Völkerrechtsgemeinschaft, Wien / Berlin (Verlag von Julius Springer) 1926.

Neil Walker (ed.) (2003), Sovereignty in Transition, Oxford / Portland/OR (Hart Publishing) 2003.

Joseph H. H. Weiler (1998), Europe: The Case Against the Case for Statehood, in: European Law Journal 4 (1998), 43-62.

Joseph H. H. Weiler (1999), The Constitution of Europe, Cambridge (Cambridge University Press) 1999.

Joseph H. H. Weiler (2000), Epilogue. Fischer: The Dark Side, in: *Christian Joerges / Yves Mény / Joseph H. Weiler* (eds.), What Kind of Constitution for What Kind of Polity? Responses to Joschka Fischer, San Domenico (Robert Schuman Centre) 2000, 235-247.

Erika de Wet (2006), The International Constitutional Order, in: International & Comparative Law Quarterly 55 (2006), 51-75.

Bruno de Witte (1999), Direct Effect, Supremacy and the Nature of the Legal Order, in: *Paul Craig / Gráinne de Búrca* (eds.), The Evolution of EU Law, Oxford (Oxford University Press) 1999, 177-213.

Bruno de Witte (2007), Article I-6, in: *Laurence Burgorgue-Larsen / Anne Levade / Fabrice Picod* (eds.), Traité établissant une Constitution pour l'Europe – Commentaire article par article, Vol. 1, Brussels (Bruylant) 2007, 106-116.

Jacques Ziller (2005), The European Constitution, The Hague (Kluwer) 2005.

Jacques Ziller (2007), Il nuovo Trattato europeo, Bologna (Il
    Mulino) 2007.

Hervé Bribosia

The Main Institutional Innovations
of the Lisbon Treaty

I. Introduction

The bulk of the institutional reform resulting from the Lisbon Treaty (LT) was taken from the Constitutional Treaty (CT). This probably reflects the fact that the institutional substance of the CT was not perceived as having contributed to its rejection.

In fact, the most delicate institutional issues like the composition of the Commission, the definition of qualified majority voting (QMV) or even the composition of the European Parliament (EP) have never been the main concern of the European citizens. But they have always been very sensitive questions for the Member States and their governments. These issues were the 'leftovers' of the Amsterdam Treaty and were dealt with by the Nice Treaty in a very unsatisfactory way – so unsatisfactory that, one year later, the Laeken Declaration paved the way for their reconsideration. Even during the European Convention, these institutional issues were not addressed using the usual method of the Convention. They were again largely revisited during the 2004 IGC.

One must confess that it is not easy to retrace the evolution of these traditional institutional issues, nor to work out the legal foundations of the current situation. Having in one's hands the latest consolidated version of the treaties is not enough. You still need the Nice Protocol on Enlargement (including the related Declaration on Enlargement 'EU 27'), and above all the last two Accession Treaties (AT). Yet this is the situation which will remain until the LT is ratified by the 27 Member States and enters into force.

It is then that one realises the value of one single treaty (like the CT) replacing all the others. Now, to tell the truth, the LT does not only borrow most of the substance of the institutional provisions of the CT, but also the way in which these provisions have been redrafted to make them clearer. Likewise, the new Treaty on the European Union (TEU-L) comprises more institutional provisions than before, namely, the most significant ones stemming from the first part of the CT (and, to an even greater extent, those regarding the Commission).

One difficulty lies in the LT's transitional provisions regarding the institutions. Some of the reforms would enter into force immediately – on 1 January 2009 for the High Representative and the President of European Council – some in the course of 2009 (new composition of the EP, election of the President of the Commission by the EP), and others in 2014 ('small' Commission, new definition of QMV).

In this chapter, I will sketch the main institutional changes provided by the LT, regarding the European Parliament, the European Council and its President, the Council and its Presidency and the European Commission. Where relevant, the differences between the LT and what the CT had foreseen will be underlined. I will first set out what the new institutions and institutional players are, and point to some new terminology for them. Although there are a number of innovations concerning the Court of Justice, these will not be addressed in this contribution.

II. New institutions, new names

As in the CT, there are two new institutions, the European Central Bank (ECB) and the European Council.

The institutionalisation of the ECB should not have significant implications, as it already has a legal personality. However, it should bring to an end speculation regarding the ECB's status as an autonomous sectoral organisation.[1] The new European Council replaces the current European Council as a political body and the Council configuration composed of 'Heads of State or Government' (on this topic, see below). But unlike the CT which considered the ECB and the Court of Auditors as 'other institutions', the LT does not make any such distinction.

There are also new names.

Thus the new 'Court of Justice of the European Union' comprises the 'Court of Justice' and the 'General Court' ('*Tribunal*' in French), instead of the current 'Court of First Instance'. There are no longer any 'judicial panels' ('*chambres juridictionnelles*'), but 'specialised courts' attached to the General Court ('*tribunaux spécialisés*'). One of these has already been created (before the end of 2004): the *EU Civil Service Tribunal*. However, the LT does not adopt the title 'Council of Ministers' proposed by the CT, and thus the current official name 'Council of the EU' will remain. As for the European Commission, it would be odd to keep its official title 'Commission of the European Communities' since the European Community (but not the Euratom Community) will be replaced by the Union.

---

1   *Zilioli / Selmayr* (2000). On the topic, see in this volume the chapter by *Antonio Saínz de Vicuña*.

   Then there are new institutional players. Thus the High Representative of the Union for Foreign Affairs and Security Policy (currently "for CFSP") basically takes up the institutional role of the
Union Minister for Foreign Affairs in the CT. Appointed by the
European Council (by QMV), he will play a role in CFSP similar to
the one played by the Commission in Community matters, namely
initiating and implementing the policy, as well as the external representation of the Union. He wears two hats, or even three: one as a
Vice-President of the European Commission, in charge of the external relations portfolio, the above-mentioned one in CFSP, and the
one of permanent president of the *Foreign Affairs Council*, which
will most likely cover both CFSP and all the external action of the
Community. As a result, it was difficult for him to wear yet another
hat as General Secretary of the Council, as is the case today.[2]

   The national parliaments are other potential institutional players in the law-making process of the EU (see Art. 12 TEU-L).
However, one could wonder whether the 'legislative' activity of the
EU was the right target, given the role of the EP in the ordinary legislative procedure. In fact, their involvement in the adoption of
non-legislative acts would have been more appropriate where the
role of the Council is predominant or even exclusive. The same is
true for the treaty amendment procedures (although some progress
has been made in that respect, including the so-called "*passerelle*"
procedure). It appears that the promoters of the role of national parliaments had in mind a counterbalance to the supranational decision-making process, rather than more control over their respective
governments acting in the Council. Thus the former Commissioner
Michel Barnier had suggested during the Convention that the national parliaments could attend the sessions of the Council, but the
idea was far from being endorsed. In other words, the new role of
the national parliaments could be seen as a new kind of intergo-
vernmentalism in the EU setting. Only time will tell to what extent
the national parliaments may affect the law-making process of the
EU, notably in the assessment of compliance with the subsidiarity
principle. They are not likely to have a great deal of influence,
which may be not all too negative.[3]

   One could mention yet another potential future institutional
player, namely the European Prosecutor in criminal matters. Its cre-

---

2   On the topic, see in this volume the chapter by *Christine Kaddous*.

3   On this argument, see *Bribosia* (2007), 424-428.

ation is foreseen by the LT, but would require unanimous agreement.

Let us now return to the usually sensitive institutional issues.

III. The European Parliament

A. Powers of the EP

The EP is number one on the list of institutions in the Treaty and the great winner of the institutional reform. The number of cases where it co-legislates with the Council has doubled, up to 90 all together (formerly co-decision, now the 'ordinary legislative procedure'). As the annual budgetary procedure has transformed itself into a sort of new co-decision procedure, its powers have increased as regards compulsory expenditure (two thirds of the annual budget). The distinction between compulsory and non-compulsory expenditure has indeed been abolished. The EP's control over the 'executive' functions of the Commission has been increased both via the new system of delegated legislation, and via its future influence to devise the comitology system (which will be reviewed by co-decision). Eventually, the political control of the EP will also be increased as it will 'elect' the President of the Commission.[4]

B. Composition of the EP

The composition of the EP is a perfect example of the complexity of the evolution of the legal framework of an institution.

1. Current situation

To date, the maximum number of MEPs and the distribution of seats between Member States have been determined by the Treaties, in particular by the last two Accession Treaties.

After the accession of Finland, Sweden and Austria, the number of MEPs rose from 567 to 626. This number will remain stable during the 1999-2004 EP session, although the Amsterdam Treaty had provided for a maximum of 700 MEPs. In view of the coming enlargements, the Nice Treaty raised this ceiling to 732, while the Declaration on Enlargement 'EU 27' provided for the future distribution of seats between the 15 Member States (sharing 535 seats amongst themselves) and the 12 new Member States to come (sharing amongst themselves the remaining seats).

---

4   On the topic, see in this volume the chapter by *Paul Craig.*

Since only 10 new Member States joined before the 2004 elections, Bulgaria and Romania's 50 seats were re-allocated amongst the 25 Member States in the Accession Treaty of 16 April 2003. The distribution of seats for the 2004-2009 EP session can therefore be found in the 2003 Accession Treaty (Art. 11 of the Act annexed to the Treaty). When Bulgaria and Romania joined mid-term in 2007, they were allocated their 50 seats (plus 3 more). This is why there are at present 785 MEPs, namely 732 plus 53. The extra seats above the ceiling of 732 were provisionally allowed by the Nice Protocol on Enlargement.

To sum up, there were 732 MEPs at the beginning of the 2004-2009 EP session, and as of 1 January 2007, there are 785 MEPs.

Regarding the 2009-2014 EP session, the last Accession Treaty of 25 April 2005 increases the maximum ceiling from 732 to 736 in order to make up for the unfair allocation of seats to both Hungary and the Czech Republic in Nice. They were both given two more seats each. Apart from that, the distribution of the EP seats basically corresponds to the allocation already provided for in the Nice Declaration on Enlargement 'EU 27'. The seats will be allocated in this way unless the LT enters into force in due time.

2. The 2009-2014 EP session following the Lisbon Treaty

If the LT enters into force in time for the next elections in June 2009, the ceiling would be raised to 751, i.e. one more than in the CT. It also sets maximum and minimum thresholds of 96 seats (3 less for Germany than the figure in the 2005 Accession Treaty) and 6 seats (1 more for Malta than the figure in the 2005 Accession Treaty).

The main new feature (already in the CT) is that the actual allocation per Member State will no longer be determined by the Treaty but by a decision taken by the European Council, by unanimity, on a proposal from the EP. The only indication given by the LT is the principle of *degressive proportionality* of the citizens' representation, which basically had already governed all the previous allocations.

According to the CT, such a decision was to be taken in due time for the 2009 elections. The June 2007 European Council (which established the mandate for the IGC) kept the idea of a new allocation to be ready in time for the next elections. The allocation of EP seats was also seen by some as a part of the whole new institutional package deal. Therefore the European Council called for the EP to make a proposal.

The EP did so quickly in its Resolution of 11 October 2007, following an in-depth report on the topic by *A. Lamassoure* and *A. Severin*. Their approach was to start from the allocation currently planned for 2009 (in the 2005 Accession Treaty), while taking into account the new thresholds. The Resolution then redistributes the 16 free 'remaining seats' (750 minus736 minus 3 plus1 = 16), following a pragmatic interpretation of degressive proportionality, close to the current allocation. As a result, the changes are as follows:

- Germany: minus 3
- Malta: plus 1
- Spain: plus 4[5]
- France, Sweden, Austria: plus 2 for each
- UK, Poland, Netherlands, Bulgaria, Latvia & Slovenia: plus 1 for each.

The EP's proposal stipulates that this allocation will have to be revised for the following elections (2014 - 2019). A new systematic formula would enable the evolution of the populations of the Member States and the accession of new Member States to be taken into account (until then, future Accession Treaties would again provide for the ceiling of 750 to be exceeded provisionally).

The IGC endorsed the EP's proposal (see Declaration No 5 of the Final Act to the LT), but decided to give one extra seat to Italy; the new ceiling in the Lisbon Treaty is thus 751 ("750 plus the President"). The EP is likely to modify its proposal in this way, and the European Council will then be able to pass the Decision on seat allocation as soon as the LT enters into force.

Two remarks to conclude on the composition of the EP. In the CT, delaying the allocation of EP seats was seen as an advantage in the already complex negotiation. In the LT, it is seen as part of the package deal. In the CT, the reform of the EP's composition ran parallel to the new definition of QMV, as both deal with the criteria of population. They were thus both planned for 2009. In the LT, the new definition of QMV is delayed until 2014, but not the composition of the European Parliament.

---

5   Spain is regaining the seats that it had traded off against extra relative weight in the Nice definition of QMV.

III. The European Council

At present, there is a difference between the European Council and the Council meeting in the composition of Heads of State or Government.

The European Council is an informal body providing the Union with the necessary impetus for its development and defining political directions (in general, but also in CFSP and AFSJ, in particular). It includes the President of the Commission. In practice, it operates by consensus.

The Council meeting composed of Heads of State or Government is a configuration of the Council which is entitled to pass legal acts, voting by QMV or unanimity. This is the case, for example, for the appointment of the Commission President (by QMV), for the decision on the transition to the third stage of EMU (by QMV), or for the decision establishing a breach by a Member State of a basic principle of the EU (unanimity).

In the Amsterdam Treaty, the distinction is actually slightly blurred in two cases where the European Council also acts as an institution, and even votes.[6]

The 'institutionalisation' of the European Council is therefore a logical evolution. As a consequence, it will be subject to the same constraints as the other institutions. Its powers are attributed and are subject to the subsidiarity principle. Its action is subject to the jurisdiction of the Court of Justice, etc. However, such institutionalisation could have amounted to the mere formalisation of the corresponding Council configuration, acting at the level of Heads of State or Government (which is still not ruled out in the future). Instead the decision was deliberately taken to create a brand new institution separate from that of the Council of the EU, which is likely to complicate the institutional setting as a whole.

A. Composition and functioning

The European Council is composed of the Heads of State or Government, the President of the European Council (who is supernumerary in terms of nationality) and the President of the Commission (as is now the case). The High Representative is not a member but is invited to participate on a regular basis. The Heads of State or

---

6   Decision to have a common defence (Art. 17 TEU); decision by unanimity to consider important reasons of national policy where a QMV is opposed by a Member States in CFSP (Art. 23.2 TEU).

Government can be accompanied by a national Minister (not necessarily the Minister for Foreign Affairs), and the President of the Commission by a Commissioner.

The European Council meets twice per semester in Brussels. It remains to be seen if informal meetings will continue to be held in the Member State holding the rotating Presidency. Its Secretariat is provided by the General Secretariat of the Council.

B. Powers of the European Council

The new European Council continues to hold most of its previous powers and responsibilities (and those of the Council in its Heads of State or Government configuration), but is also entrusted with many new powers. There are around 35 legal bases concerning the European Council (instead of 8 or 9 in the current Treaties). They reflect the various functions of the European Council.

It gives political guidance[7] notably by defining the strategic interests and objectives in CFSP.[8]

It plays the role of a 'broker' in what is known as the emergency brake procedure, where a Member State may invoke fundamental aspects of its national systems (social security, criminal matters),[9] rather like in the Luxembourg Compromise. The last IGC added two new cases of this kind (police co-operation and creation of the European prosecutor): the European Council can either require the Council to reach agreement or let the legislative process continue within the framework of the enhanced co-operation mechanism.[10]

The European Council is in charge of appointing people to the most senior positions: its own President,[11] the Commission and its President,[12] the High Representative,[13] and the members of the Executive board of the ECB.[14]

---

7   Art. 15.5 TEU-L.

8   Art. 22.1 and 26 TEU-L.

9   Art. 48, 82, 83 TFEU (comp. art. 31 TEU-L regarding CFSP).

10   Art. 86.1 and 87 TFEU.

11   Art. 15.5 TEU-L.

12   Art. 17.7 TEU-L.

13   Art. 18.1 TEU-L.

14   Art. 283 TFEU. In the current Treaties, this last appointment is the result of a 'common agreement' of the Heads of State or Government.

It 'shall not exercise legislative functions'. Nevertheless, it passes 'normative' decisions, for example, on the composition of the EP,[15] on the configurations of the Council, and on the rotating presidency of the Council.[16] The European Council (the Council in the current Treaties) is also entitled to modify the number of members of the European Commission.[17] In other words, it exercises a quasi-constitutional function.

The European Council also enjoys a central position in treaty amendment procedures, both the ordinary and simplified procedures. In particular, it triggers what are known as *passerelle* mechanisms, which involve changing the decision-making procedures into QMV or the ordinary legislative procedure.[18]

C. Voting rule

The LT formalises the practice of consensus in the European Council, which is quite unusual for an 'institution', unless a voting rule is provided for in the Treaty.[19] This is actually the case for over half of the legal bases. Unanimity is provided mainly for its quasi-constitutional function; QMV mainly for appointments; and even a simple majority is provided for, such as for the adoption of Rules of Procedure, or to take the decision not to convene a Convention.

In general a voting rule corresponds to the adoption of a legal act, and consensus corresponds with a political action.[20] Where there is a vote, the President of the European Council (who is supernumerary) and the President of Commission (who is currently not a member of the Council configuration) do not take part. This was not mentioned in the CT. But there is already a controversy as to whether their exclusion from voting applies only to QMV, as opposed to unanimity cases.

D. The President of the European Council

At present, the rotating Presidency system applies to both the Council and the European Council. One of the main innovations of the

---

15 Art. 14.2 TUE-L.

16 Art. 236 TFEU.

17 Art. 17.5 TEU-L.

18 Art. 48.6 et 48.7 TEU-L.

19 Art. 15.4 TEU-L.

20 But not strictly: the current cases where the European Council votes still apply (see above).

CT, taken up by the LT, is the establishment of a more permanent Presidency of the European Council. The Presidency will now be assumed by a President 'elected' by the European Council for a term of 2 ½ years, renewable once. It is a full-time job, not compatible with any national office (which is why he is supernumerary). The purpose of this innovation is to ensure the continuity and the efficiency of the work of the European Council.

The functions (and powers) of the President are still to be defined in practice, but one thing is certain: he will not be limited to merely 'chairing' the meeting (the IGC 2004 had already discarded the term 'Chairman' chosen by the Convention). One might assume that his functions will basically be the same as that of a rotating Presidency, but on a longer-term basis. He will conduct the work of the European Council. He will prepare for it and ensure that it is followed up. Given the new powers of the European Council (see above), this potentially represents a considerable amount of work. Above all, he will, 'at his or her level', ensure the external representation of the Union.

Some questions remain unanswered, in particular as regards the consequences of breaking the unity of the 'chain of command' between the Council and European Council (see below). What will be the President's relationship with the High Representative in terms of the external representation of the Union? Will he be seen as a rival by the President of the Commission, who has had the advantage until now of being the only permanent top figure? What administrative means will be available (the number of 60 members of specific staff has been mentioned)?

IV. The Council of the EU

The LT provisions on the Council are the outcome of a long process of self-reform (*Trumpf-Piris* report and Helsinki conclusions in 1999, Seville conclusions in 2002).

A. Configurations of the Council

The Council of the EU is one single institution representing the Member States, and is composed of Ministers from national (or regional) governments. In practice, it works in various sectoral configurations, which at present amount to nine, including the General Affairs and External Relations Council (GAERC), which is composed of national Ministers for Foreign Affairs.[21]

The LT splits the GAERC and formalises the existence of two configurations, namely the General Affairs Council (GAC) and the Foreign Affairs Council (FAC).

The GAC's role will be to ensure the consistency of the work of the other configurations (within the framework of a multiannual programme, see below). It will prepare and carry out the follow-up of the work of the European Council (in liaison with the Commission and the President of the European Council). As to the FAC, it will deal exclusively with the external action of the EU in general. It will be 'presided over' by the High Representative for Foreign Affairs and Security Policy.

The other configurations will remain those currently in place until they are formalised and/or adapted by a decision of the European Council (acting by QMV).

One might remember that the Convention's idea to set up a Legislative Council was already discarded by the 2004 IGC. Some had in mind to actually foreshadow a second legislative assembly as in a Federal system. The idea was also therefore to identify the precise executive function of the Council, which would have corresponded to what were then known as 'non-legislative acts'. This innovation was equally often associated with the appointment at national level of a sort of super Minister for European Affairs to sit at the Legislative Council. He would merely have been 'assisted' by the sectoral Ministers. This latter potential implication contributed to the idea's lack of success, as it could have altered the internal political habits of the Member States. However, in my view, the sectoral configurations could have been retained, be in only for non-legislative activities.

Be that as it may, although the concept of 'European Law' has also been dropped by the LT, the distinction between legislative and non-legislative acts has been preserved (by referring or not referring to a legislative procedure in the legal bases of the treaty). This dis-

---

21   The nine configurations are: General Affairs and External Relations, Economic and Financial Affairs, Cooperation in the fields of Justice and Home Affairs (JHA), Employment, Social Policy, Health and Consumer Affairs, Competitiveness, Transport, Telecommunications and Energy, Agriculture and Fisheries, Environment, Education, Youth and Culture.

tinction has several implications,[22] one of which is that each Council configuration will meet in public when it deliberates on legislative acts.

Furthermore, it is not ruled out that, sooner or later, the composition of the General Affairs Council will differ from that of the Foreign Affairs Council, and will be composed of national Ministers specialising in European Affairs so as to ensure the co-ordination of the work of the Council.

B. The Presidency of the Council

At present, the Presidency is held by a Member State and rotates every six months. The main advantage of this system resides in the unity in the 'chain of command' for all Council configurations, Coreper and various other committees, down to all the working groups. The drawback is the lack of continuity and, for some, also the lack of efficiency of the work of the Council. For smaller or newer Member States, the task can appear very demanding indeed.

Although there were quite a number of ideas and proposals to reform the Presidency of the Council, the Lisbon Treaty, like the CT, finally took a rather conservative line.

Of course, the establishment of a permanent President for the European Council (a 2 ½ year renewable term) and for the Foreign Affairs Council (in principle for 5 years, i.e. the term of the Commission, as one of its Vice-Presidents) is a considerable innovation which meets the need for continuity.

As for the other configurations of the Council (including the GAC), there is a new system of *Team Presidencies* which should be pre-established for each 18-month period, and which are composed of three Member States, *'taking into account their diversity and geographical balance within the Union'*. As a result, each Member State still holds the Presidency for six months in turn, but it operates on the basis of a common programme. The Team Presidency should improve the continuity of the work of the Council (at least for each 18 month period). Furthermore, each Member State can be assisted by the two others, and the group can agree on special arrangements, probably including delegating (but not sharing) the chairs of some configurations, committees and working groups. In

---

22   Regarding access to documents, individual access to the ECJ, and notably the role of national parliaments as far as subsidiarity is concerned.

practice, the system of team presidency has already been at work since the last German presidency (with Portugal and Slovenia).

C. Assessment of the Council's presidency

The new Presidency of the Council is thus pragmatic and in many respects similar to the current one. With 27 Member States, each of them will still have to wait almost 14 years to have its turn, but the system is flexible. It can be organised by a decision of the European Council and implemented or adapted by the Council, both acting by QMV, and there can be internal arrangements within the teams. The only requirement imposed by the Treaty is the principle of equal rotation.

However, there is a major danger resulting from the fragmentation of the unity of the Presidency and of its 'chain of command'.[23] There may result a lack of co-ordination, or even a rivalry, between the President of the European Council and the rotating Presidency of the Council, not only as regards the work of the European Council, which is still supposed to be carried out 'on the basis of the work of the GAC', but also as regards the work of the Council.

Will the President of the European Council intervene in the GAC or even in the sectoral configuration of the Council? What will be the relationship between the President of the European Council and the Head of State or Government holding the rotating Presidency (in particular where it is held by a large Member State)? Who will set up the *multiannual programme* for the activity of the GAC, and thus of the Council as a whole (see on this point Art. 3 in the draft decision, provided for in Declaration No. 6)? Who will eventually give the general political guidance? Who will be responsible for the achievements of the six month Presidency? Last but not least, who will preside over the IGCs?

More generally speaking, the Presidency is fragmented into five different systems of responsibility – not only the President of the European Council and the rotating Member State, but also the Team Presidency as such, the High Representative and the President of the Eurogroup. Such fragmentation might not ensure the consistency and efficiency of the Presidency of, or rather in, the European Union, and the risk of dilution of responsibility is real. The external representation of the Union will be even more fragmented as one may add to this list the President of the Commission

---

23   Conversely the unity between the GAC and the Coreper is preserved.

and some Commissioners (e.g. responsible for trade or aid), as well as the Foreign Minister of the rotating Presidency.

In order to ensure the coherence of the system, there will be a strong need for consultation and co-ordination procedures between all these players, and perhaps even some collegiality. Co-ordination will have to govern the programming of the Council's work (for 2 ½ years, 18 months, and 6 months).[24] The General Affairs Council might eventually play this role of co-ordination, which has remained quite theoretical until now.

D. The definition and scope of qualified majority voting[25]

The extension of qualified majority voting (by QMV) to 45 new cases in the LT is one of the main institutional improvements (although it already stems from the extension of the co-decision procedure in around 30 cases). This makes the definition of QMV an all the more important and sensitive issue. It affects not only the efficiency of the decision-making process, but also the relative weight of each Member State in that process. For some however, the definition of QMV is less important than the generalisation of QMV across the board, as that is the most determining factor in the negotiation pattern.

The new definition of QMV devised in the CT is preserved by the LT. It still requires 55 % of the Member States,[26] representing 65 % of the population of the Union, whereas a blocking minority must include at least four Member States. But the reform is delayed until 1 November 2014 (instead of 2009 in the CT), so that the Nice system will continue to apply until then. And from that date until the end of March 2017, a Member State can still require the application of the Nice system (see the Protocol on Transitional Provisions).

This is the first part of the compromise which mainly pertained to accommodate Poland with the new double majority. The other part of the compromise was to revisit the *new Ioannina* procedure devised in the CT concerning the implementation of the new double majority: where three quarters of the blocking minority is reached – in terms of Member States (45.1 % of the Member States) or of the EU population (35.1 % of the EU population) – the adoption of the

---

24   CEPS / EGMONT / EPC (2007), 50.

25   On this topic, see in this volume the chapter by *Bruno de Witte*.

26   Including 15 Member States, but this condition will always be fulfilled following the accession of the last two Member States.

decision by QMV may be delayed 'within a reasonable time' in order to look for 'a satisfactory solution to address the concerns' raised by the minority of Member States and for a 'wider basis of agreement in the Council'.

In the LT, the same procedure will be applicable only during the transitional period of 2014 and 2017. Afterwards, the system will still apply, but the proportion of the blocking minority required to trigger the Ioannina procedure will be lowered from 75 % to 55 %. This means that two large Member States will be able to use it, which is a little worrying with regard to the efficiency of the decision-making process.

As in the CT, the Ioannina procedure is established in a draft decision of the Council which would apply as soon the LT itself enters into force.[27] The peculiarity of this draft decision is that it does not seem to have any legal basis (actually like the original Iaonnina Decision of 1994), and there is thus no predetermined procedure for possible future modifications. This was the ultimate compromise: instead of engraving Ioannina in primary law (as requested by the Polish delegation), there is a protocol annexed in the LT providing that any 'draft' which aims to abrogate or amend the Ioannina procedure shall be preceded by a deliberation of the European Council, acting by consensus.

V. The composition and appointment of the European Commission

Although the powers of the Commission are more detailed in the provisions of the CT, and now of the LT, the substance of these powers is basically the same as today. Its executive powers have even been strengthened, notably via the new system of legislative delegation to the Commission. Consequently, what is known as the Comitology system (provided for the implementation of EU legislation) will have to be reformed, this time by the ordinary legislative procedure (and not just in the Council), which may improve the position of the Commission in relation to the Council. But an agreement to revise the Comitology decision of July 2006 is yet to be found.

In this Chapter I will address the issue of the composition and the appointment of the Commission and its President.

---

27 See the Declaration No. 7 in the Final Act of the LT.

A. Composition of the Commission

The current *Barroso* Commission (2004-2009) is composed of one Commissioner per Member State.

One may remember that by the end of the *Prodi* Commission (May 2004) there were 30 Commissioners (20 + 10 coming from the 10 new Member States). The term of the *Prodi* Commission expired slightly earlier than foreseen (31 October 2004 instead of 1 January 2005), and the following Commission (the current *Barroso* Commission) was composed for the first time of one Commissioner per Member State. The large Member States gave up their second Commissioner as a trade-off for the anticipated application of the new definition of QMV. The link between these two institutional issues results from the Nice compromise. But in order to find the legal foundations of these developments, it is necessary to consult the Act annexed to the 2003 Accession Treaty (i.e. concerning the 10 new Member States), in its Part V, Article 45. This is another example of the complexity mentioned in the introduction to this Chapter.

What about the composition of the Commission for its 2009-2014 term? According to the Nice Protocol on Enlargement, from the beginning of the new term after the accession of the 27th Member State, the Commission could no longer be composed of one Commissioner per Member State. Its size would have to be reduced to less than the number of Member States. The actual number and further details regarding the system of equal rotation would have to be determined beforehand by the Council, acting by unanimity. This would be the situation if the LT did not enter into force in time for the next appointment of the Commission.

However, if the LT does enter into force in time, the Commission will continue to be composed of one national per Member State for its 2009-2014 term. This was already the solution provided for in the CT. The idea of the European Convention to make a distinction between voting and non-voting Commissioners had not been taken up by the 2004 IGC.

As for its 2014-2019 term, the Commission will be reduced to 2/3 of the number of Member States (i.e. 18 members in 'EU 27'), including the President and the High Representative. The basic elements of the system of equal rotation are the same as in the Nice Protocol on Enlargement: *"Member States shall be treated on a strictly equal footing"*. Likewise, the Commission shall be composed so *"as to reflect satisfactorily the demographic and geo-*

graphical range of all the Member States". The number of Commissioners could be adapted without treaty revision, by the European Council acting unanimously (as is currently the case, but by the Council).

The reasons for reducing the size of the Commission are basically to make it more efficient and more consistent, and to strengthen its collegiality. One could add that a reduced Commission would make it more legitimate and respected by the Council, in particular by the large Member States. The *one per Member State* composition could indeed reflect an intergovernmental conception which is less acceptable to the largest Member States as they would fear, in this case, that they might be outvoted by a majority of small or very small Member States. The idea is also that a 'small' Commission would be able to re-introduce voting, which is apparently very rarely the case at present.

The drawback of a 'small' Commission is the lack of political support and acceptance by frustrated Member States not 'represented' in the Commission (again particularly for the largest Member States). From this point of view, the Commission would become a weaker Commission (especially given the new figure of the President of the European Council, who could be perceived as a new interlocutor for the large Member States).

In order to solve this problem, a Declaration (No 10) in the Final Act of the LT recommends that the Commission ensures full transparency in relation to all Member States, shares information and consults all of them. It should also take the "appropriate organisational arrangements" to make sure that the social, economic and political realities of all Member States are taken into account.

Some still wonder however about the political feasibility of the strict equal rotation system which has still to be determined (by unanimity) in the European Council, although the LT does not seem to leave much room for manoeuvre. It remains indeed to be seen to what extent the largest Member States will accept it (although only two large Member States would probably not be represented in each Commission).

B. The appointment of the Commission and its President

The current *Barroso* Commission was appointed following the procedure ultimately amended by the Nice Treaty.

The Commission President was nominated by the European Council (by QMV, but in practice still by quasi-consensus), and appointed after the approval of the EP. He thus enjoys a double legitimacy, from the EP and from the national governments.

According to the LT (as was already the case in the CT), the European Council (still by QMV) will propose a candidate, to be *elected* by the European Parliament (the majority of its component, thus more difficult than at present). The proposal will also have to 'take into account the result of the EP election'.

There is thus a slight formal strengthening of the EP, but one could wonder whether this will bring about any real change in practice. The majority (albeit a coalition) in the EP will want to appoint a person of the same political allegiance, as is currently the case. Surely the EP election campaign could be more personalised, and thus more visible, if a candidate for the Presidency of the Commission was chosen beforehand by the political parties. But this could also have been achieved in the current system.

The rest of the Commission will basically be appointed as it is today: suggestions by the Member States (for 'their respective candidates', at least until 2014), adoption of the list of candidates by the Council (by QMV), common agreement with the President-elect, approval of the body by the EP, in practice after hearings and formal appointment of the Commission by the European Council. However, as already mentioned, the Commission will include the High Representative as Vice-President of the Commission. He is appointed by the European Council, with the 'agreement of the President of the Commission'.

Two more changes brought about by the LT are worth mentioning: the Commissioners have to be chosen on the grounds of 'European commitment', and the position of President of the Commission is strengthened, as he could henceforth request a Commissioner to resign without the approval of the college.

The process of 'Parliamentarisation' of the political system of the Union has thus been confirmed by the LT. The main aspects are the election of the President of the Commission and the approval of the college by the EP, QMV in the European Council in the process of appointment, and the motion of censure reserved exclusively to the EP.

However further (parliamentary) politicisation could undermine the Commission's claim for independence and objective expertise in representing the Community's interest, in particular when exercising regulatory and adjudication functions. It also aggravates the risk of loosening the bond between a 'small' Commission and the Member States not represented in it.

Two ideas have already been put forward to rebalance the Commission if it were 'captured' by the EP to too great an extent. One would be to confer the right to censure the Commission not only upon the EP, but also upon the European Council. Another one would be to allow the European Council to dissolve the EP. However, it may well be the case that the European Council and its President already modify the present balance, as the Commission may have to respond more to its political guidance.

VI. Concluding remarks

The main institutional innovations in the LT are basically the same as those provided for in the CT. Those include "new institutions" in the case of the European Council and the European Central Bank, new institutional players, like the European Council President, the High Representative or the national Parliaments, and some new terminology.

The LT's main compromise (actually already secured during the European Convention) results in the trade off of a full-time permanent President of the European Council against the election of the President of the Commission by the EP. By comparison, the Nice compromise was to trade off the second Commissioner of the large Member States against a new definition of QMV which worked in their favour.

One difference with regard to the CT concerns the composition of the EP: this time it is (indirectly) part of the Lisbon package deal, and could already apply to the next elections of the EP. In addition, the outcome concerning the new definition of QMV (double majority) has been delayed until 2014 rather than being applicable at the same time as the new composition of the EP, given the connection with the criterion of population representation in both cases. The year of 2014 is also the time for the reduction in size of the European Commission, which brings us back to the spirit of the institutional compromise in Nice (i.e. linking the reform of the Commission to the new definition of QMV). Finally the new Ioannina procedure will become more restrictive after 2017.

In principle, the High Representative and the President of the European Council should be appointed on 1 January 2009, or as soon as the entry into force of the LT. But there is a claim for a general political package, including the appointment of the new Commission and its President, namely after the next election of the EP in June 2009. Such a claim reflects notably the Declaration No 6 annexed to the final act which underlines some kind of new institutional "magic rule", namely the *"need to respect the geographical and demographic diversity of the Union and its Member States"* for the nominations of the three top figures. [28] Moreover, if such a package of nominations is not respected the first time, it will be more difficult to put together such a package in the future, although it is always possible to delay the moment when the nominees actually enter into office. Appointing the High Representative in early 2009 would prevent the European Parliament from approving the appointment of the new High Representative. It would also imply reshuffling the portfolios in the current Commission: the present Commissioner in charge of external relations (Mrs *Ferrero-Waldner*) would have to change her portfolio, and the Commissioner sharing the same nationality as the new High Representative would have to be dismissed.

The institutional outcome of the Lisbon Treaty is paradoxical in two respects. Firstly, although the main purpose of the reform was to clarify the responsibilities, the new system will be based to an even greater extent on co-ordination and co-operation between even more institutions and institutional players. Secondly, although institutional reform was considered urgent at the time of the Amsterdam treaty in view of further EU enlargements, the core of the innovations will not enter into force until 2014, let alone 2017. Some will argue that in the meantime, the practice has already adapted itself to the needs ...

During the European Convention, the motto was to strengthen the three sides of the institutional triangle, without affecting the overall institutional balance. All in all, however, and this will appear in other chapters of this Volume devoted notably to the decision-making process and the role of the European Parliament, the institutional balance has not been left untouched. The EP is the great winner, notwithstanding the new role of the national parlia-

---

28 As mentioned above, a similar rule applies in defining the equal rotation between the Member States. Thus the Presidency of the Council has to be organised *"taking into account their diversity and geographical balance within the Union"* and the future 'small' Commission be composed so *"as to reflect satisfactorily the demographic and geographical range of all the Member States"*.

ments in the legislative process. The European Council is also gaining many new powers, and is strengthened by its institutionalisation and its permanent President. As to the European Commission, its executive powers (including delegated legislation) have also been strengthened, but its role in the political programming and in the legislative process may have been slightly undermined. It is then probably the Council of ministers whose influence has been most diminished, or the Member States who have shared more of their sovereignty. In that respect, the Community method has not only been reasserted, but also reinforced mainly through the extension of QMV and the legislative procedure.

The fact remains however that the new institutional setting of the Union remains *sui generis*. Once again, its reform has not been guided by a vision of a pre-existing political regime, in spite of some new steps made towards a parliamentary model.

References

Hervé Bribosia (2007), Subsidiarité et repartition des competences entre l'Union et ses Etats members, in: *Giuliano Amato / Hervé Bribosia / Bruno de Witte* (eds.), Genesis and Destiny of the European Constitution, Brussels (Bruylant) 2007, 424-428.

CEPS, EGMONT and EPC (2007), Joint Study, The Treaty of Lisbon: Implementing the institutional innovations, Brussels, November 2007 (available at: http://shop.ceps.be/downfree.php?item_id=1554).

Jean-Paul Jacqué (2005), Les institutions, in: *Marianne Dony / Emmanuelle Bribosia* (eds.), Commentaire de la Constitution de l'Union européenne, Brussels (Editions de l'Université) 2005, 141-168.

Paolo Ponzano (2007), Les institutions de l'Union, in: *Giulio Amato / Hervé Bribosia / Bruno de Witte* (eds.), Genesis and Destiny of the European Constitution, Brussels (Bruylant) 2007, 439-484.

Chiara Zilioli / Martin Selmayr (2000), The European Central Bank: an Independent specialized organization of Community Law, in: Common Market Law Review 37 (2000), 591-644.

Bruno de Witte

Legal Instruments and Law-Making in the Lisbon Treaty

I. Introduction

The system of sources of EU law consists roughly speaking of five major elements: at the summit of the legal hierarchy are the founding (or 'basic') Treaties themselves, essentially the EC and EU Treaty; next in rank are the unwritten general principles of EU law which play an important role in the case law of the ECJ; then come the international agreements concluded by the EC and the EU which must be in conformity with the founding Treaties and the ge-

neral principles but prevail over the rest of EU law; then we have
the binding acts adopted by the EU institutions; and finally (a distinctive characteristic of EU law) a proliferation of various semi-
legal acts known under the generic name of 'soft law'. The Lisbon
Treaty will leave these five major components[1] as well as their hierarchical relationship intact, with one complication, namely the fact
that fundamental rights will have an ambiguous legal status: they
will partake of the supreme legal status accorded to the founding
Treaties (through the *renvoi* clause of Article 6(1) TEU-L), but will
also continue to be part of the general principles of Union law.

In view of this general continuity between the pre- and post-
Lisbon regime of sources of EU law, I have chosen to concentrate
instead, in this paper, on one particular element of the system of
sources which will be the object of a major 'internal' reshuffle in
the Lisbon Treaty, namely the binding acts adopted by the EU institutions – what is more commonly known in the Brussels jargon
(which I will adopt here) as the *legal instruments*. The way in
which these legal instruments are enacted, that is the *law-making
procedures*, will change less than the system of instruments itself,
although some notable changes concerning the former are worth
highlighting.

The structure of the paper is then as follows: after a section in
which I will sketch in very broad lines the current system of legal
instruments, I will highlight, in section III., the main relevant phases of the reform process that took place between 2001 and today,
after which I will present the main changes made by the Lisbon
Treaty to the legal instruments themselves (section IV.) and to the
law-making procedures (section V.).

II. The Current[2] System of Legal Instruments

The most important current Treaty provision dealing with legal instruments is Article 249 TEC, the first paragraph of which lists a
number of them:

---

1   This is not meant to minimise the legal importance of the fact that the
     EC Treaty will be called Treaty on the Functioning of the European
     Union. What is presented in the Lisbon Treaty as a simple change of
     name is, in fact, accompanied by a number of legal implications.

2   Throughout this paper, when using the term 'current' I refer to the
     law as it stands in 2008, that is before the entry into force of the Lis-
     bon Treaty.

"In order to carry out their task and in accordance with the provisions of this Treaty, the European Parliament acting jointly with the Council, the Council and the Commission shall make regulations and issue directives, take decisions, make recommendations or deliver opinions".

As is well known, this article gives a very incomplete indication of the legal instruments effectively used by the EU today. There is a separate range of instruments for the second and for the third pillar, which are mentioned in the Treaty on European Union, and even within the first pillar the European Union uses instruments other than those listed in Article 249; the so-called *actes atypiques*,[3] which include numerous *soft law* instruments,[4] but also an important *binding* instrument, namely the '*sui generis* decision'[5] or 'general decision', which is not the same instrument as the 'decision' referred to in Article 249.[6] The *sui generis* decision plays an important and often underestimated role in EC law;[7] they are more numerous even than directives. They are used for the enactment of

---

3   This expression is used in the internal jargon of the EU institutions and in the French legal doctrine, which has devoted particular attention to the classification of the sources of EU law. For a comprehensive analysis of the acts not mentioned in Article 249, see *Lefèvre* (2006).

4   For inventories of the variety of soft law instruments in EU law, and of the variety of the functions they fulfil, see (in addition to the work cited in the previous footnote) *Senden* (2004); *von Bogdandy et al.* (2004), 111-117.

5   This the rather lame term which is generally used in English to distinguish them from decisions in the sense of article 249 TEC (see e.g. *Lenaerts / Van Nuffel* (2005), 784).

6   This instrument is named in English 'decision', and in French '*décision*' (and they are published under those names in the OJ), but in other languages there is a separate name for it. In German, for example, the 'decisions' in the sense of Article 249 TEC are called '*Entscheidung*' whereas the decisions referred to here are called '*Beschluss*', which shows that these are truly different legal instruments. Because of the lack of a separate term, the decision-*Beschluss* is often not perceived as a separate legal instrument in the English and French language literature. This linguistic ambiguity disappears, perhaps inadvertently, in the text of the Lisbon Treaty; see discussion *infra*.

7   Among academic writers who have drawn attention to this legal instrument, see *von Bogdandy et al.* (2004), 103-106.

detailed institutional arrangements in the internal operation of the European Union, such as in laying down rules of procedure or setting up new committees or new administrative bodies. The adoption of the budget also takes the form of a *sui generis* decision, as well as the multi-annual 'action programmes' adopted in all kinds of policy areas, for example the *Socrates* programme for mobility of students and teachers and its recent successor.[8]

These various legal instruments lead, as it were, a life of their own; they are not linked to particular authors, particular procedures or particular categories of EU competence. As far as the *authors* are concerned, the first paragraph of Article 249 makes clear that each of the legal instruments mentioned may be enacted by three kinds of authors: the Commission, the Council, or the European Parliament and the Council acting jointly, and the same varied authorship applies to the *actes atypiques*. The nature of the Commission's powers implies that it normally adopts acts of an executive nature, so that it mainly uses regulations (for generally applicable executive measures) or decisions (for individual measures), although it also occasionally adopts implementing directives. The other two institutions are more obviously endowed with a legislative role, and act mainly by means of directives and regulations, as well as through *sui generis* decisions. Whether a legislative measure should be enacted by the Council acting alone, or by the Parliament and Council acting jointly, depends on the prescribed decision-making procedure. In those policy areas where co-decision applies, the acts are adopted by the Parliament and Council jointly; in the other areas, acts are adopted by the Council. This also shows that there is no connection between the type of legal instrument and the use of a particular *procedure* of decision-making, although when the title of a directive, regulation or decision indicates that it was adopted "by the European Parliament and the Council", we can normally conclude from this that it was adopted in accordance with the co-decision procedure. Finally, the use of a particular instrument is not related in a clear way to the *types of EC competence*. It is true, on the one hand, that the EC's complementary competences that do not allow for the adoption of harmonisation measures, such as those in the field of education and culture, are not exercised by means of re-

---

8   Decision No 1720/2006 of the European Parliament and of the Council of 15 November 2006 establishing an action programme in the field of lifelong learning, OJ 2006, L 327/45.

gulations and directives, but rather by general decisions and soft law measures. On the other hand, the central distinction between regulations and directives, which was originally intended to express a distinction between more and less 'supranational' areas of Community policy, has now, in practice, lost that connotation.[9] Both instruments are used today almost interchangeably in all areas of EC law and the Treaty definition of the directive (with its reference to the Member States' choice of form and methods of transposition) is no longer seen as expressing a competence limit.

The general feeling among commentators is that there are too many different EU legal instruments and that, partly because of this high number,[10] the distinctions between them are not clear. Moreover, there is some confusion, for the non-experts, between the legal instruments mentioned above (that is, formal denominations of binding and non-binding EU acts that appear, as such, in the *Official Journal*) and what can more broadly be termed 'policy instruments', that is, particular ways in which EU policies are effectuated; these policy instruments may or may not be mentioned in the Treaty text, and include: incentive measures, funds, the open method of coordination, European Council conclusions, strategies, action plans, etc. However, it would be wrong to conclude from all this that the system, either in 2001 or today in 2008, causes great problems in the day-to-day operation of the EU institutions. As was observed by the authors of a searching empirical analysis of the current system, "the structure of the legal instruments is complex and only partially determined by the Treaties, but it is not chaotic".[11] It adequately performs its technical function of providing a set of legal tools to turn EU policy into practical reality.

---

9 For a discussion of the distinction between the regulation and the directive from the perspective of the vertical division of powers between the EU and its Member States, see *Schütze* (2006), 112-129; see also that author's conclusion (at 149-151), in which he advocates a return to the 'federal rationale' by strengthening the framework character of directives, a suggestion which, as we shall see, was put on the reform agenda by the Laeken Declaration but was eventually not pursued.

10 There is no agreement on the actual number of EU legal instruments. One list, proposed by the head of the Council's legal service, contains 15 instruments: *Piris* (2006), 71.

11 *von Bogdandy et al.* (2004), 92.

III. The Reform Process from Laeken to Lisbon

The question of the reform of the system of legal instruments was put squarely on the agenda by the Laeken Declaration of December 2001 (the formal start of the Treaty revision process) which devoted a separate section to it that is worth recalling here:

"Simplification of the Union's Instruments

Who does what is not the only important question; the nature of the Union's action and what instruments it should use are equally important. Successive amendments to the Treaty have on each occasion resulted in a proliferation of instruments, and directives have gradually evolved towards more and more detailed legislation. The key question is therefore whether the Union's various instruments should not be better defined and whether their number should not be reduced.

In other words, should a distinction be introduced between legislative and executive measures?

Should the number of legislative instruments be reduced: directly applicable rules, framework legislation and non-enforceable instruments (opinions, recommendations, open coordination)?

Is it or is it not desirable to have more frequent recourse to framework legislation, which affords the Member States more room for manoeuvre in achieving policy objectives? For which areas of competence are open coordination and mutual recognition the most appropriate instruments? Is the principle of proportionality to remain the point of departure?"

It is worth exploring why the reform of the legal instruments was given such a prominent place in the Laeken Declaration whereas it had not featured much, or at all, in the previous Intergovernmental Conferences, including the IGC leading to the Treaty of Nice only one year before.[12] Even within the broad 'citizen-friendly' approach adopted by the Laeken Declaration, the need to address the seemingly technical question of the legal instruments does not immediately spring to mind as a priority. In reality, the heading 'simplification' covers a range of different concerns which include

---

12   For an insightful discussion of the reasons why the successive IGCs paid so little attention to the subject, see *Tizzano* (1996).

not only a reaction against what is called the proliferation of legal instruments, but also the idea of drawing sharper distinctions between instruments so as to relate them more closely to categories of EU competence and to the separation between legislative and executive powers. Behind these concerns expressed in the Declaration, there were also unexpressed, but perhaps politically more urgent motives, such as the desire to appear to be addressing the creeping expansion of EU competences and the wish to pave the way for an across-the-board extension of co-decision to all areas of EU policy by offering a precise and narrow definition of legislative acts.[13]

In any case, in view of the prominence given to this question in the Laeken Declaration, it is not surprising that the Convention on the future of Europe decided to set up a Working Group to deal with the question of what became rather narrowly and improperly known as 'simplification'. The tone for the Working Group's activities was set in a paper by the Presidium of the Convention which cautiously endorsed the critical view of the current system which emanated from the Laeken declaration's many interrogations.[14] The Working Group, chaired by the Convention's vice-president *Amato*, briskly took up its reformist mandate and proposed, in its final report of November 2002,[15] a number of fundamental changes, inclu-

---

13   For some contemporary reflections on the significance of this section of the Laeken Declaration, see *Lenaerts* (2002), 36-38.

14   Note by the Presidium to the Convention, *The legal instruments: present system*, CONV 162/02 of 13 June 2002. The note contains very many critical statements on the current system of instruments and law-making. It states for example, with respect to the legal instruments (at 10): "Some have seen the multiplication of instruments which has accompanied the extension of Union's policies as a factor leading to legal insecurity and one of the principal reasons for the opacity of which the Union stands accused".

15   The European Convention, Final report of Working Group IX on Simplification, 29 Nov. 2002, CONV 42/02. Some of the working documents of this Group are of special importance in order to understand the choices and institutional implications of the proposals in its report, in particular the documents with the written contributions by the heads of the Commission and Council legal services (*Michel Petite* and *Jean-Claude Piris*) and by Professor *Koen Lenaerts*: WG IX – WD 006, 007 and 008 (all still available on the European Convention's website).

ding the abolition of the separate range of legal instruments for the third pillar (following logically from the proposed abolition of that pillar), and a major change in the denomination of the most important instruments so that in future a regulation having a legislative character would instead be a "law of the EU" and a directive having a legislative character would become a "framework law of the EU". The term "directive" would disappear from sight after a long and glorious life, whereas the "regulation" would survive as a denomination reserved for sub-legislative general acts. The laws and framework laws would, in most cases, be adopted according to the co-decision procedure which, to emphasise this fact, was to be re-baptised as the "ordinary legislative procedure".

These and other changes proposed by the Working Group found their way into the final text of the Constitutional Treaty.[16] In fact, there was very little debate on this question in the later stages of the Convention, probably because the matter seemed too technical for most Convention members. There was equally little debate about the legal instruments and law-making procedures in the subsequent IGC, except of course on the high-profile question of which policy areas would be subject to co-decision, and which not. The one relevant change, at that stage, was that the IGC decided to undo the proposed creation of a special Council formation for legislative matters, and to preserve instead the current system whereby all Council formations can act both in a legislative and an executive capacity.

It is difficult to imagine that many French or Dutch voters have cast a 'No' vote in the referendum on the Constitutional Treaty because of that treaty's provisions dealing with the sources of law and the law-making procedures. And yet, despite the lack of visible political controversy specifically on these matters, this major element of the reform process became a collateral victim of the referendum debacle. It was considered, during the diplomatic talks leading to the European Council mandate of June 2007, that the de-constitu-

---

16   There are numerous commentaries of the reforms of legal instruments contained in the Constitutional Treaty, including the following: *Stancanelli* (2007); *Lenaerts / Desomer* (2005); *Craig* (2004); the commentaries on Articles I-33 to I-39, in *Burgorgue-Larsen et al.* (2007); *Van Raepenbusch* (2005); *Blanchet* (2005); *Louis / Ronse* (2005), 211-220; *Rideau* (2004); *Best* (2003); *Liisberg* (2006); *Celotto* (2003); *Tiberi* (2003).

tionalisation operation should also involve the elimination of the terms "law" and "framework law",[17] which perhaps sounded too much like the legal instruments of a European super-state. Instead, it was decided that the familiar instruments "regulation", "directive" and "decision" would be retained. This is considered by many commentators as a loss from the perspective of involving citizens more closely in the operation of the EU, since the term law may be more evocative than that of regulation or directive. However, there are advantages to this return to familiar terminology. One advantage is that it preserves continuity in the evolution of EU law. With the introduction of laws and framework laws, we would have had for many years the coexistence of old-style regulations and directives with new-style laws and framework laws, presumably all having the same rank in the hierarchy of EU law. Another weakness of the Constitutional Treaty terminology, which is now remedied, was that it had converted the regulation into an ambiguous second-order law-making instrument which could have the characteristics either of a current (implementing) regulation or of a current (implementing) directive. Finally, the proposed creation of a new instrument called "law" would have been more attractive if such laws would have been adopted according to a fixed legislative procedure, namely co-decision. This aim had been formulated by a number of actors during the early stages of the Convention, including in a memorandum of the Commission expressing its official views on institutional reform.[18] This ambition was abandoned in the face of political reality (i.e. the resistance of most member state governments) and, as we will see, the Convention's draft Constitutional Treaty and all subsequent Treaty versions provided for a variety of legislative procedures alongside co-decision, so that the terms law and framework law did not convey the unambiguous 'democratic' message which their promoters had envisaged.

Apart from the shedding of the laws and framework laws, most other changes in the system of legal instruments proposed in the

---

17   Draft ICG Mandate (Annex 1 to the Conclusions of the European Council of 21/22 June 2007), para. 3.

18   *For the European Union. Peace, Freedom, Solidarity,* Communication of the Commission on the Institutional Architecture, COM (2002) 728 of 1 December 2002, at 6: "the codecision procedure should be applied without exception to the adoption of all European laws".

Constitutional Treaty have been preserved in the Lisbon Treaty, so
that if this Treaty enters into force, we will see a rather significant
reform of their current regime. In what follows, I will first examine
the changes in the system of legal instruments, and subsequently the
changes in the law-making procedures, although these two questions are rather closely related under the new Lisbon regime (in any
case more closely than in the current Treaty system).

IV. Changes in the System of Legal Instruments

A. Disappearance of the third pillar instruments

The most obvious change brought about by the Lisbon Treaty is the
disappearance of the special set of legal instruments for what is today the law of the third pillar. Framework decisions and conventions will no longer be available as instruments for the European
Union's policy in the field of police and criminal justice co-operation. In this field, the 'mainstream' legal instruments will be used.
These include the *decision*, in accordance with the new meaning given to that instrument in Article 288 TFEU, which is different from
the specific meaning of the current third pillar decision.

    Conventions between the Member States will be abandoned as
official EU legal instruments. Not only the third pillar conventions
referred to in Article 34(2)(d) TEU will disappear, but Article 293
TEC, which provides for inter-state conventions in the first pillar
was similarly repealed. Inter-state conventions have proved to be a
disappointment particularly because they typically require ratification by the national parliaments which makes their entry into force
and subsequent amendment a very cumbersome process.[19] This
does not mean that the Member States will no longer be permitted
to conclude international agreements between themselves in connection with the operation of the European Union, but these agreements will no longer be mentioned as a normal category of instruments of EU law. The *framework decision*, on the other hand, will
simply be replaced by the directive. The current Treaty definition of
framework decisions is already demonstrative of their great functional similarity to directives, and practice shows that they are in-

---

19   For example, three Protocols amending the Europol Convention have
    been adopted, but none of them had come into force, a fact which, in
    2006, prompted the European Commission to propose the replace-
    ment of the Convention by a Council decision. As I write, the Coun-
    cil is close to adopting that decision.

deed used for the same purpose, namely to harmonise national law, and that they raise the same issues of (non-)implementation as directives.[20]

This is not the first time that a Treaty revision abolishes existing legal instruments. The same thing happened when the Treaty of Amsterdam modified the system of legal instruments to be used in the third pillar. Under the Treaty of Maastricht regime, co-operation in the fields of justice and home affairs took place by means of joint positions, joint actions and conventions between the Member States.[21] The two former instruments turned out not to be very practical. The difference between them was not clear and their legal nature (above all the question of their binding force) was subject to much dispute. In the Treaty of Amsterdam, joint positions were in effect retained, but were now baptised "common positions" whereas the joint action instrument was abolished and replaced by two new instruments: framework decisions and decisions. The abolition of a legal instrument, then in Amsterdam as now in Lisbon, raises the question of the *transition* from the old to the new system. This time, the transition is more radical, since the change from framework decisions to directives will have important consequences in terms of judicial control and domestic effect.[22] The Constitutional Treaty dealt with this in very broad terms, in its general Article IV-438 on succession and legal continuity in which was stated: "The acts of the institutions, bodies, offices and agencies adopted on the basis of the treaties and acts repealed by Article I-437 shall remain in force. Their legal effects shall be preserved until those acts are repealed, annulled or amended in implementation of this Treaty." Since the Lisbon Treaty, unlike the Constitutional Treaty, does not repeal and replace the existing Treaties, the general "succession and legal continuity" Article has also disappeared.[23] Instead, we have a miscella-

---

20 See *Borgers* (2007).

21 Art. K.3(2) TEU, in its Maastricht version.

22 To name just the principal differences: in terms of judicial control, the Commission cannot bring actions for infringement against Member States for their failure to correctly implement framework decisions, whereas it can do so for directives; and in terms of domestic effect, the TEU currently excludes the direct effect of framework decisions, whereas directives can have (vertical) direct effect.

23 There is still a 'replace and succeed' clause in the Lisbon Treaty but it refers only to the European Community as an organisation (which

neous Protocol on transitional provisions,[24] whose very complicated Title VII deals with the legal effects of the existing acts in the field of criminal justice and police co-operation. Basically, the intergovernmental characteristics of those acts (no Commission infringement actions and limited judicial control powers of the ECJ) will remain in place for another five years unless such acts are amended within that period. The question of their domestic effect in the legal orders of the Member States (in particular whether or not they can have direct effect) is not expressly addressed in the Protocol and is therefore a matter of speculation.

B. Specificity of CFSP legal instruments

The 'merger', described above, of the legal instruments of what are currently the first and third pillars will not be extended to the second pillar. In the field of common foreign and security policy, regulations and directives will not be any more available than they are now. The central legal instrument in this field will become the *decision,* which will replace the variety of binding instruments currently in use for CFSP, namely the joint actions, common positions and decisions. This is a major terminological simplification, although it should be kept in mind that these CFSP decisions will be used for a variety of different purposes[25] corresponding to the purposes for which, today, different CFSP instruments are used. In this sense, the terminological simplification is somewhat deceptive. Also, it is not made clear whether the decision mentioned in the TEU-L as the single legal instrument for CFSP is, in fact, the same legal instrument as the decision mentioned in the new Article 288 TFEU (on which see below), to be used in all other areas of EU policy. The drafters of the Lisbon Treaty probably did not intend them to be the same instrument, because otherwise they would be importing into the field of CFSP an instrument which is capable of having direct effect in national legal orders! It is however unfortunate that this major ambiguity has been left unresolved.

---

is absorbed by the European Union – see Article 1, third para. TEU-L) and not to the EC Treaty instrument which is not replaced but 'only' amended.

24   OJ 2007, C 306/159.

25   See Article 25(b) TEU-L.

C. A new hierarchy of legal instruments

There will also be a significant reform of the regime of 'mainstream' legal instruments, that is, those instruments to be used in all areas of EU law except for CFSP and EMU which have their own special rules. All the relevant rules which, in the Constitutional Treaty, were contained in the 'fundamental' Part I, were eventually incorporated by the Lisbon Treaty into the Treaty on the Functioning of the European Union, the successor to the EC Treaty. They are placed towards the end of that treaty (which is the place where they are situated in the EC Treaty today), so that, when one reads the TEU-L and TFEU from the start, one first finds multiple references to the adoption of directives, regulations or decisions before one actually finds a general provision indicating that these are the binding legal instruments at the disposal of the EU. So, the Lisbon Treaty reform is structurally less transparent and coherent than the Constitutional Treaty on this question, as on many others.

As was mentioned above, the Constitutional Treaty contained a radical terminological novelty by introducing the new instruments of "laws" and "framework laws" to replace regulations and directives having a legislative character. This innovation was undone by the Lisbon Treaty, so that regulations and directives will continue to be, as today, the main legislative instruments of the European Union. However, the related ambition of introducing a clearer hierarchy within the system of EU acts was not abandoned. The amorphous current system, in which the distinction between legislative and executive acts is not made visible by the denomination of the act (for instance, a regulation can be used both for very important legislative measures taken in co-decision and for very lowly implementing measures taken by the Commission), will be replaced by a more detailed typology of acts in which that distinction will be clearly expressed.

Legal hierarchy is not absent from the current EU system, but it is not apparent from the denomination of the act. In practice, the text of a regulation frequently provides that implementing measures must be taken either by a Community institution (usually the Commission) or the Member States, or both. Implementation by the Commission frequently takes place by means of individual decisions, but often also by means of (further) regulations, but the implementing decision or regulation must be in conformity with the basic regulation. There is thus a judicially enforceable legal hierarchy between two legal instruments which have the same denomination. In some cases, one even finds a 'cascade of regulations': the general policy framework is laid down in a Council regulation, which is then implemented by means, first, of a series of general executive Council regulations and, secondly, of a series of more detailed Commission regulations. This situation illustrates well how little the denomination of the act tells us about the legislative or executive nature of the act.

In the new Article 288 of the TFEU, we find apparently the same three types of binding legal instruments as are currently listed in Article 249 TEC, namely *regulations*, *directives*, and *decisions*. However, each of these instruments will, in the future, be available at three different levels of law-making: for 'true' legislation, for the adoption of delegated acts and for the adoption of implementing acts. Their position at one of these three levels will be indicated in the formal denomination of the act.

The upper tier is formed by what the new Treaty text calls *legislative acts*. This term does not indicate a particular legal instrument, but the particular nature that some regulations, directives or decisions will possess, and others not. Curiously enough, this particular legislative nature will not be determined by their actual content, but merely by the use of a particular procedure, as is stated by the new Article 289(3) TFEU: "Legal acts adopted by legislative procedure shall constitute legislative acts".[26] In other words, future EU acts directly based on Treaty articles that prescribe the use of the ordinary or special legislative procedure will, for that reason only, be considered as legislative acts. For example, Article 82(1) TFEU states that "the European Parliament and the Council, acting in accordance with the ordinary legislative procedure, shall adopt measures to ... (c) support the training of the judiciary and judicial staff; (...)". Therefore, European judicial training programmes will be legislative acts, despite the fact that, in terms of their content, they will appear 'administrative' rather than 'legislative'.

The main novelty of the post-Lisbon regime is that a new intermediate level of law-making, between the purely legislative and purely executive, will be introduced, namely the *delegated acts*. These will be adopted by the Commission in order to "supplement or amend certain non-essential elements of the legislative acts". In contrast to implementing acts, these delegated acts may thus actual-

---

26   There will not be a single legislative procedure, though; see *infra*, section IV.

ly modify a legislative act, albeit only on non-essential points. Such modifications can occur only if a specific delegation is made within the relevant legislative act, and they will be subject to control by the institutions that have adopted that act, that is, normally speaking, by Council and Parliament.[27] In order to evaluate the novelty of this new Treaty provision, one must remember that the practice whereby the Commission is given the power to amend or supplement legislative acts already exists today, but this practice is considered to be covered by the Commission's general implementation powers and has no explicit Treaty basis.[28] So, under the current system, there was for a long time no need to sharply distinguish between "amending or supplementing measures" and "implementing measures", a distinction which is often not obvious, particularly in the case of broad framework legislation.[29] However, the disadvantage of this lack of differentiation is that, to use the words of the Convention Working Group's final report, "the legislator is obliged either to go into minute detail in the provisions it adopts, or to entrust to the Commission the more technical or detailed aspects of the legislation as if they were implementing measures".[30] In reality, the dilemma is not as stark as it is presented in the Working Group report because the existence of the comitology system means that the detailed aspects are "entrusted" to the Commission subject to an

---

27 See the new Article 290 TFEU for the details of this new legal regime.

28 See *Piris* (2006), 73: "Practice to date under the expression 'implementing powers' has combined two types of power which are different in nature: the power to adopt a normative act which amends or supplements the basic legislative act itself, on the one hand, and the power to implement, or to execute at EC level, all or part of a legislative act, on the other hand".

29 See for example the Directive of 3 December 2001 on general product safety (OJ 2002, L 11/4). It does not contain substantive safety standards itself, but leaves it to the European Commission to set safety requirements for particular products, which are then to be implemented by private standardisation bodies. One recent example is the Commission Decision of 25 March 2008 on the fire safety requirements to be met by European standards for cigarettes (OJ 2008, L 83/35). Is this a measure which "supplements" or only "implements" the Directive?

30 The European Convention, Final report of Working Group IX on Simplification, 29 Nov. 2002, CONV 42/02, 8.

external check on its activities. That check was traditionally exercised by the Council and not by the other branch of the legislative power, the EP. However, in 2006, a new comitology procedure was
added to the three existing ones, namely the so-called regulatory
procedure with scrutiny. This applies to cases in which a committee
considers Commission drafts for amendment of non-essential parts
of EC legislation adopted under co-decision. Since such Commission measures can be considered as quasi-legislative acts (they involve actual changes, albeit of a technical nature, to EC legislation),
rather than mere implementation, it was thought proper to allow
each of the two legislative organs, the Council and the European
Parliament, to scrutinise and actually overturn an opinion of the
committee involved.[31] This mechanism partially prefigures the control mechanism which the new Treaty will require for delegated
acts. So, seen from this perspective, the new category of delegated
acts has not come out of the blue, but is rather the latest development in a long-standing bargaining process between the EU institutions on where to draw the line between the role of the legislative
and the executive, and on how to organise oversight by the legislator on acts adopted by the executive.[32] It remains to be seen in actual practice whether the creation of a formal distinction between
delegated acts and 'pure' implementing acts will add to the transparency and accountability of EU decision-making, and how it will affect the power relations between the EU institutions.[33]

So, to repeat and conclude on this point, there will be three
versions of each of the three binding legal instruments of 'mainstream' EU law: legislative regulations, directives and decisions;
delegated regulations, directives, and decisions; and implementing
regulations, directives and decisions.[34] The nature of the act will be
visible from its title. Indeed, it is specified that the adjective "dele-

---

31   Council Decision 2006/512 amending Decision 1999/468, of 17 July
     2006, OJ 2006, L 200/11. See Editorial Comment, *Common Market
     Law Review* 43 (2006), 1245-1250.

32   It is worth noting, though, that this evolution took the form, most of
     the time, of interstitial change in between Treaty revision rounds,
     whereas this time a change is entrenched through formal treaty
     amendment (see, on the earlier evolution process, *Bergström et al.*
     (2007)).

33   See, on these questions, the chapter by *Paul Craig* in this volume.

34   See *Ziller* (2007), 133.

gated" shall be inserted in the title of delegated acts and that the word "implementing" shall be inserted in the title of implementing acts.[35] Therefore, regulations, directives and decisions without any of these two adjectives in their title will normally[36] be legislative acts. This will certainly add to the transparency of EU law, compared to the present situation, in that the title will give some additional indication as to the nature of the instrument.

D. A decision is not a decision

It is worth noting that in this new multi-tiered system, *decisions* will be available at all three levels. This shows that the Lisbon-style decision will not be identical to what is now called decision in Article 249 TEC, but will be some kind of conceptual blend of the decision in the sense of Article 249 TEC (which is normally an individual administrative act, called *Entscheidung* in German) with the *sui generis* decision (which is currently used for the adoption of certain legislative and general administrative acts, and in German is called *Beschluss*).[37] The future decision will fulfil the rather different functions currently fulfilled by these two different types of instruments. Its ill-defined nature is not adequately rendered by the definition in Article 288 TFEU: "A decision shall be binding in its entirety. A decision which specifies those to whom it is addressed shall be binding only on them". This definition comes very close to the current definition of the decision in Article 249 TEC Treaty and would seem to give the impression that we are still faced with the same instrument as before. In fact, it is *not* the same legal instrument, as becomes visible if, instead of the English or French versions, one reads the German or Dutch versions of the new Treaties: the word *Beschluss* appears instead of *Entscheidung*, and the word *besluit* instead of *beschikking*. So, what is happening, without any publicity or explanation, is that one of the age-old legal instruments of EC law, the decision of Article 249 TEC, is being eliminated. But, one may wonder, if the decision is to become a *passe-partout* legal instrument, what is then the distinction between a decision and a regulation? Would it not have been more transparent (and closer to the practice in national constitutional law) to use the regulation

---

35   See respectively Article 290(3) and Article 291(4) TFEU.

36   Subject to an anomalous exception which I will mention below in section V.C.

37   See *supra*, section II.

for all the 'general measure' functions of the decision, and reserve the term decision for individual administrative acts only? Moreover, as was already mentioned above, there is considerable ambiguity on the question whether the decision mentioned in Article 288 TFEU is the same instrument as the decision mentioned in Article 25 TEU-L to be used for CFSP purposes.

E. The choice between legal instruments

The Laeken Declaration had given considerable importance to the question of which legal instrument should be used for which purpose or in which policy area.[38] It asked among other things whether the principle of proportionality should "remain the point of departure"? Well, of course it does. Proportionality is, after all, the most enthusiastically embraced (and most unpredictable) principle of EU law these days. It is already the case in the current regime that whenever the Treaty legal basis allows the EU institutions a choice between different legal instruments (which is most of the time), that choice is constrained – at least in matters of EC law, if not EU law – by respect for the principle of proportionality. This results from the Protocol on subsidiarity and proportionality which states that "Other things being equal, directives should be preferred to regulations and framework directives to detailed measures". The norm which makes proportionality relevant for the choice of instrument will, through the Lisbon Treaty, be taken out of the Protocol on subsidiarity and proportionality and be inserted in the Treaty section dealing with instruments, more precisely in Article 296 TFEU, first paragraph: "Where the Treaties do not specify the type of act to be adopted, the institutions shall select it on a case-by-case basis, in compliance with the applicable procedures and with the principle of proportionality". One may note that the priority given to directives "other things being equal" is no longer there, which make sense, given that that sentence might have expressed a political message but was of little use or effect in practice. Nevertheless, the aspiration expressed at the start of the Treaty reform process, in-

---

38   See the following paragraph in the Laeken Declaration (already cited above in section III.): "Is it or is it not desirable to have more frequent recourse to framework legislation, which affords the Member States more room for manoeuvre in achieving policy objectives? For which areas of competence are open coordination and mutual recognition the most appropriate instruments? Is the principle of proportionality to remain the point of departure?"

cluding in the Laeken declaration, to "have more frequent recourse to framework legislation" is not translated into a concrete legal rule in the new Treaty text – except perhaps for the fact that the new subsidiarity monitoring mechanism might allow national parliaments to press for leaving the Member States "more room for manoeuvre", even though formally speaking the standard these national parliaments must use is that of subsidiarity rather than proportionality.[39]

The reference in Article 296 to the "applicable procedures" is more meaningful than before. Whereas, as was mentioned above, the current legal bases in the Treaty often leave the choice of instruments wide open, the Lisbon Treaty (as in the Constitutional treaty) make an effort to specify in the legal basis article which instrument(s) the EU may use in order to attain the policy ends defined in that article. So, in a number of cases, it is now specified that the EU should act by means of either regulations or directives, although in many other cases, the legal basis articles still use *passe partout* terms such as "provisions" or "measures", which allow for an *ad hoc* choice of the instrument by the institutions.

V. Changes in the Law-Making Procedures

A. Ordinary and special legislative procedures

As far as legislative decision-making is concerned, there will be no major changes in the procedures themselves, but the relative importance of the various procedures will change. As before, there will be no single unified procedure for making EU legislation, but the co-decision procedure (which, in its operation, will not be modified[40]) will henceforth be called the *ordinary legislative procedure* (Article 289(1) TFEU). All the remaining procedures (including mainly the consultation and assent procedures) will be called *special legislative procedures*. This change of terminology is justified by the fact that co-decision will, once again, be extended to new areas of policy-making beyond those to which it currently applies, including im-

---

39   Both quotes in the sentence are from the Laeken declaration (see section III. above for the full text of the relevant paragraph of the declaration).

40   The formulation of the Treaty article is slightly modified compared to the current Article 251 TEC in order to make the procedure more accessible to the reader, but there are no changes to the substance.

portant areas such as agriculture, external trade, 'legal' migration,
and police and criminal justice co-operation. It will indeed become
the main procedure through which EU legislation is adopted. This
confirmation of the central role of co-decision is, however, accompanied by a number of new derogations and exceptions which de-
tract from the transparency of the future law-making system. One
derogation is that the Commission will share its power of initiative
with a group consisting of at least a quarter of the Member States in
matters of criminal justice and police co-operation (Article 76
TFEU). A second derogation consists of the so-called 'emergency
brakes' provided for in some sensitive policy areas, that allow single Member States to suspend the co-decision procedure and refer
the file for discussion at European Council level.[41] The most far-
reaching exception to normal co-decision is the non-participation of
certain states in the adoption of a legislative act by means of a so-
called opt-out. The current opt-outs for Denmark, Ireland and the
United Kingdom in the area of migration, asylum and co-operation
in civil matters will be preserved, but in addition the United Kingdom and Ireland will benefit from a new and very complex opt-out
in the area of police and criminal justice (this was the price which
the UK government exacted in return for allowing the ordinary
legislative procedure to be applied in this field). Confusingly, this
major derogation to the normal legislative procedure is not made
visible in the text of the TFEU, but appears only in special
Protocols attached to the Treaty.

More generally speaking, there will not yet be a single legislative procedure in tomorrow's European Union. There will still be
many cases in which the Treaty provides for special legislative procedures,[42] mainly in the 'intergovernmental' matters where the
Council will be the sole author of legislation and / or where the
Council will have to act by unanimity rather than qualified majority.
In all those cases, the relevant legal basis of the Treaty refers to the
adoption of the act "in accordance with *a* special legislative procedure" rather than "in accordance with *the* ordinary legislative proce-

---

41   For example, under Article 82(3) TFEU, if the State considers that a
      draft directive would affect fundamental aspects of its criminal justi-
      ce system.

42   There were 30 such cases in the Constitutional Treaty; see the list
      provided by *Stancanelli* (2007), 529-530. Practically all of these were
      copied into the Lisbon Treaty.

dure". One may note the slightly different wording which expresses the fact that there is one single ordinary procedure, but a number of different special procedures. One consequence of the continued plurality of legislative procedures is that there will still be occasions (although fewer than now) for legal basis disputes between the institutions, or between the institutions and some Member States, since the choice of a Treaty basis for a given measure will trigger a particular law-making procedure, and therefore also a particular balance between the institutions.

B. Executive decision-making

As far as non-legislative acts are concerned, the Lisbon Treaty introduces, as was mentioned above, a distinction between delegated acts and implementing acts. They are both to be adopted by the Commission, according to its own internal decision-making rules, but the distinction will be relevant in terms of the control mechanisms imposed on the Commission when it enacts such measures. In the case of 'pure' implementing acts, the Commission's power will remain subject to the current Comitology system, or rather a variation thereof that will be adopted after the entry into force of the Lisbon Treaty.[43] In the case of delegated acts, which will supplement or amend legislative acts, the Commission will be subject to a new and stricter control mechanism which, according to the new Article 290 TFEU, will either allow the European Parliament or the Council to revoke the delegation; or permit the entry into force of the delegated act only if the Parliament or Council have not objected to it within a given period of time. The precise terms of these new control mechanisms need to be worked out, perhaps by means of an inter-institutional agreement.

Still as regards administrative decision-making, it is worth noting that neither the Convention nor the various IGCs have attemp-

---

43 See Article 291(3) TFEU. The fact that the existing Comitology mechanism must be revised after the entry into force of the Treaty of Lisbon is not expressly mentioned, but results implicitly from the text of the Article where it states that the control mechanism must be adopted "by means of regulations in accordance with the ordinary legislative procedure", whereas currently they are adopted by means of Council decisions. So, the current Comitology decision will have to be revised in order to allow the European Parliament to exercise its new co-decision powers in this respect (and in order to transform it into a regulation).

ted to codify the main rules for the establishment of *agencies* and their own decision-making, despite the fact that these have become increasingly important parts of the EU administration. Agencies have been included, by the Treaty of Lisbon, within the scope of application of the general rules relating to transparency, judicial control and fundamental rights protection, but their decision-ma-king mechanisms will still be dealt with in an ad-hoc manner with-out any overarching principles laid down in the Treaty.

C. Extra-legislative rule making and the incomplete hierarchy

The amended Treaty on European Union indicates that, in the field of CFSP, both the Council and the European Council will have the power to adopt decisions, but adds that "the adoption of legislative acts shall be excluded" (Article 24(1) TEU-L). So, we will have binding legal instruments that are not legislative acts, but are not delegated or implementing measures either. In other words, these acts do not fit in the hierarchical three-level model sketched above, but will have a separate existence outside this hierarchy. During the Convention and the IGCs they were often referred to as "autono-mous acts", in analogy with the *règlements autonomes* in French constitutional law.[44] This is not just a specific feature, among many others, of the CFSP legal order. More surprisingly, we will find the same phenomenon of legal acts that are not legislative acts though they look very much like them in more traditional areas of EU law. For example, in the field of competition law, Article 103 TFEU sta-tes that "the appropriate regulations and directives to give effect to the principles set out in Articles 101 and 102 shall be laid down by the Council, on a proposal from the Commission and after consul-ting the European Parliament".[45] What is referred to here are acts such as Regulation 1/2003 on the modernisation of competition law, which is a legislative measure by any standard meaning of that term. Yet, Article 103 does not say that these acts will have to be made either through the ordinary or through a special legislative procedu-re, and therefore they will not be "legislative acts" in the sense of the Lisbon Treaty! This qualification as non-legislative acts seems

---

44   *Ziller* (2005), 469.

45   These are the Treaty articles laying down the substantive principles of competition law, corresponding to the current Articles 81 and 82 TEC.

rather arbitrary.[46] The same is true for Council acts setting out general rules in the field of state aid (Article 109 TFEU), and there are a number of other cases.[47] The fact that we will have important binding instruments, in traditional fields of EU law, that will be neither legislative nor executive, formally speaking, makes a bit of a mockery of an otherwise careful effort to establish a distinction between legislative and executive acts of EU law.[48]

This 'incomplete hierarchy' is not just an aesthetic failing of the simplification effort. Practical legal consequences will flow from the identification of an act as being legislative, executive or neither of the two. One consequence is the existence or not of an obligation for the Council to deliberate in public. This obligation only applies to legislative acts,[49] and therefore the scope of this obligation will be narrower than the current situation where the Council's Rules of Procedure provide for public deliberation (subject to exceptions) for a more broadly defined category of legislative acts which includes, among others, Council acts in the field of competition and state aid.[50] Another practical consequence relates to the new role of national parliaments in monitoring respect for the principle of subsidiarity. This role is limited to draft legislative acts only and will therefore not apply to the *règlements autonomes*.[51] Finally, the distinction may be relevant to the new definition of the in-

---

46 See, for early criticism of the Convention draft using this specific example, *Dougan* (2003), 784.

47 In his analysis of the Constitutional Treaty, *Stancanelli* (2007), 532-534, lists 76 legal bases for non-legislative acts of the Council, and 17 for the European Council. However, this list includes a number of organisational measures, appointments, etc., which do not have a law-making character.

48 *Stancanelli* (2007), 517, describes it more gently: "une exception de taille à l'articulation rigoureuse entre la fonction législative et la fonction exécutive".

49 Article 16(8) TEU-L.

50 See *Liisberg* (2006), 161. The current regime of Council publicity is outlined in Article 8 of the Council's Rules of Procedure as last amended by Council Decision of 15 September 2006, OJ 2006, L 285/47. See, on the background and significance of the latest reform in 2006, *de Leeuw* (2007).

51 See the new text of the Protocol on the application of the principles of subsidiarity and proportionality.

dividual right to challenge EU acts directly before the European Court: it will apply to "regulatory acts",[52] but this term is not further defined. Presumably it does not cover legislative acts, but it does cover delegated acts and autonomous non-legislative acts such as those mentioned above? We are not clearly told the answer. This is a case of very sloppy treaty drafting, which remained in place all the way from the original Draft Constitutional Treaty proposed by the Convention until the Lisbon Treaty.

D. Codification of interinstitutional agreements

The interinstitutional agreement (IIA) is a source of law that plays an increasingly important role in regulating the relations between the EU institutions in the legislative and budgetary field.[53] As the name indicates, these are agreements concluded between two or more of the EU institutions. They are intended to smoothen the operation of the inter-institutional process by adding more detailed rules of behaviour to the often very laconic Treaty language. These agreements are usually published in the C series of the *Official Journal* and do not create legal obligations for third parties. Between the institutions themselves, the agreements may or may not have binding legal force, but they certainly are considered by their signatories as being authoritative guidance for their action. The practice of interinstitutional agreements was confirmed by Declaration No. 3 attached to the Treaty of Nice, although here the Member States implied that such agreements can only be concluded by all three institutions (Council, Commission and Parliament), while in practice sometimes agreements are concluded between only two of these institutions. Now, with Lisbon, IIA's are being dealt with in the Treaty text itself, namely in the new Article 295 TFEU[54] which, significantly, is not inserted in the Treaty section on legal instruments but in the subsequent section dealing with decision-making procedures. So, IIA's are seen as an ancillary legal mechanism to be used in the specific context of the inter-institutional decision ma-

---

52   New Article 263 TFEU.

53   For an analysis of their role and legal nature, see for example: *von Alemann* (2006); *Eiselt / Slominski* (2006); *Driessen* (2007).

54   "The European Parliament, the Council and the Commission shall consult each other and by common agreement make arrangements for their cooperation. To that end, they may, in compliance with the Treaties, conclude interinstitutional agreements which may be of a binding nature".

king procedures. That makes it questionable whether such agreements are a true legal instrument that could be used also to deal with questions that have an extra-institutional dimension. At any rate, the definition of Article 295 would not cover the Charter of Fundamental Rights which, because of the fact that it was proclaimed by the presidents of the three institutions, was occasionally qualified in the literature as an interinstitutional agreement.

E. The Open Method of Co-ordination: a twilight existence

There has been, in the last decade, an upsurge of academic interest and effective use of what is generally termed the open method of co-ordination (OMC), although in reality this term hides a number of individual methods that are partially different in each relevant policy area, including employment, macro-economic policy, social exclusion and education, to name but a few.[55] The term "open method of co-ordination", which was coined by the Lisbon European Council in 2000, does not figure in the current text of the Treaties, but the Laeken declaration referred to it, and the Convention's Working Group on simplification recommended that "constitutional status should be assigned to the open method of coordination, which involves concerted action by the Member States outside the competences attributed to the Union by the treaties".[56] This sentence expresses a curious miscomprehension of the OMC (it is clearly not used *outside* but *inside* the EU's competences), which is symptomatic of the lack of sustained attention accorded to it by the Convention. In the end, and despite some protests from academics,[57] the Convention decided not to give a comprehensive constitutional status to the OMC, but rather, by way of compromise, a description of a method of action which corresponds to the OMC – but without using the term – was included in the Treaty articles dealing with the policy areas of public health, industry and research. In addition, the existing, and differently formulated references to policy co-ordination were kept for the areas of economic union and employment. This fragmented and unsatisfactory approach was maintained in the

---

55 The very rich literature describing the various forms taken by the OMC includes: *Armstrong / Kilpatrick* (2007); *Szyszczak*, (2006).

56 The European Convention, Final report of Working Group IX on Simplification, 29 Nov. 2002, CONV 42/02, 7.

57 See *de Búrca / Zeitlin* (2003).

Lisbon Treaty[58] so that the question inevitably arises: given that the Lisbon Treaty formally recognises the use of the method in certain areas, does this mean that it may not be used in other policy areas where it is currently used (such as education) or where it might be used in the future (such as immigration)?

VI. Conclusion

The final report of the Convention Working Group on simplification of instruments started by stating that nothing is more complicated than simplification, and then valiantly went on to propose a large number of quite radical changes to the current system of legal instruments and decision-making. The complication of the reform operation was partly due to the fact that the nomenclature of legal instruments is not a purely technical matter, but is bound up with broader constitutional questions of the division of competences between the EU and its Member States, and the balance between the EU institutions. The end result is a major reform (the biggest reform of the system of legal instruments and law-making since the 'proliferation' brought about by the Maastricht Treaty), but not one that simplifies much. There are some genuine simplifications, such as the elimination of the separate range of instruments for the third pillar (but this is just the consequence of the agreement to merge the first and third pillar), and there are interesting attempts, inspired by separation-of-powers considerations, to define what legislation is – as opposed to executive action – and what the normal way for adopting such legislation is. However, these attempts have not been entirely successful: (a) legislative acts are defined in purely procedural terms, not in terms of their content, so that there is no intrinsic 'lower limit' to the content of these legislative acts; (b) a number of acts, in CFSP but also elsewhere, will be neither legislative nor executive but 'something else'; (c) and there will still be many different ways in which EU legislation is made alongside co-decision. In addition, the reform process has introduced some new complications which do not exist in the current system: (a) it has rendered the instrument called "decision" more fuzzy by mixing together different legal instruments which have little to do with one another; (b) it has introduced a formal category of delegated acts, which may

---

58   The three identically phrased references to the method, in relation to public health, industry and research, can be found in Articles 168, 173 and 179 TFEU.

lead to new institutional line-drawing disputes, without perhaps much tangible benefit in terms of efficiency or democratic accountability; (c) and it has left unclear the legal characteristics of the decisions that will be the new catch-all legal instruments for CFSP. In conclusion, it is not obvious that the new post-Lisbon regime will actually lead to a simplification of EU law which, as was mentioned above, was a central aim of the Convention on the Future of the Union when it started discussing this matter in 2002.

There is another dimension of the reform that was prominently mentioned in the Laeken Declaration but was gradually left aside during the process, namely the use of the system of legal instruments for fine-tuning the competence relations between the EU and its Member States. Proposals to connect particular types of instruments with particular categories of competence (e.g. the sole use of non-binding instruments in areas of complementary competences) were rightly rejected by the Convention and subsequent IGCs. But the stated ambition of leading the directive (or framework law, as it was briefly called) back to its origin as an instrument leaving considerable *substantive* discretion to the Member States was also abandoned along the way. The definition of the directive has not changed with the Lisbon Treaty, and there is no indication that the current practice of occasionally very detailed directives will be discontinued. Again, the preservation of this instrumental flexibility for the EU legislator is probably a good thing. But then, if the reformers were unable or unwilling to introduce a sharper distinction between "directly applicable rules" and "framework legislation" (to use the words of Laeken), would it not have been logically consistent to abolish the distinction between directives and regulations, and to replace them with one single legislative instrument?[59]

---

59 Such a merger of the regulation and directive has occasionally been proposed, for example in the Draft Treaty on European Union adopted by the European Parliament in 1984 (the '*Spinelli* Draft'), and also more recently (during the Convention period) in the *Penelope* document prepared by a working group within the Commission. The move to a single law-making instrument would not have meant less autonomy for the Member States, since the amount of uniformity would, like today, be decided by the EU legislator on a case-by-case basis. But clearly the scrapping of the directive was taboo, since it would have run against the subsidiarity rhetoric which is such a striking characteristic of the Lisbon Treaty.

References

Florian von Alemann (2006), Die Handlungsform der interinstitutionellen Vereinbarung, Berlin (Springer) 2006.

Kenneth Armstrong / Claire Kilpatrick (2007), Law, Governance, or New Governance? The Changing Open Method of Coordination, in: The Columbia Journal of European Law 13 (2007), 649-677.

Carl-Fredrik Bergström / Henry Farrell / Adrienne Héritier (2007), Legislate or Delegate? Bargaining over Implementation and Legislative Authority in the EU, in: West European Politics 30 (2007), 338-366.

Edward Best (2003), Decision-Making and the Draft Constitution: have we really cleaned up our legal acts?, in: Intereconomics 38 (2003), No. 4, 170-175.

Thérèse Blanchet (2005), Les instruments juridiques de l'Union européenne et la rédaction des bases juridiques: situation actuelle et rationalisation dans la Constitution, in: Revue trimestrielle de droit européen 41 (2005), No. 2, 319-343.

Armin von Bogdandy / Jürgen Bast / Felix Arndt (2004), Legal instruments in European Union law and their reform: a systematic approach on an empirical basis, in: Yearbook of European Law 23 (2004), 91-136.

Matthias J. Borgers (2007), Implementation of Framework Decisions, in: Common Market Law Review 44 (2007), 1361-1386.

Gráinne de Búrca / Jonathan Zeitlin (2003), Constitutionalising the Open Method of Coordination: A Note for the Convention, (= CEPS Policy Brief No. 31, March 2003), Brussels (CEPS) 2003.

Laurence Burgorgue-Larsen / Anne Levade / Fabrice Picod (eds.), Traité établissant une Constitution pour l'Europe – Commentaire article par article, Vol. 1, Brussels (Bruylant) 2007.

Alfonso Celotto (2003), La 'legge' europea, in: *Alberto Lucarelli / Andrea Patroni Griffi* (eds.), Studi sulla costituzione europea – Percorsi e ipotesi, Naples (Edizioni Scientifiche Italiane) 2003, 209-219.

Paul Craig (2004), The hierarchy of norms, in: *Takis Tridimas / Paolisa Nebbia* (eds.), European Union Law for the Twenty-

First Century. Rethinking the New Legal Order, Oxford (Hart) 2004, 75-93.

Michael Dougan (2003), The Convention's Draft Constitutional treaty: bringing Europe closer to its lawyers?, in: European Law Review 28 (2003), 763-793.

Bart Driessen (2007), Interinstitutional Conventions in EU Law, London (Cameron May) 2007.

Isabella Eiselt / Peter Slominski (2006), Sub-constitutional engineering: negotiation, content, and legal value of Inter-institutional Agreements in the EU, in: European Law Journal 12 (2006), 209-225.

Magdalena Elisabeth de Leeuw (2007), Openness in the legislative process in the European Union, in: European Law Review 32 (2007) 295-318.

Silvère Lefèvre (2006), Les actes communautaires atypiques, Brussels (Bruylant) 2006.

Koen Lenaerts (2002), La déclaration de Laeken: premier jalon d'une Constitution européenne?, in: Journal des tribunaux – Droit européen 10 (2002), 29-43.

Koen Lenaerts / Marlies Desomer (2005), Towards a hierarchy of legal acts in the European Union? Simplification of legal in-struments and procedures, in: European Law Journal 11 (2005), 744-765.

Koen Lenaerts / Piet van Nuffel (2005), Constitutional Law of the European Union, London (Sweet&Maxwell) ²2005.

Jonas Bering Liisberg (2006), The EU Constitutional Treaty and its distinction between legislative and non-legislative acts, in: *Brigitte Egelund Olsen / Karsten Engsig Sørensen* (eds.), Regulation in the EU, Copenhagen (Thomson) 2006, 133-168.

Jean-Victor Louis / Thierry Ronse (2005), L'ordre juridique de l'Union européenne, Brussels (Bruylant) 2005.

Jean-Claude Piris (2006), The Constitution for Europe: A Legal Analysis, Cambridge (Cambridge University Press) 2006.

Sean van Raepenbusch (2005), Les instruments juridiques de l'Union européenne, in: *Marianne Dony / Emmanuelle Bribo-sia* (eds.), Commentaire de la Constitution de l'Union euro-péenne, Brussels (Editions de l'Université) 2005, 203-218.

Joël Rideau (2004), Présentation des actes juridiques dans la Cons-
titution, in: *Enrique Álvarez Conde / Vicente Garrido Mayol /
Susana García Couso* (eds.), Comentarios a la Constitución
Europea, Valencia (Tirant lo Blanch) 2004, 293-334.

Robert Schütze (2006), The Morphology of Legislative Power in
the European Community: Legal Instruments and the Federal
Division of Powers, in: Yearbook of European Law 25 (2006),
91-152.

Linda Senden (2004), Soft Law in European Community Law: Its
Relationship to Legislation, Oxford (Hart) 2004.

Paolo Stancanelli (2007), Le système décisionnel de l'Union, in:
Giuliano Amato / Hervé Bribosia / Bruno de Witte (eds.),
Genesis and Destiny of the European Constitution, Brussels
(Bruylant) 2007, 485-543.

Erika Szyszczak (2006), Experimental Governance: The Open
Method of Coordination, in: European Law Journal 12 (2006),
486-502.

Giulia Tiberi (2003), La semplificazione degli atti dell'unione
Europea e il metodo di coordinamento aperto, in: *Alberto
Lucarelli / Andrea Patroni Griffi* (eds.), Studi sulla costituzione europea – Percorsi e ipotesi, Naples (Edizioni Scientifiche Italiane) 2003, 221-243.

Antonio Tizzano (1996), The Instruments of Community Law and
the Hierarchy of Norms, in: *Jan A. Winter / Deirdre Curtin /
Alfred E. Kellermann / Bruno de Witte* (eds.), Reforming the
European Union – The Legal Debate, The Hague (Kluwer Law
International) 1996, 207-219.

Jacques Ziller (2005), National constitutional concepts in the new
Constitution for Europe. Part two, in: European Constitutional
Law Review 2 (2005), 452-480.

Jacques Ziller (2007), Il nuovo Trattato europeo, Bologna (Il Mu-
lino) 2007.

Paul Craig

The Role of the European Parliament
under the Lisbon Treaty

This chapter seeks to address the likely impact of the Lisbon Treaty on the European Parliament and its role in the decision-making process. I shall begin by considering the role of the EP in relation to the legislative process, and then consider the powers accorded to the EP in relation to other matters such as the appointment of Commission and the President thereof and its power over the dismissal or censure of the Commission. It is important to understand that the formal legal powers accorded to the EP by the provisions of the Lisbon Treaty are only part of the story and that these must be seen against the backdrop of how the institutions have interacted in the past and how are they are likely to do so in the future.

I. The EP and the Legislative Process: The EP as 'Winner'

There is a real sense in which the EP emerged as a winner in the Lisbon Treaty and this is so notwithstanding the qualifications that will be made to this picture in the ensuing discussion. The principal evidence for this is to be found in the provisions concerning the legislative process, and more specifically to those concerning the ordinary legislative procedure.

In relation to 'primary legislation', inter-institutional balance, as opposed to separation of powers, has characterised the relationship, de jure and de facto between the major players. The Commission has retained its 'gold standard', the right of legislative initiative. The EP and the Council both partake in the consideration of legislation and do so now on an increasingly equal footing. The EP and the Council are said to exercise legislative and budgetary functions jointly.[1] This is embodied in Article 14(1) TEU-L, which provides that the European Parliament shall, jointly with the Council, exercise legislative and budgetary functions, and this provision is replicated in relation to the Council in Article 16(1) TEU-L.

The co-decision procedure is now deemed to be the ordinary legislative procedure,[2] and this procedure consists in the joint adoption by the European Parliament and the Council of a regulation, directive or decision on a proposal from the Commission. The reach of the ordinary legislative procedure has been extended to cover more areas than hitherto, including, for example, agriculture,[3] ser-

---

1   Art 14(1) and Art 16(1) TEU-L.

2   Arts 289 and 294 TFEU.

3   Art 43(2) TFEU.

vices,[4] asylum and immigration,[5] the structural and cohesion funds,[6] and the creation of specialised courts.[7]

This development is to be welcomed. The co-decision procedure has worked well, allowing input from the EP, representing directly the electorate, and from the Council, representing state interests. It provides a framework for a deliberative dialogue on the content of legislation between the EP, Council and Commission. The extension of the ordinary legislative procedure to new areas is a natural development, building on what has occurred in earlier Treaty reform. It enhances the legitimacy of Union legislation and its democratic credentials by enabling the EP to have input into the making of legislation in these areas.

We should nonetheless be mindful of the way in which co-decision has operated more recently, which has reduced, or carries the danger of reducing, the 'space' for meaningful dialogue within the co-decision procedure. The institutionalisation of trialogues has been of particular importance in this respect.[8] The trialogue contains representatives from the Council, EP, and Commission, normally no more than ten, from each institution. These informal meetings have been common since the mid-1990s and were originally devised so as to precede and exist alongside formal meetings of the Conciliation Committee with the object of facilitating compromise. There is however now evidence that they have moved 'earlier up' in the co-decision process, such that trialogues are now increasingly commonly used to broker inter-institutional compromise prior to second reading, thereby limiting the potential for meaningful dialogue by a broader range of members of the EP and Council.[9]

---

4   Art 56 TFEU.
5   Arts 77-80 TFEU.
6   Art 177 TFEU.
7   Art 257 TFEU.
8   European Parliament (2004), 13-15; *Shackleton / Raunio* (2003), 177-179.
9   I am grateful to *Deirdre Curtin* for this point, see *Curtin*, (forthcoming).

II. The EP and the Legislative Process:
Delegated and Implementing Acts

The role of the EP in relation to the legislative process would however be incomplete without consideration of the provisions concerning delegated and implementing acts under the Lisbon Treaty.
Bruno de Witte has already provided a valuable analysis of these
provisions[10] and the discussion that follows builds on those foundations.

A. Delegated and Implementing Acts:
The Provisions of the Lisbon Treaty

It will be remembered that the Constitutional Treaty introduced a
hierarchy of norms, which distinguished between different categories of legal act, and used terms such as 'law', 'framework law' and
the like.[11] The European Council of June 2007, which initiated the
process leading to the Lisbon Treaty, decided that the terms 'law',
and 'framework law' should be dropped. The rationale given was
that the Lisbon Treaty was not to have a 'constitutional character',[12]
although it is not readily apparent why the terminology of 'law' or
'framework law' should be assumed to have a constitutional character. It was nonetheless decided to retain the existing terminology
of regulations, directives and decisions.

A version of the hierarchy of norms is however preserved in
the Lisbon Treaty, which distinguishes between legislative acts,
non-legislative acts of general application and implementing acts.

Thus Article 289 TFEU defines a legislative act as one adopted
in accord with a legislative procedure, either the ordinary legislative
procedure, which is the successor to co-decision, or a special legislative procedure.

Article 290 TFEU deals with what are now termed non-legislative acts of general application, whereby power to adopt such acts
is delegated to the Commission by a legislative act. Such non-legislative acts can supplement or amend certain non-essential elements of the legislative act, but the legislative act must define the
objectives, content, scope and duration of the delegation of power.
The essential elements of an area cannot be delegated. The legislative act must specify the conditions to which the delegation is sub-

---

10   Contribution of *Bruno de Witte* to this volume, Chapter V.

11   Arts I-33-39 CT.

12   Brussels European Council, 21-22 June 2007, Annex 1, para 3.

ject. Such conditions may allow the EP or the Council to revoke the delegation; and / or enable the EP or the Council to veto the delegated act within a specified period of time.

The third category in the hierarchy of norms, implementing acts, is dealt with in Article 291 TFEU. Member States must adopt all measures of national law necessary to implement legally binding Union acts. Where uniform conditions for implementing legally binding Union acts are needed, those acts shall confer implementing powers on the Commission, or, in certain cases on the Council. It is for the EP and Council to lay down in advance the rules and general principles concerning mechanisms for control by Member States of the Commission's exercise of implementing powers.

B. Non-Legislative Acts: The Implications for the Role of the EP

1. A formal distinction

We should recognise at the outset that the distinction between legislative and non-legislative acts is formal in the following sense. Legislative acts are defined as those enacted via a legislative procedure, either ordinary or special; non-legislative acts are those that are not enacted in this manner. This should not however mask the fact that the latter category of delegated acts will often be legislative in nature, in the sense that they will lay down binding provisions of general application to govern a certain situation. This is implicitly recognised in the nomenclature used in the Lisbon Treaty, which speaks of delegated acts having 'general application'. This moreover accords with the use made of 'secondary regulations' under the regime prior to the Lisbon Treaty. Such regulations were and are very commonly used to flesh out the meaning, scope or interpretation of provisions in the relevant 'parent regulation' in a manner analogous to the use made of delegated legislation, secondary legislation or rulemaking in national legal systems. It is interesting to contrast the label attached to delegated regulations in the Constitutional Treaty and non-legislative acts in the Lisbon Treaty, with the Convention on the Future of Europe Working Group's more honest depiction of these acts as a new category of legislation.[13]

---

13   Final Report of Working Group IX on Simplification, CONV 424/02, Brussels 29 November 2002, 8.

2. The Political History

It is important to be aware of the significant 'history' that underlies
these provisions on the hierarchy of norms. The Commission's primary goal has been to dismantle the established Comitology regime, at least insofar as it entails management and regulatory committees. It has supported the *ex ante* and *ex post* constraints on non-
legislative acts contained in Article 290 TFEU in the hope that the
Member States might then be persuaded to modify the existing
Comitology oversight mechanisms for delegated regulations.[14]

The Commission's desire to have greater autonomy over this
area has been apparent for some time,[15] and was an explicit feature
of the White Paper on *European Governance*.[16] The key to the
White Paper was the Commission's conception of the 'Community
method',[17] with the Commission representing the general interest
and the Council and the EP as the joint legislature, representing the
Member States and national citizens respectively. This is in itself
unexceptionable. It is the implications that the Commission drew
from it that are contentious.

It was, said the Commission, necessary to revitalise the Community method.[18] The Council and the EP should limit their involvement in primary Community legislation to defining the essential elements.[19] This legislation would define the conditions and
limits within which the Commission performed its executive role. It
would, in the Commission's view, make it possible to do away with
the Comitology committees, at least so far as they had the powers
presently exercised by management and regulatory committees.

---

14 *European Governance*, COM(2001) 428 final, paras 20-29; *Institu-*
    tional Architecture, COM(2002) 728 final, paras 1.2, 1.3.4; Proposal
    for a Council Decision Amending Decision 1999/468/EC Laying
    Down the Procedures for the Exercise of Implementing Powers Con-
    ferred on the Commission, COM(2002) 719 final, 2; Final Report of
    Working Group IX on Simplification, CONV 424/02, Brussels 29
    November 2002, 12.

15 Cf. *Bergström* (2005).

16 COM(2001) 428 final. The White Paper provoked a variety of critical
    comment, see *Joerges / Mény / Weiler* (2001).

17 COM(2001) 428 final, 8.

18 *Ibid* 29.

19 *Ibid* 20.

There would instead be a simple legal mechanism allowing the Council and EP to control the actions of the Commission against the principles adopted in the legislation. The possibility of enhancing the Commission's control over delegated regulations by abolishing or amending the Comitology procedure was raised again by the Working Group on Simplification.[20]

It remains to be seen whether the Commission is successful in this regard. It also remains to be seen whether the controls embodied in Article 290 will be effective, if the Comitology regime is dismantled.[21] Let us assume for the sake of argument that the only controls on non-legislative acts are those set out in Article 290 TFEU, and that this does not include Comitology type controls of the kind that are mentioned explicitly in relation to implementing acts.

3. The EP and Delegated Acts: The Positive Interpretation

The controls contained in Article 290 TFEU are important, more especially so since they accord to the EP the simple power to reject a non-legislative act. Viewed from this perspective, the EP emerges as a winner from the Lisbon Treaty in relation to delegated acts as well as legislative acts, because it is accorded an important power that it did not have hitherto. This may well prove to be so, but the picture in this area is more complex and less certain for a number of related reasons.

4. The EP and Delegated Acts: A More Cautious Interpretation

There are a number of reasons to be more cautious about the overall impact on the EP of the new regime concerning delegated acts.

First, we should be mindful of the trade-off that is inherent in this schema for non-legislative acts. In essence the pre-existing regime was based on generalised ex ante input into the making and content of the delegated norms, with the possibility of formal recourse to the Council in accord with the Comitology procedures. It allowed for regularised, general and detailed input into the content of such norms by Member State representatives, with increasing control exercised by the EP, more especially since the 2006 reforms. The Lisbon Treaty is premised on a system of ex ante speci-

---

20 Final Report of Working Group IX on Simplification, CONV 424/02, Brussels 29 November 2002, 12.

21 *Craig* (2004), Chap 5; Craig (2006), Chap 4.

fication of standards in the primary law, combined with the possibility of some control ex post should the measure not be to the liking of the EP or Council.

Secondly, the controls contained in Article 290(2) TFEU are not mandatory. The conditions of application to which the delegation is subject 'shall' be determined in the legislative act. These 'may' entail the possibility of revocation of the delegation by the EP or the Council, or a condition whereby the delegated regulation enters into force only if there is no objection expressed by the EP or the Council within a specified period of time. These controls will therefore only operate where they are written into the legislative act.

Thirdly, the methods of control contained in Article 290(1) TFEU will be difficult to monitor and enforce. It is true that the non-legislative acts can only amend or supplement 'certain non-essential elements of the legislative act', and cannot cover the 'essential elements of an area'. These must be reserved for the legislative act, which must also define the 'objectives, content, scope and duration of the delegation of power'. It will often be difficult for the Council and the EP to specify with exactitude the criteria that should guide the exercise of delegated power by the Commission. The Council and the EP will often have neither the knowledge, nor the time to delineate in the legislative act precise parameters for the exercise of regulatory choices. The real issues about the assignment of regulatory risks and choice will often only be apparent when the matter is examined in detail. It was for these very reasons that the Comitology process was first created. It will therefore not be easy for the legislative act to define with precision the 'objectives, content, scope and duration' of the delegation.

If these requirements are to be taken seriously then there will have to be oversight by, *inter alia*, the Community courts. They will have to enforce a non-delegation doctrine, striking down delegations where the legislative act was insufficiently precise about the 'objectives, content, scope and duration' of the delegation. Whether the Community courts would be willing to do this with vigour remains to be seen, and history does not indicate vigorous judicial enforcement of such criteria by the Community courts.[22]

---

22 See, e.g., Case 156/93 *European Parliament v Commission* [1995] ECR I-2019; Case 417/93 *European Parliament v Council* [1995] ECR I-1185. Experience from other legal systems is mixed. The non-

It would of course be open to the Community courts to review compliance with these criteria more forcefully than it has done hitherto, and it might choose to do so precisely because there will not be the Comitology controls that existed hitherto. It should nonetheless be recognised that even if this were to happen the controls contained in Article 290(1) would still be of limited efficacy. This is because even if the EP and Council take seriously the obligation to specify the essential elements in the legislative act, and even if compliance with these criteria is taken seriously by the Community courts, important regulatory choices, and issues of principle will still be dealt with through delegated acts. This is because the legislative act itself will often be set at a relatively high level of generality, since the Council and the EP will often have neither the knowledge, nor the time to delineate in the legislative act precise parameters for the exercise of regulatory choices with the consequence that the meaningful issues only become apparent when the provisions of the legislative act are worked through in greater detail in the delegated acts.

Fourthly, we should also be mindful of the limits to the controls set out in Article 290(2) TFEU. We have already seen that these controls are not mandatory. Article 290(2) states that the conditions of application to which the delegation is subject *shall* be explicitly determined in the legislative act and that they *may* consist of revocation of the delegation, and / or entry into force only if there is no objection from the Council or the EP. The wording of the analogous provision in the Constitutional treaty was consciously altered to make it clear that 'these conditions do not constitute a mandatory element of such a law or framework law'.[23] Let us assume, however, that such controls are imposed in the relevant legislative act that governs an area. We should nonetheless be mindful of the limits of these controls.

Revocation of the delegation might be useful as an ultimate weapon, but it is ill-suited by its very nature to fine-tuned control over the content of a particular non-legislative act. This can only be achieved by recourse to the other control specified, the prevention

---

delegation doctrine in the USA has, for example, provided little by way of control of broad regulatory choices accorded to agencies, *Aman / Mayton* (2001), Chap 1; *Rogers / Healy / Krotoszynski* (2003), 312-345.

23   CONV 724/03, Annex 2, 93.

of entry into force of a delegated regulation to which the EP or Council objected. It should be noted that neither the Council nor the EP is accorded any formal right to propose amendments to delegated acts, but only the power to prevent their entry into force. The threat of use of the latter power might be used as de facto leverage to secure amendment to a delegated act, but this does not alter the fact that Article 290(2) does not contain any formal power to amend.

The exercise of the 'veto' power is moreover crucially dependent on knowledge and understanding of the relevant measure. Neither the Council nor the EP will be in a position to decide whether to object to the measure unless they understand its content and implications. The Member State representatives on the Council clearly have neither the time nor expertise to perform this task unaided. The committees of the EP might develop such expertise, but have not yet done so in a sustained and systematic manner across all areas of EU law. They have hitherto been able to draw on informational resources from the Comitology committees, in order to understand the relevant measure and decide whether to object to it. Assuming that such committees cease to operate in relation to delegated acts, then the relevant EP committee will have significantly less material to help it to comprehend the relevant measure and decide whether to object to it. Even if advisory committees of Member State representatives are retained under the new regime, there is no certainty that the EP would be able to access any information about the content of the delegated act in the manner that it has done hitherto

These difficulties would be more pronounced given that the EP and Council would have to raise any such objection within a period specified by the legislative act. The period will vary depending on the area, but it will probably be relatively short.[24] The Council and EP would therefore have to 'get their act together' pretty quickly if either institution sought to prevent the non-legislative act becoming law.

---

24 The amendment to the Second Comitology Decision specifies a period of four months for the EP to oppose a measure under the 2006 reforms, but this is premised on the continued existence of Comitology committees, which means that the measure would have received detailed scrutiny already, albeit by committees on which Member State interests were represented.

It might be argued that the concerns expressed above are misplaced or overplayed because non-legislative acts will, in any event, only deal with relatively minor technical matters. This will not withstand examination. The very depiction of delegated acts as non-legislative serves, whether intentionally or not, to dispel fears that the Commission is making legislative choices of its own volition. The reality is that secondary regulations often deal with complex regulatory choices or policy issues, which are not rendered less so by the fact that they are concerned with matters of detail or technicality. To the contrary, the devil is often in the detail, which is of course the very reason why the Comitology committees were created in the first place, so as to allow Member State oversight of these complex regulatory choices.[25] The fact that the matters are often complex and detailed does not alter this important fact. The committees were created precisely because the Member States sought greater regulatory input into the detail of secondary regulations than allowed for in the then existing Treaty provisions. Comitology-type committees were created as soon as the need to delegate extensive powers to the Commission became a reality. They have been part of the institutional landscape for over forty years. They were established to accord Member States an institutionalised method for input into the content of delegated legislation. These regulatory choices will not disappear. They will continue to be made through the new style non-legislative acts, and these will, so it is intended be made against the background of less detailed primary legislative acts.

C. Implementation Acts: The Implications for the Role of the EP

The Lisbon Treaty, following the Constitutional Treaty, also makes provision for implementation acts in Article 291 TFEU, which are distinct from non-legislative acts, which are dealt with in Article 290 TFEU. Assessment of the implications of Article 291 for the role of the EP is predicated on addressing two issues: when Article 291 will apply and the role of Comitology therein. These will be considered in turn.

1. The Sphere of Application of Article 291

The first issue, when Article 291 will apply, appears to be answered by the wording of the Treaty article: where uniform conditions are required for implementing legally binding Union acts, those acts

---

25   *Joerges / Vos* (1999); *Andenas / Türk* (2000); *Bergström* (2005).

shall confer implementing powers on the Commission, or, in certain cases on the Council. Matters are not quite so simple.

Binding legislative acts can take the form of regulations, directives and decisions. This follows from Article 289 TFEU, which lists these measures and provides that whenever they are adopted pursuant to a legislative procedure they constitute legislative acts. Binding non-legislative acts, deemed delegated acts, can also, in principle take the form of regulations, directives or decisions, although regulations have been most commonly used hitherto as the legal medium for the passage of secondary legislation.[26] We need however to tread carefully to see precisely when Article 291 will come into play.

If the primary legislative act is a regulation, as defined in Article 288 TFEU, then it is directly applicable within the Member States' legal systems, and is binding as to means as well as ends. It does not require adoption or transformation before it acquires legal force within those systems, and the ECJ has moreover held that they should not normally be cast into national legislation.[27] It is therefore difficult to see how the need for 'uniform conditions for implementing legally binding Union acts' justifying conferral of implementing powers on the Commission would be of relevance in relation to such legislative acts themselves, given that they are directly applicable.[28] The primary legislative regulation might itself specify in detail the way in which it is to be implemented, which

---

26 The Working Party on Simplification considered that it would be possible for implementing acts to be made pursuant to delegated acts, as well as legislative acts, and this is clearly correct in principle, given that delegated acts are legally binding, Final Report of Working Group IX on Simplification, CONV 424/02, Brussels 29 November 2002, 9-11.

27 Case 34/73, *Variola v Amministrazione delle Finanze* [1973] ECR 981

28 It is true that a regulation might require consequential changes in other areas of national law, but where this is so the nature of those amendments are bound to differ as between the Member States, precisely because their previous laws in the area will often be very different. It will not therefore be possible to contemplate uniform changes to these other national legal provisions that could be stipulated by the Commission. The Member States would simply have the obligation, pursuant to Article 291(1), to adopt all measures necessary to implement legally binding Union acts.

would then be directly applicable in the same way as the remainder of the regulation. This does not however serve to explain the conferral of implementing powers on the Commission, since by definition the job would have been done by the primary legislative act itself. Where the legislative act is a regulation there is therefore no need for recourse to Article 291 in relation to implementation of that legislative act itself. Article 291 would be used to enact implementing norms made pursuant to the legislative act, in circumstances where the conditions warrant uniform conditions of implementation. Thus there could be instances where past experience reveals that a primary legislative regulation in a particular area has been implemented somewhat differently within different Member States and that greater uniformity is required. Thus when a new version of the primary legislative regulation is enacted it could contain power for the Commission to enact uniform implementing measures, without the need to amend the primary legislative act itself. Whether recourse to Article 291 by the Commission is warranted would however depend upon the nature of any measures introduced. It should be remembered that Article 290, which deals with non-legislative acts, is operative whenever the primary legislative act is supplemented or amended by a later measure. There may therefore be difficult borderlines between instances of 'pure implementation', where recourse to Article 291 is warranted, and those instances where the later measures in effect 'supplement or amend' the primary legislative act, where recourse should be had to Article 290.

We must be equally careful when considering the application of Article 291 where the primary legislative act is a directive. The very nature of a directive leaves Member States with discretion as to means of implementation. That is its very *raison d'être*. It would therefore be odd, to say the least, to enact a directive, but to empower the Commission to impose uniform conditions for implementation. The reality is that if the Commission's power to impose uniform conditions for implementation were to be used in relation to directives it would radically alter their nature. It would create a new hybrid species of primary legislative act, in which the means of implementation, normally left to the discretion of the Member States, would be exercised by the Commission. Once again the proper sphere for application of Article 291 would be in situations where it is thought necessary to accord the Commission uniform powers to make implementing measures pursuant to some aspect or article of the legislative directive, not the directive itself. Once again, as in the discussion in the previous paragraph, there could be difficult borderline issues as to whether such measures fell within Article 291, or whether they should be regarded as coming within Article 290, because they supplement or amend the primary legislative directive.

It might be possible to envision circumstances in which Article 291 could be used where the primary legislative act was a decision of the more generic kind. Article 288 TFEU contemplates two kinds of decision, the most common being a decision addressed to a particular individual or firm, as exemplified by cartel decisions imposing fines. There can however also be decisions of a more generic nature, which are not addressed to a particular person.[29] There could be circumstances where such decisions require uniform methods of implementation, thereby triggering the Commission's powers to devise uniform implementation pursuant to Article 291(2). This same Article also expressly contemplates the Council imposing uniform conditions for implementation pursuant to Articles 24 and 26 TEU-L, which are concerned with the CFSP.

The reasoning in the preceding paragraphs concerning the circumstances in which the Commission is justified in imposing uniform conditions of implementation is equally applicable where the legally binding act takes the form of a non-legislative act made pursuant to Article 290 TFEU. This is because the reasoning set out above would also be operative where the non-legislative act took the form of a delegated regulation or delegated directive. This is subject to the following caveat. It would seem possible in principle for the Commission to enact, for example, a delegated regulation, for the Commission to decide that uniform implementing conditions are required, and for the Commission to then give itself the implementing power in the delegated regulation. This seems to follow from a reading of the Articles of the Lisbon Treaty. Whether it is desirable in normative terms is far more contestable. It would, if used in this manner, certainly increase the Commission's degree of control over the legislative process taken as a whole. The only formal constraints on this happening would be the possibility for the Council or EP to object to the entry into force of such a delegated regulation pursuant to Article 290, or through Comitology to the extent to which it might still exist pursuant to Article 291(3).

---

29   Contribution of *Bruno de Witte* to this volume, Chapter V.

2. Implementing Acts, Comitology and the EP

We can now consider the second issue, the role of Comitology in relation to implementation acts. There are four points to note in this regard.

First, the continuance of Comitology is expressly envisaged by Article 291(3), which provides that where uniform conditions for implementation are needed and therefore the requisite powers have been conferred on the Commission, the EP and the Council shall lay down in advance by means of a legislative regulation enacted by the ordinary legislative procedure the rules and principles concerning mechanisms for control by the Member States of the Commission's implementing powers.

Secondly, there is however nothing in Article 291(3) which stipulates the form or nature of the controls over the Commission's implementing powers. They might simply replicate the existing Comitology regime. It is more likely that they will not do so. It should be noted in this respect that the wording of Article 291(3) is framed in terms of 'control by Member States'. It is not even framed in terms of the Council, and says nothing of control by the EP. It is therefore questionable whether provisions which gave the EP some control over such matters would be interpreted to be *intra vires* that Article. It is in any event doubtful, given the *raison d'être* of Article 291, whether the Commission would conceive of the EP as having any proper role in relation to such matters, given that they are meant to be about 'pure implementation', and therefore of concern for the Member States either in their individual guise, or through the collectivity of the Council.

Thirdly, the circumstances in which any Comitology regime would operate would however be subject to the limits discussed in the previous section. Furthermore, the divide between instances where Article 290 should apply, because the further act supplemented or amended the delegated act, and those instances where recourse could properly be had to Article 291 and implementing acts, could be problematic. It could also lead to inter-institutional litigation, more especially so if, as is likely to be the case, the EP is given no role in relation to implementation acts. Assuming this to be so, there could well be instances where the Commission seeks to have recourse to implementation acts, and this is challenged by the EP on the ground that the relevant measures either supplement or amend the legislative act, and hence should have been made pursu-

ant to Article 290, thereby enabling the EP and Council to exercise
the controls specified in that Article.

Fourthly and finally, we should be mindful of the change that
the Lisbon Treaty could bring about in relation to the passage of
acts other than legislative acts. The preceding discussion has been
premised on the assumption that Comitology and its attendant procedure applies only in relation to implementation acts, and not in
relation to non-legislative acts, although this assumption will be
questioned below. The assumption is premised on the fact that there
is no mention of Comitology procedures in Article 290, which deals
with non-legislative acts. If this assumption proves correct then it
will represent a marked change in the Community regime. The
'cause' of this shift resides ultimately in ambiguity as to the meaning of the word implementation. It can bear the meaning that it has
in the current Article 202 TEC: delegated rulemaking or decision-
making subject to Comitology conditions. Implementation can also
mean the execution of other norms, whether Treaty provisions, primary laws or delegated regulations: the relevant norm will be applied or executed, but without any supplementation or amendment.
The Comitology procedure has hitherto applied to implementation
that included the first sense of this term: it was the condition attached to delegated rulemaking or decision-making by the Commission. The discussion in the Convention on the Future of Europe revealed an important shift in thought. The Comitology procedures
were not mentioned in relation to the making of delegated regulations, even though this was the true analogy with the status quo
ante, the implication being that they would be replaced by the controls in Article I-35(2) CT, now replicated in Article 290(2) TFEU.
The Convention documentation considered the legitimacy of
Comitology primarily in the context of implementing acts covered
by Article I-36, where the emphasis was on implementation in its
second sense, as execution or application. This was apparent in the
literature from the Working Group.[30] It was apparent again in the
Convention comments on Article I-36(3), which provision allowed
for Member State control over implementing acts.[31] The Presidium
stated that several amendments were opposed to the current committee mechanisms, and wished to delete this Article, while other

---

30   Final Report of Working Group IX on Simplification, CONV 424/02,
     Brussels 29 November 2002, 9.

31   CONV 724/03, Annex 2, 94.

comments proposed confining the control mechanisms to advisory committees alone. The Presidium considered that this was a matter for secondary legislation and therefore did not amend the Article. The assumption was therefore that in the future Comitology would be relevant only in the context of implementing acts, and not in relation to delegated regulations, even though this was in stark contrast to the circumstances where Comitology is currently used.

III. The EP and the Legislative Process: Conclusion

The EP undoubtedly emerged as a winner from the Lisbon Treaty in relation to the passage of legislative acts: the formal endorsement of the EP as co-legislator with the Council, combined with the extension of the ordinary legislative procedure to new areas will strengthen the EP's role in relation to the primary legislative acts.

The position of the EP in relation to non-legislative acts is more equivocal. It is true that Article 290 TFEU strengthens the EP's powers by according it a general right to reject such an act if it so wishes. The difficulties with the regime of ex ante and ex post controls embodied in Article 290 have however been set out above. The reality is that non-legislative acts will continue, as they have done hitherto, to address matters of importance that involve the making of contentious value judgments. The Article 290 regime on its face does not allow for input into the making of such norms by either the EP or the Council, nor does it formally contain any power to amend. The ability of either Council or the EP to reject a non-legislative act is therefore crucially dependent on developing an understanding of the measure within the time limit laid down in the legislative act in order to decide whether they wish to oppose it.

It remains to be seen whether Comitology will disappear from the 'world of non-legislative acts'. A touch of political *realpolitik* is warranted here. The Member States are unlikely to accept the abolition of a regime whereby they can have input into the making of non-legislative acts. They have insisted on this for forty years, and it is difficult to see why they would dismantle a regime that has allowed them input into the content of such norms while they are being formulated. It is equally doubtful whether they would accept the downgrading of all such committees to become merely advisory committees, thereby doing away with management and regulatory committees. If this were to happen, if the regulatory regime of the last forty years were to be discontinued, the Council would in any event quickly recognise that it could only make meaningful judgments as to whether to oppose a particular non-legislative act if it had the knowledge from which to make such a considered judgment. It would therefore have to re-create some form of committee system to oversee the content of non-legislative acts, which would of course be déjà vu all over again.

IV. The EP and Executive Power

The discussion thus far has been concerned with the role of the EP in relation to the legislative process under the Lisbon Treaty. The analysis now turns to consideration of the EP's powers in relation to executive organs.

We can begin by considering the election of the Commission President. The relevant provisions of the Lisbon Treaty mirror those of the Constitutional Treaty. Article 14(1) TEU-L provides, *inter alia*, that the EP shall elect the President of the Commission.[32] The retention of state power is however apparent in Article 17(7) TEU-L.[33] The European Council, acting by qualified majority, after appropriate consultation, and taking account of the elections to the EP, puts forward to the EP the European Council's candidate for Presidency of the Commission. This candidate shall then be elected by the EP by a majority of its members. If the candidate does not get the requisite majority support, then the European Council puts forward a new candidate within one month, following the same procedure.

The Lisbon Treaty also follows the Constitutional Treaty in relation to the election of the other members of the Commission. Article 17(7) TEU-L provides that the Council, by common accord with the President-elect, adopts the list of the other persons whom it proposes for appointment as members of the Commission, these having been selected on the basis of suggestions made by Member States. The President, the High Representative of the Union for Foreign Affairs and Security Policy and the other members of the Commission are then subject as a body to a vote of consent by the European Parliament. It can therefore be expected that the EP will continue with its 'senate-like' confirmation hearings of proposed Commissioners, in which it subjects aspirant holders of such posts to fairly intense scrutiny to determine their expertise and likely ap-

---

32   The equivalent provision was Art I-20(1) CT.
33   The equivalent provision was Art I-27(1) CT.

proach to the area over which they are to have responsibility. It should nonetheless be noted that Article 17(7) TEU-L provides once again for the retention of state power, in that while the EP's consent is necessary for the appointment of the President, High Representative and members of the Commission, the actual formal appointment rests with the European Council, acting by a qualified majority. This is in accord with the final version of the Constitutional Treaty.[34]

It is interesting to reflect on the way in which state power and control has been 'ratcheted up' in relation to appointment of the Commission. The version of the Constitutional Treaty produced by the Convention on the Future of Europe and submitted to the IGC differed from the above. It provided that each Member State established a list of three persons whom it considered suitable to be Commissioner, that the President-elect made the choice from within each list, and that the final list was then to be collectively approved by the EP.[35] The final version of the Constitutional Treaty made changes in this respect as a result of discussions in the IGC. State power was enhanced in two complementary ways: it is now the Council, in accord with the President-elect, which adopts the list of proposed Commissioners, and it is now the European Council that makes the formal appointment of the Commission, after the EP has given its consent.

The EP has retained its 'nuclear-strike' power in relation to censure of the Commission. Thus Article 17(8) TEU-L stipulates that the Commission is responsible to the EP, and that if the EP votes in favour of a censure motion the members of the Commission must resign and the High Representative of the Union for Foreign Affairs and Security Policy must resign from the duties that he carries out in the Commission.

V. The EP, Policy and Politics

It is interesting to reflect briefly on the impact of the preceding provisions on the functioning of the EU, and more particularly the extent to which they will render the system more truly 'parliamentary' than hitherto. There is no doubt that there is some movement in this direction. Thus, while the European Council retains ultimate power

---

34   The relevant provision of the CT was Art I-27 CT.

35   CONV 850/03, 18 July 2003, Art I-26(2).

over choice of Commission President, it is unlikely to attempt to
force a candidate on the EP that is of a radically different persuasion from the dominant party or coalition in the EP.

The rules contained in the Lisbon Treaty on this issue generally cohere with recent practice, and they go some way to improving the linkage between policy and politics in the EU. Insofar as the
EU has been depicted as a polity in which policy is divorced from
party politics, a formal linkage between the dominant party / coalition in the EP and the appointment of the Commission President
serves to strengthen the connection between policy and party politics, the assumption being that the designated President of the
Commission will share similar political views on policy to that of
the dominant party in the EP.

We should nonetheless be mindful of the obstacles that subsist
to a closer link between policy and politics in the EU, even after the
Lisbon Treaty reforms. Four such factors deserve mention.

First, the President of the Commission may well be *primus
inter pares*, but he or she is still only one member of the Commission team. The other Commissioners will not necessarily be of the
same political persuasion as the President or the dominant party in
the EP, and it has been common for Commissioners to come from
varying political backgrounds. Thus even if there is some common-
ality of view between President and EP in terms of politics and
policy, this will not necessarily be shared by all Commissioners.
Nor, insofar as this is perceived to be a problem, which is itself
open to debate, can it be resolved through EP hearings of individual
Commissioners.

Secondly, and even more importantly, is the fact that the policy
agenda in the EU is of course not exclusively in the hands of the EP
and / or Commission. The Council and the European Council both
have input both de jure and de facto into the policy agenda for the
EU. The extended Presidency of the European Council is likely to
increase this tendency further, since the incumbent of the office will
have the time and opportunity to develop a set of ideas for the EU
in the way that the pre-existing regime of six-monthly rotating
presidencies precluded. It should moreover be noted that the Lisbon
Treaty, like the Constitutional Treaty, accords the Commission the
power to initiate the Union's annual and multiannual programming
with a view to achieving interinstitutional agreements.[36] This is ex-

---

36   Art 17 TEU-L.

plicitly premised on the assumption that other institutional players will and should have an impact on the development and shape of politics and policy. Thus even if the EP and Commission President were very closely allied in terms of substantive political vision for the EU, the policy that emerges will necessarily also bear the imprint of the political vision of the Council and European Council.

Thirdly, the absence of a developed party system at the EU level also serves to limit the extent to which the gap between politics and policy can be narrowed within the EU. A coherent political agenda will normally emerge at national level, precisely because it is developed by rival parties, which formulate the contending political packages to voters who then choose between them. The absence of a developed party system at the EU level, means that elections to the EP are, as is well known, fought by national political parties in which national political issues often predominate, with the result that there is little by way of a clear political agenda on EU issues that is proffered to the voters to choose from. The MEPs will then sit within cross-national political groupings of left, centre, right wing and the like, but they will not come to the EP with a coherent left wing or right wing agenda.

A further factor that has reduced the linkage between policy and party politics in the EU concerns the very nature of the issues that the EU regulates. It is true that the scope of the EU's competence has been expanded by successive Treaty amendments. It is true also that certain of the issues which have more recently fallen within the EU's competence are by their nature highly political, such as many of the matters covered by the area of freedom, security and justice. It nonetheless remains the case that many of the most 'political' issues at national level, or matters that cause the most pronounced tensions between the left and right wing, are issues over which the EU either has no competence, or only limited competence. These issues include direct taxation, the reach and nature of the welfare state, education, crime, health and the like.

VI. The EP and the Budget

Money matters, it always has. This is a trite proposition, but it is true nonetheless. This is especially so in relation to parliaments, since they properly regard power over financial disbursements as significant in itself, and as a powerful lever through which to secure further concessions from other institutions within the polity.

The decision-making regime under Article 272 TEC was complex, but in effect gave the EP the final say over non-compulsory expenditure, with the Council having the final word over compulsory expenditure. This dichotomy led to repeated battles and skirmishes over the divide between compulsory and non-compulsory expenditure.

The decision-making regime under the Lisbon Treaty marks a significant change in this respect. Article 14(1) TEU-L provides that the EP jointly with the Council, exercises legislative and budgetary functions, and this is reiterated in Article 16(1) TEU-L from the perspective of the Council.

The detailed rules as to this joint exercise of budgetary authority are then found in the TFEU. Article 310 TFEU provides that the Union's annual budget shall be established by the EP and the Council in accordance with Article 314. The annual budget must however comply with the multiannual financial framework, which is established for five years, Article 312 TFEU. The Council, acting in accordance with a special legislative procedure, adopts a regulation laying down the multiannual financial framework. The Council acts unanimously after obtaining the consent of the European Parliament, which must be given by a majority of its component members.[37] The financial framework determines the amounts of the annual ceilings on commitment appropriations by category of expenditure and the annual ceiling on payment appropriations.

The detailed rules concerning passage of the annual budget are then set out in Article 314 TFEU. It is for the EP and the Council, acting in accordance with a special legislative procedure, to establish the Union's annual budget. This legislative procedure is close to the ordinary legislative procedure, but there are a number of differences.

In essence, the Commission produces a draft budget based on estimates submitted to it by the different institutions. This is then submitted to the EP and the Council not later than 1 September of the year preceding that in which the budget is to be implemented. The Council then adopts its position on the draft budget, giving reasons for its position, and forwards this to the EP not later than 1

---

37   The European Council may, unanimously, adopt a decision authorising the Council to act by a qualified majority when adopting the regulation of the Council, Art 312(2) TFEU.

October of the year preceding that in which the budget is to be implemented.

The EP can then within 42 days of this communication: approve the Council's position, in which case the budget is adopted; not take a decision, in which case the budget is deemed to have been adopted; adopt amendments by a majority of its component members, in which case the amended draft is forwarded to the Council and to the Commission. This then triggers a meeting of the Conciliation Committee, unless the Council signifies within ten days of receiving the amended draft that it approves all such amendments. If the Conciliation Committee meets then its task is to broker agreement between the Council and EP, in much the same way as under the ordinary legislative procedure. If the Conciliation Committee is able to agree on a joint text then this must be approved by the EP and Council, and there are detailed rules as to what should occur if either the Council or EP rejects the joint text.

Time will tell exactly how the decision-making regime under Article 314 operates. The statement of principle contained in Article 14 TEU-L that the EP exercises budgetary functions jointly with the Council, and the abolition of the distinction between compulsory and non-compulsory expenditure, both serve to increase the EP's power over the budget as compared to the pre-existing situation. It should however be recognised that the special legislative procedure set out in Article 314 contains a number of distinctive features as compared to the ordinary legislative procedure, which could serve to constrain the EP. Thus under the procedure in Article 314 it is the Council that initially communicates its position to the EP, there is nothing equivalent to the first reading by the EP under the ordinary legislative procedure. When the EP does respond to the Council's position it has no power of outright rejection at that stage, which is once again different from the position under the ordinary legislative procedure. These differences reflect the central importance of the annual budget for the EU. Having said this, the *de jure* powers accorded to the EP under Article 314 are still very significant, more especially given that they apply to all expenditure, and de facto one can expect all players, Council, EP and Commission, to be keen to reach agreement in order to secure passage of the budget and financial order within the EU.

VII. The EP and Amendment

The EP's power has also been increased by the Lisbon Treaty in relation to the amendment procedure. The position under Article 48 TEU prior to the Lisbon Treaty was that the government of any Member State or the Commission could make a proposal for Treaty amendment. It was then for the Council, after consultation with the EP, to decide whether to call for an IGC. The EP might be invited to take part in the IGC, and indeed was invited to participate in the IGC that led to the Lisbon Treaty, but the EP had no right to participate, nor did it have any formal right to propose Treaty amendments.

Article 48 TEU-L establishes an ordinary and simplified method of revising the Treaties. The details of the differences between these methods for Treaty amendment are not of immediate concern here. What is of direct relevance is the fact that under the ordinary revision procedure Member States, the Commission *and* the EP are accorded the power to propose Treaty amendments to the Council. It is then for the Council to submit such proposals to the European Council, which decides by simple majority, after consulting the Commission and EP, whether to press forward with examination of the proposed Treaty amendments. If it decides in favour of doing so, then a Convention is convened. This is composed of representatives of the national Parliaments, Member States, European Parliament and Commission. Thus under the ordinary revision procedure the EP is given the right to propose amendments and the right to participate in the Convention that discusses such amendments. It is open to the European Council to decide not to establish a Convention, because this is not warranted by the extent of the proposed amendments, and to proceed instead via an IGC, but this can only be done if the EP consents.

The EP is also included in the list of those who can submit proposals under the simplified legislative procedure for amendment of all or part of the provisions of Part Three of the TFEU relating to the internal policies and action of the Union. The decision with regard to such amendments is made by the European Council by unanimity after consulting the EP and the Commission. It must then be ratified by the Member States, as of course must any amendments made pursuant to the ordinary revision procedure.

There is little doubt that the Member States will continue to be the key players during major constitutional moments involving

Treaty amendments. Notwithstanding this, the very fact that the EP has now been included in the list of those who can propose Treaty amendment is of symbolic significance, insofar as it places the EP in parity in this respect with the Commission and Member States. It might also be of some real practical significance, since the EP might well seek to make use of this power to place an issue on the agenda for EU reform.

The fact that the EP is granted the right to participate in a Convention established pursuant to the ordinary revision procedure concretises *de jure* the *de facto* gains made by the EP through its participation in the Convention that drafted the Charter and the Convention on the Future of Europe. The EP is not granted any formal right to participate in an IGC, should this be established in lieu of a Convention. However the very decision whether to opt for an IGC rather than a Convention, on the ground that the scale of the Treaty amendments does not warrant a Convention, is dependent on the consent of the EP. The EP might well use the need for its consent as leverage to press for its inclusion within the formal IGC deliberations.

VIII. Conclusion

The EP is most certainly a net beneficiary of the changes introduced by the Lisbon Treaty. This is especially so in relation to its increased powers over the passage of legislative acts and the budget. The implications of the new Treaty provisions relating to delegated and implementing acts are more equivocal. Much will depend on how such provisions are interpreted and used. The positive reading of these provisions is that the EP is also a winner in this regard, being given a clear veto power over delegated acts that it does not approve of. It has however been argued in the preceding discussion that we may need to be more cautious about the implications of these new provisions.

We should moreover not forget that the EP's overall role in the development of EU policy will also be affected by the subsequent development of new forms of governance, such as the open method of co-ordination, OMC. This has been applied to an increasingly wide range of areas, and the EP has justly expressed concern about its exclusion from such processes, or the limited involvement that it has been allowed within OMC.

References

Alfred C. Aman / William T. Mayton (2001), Administrative Law, Saint Paul / MN (West Group) ²2001.

Mads Andenas / Alexander Türk (eds.) (2000), Delegated Legislation and the Role of Committees in the EC, The Hague (Kluwer Law International) 2000.

Carl-Fredrik Bergström (2005), Comitology, Delegation of Powers in the European Union and the Committee System, Oxford (Oxford University Press) 2005.

Paul Craig (2004), The Hierarchy of Norms, *Takis Tridimas / Paolisa Nebbia* (eds.), European Union Law for the Twenty-First Century. Rethinking the New Legal Order, Oxford (Hart) 2004, 75-93.

Paul Craig (2006), EU Administrative Law, Oxford (Oxford University Press) 2006.

Deirdre Curtin (forthcoming), Accountability of the Council of Ministers: The Missing Link.

European Parliament, Conciliations and Co-decision, A Guide to how Parliament Co-legislates (DV/547830EN.doc), Brussels 2004.

Christian Joerges / Yves Mény / Joseph H. H. Weiler (eds.) (2001), Mountain or Molehill? A Critical Appraisal of the Commission White Paper on Governance (= The Jean Monnet Working Papers 06/01), Brussels, July 2001 (available at: http://www.jeanmonnetprogram.org/papers/01/010601.html).

Christian Joerges / Ellen Vos (eds.) (1999), EU Committees: Social Regulation, Law and Politics, Oxford (Hart) 1999.

John M. Rogers / Michael P. Healy / Ronald J. Krotoszynski, Administrative Law, New York / NY (Aspen Publishers) 2003.

Michael Shackleton / Tapio Raunio (2003), Codecision since Amsterdam: A Laboratory for Institutional Innovation and Change, in: Journal of European Public Policy 10 (2003), 171-187.

Paolo Ponzano

'Executive' and 'delegated' acts: The situation after the Lisbon Treaty

I. Distinction between *delegated* and *executive* acts

A basic fact to be borne in mind is that the Lisbon Treaty *introduces important innovations* in relation to the Treaties currently in force. The main innovation is that it makes a *distinction for the first time* between *legislative delegation and executive delegation* (under the present treaties there is no distinction between the two and they have always been subject to the Comitology procedure).

The Treaty of Lisbon breaks new ground by establishing two separate procedures for 'delegated acts' and 'implementing measures' (in line with the practice in many national systems). In these systems, we have three different legal situations:

a) cases in which the legislator acts in his own field of competence: these are the 'laws';

b) cases in which the Executive acts in his own field of competence: these are 'executives acts' *stricto sensu* or 'ministerial decrees' (*"arrêtés ministériels"*);

c) cases in which the Executive acts in the field of competence of the legislator (either following an explicit delegation of powers or on its own initiative: in French, these acts are named *"ordonnances"* and in Italian *"decreti-legge"* or *"decreti legislativi"*).

Why was it necessary to change the present system? Principally, the need for change arose due to the difference between the 'ministerial decrees', which in our Member States fall within the 'exclusive competence' of the Minister responsible (and therefore the executive), and the 'decree laws' adopted by the government in areas which fall within the competence of the *legislature*. For example, how can the granting of financial assistance to NGOs or agricultural export refunds be equated with the *amendment of a law* adopted by the legislative body (such as the addition of some new dangerous products to a list of 30 products already voted on by the European Parliament and the Council)?

Within the European system, we need to make a similar distinction between acts adopted by the Commission in its own field of competence ('executive acts') and acts adopted by the Commission in the field of competence of the European Parliament and/or the Council ('delegated acts'). Some scholars[1] have criticised this new system as being unclear and a source of confusion. However, the same criticism could be applied to the national systems (is an Italian "*decreto-legge*" a law or a decree?)

For a long time the Council has exploited an interpretation of the Treaty which allowed it to remove 'delegated acts' from the competence of the European Parliament on the pretext that execution was the responsibility of the Member States and, at EU level, of the Commission (assisted by Committees made up of Member States' representatives). However, the new Treaty has replaced the comitology system with an arrangement whereby the *Commission takes responsibility for delegated acts* under the *direct control* of the European Parliament and the Council (giving each of them the possibility of opposing the measure or revoking the delegation).

II. How will the Commission exercise its responsibility for delegated acts?

1. Some commentators have [2] expressed the fear that the removal of Committees for the adoption of delegated acts could deprive the Commission of the expertise required for elaborating measures. This, however, is groundless because the Commission will continue to rely on Member States' experts, even in the absence of a formal Committee which should vote by qualified majority and make appeal to the Council if there is no qualified majority.

---

1   See for instance *Bergström* (2005).

2   See the contribution of *Paul Craig* to this volume.

In other words, the *same procedure* should be followed for amending a law as *for drafting the law* (for example, if the Commission consulted Scientific Committees and / or Member States' experts when drawing up the list of 30 dangerous products, it will do the same when it wants to add a thirty-first product or amend the annexes to the REACH Regulation, consulting the *same bodies* as for the original act). Therefore, the main difference between the procedure before and the procedure after the Lisbon Treaty will be that a possible negative opinion of Member States' experts will not provoke an appeal to the Council in order to modify the Commission's draft.

2. A special case is that of the *Lamfalussy* acts for *financial services* (where the Commission adds some provisions to the law instead of *amending* the annexes). For this sector, the Intergovernmental Conference adopted a declaration (n. 39) by which the Commission confirmed *its established practice of consulting the competent national experts.* Why this declaration? It is a result of the fact that the Finance Ministers are well aware that the national experts de facto *dictate* several provisions to the *Commission's departments* in the financial services field. However, even in this sector, the Member States *agreed not to request that the existing Committees be retained,* provided that the Commission *maintained the current practice.* Even if this commitment has not been extended to other sectors (where it was not a matter of adding new elements to *an act* but only of amending *the annexes* to a directive to bring them into line with scientific, technical or economic progress), it will clearly be in the interests of the Commission's departments to consult the same experts who helped them to prepare the original proposal before tabling a 'delegated act' amending the annexes. In conclusion, the Commission will continue to request the assistance of an advisory working group of national experts before submitting the delegated acts to the European Parliament and the Council.

It is certainly true – as *Craig* underlines in his contribution to this book – that the Comitology procedure provides the Commission with more expertise on regulatory choices than a mere political control ex-post from the European Parliament and the Council. However, if the Commission's departments play the game correctly, they will dispose of the same expertise on regulatory choices while allowing the legislator to ex-

ercise a political control over the content of an act falling
within his field of competence. Moreover, the same problem
arises for the British government when it submits a 'delegated
act' to the House of Commons in order to get its tacit assent
within a very short period of time.

III. The problem of 'supplementing' measures

Some attendees to the Florence Conference wonder why the Member States have accepted to extend the powers of 'delegated acts' to
the 'supplementing measures' instead of limiting these ones to the
'amending measures'.

The work of the *'Amato* Group' on simplification can help in
providing an answer to this question. The members of the *'Amato*
Group' are aware of several cases for which the Commission has
been authorised by the legislator to adapt a previous regulation or
directive to a technical, scientific or economic progress (by the
means of a new proposal amending or supplementing the annexes in
the previous acts – see, for instance, the REACH regulation). But
the members of the Group are also aware of the new procedure introduced more recently by the Council, the so called *"Lamfalussy
procedure"*. According to this procedure, the Commission has been
delegated the power not only to amend one or more annexes in previous acts, but also to complete (or *supplement*) *the legislative act
i t s e l f with new provisions. In this way the legislator uses the
Commission as a means of speeding up the adoption of these provisions and avoids a new codecision procedure*! These could be
measures of a general nature which add new elements to the legal
framework of the legislative acts. Some examples of this kind of
measure can be found in Directive 2003/6/CE on market abuse (art.
6, par. 10), in Directive 2003/71/CE related to the prospectus (art.
2, par. 4) or in Directive 2004/109/CE on transparency (art. 21, par.
4).[3]

In other words, this delegation of powers does not limit the
Commission's ability to *formally modify* the annexes of the concerned regulations / directives, but precisely to complete (or supplement) the legislative act with *other provisions* that the legislator
could have adopted at the same time. It is true that the PRAC pro-

---

3   Examples from *Szapiro* (2006), 573.

cedure[4] attempted to cover this legal situation by using the words *"amending the legislative act by supplementing the instrument or by deleting some elements"*, but we can easily check that this expression covers the same legal situation (the *Lamfalussy* procedure) with other words. In fact, the list of priority acts which require an *alignment* of existing acts to the new procedure (PRAC) rightly covers the directives in which the *Lamfalussy* procedure is applied. Therefore, the Member States were aware of the consequences when they added the word *"supplement"* both in the *Comitology decision* of July 2006 and in the Lisbon Treaty.

IV. Implementing measures (or executive acts)

The situation is different for *implementing measures in the strict sense*. In this case, the committees of Member States' representatives *remain due to the fact that the Treaty provides for the monitoring of such measures by the Member States* (and not by the legislator, unlike delegated acts).

However, even the comitology system has to change, firstly because the general decision will be adopted by codecision procedure by the two co-legislators (the European Parliament having a right of veto and the Council acting by qualified majority and no longer by unanimous vote), and secondly because control of the measure *by the Member States* would seem to rule out any appeal to the Council (which would moreover be difficult for Parliament to accept unless it too had a *right of appeal*, which seems to be out of the question for *strictly implementing measures*).

On the other hand, the European Parliament might wish to retain its present *right of scrutiny in cases in which the Commission exceeds its powers* (it has exercised this right of scrutiny only *six times since 2000 in respect of more than 5000* executive measures, and got through in only one case. In all other cases the Parliament challenged de facto the content of the measure and not *'the abuse of power'* of the Commission).

The maintenance of Management and Regulation Committees as such will be problematic because a negative opinion from these Committees (following different procedures) currently provokes an appeal from the European Commission to the Council (while, in the

---

4   See the new *Comitology decision* adopted by the Council in July 2006.

new system, the European Parliament cannot accept an appeal just to the Council. Therefore, it might be possible that the Commission will propose the maintenance of the current negotiations at the level of the Committees of Member States' representatives and will suggest that it could not adopt a measure without obtaining a favourable opinion from these Committees.[5]

In his contribution to this volume, *Paul Craig* seems to exclude the possibility of recourse to an implementing measure where the legislative act is a regulation or a directive. It is true that most of the 'implementing measures' come from decisions by the legislator (for instance, all the programmes providing financial support from the Union). However, in reality, the legislator delegates a significant amount of powers to introduce implementing measures both through regulations or directives (see the agricultural or fishing regulations as well as the environmental directives for the authorisation of GMO products). Moreover, the implementing measures do not only cover measures of a general nature, but also individual measures (authorisation of individual products, derogation for a Member State, import ban or closure of a fishing zone, etc.).

In his paper, *Paul Craig* also expresses the fear that it could be difficult to draw a border line between *delegated* and *executive* acts (with the subsequent risk that some executive measures of the Commission might be challenged by the European Parliament for *abuse of power*). However, as far as the European Parliament and the Council (as a general rule) make this distinction in the legislative act (for instance: *"the measure covered by art. X will be adopted by the Commission following the procedure of "delegated acts" and the measures covered by art. Y will be adopted by the Commission following the procedure of "executive acts"*), there will not be any legal problem with the Commission submitting implementing measures.

V. Conclusion: the 'anomaly' of the Comitology system

In the past, many commentators have challenged the fact that the European Commission has the power to modify (or complete) a law *without the assent (tacit or explicit) of the legislator*. The Lisbon

---

5   Another solution could be that, in the absence of a qualified majority within the Committees, the Commission will make appeal to the same Committee meeting at ministerial level.

Treaty has remedied this situation. As far as efficiency is concerned, it would be useful if the Commission could modify (or complete) a law by an *executive* act with the agreement of a Committee of Member States' representatives (for instance, the REACH regulation which has about a thousand pages of annexes). However, as far as the democracy of the Union is concerned, this 'anomaly' in the institutional decision-making process of the European Union had to be modified.[6] It would be a shame if the loss of the previous system is regretted on the basis that it was more efficient the moment the Lisbon Treaty changes the Comitology system making it more transparent and 'democratic'!

In conclusion, we can keep saying that, when the Executive acts in the field of competence of the legislator, the maintenance of the Comitology system would be an *anomaly*, while the *legislative delegation* is the right rule.

References:

Carl-Fredrik Bergström (2005), Comitology, Delegation of Powers in the European Union and the Committee System, Oxford (Oxford University Press) 2005.

Manuel Szapiro (2006), Comitologie: retrospective et prospective après la reforme de 2006, in: La Revue du Droit de l'Union européenne 501 (2006), 545-586.

---

6   During a hearing in the 1990's within the European Parliament, where I described very deeply the consensual and efficient system of Comitology, the MEP *Voggenhuber* replied: "this is a typical speech of a European official. The problem is not the efficiency of the Comitology system, but its 'non-democratic' nature!"

Jan Wouters / Dominic Coppens / Bart De Meester

The European Union's External Relations after the Lisbon Treaty

"We aim at shaping globalisation in the interests of all our citizens, based on our common values and principles. For this even the enlarged Union cannot act alone. We must engage our international partners in enhanced strategic cooperation and work together within stronger multilateral organisations. The Lisbon Treaty, in setting a reformed and lasting institutional framework improves our capacity to fulfill our responsibilities, respecting the core principles enshrined in the Berlin declaration. It will bring increased consistency to our external action".[1]

I. Introduction

The aspirations with regard to the Lisbon Treaty in the above-mentioned excerpt from the 'Declaration on Globalisation' which the European Council adopted on 14 December 2007 seem to be modest when compared to what was expected from the European Union (the 'Union' or 'EU') as an external actor in the run-up to the Treaty establishing a Constitution for Europe (the 'Constitution'). Indeed, the Laeken Declaration envisaged developing "the Union into a stabilizing force and a model in the new, multipolar world".[2] Six years later, after the failure of the ratification of the Constitution, the role of the Lisbon Treaty (with regard to external relations) appears only to be to "bring increased consistency to [the] external action [of the Union]".

The present contribution aims to examine whether the Lisbon Treaty[3] has the potential to do more, namely to transform the Union into an efficient global actor. We address the specific modifications which the Lisbon Treaty makes to the Treaty on European Union ('TEU-L')[4] and to the Treaty establishing the European Community

---

1   European Council, *Presidency Conclusions – Annex on 'EU Declaration on Globalisation'*, 14 December 2007.

2   Laeken Declaration on the Future of the European Union, annexed to the Presidency Conclusions of the European Council summit, 14-15 December 2001, section II.

3   Treaty of Lisbon amending the Treaty on European Union and the Treaty establishing the European Community, signed at Lisbon, 13 December 2007, OJ 2007, C 306/1. Abbreviation: Lisbon Treaty.

4   Article 1 Lisbon Treaty. Note that we refer to the new numbering of the TEU-L. If we refer to an older version of a provision in the TEU, we will indicate '*ex*' before the Article.

(now re-named the Treaty on the Functioning of the European Union, 'TFEU').[5] The question regarding the efficiency of the Union as a global actor after Lisbon is tackled with particular attention to the following two sub-questions. First, we will consider whether the modifications of the Lisbon Treaty are in line with the modifications proposed in the Constitution. As will be seen in the following discussion, many amendments are copied directly from the Constitution. Nonetheless, in other respects the contents of the Lisbon Treaty are different in comparison to what was proposed in the Constitution. We will consider whether the Lisbon Treaty succeeds in addressing thorny issues that were identified with regard to the Constitution by scholars before and during the negotiation process of the Lisbon Treaty. An important example is that of the possible extension of the principle of primacy to the area of the Common Foreign and Security Policy ('CFSP'). Second, we will consider whether the amendments are merely a codification of the case-law of the European Court of Justice ('ECJ') with regard to external relations or whether they go beyond this case-law and break new ground.

The paper is divided into five sections. In the first section, we address the general framework for external action by the Union. The Lisbon Treaty aims to avoid dichotomies between economic and political external policy of the Union. This was done through a number of substantive amendments, such as the centralisation of the objectives of external action. However, institutional modifications too were made, notably by creating the new function of High Representative of the Union for Foreign Affairs and Security Policy ('High Representative') and by laying the basis for the European External Action Service. The role of the High Representative and of the European External Action Service will be analysed in the second section of the paper. We will consider their potential in terms of consistent external action. In a third section, the EU's CFSP is addressed. The fact that this policy field still takes a specific place in the law of the Union (*infra*, II) leads us to devote a separate section of the paper to it. Thereafter, the more general provisions on the conclusion of international agreements are considered, which

---

5   Article 2 Lisbon Treaty. Note that we refer to the TEC when we refer to the Treaty on the European Community, before the amendments by the Treaty of Lisbon. We use 'TFEU' if we refer to the new re-numbered and re-named Treaty on the European Community.

allows us to address some major modifications of external Union competences. We will consider whether the case-law on the external competences of the Union is reflected in the provisions of the TFEU. Furthermore, we will pay particular attention to the hierarchy of norms between international law, Union law and the law of the Member States. Finally, in the fifth section, we will address the modified provisions in the TFEU relating to restrictive measures, as well as the judicial protection that is put in place with regard to such measures.

II. General framework for external action

One of the principal aims behind the constitutional process was to provide the EU with the tools to enable it to become a global actor not only in the economic sphere but also in the political sphere. This required a stronger institutional and legal framework for the Union's foreign policy and guarantees for better coherence between the economic and political aspects of its external relations. Unfortunately, with the abandonment of "the constitutional concept",[6] the constitutional objectives of coherence and transparency also seem to have been abandoned, at least formally.

Unlike the Constitution, which brought together the different aspects of the Union's external action, the Lisbon Treaty formally separates CFSP from the other areas of EU external relations because, in the words of *Javier Solana*, this separation was "important conceptually" to the UK.[7] Therefore, the TEU-L contains a new Title V 'General Provisions on the Union's External Action *and Specific Provisions on the Common Foreign and Security Policy*' (emphasis added), whereas all other aspects of the Union's external action are found in the new Part V of the TFEU, 'External Action by the Union'. To be sure, this formal separation of CFSP does not bear significant legal consequences because it is explicitly stated that the TEU-L and TFEU "have the same legal value"[8] and, as elaborated below, CFSP must be driven by the same cluster of objectives as the other aspects of the Union's external action. The distinctive nature of the CFSP is further emphasised by two declara-

---

6   European Council, *Presidency Conclusions – Annex 1: IGC Mandate*, 21/22 June 2007.

7   United Kingdom (2008a), 31.

8   Article 1, para 3, TEU-L.

tions concerning the CFSP (Nos. 13 and 14) attached to the Lisbon Treaty, which emphasise that it does not affect the power of Member States to conduct their foreign policy (Nos. 13 and 14) and that it increases neither the power of the Commission to initiate decisions nor the power of the Parliament in this domain (No. 14) (see *infra*).

Like the Constitution, the Lisbon Treaty also formally abolishes the three-pillar structure, introduced by the Maastricht Treaty in 1992. The European Union replaces and succeeds the European Community[9] and is given legal personality.[10] Under the current Treaties, only the European Communities had been granted legal personality[11] explicitly and enjoyed international legal personality,[12] even though it can be argued that the Union was implicitly provided with legal personality, especially since the Treaty of Nice.[13] Nevertheless, the TEU makes it clear that the Union is able to conclude agreements on the international forum (see *infra*). Moreover, the existing variety of instruments in CFSP is abandoned: the EU shall conduct the CFSP by defining general guidelines, by adopting decisions and by strengthening systematic policy co-operation between the Member States (Article 25 TEU-L).[14] The Lisbon Treaty adopts the distinction provided for in the Constitution between legislative acts and implementing[15] (or delegated[16]) acts and confirms that acts in the field of CFSP cannot be of a legislative nature.[17] The Com-

---

9   Article 1, para 3, TEU-L.

10   Article 47 TEU-L.

11   Article 281 TEC; see also, for Euratom, Article 184 TEAEC.

12   See for example ECJ, *Commission versus Council*, Case 22/70, [1971] ECR 263, paras 13-14. See also *Eeckhout* (2004), 94.

13   See *Wouters* (2002), 63. See also *Eeckhout* (2004), 160; *Lenaerts / Van Nuffel* (2005), 816-817, para 19-003.

14   'Decisions' incorporate the previous 'common strategies', 'common positions' and 'joint actions'. See also Article 288 TFEU elaborating the different types of legal acts, which are essentially the same as under the current treaties (regulations, directives, decisions, recommendations and opinions).

15   Article 291 TFEU.

16   Article 290 TFEU.

17   Article 24(1), para 2, TEU-L. However, the Lisbon Treaty does not retain the new transparent typology introduced by the Constitution to distinguish legislative acts (e.g. law and framework law for legisla-

munity method for decision-making is generalized to all domains of Union action, with the field of the CFSP as the sole exception once again, including the Common Security and Defence Policy ('CSDP'), which remains "subject to specific rules and procedures".[18] If one accepts that the pillar structure refers to different sets of decision-making, the second pillar, as *Kurpas* correctly argues, *de facto* thus remains in place.[19] A careful reading of the provisions on CFSP in general as well as on CSDP, carried out here, will clarify these specific elements, but will at the same time reveal that the modifications inscribed in the Constitution are all transferred to the TEU-L.

In line with the Constitution, the Lisbon Treaty also clusters in the TEU-L the objectives of the EU's external action, which are currently divided over different areas of competence.[20] Article 3(5) of the TEU-L describes the objectives of the Union's external action:

> "In its relations with the wider world, the Union shall uphold and promote its values and interests. It shall contribute to peace, security, the sustainable development of the Earth, solidarity and mutual respect among peoples, free and fair trade, eradication of poverty and the protection of human rights, in particular the rights of the child, as well as to the strict observance and the development of international law, including respect for the principles of the United Nations Charter".[21]

These objectives, which the Union should thus not only "uphold" but also actively "promote", are elaborated upon further in Article 21 TEU-L, which in paragraph 2 lists eight specific objectives that, according to paragraph 3, must be respected and pursued

---

tive acts) from implementing acts. Under the Lisbon Treaty, regulations, directives or decisions are legislative acts *if* adopted by the legislative procedure (see Article 289 TFEU).

18   Article 24(1), second para, TEU-L.

19   *Kurpas* (2007), 2. *Solana* also acknowledged that the second pillar is maintained. See United Kingdom (2008a), 31.

20   The objectives of the CFSP are listed in *ex* Article 11 TEU, while the objectives of the common commercial policy can be found in Article 131 TEC and those of development co-operation in Article 177 TEC.

21   This is similar to Article I-3(4) of the Constitution.

in developing and implementing the different areas of the Union's external action.[22] Such a common set of goals is a prerequisite for a coherent external policy. It requires, for example, that the Common Commercial Policy ('CCP') not only pursues trade-related objectives as stated in the current Article 133 TEC, but takes into account and even contributes to other dimensions, such as human rights and sustainable development.[23] After the Lisbon Treaty, there is thus no doubt anymore as to whether there is a legal basis for including human rights clauses or other 'essential elements' clauses in association agreements or international trade agreements.[24]

However, the TEU-L only lists the various objectives. It does not link them to one another. Nor does it offer a mechanism for prioritising or resolving (potential) conflicts between the objectives.[25] It has been regretted, for instance, that the objective of peace and security is not linked to the aim of poverty eradication. Recognition of the complementarity of these objectives could have strengthened the importance of development co-operation in the EU's external action.[26] Nonetheless, Article 208(1) TFEU obliges the Union to take account of the objectives of development co-operation in the policies that it implements which are likely to affect developing countries.

The Council and the Commission, assisted by the High Representative of the Union for Foreign Affairs and Security Policy (the 'High Representative'), are responsible for ensuring consistency between the different areas of the Union's external action and between these and the internal action and must co-operate to that effect.[27] On the other hand, the TEU-L also stipulates in Article 18(4) that the High Representative must ensure the consistency of the Union's external action. A key question of course remains what tools these actors employ to fulfil this task. A first instrument to secure consistency is not placed in their hands but in the hands of the European Council, which can adopt by unanimity decisions on

---

22 See also Articles 21(1) TEU-L, 23 TEU-L and 205 TFEU.

23 See *Krajewski* (2005).

24 See *Brandtner / Rosas* (1998); *Cannizzaro* (2002); *Cremona* (1996).

25 See *Cremona* (2004).

26 See *Mackie et al.* (2003), para 19.

27 Article 21(3), para 2 TEU-L, which is similar to Article III-292(3) Constitution.

strategic interests and objectives along the entire spectre of the Union's external action.[28] Unlike the common strategies that could be adopted under *ex* Article 13 TEU, these decisions are not restricted to the CFSP domain but are explicitly said to "relate to the common foreign and security policy and to other areas of the external action of the Union".[29] This implies that the European Council's role in the Union's external action is increased, which might strengthen the Member States' leverage over 'Community' policies. But it also means that the European Council can contribute to ensuring consistency in this field of action – and presumably at a more authoritative level than the Commission, the Council and the High Representative. In the next section, we will analyse which instruments the High Representative has at his disposal to ensure consistency in the Union's external action.

III. High Representative and European External Action Service

A. High Representative

Many considered the creation of the 'Union Minister for Foreign Affairs' one of the Constitution's most important innovations. It is therefore important, and positive, that this position of 'bridge builder', admittedly under the 'new' title of 'High Representative of the Union for Foreign Affairs and Security Policy', is maintained under the Lisbon Treaty without substantive modifications. He / she thus only lost the title of 'Minister', mainly because of the UK's resistance to the title of 'Minister', but not to his / her double hat.

The High Representative as designed in the Lisbon Treaty should serve to bridge various tensions that *hic et nunc* appear in the Union's external action. First, within the external aspects of Community policies there is an institutional tension between the Commission and the Council as Member States' influence is often tempered by decision-making based on qualified majority voting ('QMV'). Second, a tension exists between Community external policies, traditionally with a primary focus on the economic sphere,

---

28   Article 22(1), para 1, TEU-L. These decisions are taken on a recommendation from the Council, adopted by the latter under the arrangements laid down for each area and the High Representative, in the field of CFSP, and the Commission, for other areas of external action, may submit joint proposals to the Council.

29   Article 22(1), para 2, TEU-L.

on the one hand, and CFSP, focusing on political areas, on the other. This second source of tension also has an institutional dimension of a vertical nature (Commission *versus* Member States) since, in the area of CFSP, the Member States remain the main players through the unanimity requirements in the Council and European Council (see also *infra*). In order to transcend these complexities, the Lisbon Treaty introduces the position of the dual-role High Representative. The High Representative has a double hat in the sense that he/she combines the position of the current High Representative for the CFSP (Council) with the function of Commissioner for External Relations (Commission).[30]

The High Representative's dual nature and mandate is reflected in the conditions of appointment, the institutional position and the range of competences. First of all, the High Representative is appointed by the European Council, acting by QMV, with the agreement of the President of the Commission (Article 18(1) TEU-L).[31] The same procedure can be used to end the mandate of the High Representative. However, since the High Representative also wears a Commission hat, the European Parliament receives an indirect say in his / her appointment, since the Commission as a body is subject to a vote of consent by the European Parliament.[32] Likewise, the Parliament may vote a censure motion on the Commission resulting in the resignation of the Members of the Commission as a body and the High Representative "in the duties that he carries out in the Commission".[33] In this situation, the High Representative retains his position in the Council until the appointment of a new Commission.[34] Moreover, the President of the Commission can request that the High Representative, like all other Members of the

---

30 In fact, the Council-hat of the new High Representative is much more elaborated than the current role of the High Representative. Pursuant to *ex* Article 18(3) TEU, the current High Representative merely assists the Presidency and he does not formally have the right of initiative. The High Representative will thus indeed be, as the current High Representative Solana has put it, the "same name with a different function". See United Kingdom (2008a).

31 The same procedure applies in the event of resignation, compulsory retirement or death of the High Representative (Article 246 TFEU).

32 Article 17(7), para. 3, TEU-L.

33 Article 17(8) TEU-L.

34 This aspect is not clearly spelled out in the Lisbon Treaty.

Commission, resigns, but in the High Representative's case this should be done "in accordance with the procedure set out in Article 18(1) TEU-L"[35] – which implies that the European Council must also agree.

Second, the High Representative's institutional position mirrors his / her double hat. On the one hand, the High Representative will preside over the Foreign Affairs Council, one of the configurations of the Council, which elaborates the Union's external action on the basis of strategic guidelines formulated by the European Council and ensures that the Union's action is consistent (see *supra*).[36] In addition, the High Representative will take part in the work of the European Council, consisting of the Heads of State or Government, together with its President and the President of the Commission.[37] He will thus have a more privileged position in the European Council than national Ministers or Commissioners, who may assist the European Council upon invitation.[38] This being said, the High Representative is not a 'member' of the Council or European Council and does not have a voting right.[39] On the other hand, the High Representative will also be one of the Vice-Presidents of the Commission.[40] He / she will be a full member of the Commission and shall accordingly take part in the latter's decision-making process.

Third, the High Representative's competences and responsibilities encompass the different fields of the Union's external action.

The High Representative shall together with the Member States put the CFSP into effect, in accordance with the Treaties.[41] In particular, his duties range from preparation (through the right of

---

35   Article 17(6) TEU-L.

36   Articles 18(3) and 16(6) TEU-L. The Presidency of the other Council configurations is held by the Member States representatives in the Council on the basis of equal rotation (Article 16(9) TEU-L).

37   Article 15(2) TEU-L.

38   Article 15(3) TEU-L.

39   Articles 15(2) and 16(2) TEU-L. The President of the European Council and the President of the Commission also do not take part in the vote of the European Council (Article 234 TFEU).

40   Article 17(4) TEU-L.

41   Article 24(1), para 2, TEU-L.

initiative), management and implementation (including, to some extent, the oversight of Member States' implementation[42]) to the Union's external dialogue with third parties and representation in international organisations and at international conferences.[43] For example, the High Representative shall be asked by Member States that sit on the Security Council, to defend the Union's position therein.[44] Obviously, this presupposes a common position and thus a European decision that still requires in principle unanimity (see *infra*); in other words, the High Representative's new position does not as such reduce the power and competences of Member States sitting on the Security Council.[45] Moreover, even within the domain of the CFSP, the High Representative will not entirely fulfil *Kissinger*'s demand for a 'single European telephone number', since the President of the European Council will, pursuant to Article 15(6) TEU-L, "at his level and in that capacity", ensure the Union's external representation in the field of CFSP "without prejudice to the powers of the High Representative (...)". This vague description might suggest that the President of the European Council is supposed to meet with Heads of State and Government of third countries but it does not at all create a clear division of tasks.[46] One may wonder whether the Lisbon Treaty did not create a new type of rivalry in the EU's foreign relations system, certainly given the permanent position of the President, who will be elected for two and a half years (abolition of the 6-months rotating system).

---

42 See Article 24(3) TEU-L.

43 Article 27(1) and 27(2) TEU-L.

44 Article 34(2), para 3, TEU-L.

45 Moreover, Member States which are members of the Security Council must defend the positions and the interests of the Union, "without prejudice to their responsibilities under the United Nations Charter" (Article 34(2), para 2, TEU-L). This qualification, which is inspired by *ex* Article 19 TEU, seems to imply that these Member States can deviate from a position of the Union in case the urgency of the situation demands prompt action from the Security Council. See *Eaton* (1994). One may note that the distinction between rotating and permanent members has been deleted, which is to be welcomed.

46 For example, it is unclear under the Lisbon Treaty who would lead the negotiations on behalf of the UN or EU-3 with Iran over the nuclear crisis. Example provided by *Quille* (2008), 4.

Within the Commission, the High Representative has a broad range of duties since he / she shall be responsible for tasks incumbent on the Commission in external relations and for co-ordination of other aspects of the Union's external policy.[47] The High Representative should therefore not only build bridges between the Commission and the Council (and European Council) but also between the various Commissioners responsible for different aspects of the external policies[48] and even, one may add, the Commissioners responsible for internal policies which – as practice shows – increasingly have their own external dimensions. One may wonder to what extent the voice of the High Representative might be lowered within the Commission because of the strengthened role of the President of the Commission with respect to the internal organisation of the Commission and the resignation of individual Commissioners (see *supra*).[49]

It can thus be expected that a new form of 'troika' will come about on the international scene[50]: the High Representative will be flanked by the President of the European Council, with a vaguely formulated job description[51] but a long term in office and thus an enduring voice in the field of CFSP, on the one side, and the President of the Commission, playing the first fiddle in the Commission, on the other side. Whether this multiplicity of voices will sound harmonious will largely (arguably too largely) depend on the chemistry between their personalities. Observers also point to the successive Council presidencies which will "linger on the sidelines" in the external action of the Union.[52]

Fourth, the High Representative's dual functions call for dual loyalty: as a Member of the Commission, subject to this institution's collegiate nature, and as President of the Foreign Affairs Council. Theoretically, this loyalty is defined by Article 18(4)

---

47   Article 18(4) TEU-L.

48   See *Allen* (2004), 2.

49   Article 17(6) TEU-L.

50   See, for example, *Missiroli* (2007), 19-20.

51   Article 15(6) TEU-L.

52   Indeed, the rotating presidency, though in a reformed manner, will *inter alia* remain in place in the General Affairs Council (which deals with enlargement) and the COREPER. See CEPS / EGMONT / EPC (2007), 129.

TEU-L, which declares that in exercising his responsibilities within the Commission, and only for these responsibilities, the High Representative shall be bound by Commission procedures to the extent that this is consistent with his role in the CFSP field and position in the Council. However, in practice, it remains to be seen how the High Representative "will be able to ride two horses at once".[53] It is not only institutionally a very delicate assignment, but also practically an extremely demanding – and quite possibly too demanding – job description for one person. However this may be, the suspicion that the High Representative might become a kind of Trojan horse for the Commission might have some merit.[54] He / she is indeed strongly linked to the Council and the European Council and therefore to the Member States and the more intergovernmental dimension of the EU (cf. the procedure for his appointment and resignation). Nevertheless, at least theoretically, the President of the Commission's competence to order the High Representative's resignation, albeit with the European Council's approval, might prove a useful instrument in disciplining the latter from a communautarian perspective. The High Representative's link to the Council and European Council and the persistently inter-governmental nature of CFSP will in any event make the opposite effect, namely a 'communitarisation' of CFSP, highly unlikely. Besides, Declaration No. 14 underlines that the creation of the High Representative and the European External Action Service will not affect Member States' power to formulate and conduct their foreign policy.

Next to the question of whether one person will in practice be able to shoulder this demanding job,[55] an important reason why the High Representative might not be able to meet high expectations is that the Lisbon Treaty does not sufficiently neutralise the duality within the Union's external policy to enable him to execute its dual functions. First, the High Representative's position does not alter the dividing lines between the Commission and the Council concerning external relations. The implementation of the EEAS (see *infra*) cannot leave this sensitive relationship untouched. Second, although the pillar structure is formally abandoned, the CFSP clearly holds a specific intergovernmental position in the Lisbon

---

53   *Hill* (2003), 2.

54   See *Wouters* (2004).

55   See, for example, the discussion in the United Kingdom (2008a), 55-56.

Treaty and, as elaborated below, the High Representative is not equipped with powerful instruments within the CFSP to bring coherence to the different domains of the Union's external action. Third, the Lisbon Treaty's emphasis on the distinct nature of the CFSP reveals the reluctance of some Member States to diminish their influence in the field of CFSP. Politically, Member States thus hold different views on the 'bridging' and 'autonomous' role that the High Representative will be able to play. In this respect, the vision of the UK Government, as expressed by its Foreign Secretary, is telling: "the Commission role of the High Representative is quite limited. His primary function is to carry out the wishes of the Council of Ministers".[56]

B. European External Action Service

Article 27(3) of the TEU-L introduces the European External Action Service ('EEAS'):

> "In fulfilling his mandate, the High Representative shall be assisted by a European External Action Service. This service shall work in cooperation with the diplomatic services of the Member States and shall comprise officials from relevant departments of the General Secretariat of the Council and of the Commission as well as staff seconded from national diplomatic services of Member States."

The provision's place in the Lisbon Treaty, as part of the CFSP Chapter, is not entirely fortunate given that the EEAS should precisely bridge the different components of the Union's external action and should therefore have been put under the Chapter on the Union's external action having a general application.[57] Moreover, the provision grossly understates the difficulties in working out an EEAS. The precise reach, structure and incorporation are totally left open. As mentioned, Declaration No. 14 stresses that the creation of the EEAS will not reduce the Member States' power to conduct, *inter alia*, their foreign policy and national diplomatic service. The importance and sensitivity of the subject can also be deduced from the complex decision-making process designated to set up the EEAS. It will be established by a decision of the Council on the

---

56   United Kingdom (2008a), 53.

57   Title V, Chapter 1 TEU-L.

basis of unanimity.[58] The Council must act on a proposal of the High Representative after consulting the European Parliament and after obtaining the Commission's consent. Interestingly, as under the Constitution, the preparatory work to set up this service is not made dependent on the Lisbon Treaty's ratification and entry into force but had to start, pursuant to a declaration attached to the Lisbon Treaty,[59] as soon as it was signed (13 December 2007), by the Secretary-General of the Council / High Representative for CFSP, the Commission and the Member States.

The Lisbon Treaty merely prescribes that the EEAS will be drawn from "the officials from relevant departments of the General Secretariat of the Council and of the Commission as well as staff seconded from national diplomatic services of Member States".[60] The departments that might be 'relevant' and the EEAS's institutional position are left undecided.[61]

The entire spectrum thus still remains open as to who will serve in the EEAS. At one end, one might come up with a minimalist model that includes the Director-General (DG) from the Council Secretariat together with the Commission's DG External Relations (RELEX), and with or without the Commission's current External Service. The latter currently comprises 123 Commission delegations around the world.[62] Under the Lisbon Treaty, they are set to become 'Union delegations' that represent the Union in third countries and at international organisations and are placed under the authority of the High Representative.[63] Such a minimalist model has the advantage of being realistic, also in light of the Commission's recent internal restructuring, but has the challenge of co-ordinating with the other Commission DGs dealing with external relations (Trade, Enlargement, Development, Europeaid and ECHO) that

---

58   Article 27(3) *juncto* Article 31 TEU-L.

59   Declaration No. 15. The Constitution contained a similar declaration.

60   Article 27(3) TEU-L.

61   See for an elaborated discussion on the EAAS: European Policy Centre (2007). For previous discussions on this topic, see: *Rayner* (2005); see also *Duke* (2004), 4-7; *Allen* (2004), 1-4.

62   Of which 118 in third countries and 5 at headquarters (Geneva, New York, Paris, Rome and Vienna) of international organizations (OECD, OSCE, UN and WTO).

63   Article 221 TFEU. See *Allen* (2004), 3.

would fall outside EEAS. *Rayner* developed an even more minimalist model that would be a 'virtual EEAS', leaving all relevant departments under the Council and Commission and simply providing co-ordination by a small staff under the authority of the High Representative.[64] However, as *Rayner* himself noted, such a 'virtual EEAS' would not be able to fulfil the co-ordination tasks because of a lack of influence and authority.

The other end of the spectrum would incorporate "all of the foreign policy units from the Council Secretariat, all of the External Action DGs of the Community, the Union delegations as well as Europeaid and ECHO".[65] The advantage of such maximalist model might be, as Duke indicated, the size of the EEAS and the opportunities for specialisation. However, it would require an enormous institutional reorganisation.[66]

The Lisbon Treaty does not resolve the EEAS's institutional format either. The EEAS might be an autonomous (*'sui generis'*) service, outside the Commission or the Council Secretariat, or it might be linked to either or to both.

In which direction does the preparatory work on the EEAS point so far? Some degree of preparatory work was done under the Constitution.[67] That work was halted due to the 'no' vote in France and the Netherlands. The latest formal outcome of this preparatory work was the Joint Progress Report by the Secretary-General/High Representative and the Commission of 9 June 2005.[68] This Joint Progress Report reflected a broad consensus among Member States

---

64   See *Rayner* (2005), 10.

65   *Duke* (2004), 5.

66   *Ibidem.*

67   See also *de Ruyt* (2005), 25-26.

68   This resulted from the Joint Issues Paper by the High Representative and the Commission that was subsequently discussed with Member States in COREPER as well as bilaterally. See, Council of the European Union, *Joint Progress Report to the European Council by the Secretary-General/High Representative and the Commission* (9956/05, 9 June 2005), paras 2-5 (the Issues Paper is included in Annex II). Abbreviation: *Joint Progress Report.* This report was planned to be presented at the European Council summit on 16-17 June 2005 but was dropped from the agenda because of the ratification failures. It was felt that it would send out the wrong signal if the European leaders discussed the Constitution's content.

that the EEAS should be of a '*sui generis*' nature, in the sense that it would be a service under the authority of the High Representative and not a new institution but with close links to the Council and Commission.[69] Member States also emphasised that its purpose is indeed to equip the High Representative to ensure coherence in external action. Yet, on the organisational set-up, they clearly expressed different views, ranging from a minimalist view put forward by few Member States, which would restrict it to the field of CFSP / ESDP, to a maximalist view suggested by a few others, which would also include enlargement, neighbourhood and development policies, and with the majority of Member States somewhere in between (with the only consensus being that trade would not be covered).[70] There also seemed to be consensus that the Union Delegations would be an integral part of the EEAS, but for most Member States this should not imply that all staff working in the Delegations would be part of the EEAS.[71] In that same period, the European Parliament, which only has an advisory role (*supra*), also expressed its own view on the EEAS in a resolution in which it stressed that the form the EEAS takes is "extremely important" in light of the objective of bringing more coherence in the Union's external relations.[72] The Parliament's greatest fear apparently was that the EEAS would not have an institutional link with the Commission and therefore would fall outside the latter's control.[73] Hence, the Parliament called on the Commission to strive for preserving and further developing the Community model in the field of the Union's external relations and advocated that "the EEAS should

---

69   Joint Progress Report, *loc. cit.*, supra n. 68, para 6.

70   Most Member States were of the view that the EAAS should include at least the relevant parts of the Council Secretariat (DGE and Policy Unit) and of the Commission (DG External Relations). See Joint Progress Report, *loc. cit.*, supra n. 68, para 8.

71   Joint Progress Report, *loc. cit.*, supra n. 68, para 11.

72   European Parliament, Resolution on the institutional aspects of the European External Action Service, adopted on 26 May 2005, OJ 2006, C 117 E/232.

73   See News Reports of the European Parliament, 'MEPs push to keep European diplomatic service under parliamentary control', (11 May 2005).

be incorporated, in organisational and budgetary terms, in the Commission's staff."[74]

Even though the Lisbon Treaty calls for the restart of the preparatory work (*supra*), the Council Secretariat as well as the Commission are currently completely silent on the set up of the EEAS due to the fear that this work would impede the thorny ratification process. There are even some rumours that discussions at working group level, which are likely to put the Joint Progress Report back on the table, will only resume after the entry into force of the Lisbon Treaty. Other sources, however, indicate that preparations for setting up the EEAS take place in great secrecy in high-level talks between High Representative *Solana* and Commission President *Barroso*. The European Parliament's Committee on Foreign Affairs has indicated that it is currently drawing up a report on the EEAS, and the Parliament itself has recalled its position that the EEAS should be organically linked to the Commission.[75] In the view of the spokesman of this Committee, Andrew Duff, the EEAS should be effectively established as soon as the Lisbon Treaty is ratified. Given that all options are still open and Member States as well as institutions hold different – sometimes opposite – views, it seems reasonable to expect that if an EEAS comes about by 1 January 2009, it will be in a rather embryonic, provisional form.

IV. Common foreign and security policy

As indicated above, although the pillar structure is formally abandoned, the CFSP's particular position is emphasised in the Lisbon Treaty by the formal separation of CFSP as well as Declaration Nos. 13 and 14 (*supra*). Substantively, its distinct nature becomes

---

74 Furthermore, the resolution stated that the EEAS should encompass "the units dealing with CFSP matters in stricter sense and officials holding senior positions in the delegations", while stressing that "it is not necessary to strip all the Commission directorates-general of their external relations responsibilities." Lastly, the Parliament noticed that the Commission delegations and the Council liaison offices should be merged to form 'Union embassies', headed by EEAS officials. See European Parliament, *loc. cit.*, supra n. 72.

75 See European Parliament, Committee on Constitutional Affairs, *Report on the Treaty of Lisbon* (2007/2286(INI), 29 January 2008), 77. See also, European Parliament, Resolution of 20 February 2008 on the Treaty of Lisbon (2007/2286(INI)), para 5, item e.

clear when analysing the specific CFSP provisions spelled out in the Treaty, which are similar to the Constitution.

It remains, first of all, far from clear what competence CFSP constitutes under the Lisbon Treaty. Article 2 TFEU lists the different categories of Union competences: exclusive,[76] shared[77] or supportive, coordinative or supplementary.[78] Nonetheless, CFSP is mentioned separately.[79] Therefore, some authors conclude that CFSP constitutes a kind of '*sui generis*' competence[80] or a 'non pre-emptive shared competence'.[81] Other authors' analysis of the provisions of the Constitution,[82] however, boiled down to classifying CFSP under the shared competences within the meaning of Article 2(2) TFEU because this forms the residual category.[83] In their view, the principle of pre-emption, which is a consequence of bringing CFSP under the residual category of shared competences in the sense of Article 2(2) TFEU,[84] is tempered by the fact that the Union cannot act by legislative instruments in the field of CFSP[85] (which, in any case, highlights the CFSP's specific position). However, we fail to see how the pre-emption principle would be weakened when the Union acts by 'non-legislative acts'. After all, the main difference between legislative and 'non-legislative' acts seems

---

76   Article 2(1) TFEU and 3 TFEU.

77   Article 2(2) TFEU and 4 TFEU.

78   Article 2(5) TFEU and 6 TFEU.

79   Article 2(4) TFEU.

80   See *Cremona* (2003), 1353-1354.

81   See *Cremona* (2007), 1194-1197.

82   The substantive provisions in the Lisbon Treaty are the same but, as mentioned above, Declaration No 14 and the formal separation of CFSP are new in the Lisbon Treaty. One cannot therefore exclude that their analysis would be different under the Lisbon Treaty.

83   This reasoning is based on Article 4(1) TFEU: "The Union shall share competence with the Member States where the Constitution confers on it a competence which does not relate to the areas referred to in Articles 3 TFEU *(exclusive)* and 6 TFEU *(supportive, coordinative or supplementary)*" (italics added). See *Lenaerts* (2004), 411.

84   "The Member States shall exercise their competence to the extent that the Union has not exercised its competence".

85   Article 24 TEU-L. *Lenaerts* (2004), 411.

to lie in the decision-making process.[86] Neither the scope nor the legal force is diminished by it being a 'non-legislative' act.[87] Moreover, the fact that CFSP is listed separately from the shared competence in Article 2(2) TFEU reveals the intention of the drafters that it should be treated differently, which is only reinforced by the emphasis in the Lisbon Treaty on the distinctive nature of CFSP. Declaration No. 14 also supports the reading that pre-emption is not applicable in the field of CFSP given that the provisions on CFSP do not affect the power of Member States in conducting their foreign policy. Therefore, we share the view that CFSP is not a shared competence of the type spelled out in Article 2(2) TFEU but something 'sui generis'[88] such as a shared competence without pre-emption. The related question, analysed in detail below, on whether primacy is applicable in the field of CFSP, also remains open to different interpretations.

The special nature of CFSP is corroborated by the fact that the decision-making process in this area remains strongly intergovernmental. Decision-making by unanimity within the Council remains the point of departure,[89] in spite of a Franco-German initiative during the preparatory work on the Constitution that proposed QMV as a general rule.[90] Moreover, the exceptions whereby the Council can decide by QMV are not fundamentally broadened. One circumstance is added, which was also present in the Constitution, namely:

"... when adopting a decision defining a Union action or position, on a proposal which the High Representative (...) has presented following a specific request from the European Council, made on its own initiative or that of the High Representative".[91]

---

86 Article 289(3) TFEU.

87 Regulations, directives and decisions can be 'legislative acts' if adopted by the (ordinary or special) legislative procedure or 'non-legislative acts' if adopted by another procedure. This does not influence their binding nature as defined in Article 288 TFEU but only the hierarchy among them (supremacy of legislative acts).

88 Also in this line, see European Parliament, Committee on Constitutional Affairs, *Report on the Treaty of Lisbon* (2007/2286(INI), 29 January 2008), 24.

89 Articles 31(1) TEU-L.

90 See *Wessels* (2004), 15.

91 Article 31(2), second indent, TEU-L.

Clearly, the High Representative cannot independently open the door to decision-making by QMV in the Council. With the exception of European decisions concerning the appointment of a special representative,[92] the starting point remains a decision by the European Council taken by unanimity.[93] The individual Member States thus preserve the possibility to block decision-making by QMV. Nevertheless, it cannot be excluded that the provision quoted above might generate a considerable QMV extension in practice, since a skilful High Representative, backed by a well-documented EEAS (see *supra*), could take initiatives demanding the European Council to request him / her to make a proposal to the Council that can subsequently be adopted by QMV. This 'specific request' of the European Council might in practice pass a broad and open mandate on to the High Representative. However, even when a decision is reached by QMV in the Council, Member States can still invoke the 'national interest' exception, which the Lisbon Treaty leaves unabridged.[94] Like in the Constitution, there is a specific bridging clause (*passerelle*) that enables the European Council to extend, by unanimity, the scope of QMV in the field of CFSP.[95] Thus, the Lisbon Treaty preserves a dynamic element in the CFSP by which the unanimity rule can be gradually restricted without needing to follow the procedure of treaty revision. The possibility of enhanced co-operation between some Member States, now extended to the entire spectrum of CFSP,[96] also tempers the unanimity requirement and can have a dynamising effect. However, this extension is compensated for by the fact that the Council's authorisation will have to be

---

92   Article 31(2), fourth indent, TEU-L.

93   Unanimity is the general rule for decision making by the European Council in the field of CFSP (Article 31(1) TEU-L).

94   The High Representative can play a mediating role. If no solution is found, the Council can by QMV 'kick up' the decision to the European Council which shall decide by unanimity (Article 31(2) TEU-L).

95   This specific bridging clause (Article 31(3) TEU-L) differs from the general bridging clause (Article 48 TEU-L), since the former does not require the consent of the European Parliament and does not provide for the involvement of the national parliaments.

96   Article 20 TEU-L. Under the old TEU, this is merely possible for the implementation of a joint action or common position. (*ex* Article 27b TEU).

given by unanimity, in contrast with the current situation, which merely requires QMV.[97] Moreover, Member States that enter into enhanced co-operation can decide, by unanimity, to switch to decision-making by QMV.[98] This turns enhanced co-operation into a double instrument of flexibility: a group of Member States can strengthen co-operation and agree thereby to decide by QMV in their field of enhanced co-operation.

Apart from the principle of unanimity in the Council and European Council, the marginal role of the other institutions also highlights the intergovernmental nature of the CFSP domain.[99] The Commission has even lost its autonomous right of initiative in the field of CFSP, since it is confined under the Lisbon Treaty to support proposals submitted by the High Representative.[100] Furthermore, as underlined by Declaration No. 14, the European Parliament's position in CFSP seems to have remained the status-quo, even though the Parliament itself reads a stronger role in the Treaty because it acquires a general right to be informed and consulted.[101] In fact, this right to be regularly informed and consulted as well as the obligation to duly take its view into consideration was already inscribed in the Maastricht Treaty, with the exception that this task will now rest on the shoulders of the High Representative (instead of the Presidency and the Commission).[102] The Parliament also has the right to ask questions and make recommendations not only to the Council but also to the High Representative.[103] The Parliament's link to the CFSP therefore will be mainly through the High Representative and in this way it will be in its interest to have an influential High Representative.[104] Lastly, the ECJ's jurisdiction remains,

---

97   Compare *ex* Article 27c TEU and Article 329 TFEU.

98   This specific bridging clause can be found in Article 333 TFEU.

99   See also *Dagand* (2008), 2-3.

100 Compare *ex* Article 22(1) TEU and Article 30 TEU-L.

101 In this respect, it considers Declaration No. 14 'unjustified, if not partially incorrect'. European Parliament, Committee on Constitutional Affairs, *Report on the Treaty of Lisbon* (2007/2286(INI), 29 January 2008), 27-28 and 49, footnote 1.

102 Compare *ex* Article 21 TEU and Article 36(1) TEU-L.

103 Article 36(2) TEU-L.

104 The limited role of the Parliament in the CFSP area is also visible in the Parliament's exclusion from the negotiating and concluding of

in principle excluded.[105] Compared to some ambiguity in the Constitution, the Lisbon Treaty is clear that there are only two exceptions:[106] the Court will have competence to monitor the delineation between CFSP and other fields of the Union's external action and to review the legality of decisions providing for restrictive measures against natural or legal persons (see *infra*).

With regard to CSDP[107] the provisions of the Lisbon Treaty also mirror those of the Constitution. The Lisbon Treaty acknowledges that CSDP forms an integral part of CFSP.[108] If CFSP can be labelled intergovernmental, CSDP forms the 'hyperintergovernmental' part of it.[109] The principle of unanimity in the Council applies without exception, and this cannot even be altered by the European Council because the aforementioned *passerelle* is not

---

international agreements exclusively related to CFSP (see *infra*) (Article 218(6) TFEU).

105 Article 24 TEU-L and 275 TFEU.

106 Under the formulation of the Constitution (Article III-376), the grounds for exclusion of jurisdiction were explicitly spelled out. Because this list did not refer, for example, to Article III-325(11) (concerning ECJ opinions on envisaged international agreements), it was open for interpretation whether the ECJ could provide opinions on international agreements in the CFSP field. The Lisbon Treaty, however, answers this question in the negative because the exclusion of jurisdiction in the field of CFSP is formulated more broadly: in general, the ECJ "shall have no jurisdiction with respect to the provisions relating to CFSP nor with respect to acts adopted on the basis of those provisions" (Article 275 TFEU). Similarly, Article I-16 (concerning the competence of the Union in the field of CFSP and the duty of the Member States to support the CFSP) was not listed as an exception in the Constitution. The Lisbon Treaty is now clear that the duty of cooperation of Member States in the field of CFSP (now inscribed in Article 24(3) TEU-L) falls outside the jurisdiction of the ECJ. On the open interpretation under the Constitution, see M. *Cremona* (2008), 1198-1199; Common Market Law Review (2005).

107 Title V, chapter 2, section 2 TEU-L.

108 Article 42(1) TEU-L.

109 See *Diedrichs* (2003), 4; *Diedrichs* (2004), 1. For a discussion in the UK's House of Commons Defence Committee on the future of NATO and European defence under the Lisbon Treaty, see United Kingdom (2008b), 86-90.

applicable in the field of CSDP.[110] The Lisbon Treaty broadens the reach of CSDP by widening the Petersberg tasks to include joint disarmament, military advice and assistance tasks, conflict prevention and post-conflict stabilisation.[111] The High Representative, under the authority of the Council and in close and constant contact with the Political and Security Committee ('PSC'), will be responsible for the co-ordination of civilian and military aspects of such tasks.[112] In addition, a mutual defence clause[113] and a solidarity clause are introduced.[114] All the same, the most important innovations in this field arguably lie in the instruments which the Lisbon Treaty provides to Member States willing to strengthen co-operation.[115] First, a group of Member States, which are willing and capable to carry out such a task, can be entrusted by the Council to implement a Petersberg task.[116] Second, the Treaty provides a Treaty basis for the (already existing) European Defence Agency, as an agency open to all Member States wishing to be part of it and in which specific groups shall be set up bringing together Member States in joint projects.[117] Third, Member States which fulfil higher criteria for military capabilities and which are willing to make more binding commitments, can establish a so-called 'structured co-operation'.[118] Fourth, the Lisbon Treaty introduces the opportunity for enhanced co-operation in the field of CSDP, which should be authorised by the Council acting by unanimity.[119]

---

110   Article 31(4) TEU-L.
111   Compare *ex* Article 17(2) TEU and Article 43(1) TEU-L. The extension was already agreed at the European Council in Thessaloniki (June 2003) and the Headline Goal 2010. See *Quille* (2008), 5.
112   Article 43(2) TEU-L.
113   Article 42(7) TEU-L.
114   Article 222 TFEU.
115   See *Diedrichs* (2003), 4; *Diedrichs* (2004), 1.
116   Article 44 TEU-L.
117   Articles 42(3) and 45 TEU-L.
118   Articles 42(6) and 46 TEU-L and Protocol No. 10. See *Biscop* (2008).
119   Articles 329(2) and 331(2) TFEU. The specific bridging clause between Member States engaging in enhanced cooperation cannot however be used (Article 333(3) TFEU).

In conclusion, the Union's action in the field of CFSP (including CSDP) is subject to a different set of rules (e.g. nature of this competence, decision-making procedures, judicial protection) compared to its external action in other fields. In this respect, Article 40 TEU-L highlights the importance of this distinction: the implementation of CFSP shall not affect the application of the procedures and the extent of powers of the institutions for the exercise of the Union's competence in the other fields and *vice versa*. As mentioned, the ECJ has jurisdiction on whether this provision is respected.

V. International agreements

A. Conclusion of international agreements

1. Overview

An important aspect of the external role of the Union is the conclusion of international agreements. Over the past five decades, the EC has become party to an impressive network of international agreements. However, its competence to conclude international agreements was far from uncontested, especially in the absence of an explicit general Treaty basis. An explicitation of the treaty-making competences of the Union was included in the Constitution[120] and is now incorporated in Article 216 TFEU. Furthermore, like in the Constitution,[121] the nature of the EU's external competences (exclusive, shared or complementary) is made explicit in Article 3(2) TFEU. One may wonder to what extent these provisions are simply a codification of ECJ case-law on the external competences of the EC or whether they go beyond it (V.A.2.).

The procedure for concluding international agreements by the Union has also been modified in some respects, when compared to the TEC (V.A.3.). The European Parliament's involvement – and therefore democratic legitimacy – in the process of negotiation and conclusion of international agreements has been improved. Nonetheless, the previous central role of the Commission as the Union's external negotiator may potentially be put into question when considering the provisions in the TFEU. Finally, there is no explicit provision in the TFEU that includes the possibility for the Union to

---

120 Article III-323 Constitution.
121 Article I-13 Constitution.

become a member of international organisations. This needs to be done by reference to the procedures for concluding international agreements.

2. Competence to conclude international agreements

As is known, the Constitution and the Lisbon Treaty have further elaborated the principle of conferral, under which, as is stated in Article 5(2) TFEU, "the Union shall act only within the limits of the competences conferred upon it by the Member States in the Treaties to attain the objectives set out therein. Competences not conferred upon the Union in the Treaties remain with the Member States." When the Union wants to act externally, it must thus be determined whether a competence has been conferred upon it. The external competences of the Union have mainly been clarified in ECJ case-law. The general thrust of the case-law boils down to the principle of 'parallelism' (*in foro interno, in foro externo*): if there is an internal competence of the Union, there is also external competence. From the case-law under the TEC, three different situations could be discerned: (1) the TEC gives an *explicit* competence to act externally in a certain field of competence; (2) an *implied* external competence can be derived from the explicit internal competence laid down in the TEC and (3) external action is necessary to *achieve one of the goals* of the TEC, *without an explicit internal competence* provided for by the TEC. At first sight, Article 216 TFEU seems broadly to take over these situations of external competence. Its first paragraph is formulated as follows:

> "The Union may conclude an agreement with one or more third countries or international organisations where the Treaties so provide or where the conclusion of an agreement is necessary in order to achieve, within the framework of the Union's policies, one of the objectives referred to in the Treaties, or is provided for in a legally binding Union act or is likely to affect common rules or alter their scope".

In each of the three mentioned situations, it should be determined whether the competence of the Union is *exclusive* (Member States cannot act), *shared* (Member States can act as long as the EU has not acted) or *complementary* (Member States can act next to and in addition to the EU).

The TEC granted in a limited number of cases an *explicit* competence to the EC to act externally. This was for instance the case for the CCP (Article 133(3) TEC, new Article 207(3) TFEU), but also for development co-operation (Article 177 TEC, new Article 208 TFEU). This is also reflected in the TFEU, which states that the "Union may conclude an agreement with one or more third countries or international organisations where the Treaties so provide".[122] The *nature* of the external competence at stake may also be indicated explicitly. Three types of explicit Union competences to conclude international agreements can be mentioned.

First, the Union is allowed to conclude international agreements with one or more States or international organisations in the CFSP area (Article 37 TEU-L). As elaborated above, the nature of the Union's competence in the field of CFSP is not well defined, however, and might be best categorised as a kind of *'sui generis'* competence or shared competence without pre-emption.

Second, the TFEU explicitly states that the Union may also conclude international agreements in the field of development co-operation with third countries (Articles 209(2) and 212(3) TFEU)[123] and humanitarian aid (Article 214(4) TFEU). Moreover, Article 4(4) TFEU clarifies that the nature of these Union competences is 'shared' but with the particularity that their exercise by the Union does not prevent the Member States from exercising their own competence in these fields (no pre-emption). [124]

Third, the Union is also explicitly allowed to conclude international agreements in the field of CCP,[125] which Article 3(1)(e) TFEU lists as an exclusive competence. The explicit indication in the Lisbon Treaty that the CCP in its entirety is exclusive is a major simplification compared to the complexity of the current 133 TEC and has important consequences for the external competences of the Member States. The scope of the CCP competence is clarified in Article 207(1) TFEU:

---

122 Article 216(1) TFEU.

123 This covers co-operation with developing countries: 'development cooperation' (Chapter I, Article 209(2) TFEU)) and with non-developing countries: 'economic, financial and technical cooperation with third countries' (Chapter II, Article 212(3))

124 For co-operation with non-developing countries, see Article 212(3) TFEU. This is also confirmed for development co-operation in Article 209(2) TFEU and for humanitarian aid in Article 214(4) TFEU.

125 Article 207 TFEU.

"... changes in tariff rates, the conclusion of tariff and trade agreements relating to trade in goods and services, and the commercial aspects of intellectual property, foreign direct investment, the achievement of uniformity in measures of liberalisation, export policy and measures to protect trade such as those to be taken in the event of dumping or subsidies".

Since the conclusion of international agreements with regard to trade in services and with regard to commercial aspects of intellectual property ('IP') are explicitly mentioned as falling within the scope of the CCP, the Member States will thus be excluded from adopting international agreements in this regard given that the nature of the Union competence is exclusive.[126] The intention of the

---

126 In Opinion 1/94, the ECJ had indicated that the competence of the Community to conclude agreements with regard to trade in services and the commercial aspects of intellectual property only fell within the scope of the common commercial policy as far as the cross-border provision of services is at stake without any movement of natural or legal persons, since this was similar to the cross-border trade in goods, which definitely fell within the scope of the CCP. Hence the explicit external competence with regard to CCP only covered what is called under the WTO Agreements 'Mode 1' of service provision. Other modes of service provision (Mode 2: consumption abroad of services by a consumer from another country; Mode 3: commercial presence of foreign service providers in a country and Mode 4: movement of natural persons providing services) were not covered by Article 133 TEC. (See ECJ, Opinion 1/94, *Competence of the Community to conclude international agreements concerning services and the protection of intellectual property (WTO)*, [1994] ECR I-5267, paras 44-45.) Similarly, with regard to intellectual property, according to the ECJ only those commercial aspects of intellectual property that concern the prohibition of the release into free circulation of counterfeit goods fell within the scope of common commercial policy. (See ECJ, Opinion 1/94, *Competence of the Community to conclude international agreements concerning services and the protection of intellectual property (WTO)*, [1994] ECR I-5267, para 56). The Nice Treaty extended the scope of the CCP, with respect to the negotiation and conclusion of international agreements, to trade in services and trade related aspects of intellectual property (Article 133.5 TEC). However, the *nature* of the Union's competence was disputed and it was also unclear whether it should be read in light of the broad definition of 'trade in services' in the GATS (compared to

drafters to bring the WTO agreements and negotiations within the exclusive competence of the Union confirms that 'trade in services' must be understood in its broad meaning given in the GATS (encompassing the four modes of supply).[127] What is more, the Lisbon Treaty also brings foreign direct investment ('FDI') within the scope of the exclusive CCP. One can see the inclusion of FDI in the light of the attempts within the WTO to conclude an agreement on this matter.[128] Remarkably, the Lisbon Treaty, like the Constitution, does not limit the scope to the commercial aspects of FDI, as is the case for intellectual property.[129] It has been argued that a broad in-

---

the more restrictive definition in the TEC which does not include 'commercial presence').

127 Similar to Article 133 TEC (as modified by the Nice Treaty, see *supra* n. 126), the Lisbon Treaty does not explicitly define the scope of 'trade in service'. As mentioned above, it is therefore unclear whether the broad meaning of 'trade in services' given by the GATS should be followed rather than the narrow meaning in the TEC (which excludes commercial presence). The broad interpretation is also adopted by *Eeckhout* (2004), 55; *Passos / Marquardt* (2007); *Cremona* (2001). Adopting the narrow interpretation, see *Hable* (2005), 37. As *Cremona* indicates, the relevance of this interpretative issue might be reduced given that commercial presence of service providers is also covered under the notion FDI which is included by the Lisbon Treaty. See *Cremona* (2007), 1210.

128 If one adopts the broader GATS meaning of 'trade in services', which includes commercial presence of service providers and thus FDI in the field of services, the inclusion of FDI could also be seen as a logical extension so as to bring FDI in the goods manufacturing sector within the scope of CCP. See *Eeckhout* (2004), 55; *Passos / Marquardt* (2007), 902-903. In 1995 the European Commission had already argued in favour of an exclusive competence of the EC in the field of foreign direct investment. The Commission stated that the powers of the Community in the field of investment protection could not be exercised effectively while the Member States continue to conclude bilateral treaties on investments. See European Commission, Report on the operation of the Treaty on European Union, SEC (95) 731 final, 10 May 1995, 58.

129 During the deliberations that prepared the Constitution, no discussion was held in the Working Group on the extension of CCP to investment. *Krajewski* derives from this that it was not meant to extend this competence beyond the trade-related aspects of investment measures.

terpretation of FDI, for which textual support might be found in its open formulation,[130] would exclude Member States to conclude bilateral investment treaties. But *Krajewski*, referring to the context, object and purpose as well as negotiating history, argues that only those aspects of FDI that are directly linked to international trade agreements would have the nature of exclusive Union competences.[131] From his side, *Ceyssens* argues that the Union has an exclusive competence to adopt investment policy measures, which, however, would only apply to "long-term investment enabling the investor to exercise a certain influence on an economic activity".[132] In addition, he argues that "measures to protect foreign investment

---

Otherwise, such a fundamental extension would have required serious debate. See *Krajewski* (2005), 114.

130 The text refers to FDI as such, whereas for intellectual property, there is an explicit qualification that it concerns only the trade-related aspects. One could link the reference to trade related aspects of intellectual property rights to the existence of the TRIPS Agreement in the framework of the WTO (which indeed specifically deals with *trade-related* aspects). Similarly, the existence of the TRIMS Agreement (regarding trade in goods-related investment measures) and the fact that aspects of the GATS involve investments (in particular Mode 3, i.e. commercial presence) and capital flows linked to the provision of services (see footnote 8 to Article XVI.1 GATS) could suggest that only trade-related aspects of investment are covered by CCP. However, it must be noted that also within the WTO, there was at a certain moment the intention to negotiate a multilateral agreement on investment that would go beyond aspects that were specifically related to trade in goods or services. (See the Ministerial Declaration of Singapore, WT/MIN(96)/DEC, 13 December 1996, para 20). However, this 'Singapore issue' was dropped from the Doha agenda when the 'July Decision' was adopted in 2004 (see General Council Decision of 31 July 2004, WT/GC/W/535, para g).

131 *Krajewski* (2005), 112-114. Again, it must be observed that it is not self-evident that CCP is restricted to international trade agreements. The border between trade and investment measures is rather vague. As has been indicated in the previous note (supra n. 130), international trade negotiations show a tendency of going beyond merely considering the capital flows that are linked to trade in goods or services.

132 *Ceyssens* (2005), 274-275, referring to the term 'direct investment' as interpreted by the European Court of Justice in Case C-463/00 *Commission v. Spain* [2003] ECR, I-4581.

against expropriation and to ensure fair and equitable treatment are excluded from its scope, as the EU lacks parallel internal competences".[133] Space does not permit us to enter into this discussion in depth here. One thing is clear: given the uncertainties in the scope of the new Article 207(1) TFEU, a decisive role will be played by the ECJ.[134] It would have been better if Member States had clarified this important issue in advance.

In addition, under the Lisbon Treaty, the external competence in the entire CCP domain is not confined to the conclusion of inter-

---

133 *Ceyssens* refers to Article III-315(6) Constitution, which is now Article 207(6) TFEU. This provision reads in its first part: "The exercise of the competences conferred by this Article in the field of the common commercial policy shall not affect the delimitation of competences between the Union and the Member States [...]." He argues that this sentence "could be read to ensure that external trade policy measures do not trespass in any other way on what internally would be Member States' competences." Thus, external measures in the framework of CCP (including FDI) cannot go beyond measures adopted on the basis of internal competences. *Ceyssens* identifies two policies on foreign investment that do not exist within the internal market: (1) investment protection against expropriation and (2) a general standard of fair and equitable treatment. In any case, this leads to the conclusion that the issues dealt with in present bilateral investment treaties by Member States only partly fall within the scope of the exclusive Union competence. See *Ceyssens* (2005), 279-281. One could argue, however, that the parallelism which Ceyssens sees between internal and external competences is not really supported by Article 207(6). We read Article 207(6) not as establishing "a principle of parallelism, which was alluded to by the ECJ in Opinion 1/94". The parallelism in Opinion 1/94 involved the determination of implicit external competence. Article 3(1)(e) *juncto* Article 207(1) TFEU, however, grants an *explicit* exclusive external competence, even in the absence of existing internal measures. The fact that Article 207(6) excludes an 'inverse ERTA effect' (see *infra*), indicates that the external competence of the Union can go *beyond* its internal competence. Therefore, the scope of the Union's external competence for FDI is not limited to those aspects where the Union already has exercised this internal competence.

134 As is indicated below (*infra* n. 150 and accompanying text), the Court of Justice seems rather supportive in restricting the external competences of the Member States. However, the previous discussion may indicate that good arguments can be made in both directions.

national agreements but also covers other external actions in the field of CCP, labeled as 'autonomous external measures'.[135] [136] Nonetheless, it should be highlighted that the CCP deals with the external competence of the Union and therefore does not extend to purely internal acts in these fields.[137] In this respect, Article 207(6) TFEU explicitly excludes an 'inverse ERTA effect': the exercise of the *external* competences in the CCP area (e.g. educational or cultural services) does not confer upon the Union the *internal* competence to implement these agreements internally.

Next to the explicit external competence, much more often, the TEC provided an internal competence to the EC, but did not explicitly grant power to act externally. For those cases, the ECJ case-law (especially the famous *ERTA* case) introduced the principle of parallelism: if the TEC grants internal competence and the EC has exercised this internal competence, there is an *implied* power of the EC to act also externally.[138] This would be a logical consequence of the exercised internal competence. The *nature* of the implied external competence at stake is exclusive as far as the internal competence has been exercised (*'compétence exclusive par exercice'*): independent external action by the Member States would affect the common rules established by the EC. This is a logical consequence of the duty of loyal co-operation (Article 10 TEC, Article 4(3) TEU-L).[139] This case-law seems once again to be reflected in the Lisbon Treaty: Article 216(1) *in fine* reads: "[The Union may con-

---

135 These are 'unilateral' measures (in contrast to agreements) dealing with external aspects of commercial policy (in contrast to the internal market), such as unilateral trade preferences, countervailing or anti-dumping duties. See also, *Eeckhout* (2004), 355-365.

136 This follows from the reading of Article 207(1) and 207(2) TFEU. See *Eeckhout* (2004), 55; *Cremona* (2007), 1214 (footnote 143); *Krajewski* (2005), 109.

137 *Passos* and *Marquardt* seem to hold a different view: "CCP (…) is not confined to the conclusion of international agreements but applies equally to the adoption of internal acts". See, *Passos / Marquardt* (2007), 903.

138 See ECJ, Case 22/70, *Commission v. Council (ERTA)*, [1971] ECR, 263, at 274, paras 12-19, confirmed in ECJ, Opinion 1/92, *EEA*, [1992] ECR, I-2821.

139 See ECJ, Case 22/70, *Commission v. Council (ERTA)*, [1971] ECR, 263, at 274, para 21.

clude an agreement ... where the conclusion of an agreement] is likely to affect common rules or alter their scope". The exclusive nature of the competence is indicated in Article 3(2) TFEU *in fine*: "[The Union shall have exclusive competence for the conclusion of an international agreement ...] insofar as its conclusion may affect common rules or alter their scope". What is important is that in its *opinion 1/03*, the ECJ clarified that it is not necessary that the *full* domain at stake in the international agreement already be regulated internally. The test is whether the area "is already covered to a large extent by Community rules".[140] According to the ECJ, the assessment must be based not only on the scope of the rules in question but also on their nature and content. It is also necessary to take into account "not only the current state of Community law in the area in question but also its future development, insofar as that is foreseeable at the time of that analysis".[141] The Member States thus need to give due consideration to how the internal EU legislation may evolve in the future.

Related to this, the ECJ has accepted in *opinion 1/94* that the EC may also have an external competence, even if this external competence is not explicitly provided for in the Treaties, but when the EC adopts an internal act (based on an internal competence) stating that from now on, the negotiation and conclusion of international agreements in a certain field of competence will be for the EC and not for the Member States. The *nature* of this competence is then exclusive.[142] This seems again reflected in the middle part of the new Article 216 TFEU: "[the Union has a competence to conclude international agreements when it] is provided for in a legally binding Union act". The exclusive nature of this competence is also confirmed in Article 3(2) TFEU. However, remarkably, the language used is as follows: "[there is exclusive competence to con-

---

140 See ECJ, Opinion 2/91, *Convention No. 170 of the International Labour Organization concerning safety in the use of chemicals at work*, [1993] ECR I-1061, paras 25 and 26.

141 ECJ, Opinion 1/03, *Competence of the Community to conclude the new Lugano Convention on jurisdiction and the recognition and enforcement of judgments in civil and commercial matters*, [2006] ECR I-1145, para 126.

142 See ECJ, Opinion 1/94, *Competence of the Community to conclude international agreements concerning services and the protection of intellectual property (WTO)*, [1994] ECR I-5267, para 95.

clude an international agreement when its conclusion is] provided for in a *legislative* act of the Union" (emphasis added). Legislative acts of the Union are defined in Article 289(3) TFEU as "legal acts adopted by legislative procedure".[143] A "legally binding Union act" (the language used in Article 216 TFEU to define the external competences of the Union) would then appear to be broader than merely a "legislative act of the Union" (language used in Article 3(2) TFEU). With the exception of opinions and recommendations, any legal act by the Union, whether legislative or not, is indeed binding upon the addressees of the act, by virtue of EU law.[144] Following this reasoning, both legislative and non-legislative legal acts can form the basis of implied external competence by the Union; but only when the external competence is provided for in a legislative act, an exclusive external competence would be created.

With regard to implied external competences, the ECJ has gone further and has accepted in *opinion 1/76* that there can be implied external competence for the EC *even though the internal competence of the EC has not yet been exercised*. In such cases, in order to exercise the internal competence granted in the TEC, it would be necessary to exercise the competence externally at the same time.[145] However, it should be noted that it is possible that some provisions in the TEC concerning internal competences do not include any external element: this is for example the case for the provisions on freedom of establishment (Article 43 TEC, new Article 49 TFEU) and freedom to provide services (Article 49 TEC,

---

143 Article 289(1) TFEU states that: "The ordinary legislative procedure shall consist in the joint adoption by the European Parliament and the Council of a regulation, directive or decision on a proposal from the Commission".

144 See Article 288 TFEU. Note the new heading of the chapter and of the section above this article, which refers to 'legal acts of the Union'.

145 See ECJ, Opinion 1/76, *Draft Agreement establishing a European laying-up fund for inland waterway vessels*, [1977] ECR 741, para 4. This type of competence was confirmed in ECJ, Opinion 2/91, *Convention N° 170 of the International Labour Organization concerning safety in the use of chemicals at work*, [1993] ECR I-1061, para 7. It was also referred to in ECJ, Opinion 1/94, *Competence of the Community to conclude international agreements concerning services and the protection of intellectual property (WTO)*, [1994] ECR I-5267, para 82.

new Article 56 TFEU). These provisions only apply to EU under-takings and not to undertakings from third countries.[146] An external competence would only exist as far as harmonisation measures have been adopted in these fields (on the basis of Article 95 TEC, new Article 114 TFEU or Article 308 TEC, new Article 352 TFEU).[147]

Whether the competence at stake in *opinion 1/76* is an exclu-sive one remains a matter of controversy. In later cases the ECJ seems to have avoided the issue.[148] On the basis of *ERTA*, it could be argued that the external competence can only be exclusive *after* it has been exercised. Indeed, as long as the Union has not acted, the Member States are allowed to act externally independently. At the other extreme, it could be argued that the external competence at stake is 'virtually' exclusive: even though the EC has not exer-cised the competence yet, the Member States are already excluded from acting. The middle position – the competence is exclusive as soon as it appears that the internal competence can only be exer-cised at the same time as the external competence – seems to be confirmed in *opinion 1/03*. The ECJ noted that there is exclusive external competence, "the conclusion of the international agreement being thus necessary in order to attain objectives of the Treaty that cannot be attained by establishing autonomous rules".[149] In com-bination with the further statement by the ECJ in *opinion 1/03* that the Member States need to take into account the future development of Community law,[150] this restricts the external competences of the Member States to a considerable extent.

---

146 See ECJ, Opinion 1/94, *Competence of the Community to conclude international agreements concerning services and the protection of intellectual property (WTO)*, [1994] ECR I-5267, para 81.

147 *Ibidem* paras 88-89.

148 See e.g. the *Open Skies* cases, where the ECJ stated that there was no need for the EC to exercise the external competence at the same time as the internal competence (as provided for in *Opinion 1/76*), since the EC could coordinate internally the external actions of the Mem-ber States. See ECJ, Case C-476/98, *Commission v. Germany (Open Skies)*, [2002] ECR I-9855, para 85. See *Eeckhout* (2004), 91.

149 See ECJ, Opinion 1/03, *Competence of the Community to conclude the new Lugano Convention on jurisdiction and the recognition and enforcement of judgments in civil and commercial matters*, [2006] ECR I-1145, para 115.

150 *Ibidem* para 126.

The type of external competence elaborated by the ECJ in *opinion 1/76* seems to be reflected in the middle part of Article 216 TFEU. It indicates that there is a competence for the Union to conclude international agreements "where the conclusion of an agreement is necessary in order to achieve, within the framework of the Union's policies, one of the objectives referred to in the Treaties". Article 3(2) TFEU appears to confirm the exclusive nature of the external competence by stating that the Union has exclusive competence to conclude an international agreement when it "is necessary to enable the Union to exercise its internal competence."

The basis for implied external competences, as elaborated in case-law and now laid down in the TFEU, clearly adheres to parallelism of internal and external competences: if the internal competence has been exercised, an external competence follows (*ERTA* type implied external competence); moreover, if the internal competence has not been exercised but can only be exercised by also acting externally, there is external competence (*opinion 1/76* type implied external competence). Nevertheless, the latter part of Article 216 TFEU ("the conclusion of an agreement is necessary in order to achieve, within the framework of the Union's policies, one of the objectives referred to in the Treaties") can be read as providing further competence to the Union to act externally, going beyond this 'parallelism' of internal and external competences. This phrase seems to suggest that, as soon as external action is necessary to achieve one of the objectives of the Union, the Union has competence to conclude an international agreement. Hence, that would imply that it would not even be necessary to have an explicit *internal* competence in order for the Union to be able to act externally: the need to achieve one of the objectives of the Union suffices. The middle part of Article 216 TFEU thereby appears to extend Article 308 TEC (new Article 352 TFEU) as a legal basis for action also to external action of the Union.[151] This provision has indeed been used in the past as a legal basis for the conclusion of international agreements by the EC. However, this was always in combination with an internal measure that had already been adopted on the basis of Article 308 TEC.[152] One may recall that in *opinion 2/94* the ECJ

---

151 *Lenaerts* (2004), 409-410.

152 See, for instance, the Council Decision 2006/954/EC of 18 December 2006 approving the accession of the European Community to the Geneva Act of the Hague Agreement concerning the international

held that Article 308 TEC was not an appropriate basis for accession by the EC to the European Convention on Human Rights, since
this would bring about such changes to EC law that the procedure
of Treaty amendment needed to be followed.[153] The ECJ did not,
however, exclude the possibility of Article 308 *ever* being used as a
legal basis for external competence. In *opinion 1/94* too, the ECJ
made reference to Article 308 TEC, be it in the context of defining
whether the competence to conclude GATS and TRIPS was an exclusive EC competence. The ECJ held that GATS and TRIPS came
within the competence of the EC, as far as harmonisation measures
in these fields had been adopted on the basis of Article 95 or 308
TEC. However, this was in the line of the 'parallelism' approach to
internal and external competences: if internal measures would have
been adopted on the basis of Article 308 TEC, an external competence would also exist. Nonetheless, it appears from the text of Article 216 TFEU that henceforth Article 308 TEC (new Article 352
TFEU) can *on its own* (*i.e.* without internal measures having been
adopted) provide a basis for external competence, provided that
such action is necessary to achieve one of the objectives of the
Treaties. The *nature* of this competence does not seem to be exclusive, however. Article 3(2) TFEU does not speak about an exclusive competence for the Union to conclude an agreement to achieve

---

registration of industrial designs, adopted in Geneva on 2 July 1999,
OJ 2006, L386/28 (However, there existed an internal act based on
Article 308: Council Regulation (EC) No 6/2002 of 12 December
2001 on Community designs); Council Decision 2005/523/EC of 30
May 2005 approving the accession of the European Community to
the International Convention for the Protection of New Varieties of
Plants, as revised at Geneva on 19 March 1991, OJ 2005, L192/63
(While the Council Decision indicates that the subject-matter of
UPOV falls within existing Community regulations in this field, it
does not specify these regulations) and Council Decision
2003/793/EC of 27 October 2003 approving the accession of the
European Community to the Protocol relating to the Madrid
Agreement concerning the international registration of marks,
adopted at Madrid on 27 June 1989, OJ 2003, L296/20 (However,
there existed an internal act based on Article 308: Council Regulation
(EC) No 40/94 of 20 December 1993 on the Community trade mark).

153 ECJ, Opinion 2/94, *Accession by the Community to the European
Convention for the Protection of Human Rights and Fundamental
Freedoms*, [1996] ECR I-1759, paras 28-36.

one of the objectives in the Treaties, but only "to exercise its internal competence".

Until today, many international agreements that are concluded by the EC involve not solely issues that fall exclusively within the latter's competences. In most cases, such agreements involve matters that are within the scope of the Union competences as well as matters within the scope of Member State competences. As is well-known, in such cases there will be a 'mixed agreement' to which both the EC and Member States will be a party. Before the Lisbon Treaty, the clearest example was that of the WTO agreements.[154] The wide range of issues dealt with in the agreements negotiated within the WTO context and especially the 'package approach' prevailing in these negotiations (different subject-matters are linked to each other in the negotiations and there needs to be an agreement on the full 'package') implied that the EC as well as the individual Member States needed to become parties to them. This was especially the case since, according to the ECJ in *opinion 1/94*, trade in services and commercial aspects of intellectual property rights fell only partly within the competences of the Community. Since under the Lisbon Treaty the common commercial policy has now been clarified as including services, commercial aspects of intellectual property and even foreign direct investment, it appears that all matters dealt with by the WTO fall within the exclusive competence of the Union.

Mixity will remain very important, however, when international agreements are concluded in the cases that do not cover solely issues that are fully within the competence of the Union. Even though the ECJ case-law on external competences appears to be supportive of a broad external competence of the Union, and the Lisbon Treaty does not seem to contradict this, there are still areas where the Union has no competence to act externally. This will be the case where the Union has not acted internally yet and where external action is not necessary to achieve one of its objectives. Even where the Union has a competence in all areas covered by the international agreement, the Union and the Member States might still decide to conclude a mixed agreement. Such a situation will then be a political compromise between the Member States and the Union and avoid the thorny issue of delineating the competences of

---

154 See *Steinberger* (2006).

the Union and its Member States.[155] However, this may in turn be detrimental to the consistency of the external action, since uncertainties may arise with regard to the question of who bears the responsibility for failure to comply with the international agreement (Union or Member States) or with regard to who may cast the votes (representatives of the Union or Member States) in an organ established by the mixed international agreement.[156]

3. Procedure to conclude international agreements

Whereas current EU law stipulates two tracks for the conclusion of international agreements depending on whether the Community pillar (Article 300 TEC) or the other pillars (*ex* Article 24 TEU) are at stake, the Lisbon Treaty, like the Constitution, unifies in Article 218 TFEU the procedure for concluding international agreements by the Union, though specific rules are inscribed in this provision for CFSP agreements. With respect to CCP (Article 207 TFEU) and monetary policy (Article 219 TFEU), there still exist specific rules in other provisions.

The right of initiative to conclude international agreements still lies with the Commission. Only when the international agreement relates exclusively or principally to the field of CFSP, the right of initiative lies with the High Representative.[157] After an initiative is taken, the Council will authorise the opening of negotiations and will, depending on the subject of the envisaged agreement, nominate the Union negotiator or the head of the Union's negotiation team. Hence, whereas under the TEC, the Commission was always representing the Community in negotiations, this is less evident under the TFEU.[158] This is of course related to the fact that the 'pillar-structure' disappears: "depending on the subject of the envisaged agreement", different constellations will need to be possible. When exclusively a non-CFSP external competence is at stake, the Commission will most likely be appointed as Union negotiator. However, when a matter of CFSP is at stake, the negotiator will be the High Representative. Moreover, in cases of mixed treaties, the Council will appoint the head of the negotiation team. The Council

---

155 See *Eeckhout* (2004), 198-199.

156 See *Gaja* (1983) and *Karayigit* (2006).

157 Article 218(3) TFEU.

158 Only for the CCP is the Commission is explicitly appointed as the negotiator (Article 207(3) TFEU).

may then address directives to the negotiator and designate a special committee with which the negotiator must consult during the negotiations. When the negotiations are finalised, the Council will adopt a decision to authorise the signing of the agreement.[159] Upon a proposal of the Union negotiator, the Council will finally adopt a decision concluding the international agreement.[160]

All Council decisions (authorising the opening of the negotiations, appointing the negotiator, authorising signature and concluding the agreement) are taken by QMV.[161] However, there are three exceptions to this.

First, unanimity is required when the subject-matter of the international agreement concerns an area where unanimity is also required internally in order to adopt a Union act (principle of *in foro interno, in foro externo*). Unanimity will thus, in principle, be required for the conclusion of agreements in the CFSP area. An important specification in this respect is also made with regard to CCP. The negotiation and conclusion of international agreements in the field of services and the commercial aspects of intellectual property and of foreign direct investment should be taken by unanimity if this is also to be done by unanimity internally.[162] Moreover, when international agreements are concluded in the field of trade in cultural and audiovisual services, unanimity is required where these agreements risk prejudicing the Union's linguistic and cultural diversity.[163] Similarly, unanimity is also required when international agreements are concluded in the field of trade in social, educational and health services, where these agreements risk seriously disturbing the national organisation of such services and prejudicing the responsibility of the Member States to deliver them.[164] The latter two cases of unanimity respond to the concerns of several Member States. France and the French-speaking part of Belgium are particularly concerned that the Union will commit itself to a further liberalisation of the cultural and audiovisual services markets in the framework of the WTO. The same can be said

---

159 Article 218(5) TFEU.
160 Article 218(6) TFEU.
161 Article 218(8) TFEU.
162 Article 207(4), para 2, TFEU.
163 Article 207(4), para 3, (a) TFEU.
164 Article 207(4), para 3, (b) TFEU.

for international agreements in the field of social, educational and health services. Several Member States want to maintain the freedom to distribute these services of 'general economic interest' through the State.[165] Although these seem to be only limited exceptions to QMV, they might have an important impact in practice on the conclusion of future agreements in the framework of the WTO given that, as indicated, such agreements are concluded in a single package ('single undertaking'). As a result of the 'Pastis' principle, the entire agreement will require unanimity in the Council in case one of the exceptions (e.g. educational services) is included.[166]

Secondly, unanimity is required for the conclusion of association agreements[167] and agreements of economic, financial and technical co-operation with candidate Union Members.

Finally, unanimity is also required for accession of the Union to the European Convention on Human Rights ('ECHR').[168] This has changed since the Constitution, which did not list accession to the ECHR as one of the exceptions to QMV.

Before the Lisbon Treaty, the European Parliament had no formal role *during* the negotiations on an international agreement. However, a Framework Agreement had been concluded between the Commission and the Parliament that provided for exchange of information between both institutions.[169] The Lisbon Treaty now

---

165 See in this regard the Protocol in Services of General Interest, Annexed to the TFEU.

166 As described by *Pascal Lamy*: "(...) under the Pastis principle, a little drop of unanimity can taint the entire glass of QMV water". See: *Pascal Lamy*, 'The Convention and trade policy: concrete steps to enhance the EU's international profile', speech delivered in Brussels, 5.2.2003 (available at: http://ec.europa.eu/archives/ commission _1999_2004/lamy/speeches_articles/spla146_en.htm) (visited May 25, 2008).

167 Article 198 TFEU.

168 *Ibidem* Note that the latter accession only enters into force after this has been approved by the individual Member States through their constitutional processes.

169 Annex III(ii) Framework Agreement on relations between the European Parliament and the Commission, OJ 2001, C121/122. The Commission would inform the Parliament on the preparation of agreements, draft and adopted negotiation directives. The information had to be provided to the Parliament to allow it to express its point of view and such as to allow the Commission to take into ac-

explicitly indicates that the Parliament "shall be immediately and fully informed at all stages of the procedure".[170]

The role of the Parliament at the moment of the conclusion of the international agreement has been reinforced. Pursuant to Article 218(6)(a) TFEU the Parliament has to give its consent to the Council decision to conclude the international agreement, not merely – as under the old Article 300(3) TEC – for the conclusion of association agreements, agreements establishing a specific institutional framework by organising co-operation procedures and agreements with important budgetary implications for the Union, but also for the EU's accession to the ECHR and for "agreements covering fields to which either the ordinary legislative procedure applies, or the special legislative procedure where consent by the European Parliament is required." It is interesting to note that the Parliament's consent has to be obtained as soon as the international agreement 'covers a field'[171] for which co-decision ('the ordinary legislative procedure) is also required internally. Under the TEC formula, consent was only required when, by concluding an international agreement, an amendment was made to an act that was concluded by means of co-decision.[172] Not only the requirement of a pre-existing act adopted under the co-decision procedure has been suppressed, but also fields covered by the consent procedure are now included. At first sight one may be disappointed by the exclusion of the Parliament from decisions concluding an agreement when such agreement relates *exclusively* to CFSP.[173] However, it follows from this formula that, when an international agreement includes CFSP

---

count this view. During the negotiations, the Parliament would be kept up to date. Moreover, the Parliament had to be allowed to send Members of Parliament as observers in the Community delegations. Finally, the Commission had to inform the Parliament on the conclusion of the negotiations.

170 Article 218(10) TFEU.

171 *Cremona* has noted that the phrase 'covers the field' is "potentially wider than the legal base of an agreement". See *Cremona* (2007), 1192, note 66.

172 Article 300(3) TEC.

173 However, the general right of the Parliament to be informed and to express its view as inscribed in Article 36 TEU-L (see *supra*) still applies.

issues as well as other Union competences, the Parliament will have to be involved through consultation or even consent.

All in all, these are serious improvements from the perspective of the democratic legitimacy of the EU's treaty-making practice.

Another important improvement with regard to democratic legitimacy is that the Parliament now has to give its consent in the area of Common Commercial Policy. Under the TEC, even consultation of the Parliament was excluded in this area.[174] Now, the new Article 207(3) TFEU[175] explicitly states that the procedure of Article 218 is applicable for the negotiation and conclusion of international agreements in this field. Hence the combination of Article 207(2) TFEU (which indicates that the 'ordinary legislative procedure' must be followed to adopt the internal measures defining the framework of implementing the CCP[176]) with Article 218(6)(a)(v) TFEU (which states that for international agreements that cover a field that requires the ordinary legislative procedure the consent of the Parliament has to be obtained) leads to the conclusion that the Parliament's consent will have to be obtained for the conclusion of international agreements in the field of CCP. This is a major improvement when compared to the situation under the TEC.[177]

The exclusivity of the CCP competence and the broader definition of this competence under the Lisbon Treaty carries some important consequences for national parliaments. Indeed, the fact that the CCP is now explicitly identified in Article 3(1)(e) TFEU as an exclusive competence, implies that the Member States cannot act

---

174 Parliament's consent was only required in certain situations (spelled out in Article 300(3) para 2 TEC), for example, when agreements establish a specific institutional framework by organising cooperation procedures (e.g. the Marrakesh Agreement establishing the WTO).

175 Article 133 TEC.

176 The Constitution was less clear on this issue because it did not explicitly refer to the 'ordinary legislative procedure' but merely referred to 'European laws' by which the framework for implementing CCP would be established. Most authors, however, agreed that the Parliament's consent was required in the field of CCP. See, for example, *Cremona* (2007), 1215; *Krajewski* (2005), 124-125 (with the exception of agreements which do not need to be implemented).

177 This is also welcomed by the European Parliament. See European Parliament, Committee on Constitutional Affairs, *Report on the Treaty of Lisbon* (2007/2286(INI), 29 January 2008), 37, 75, 85.

alone anymore in this field. Hence, whereas under the TEC international agreements on trade in services and commercial aspects of intellectual property rights were mixed agreements that fell partly within the exclusive competence of the Community (namely the cross-border movement of services and aspects of trade in counterfeited goods) and partly within the competence of the Member States (namely the other aspects of trade in services and intellectual property, as far as no internal Community measures were adopted in these fields), under the TFEU all these aspects fall within the exclusive competence of the Union. Therefore, to the extent that no elements of mixity appear (*supra*), national parliaments no longer have a role to play in the conclusion of international agreements in these fields. Moreover, as mentioned before, foreign direct investment is now also included in the field of the common commercial policy. Therefore, from the perspective of national (and sub-national) parliaments the democratic legitimacy appears diminished. However, it may be submitted that this is compensated by the improved involvement of the European Parliament in the conclusion of these agreements. To be sure, the representatives of the Member States in the Council remain politically accountable to their parliaments when deciding within the Council. In Member States – like Belgium – where sub-national parliaments have normally an important say in the approval of international agreements touching upon defederated competences, the latter form of accountability may not be a great consolation.

It should be noted finally that, even if the European Parliament has to give its consent in the majority of the cases for the *conclusion* of an international agreement, it does not need to give its consent for the decision to *open* the negotiations or for defining the negotiation mandate of the Union negotiator. Therefore, the Parliament may be left upon the conclusion of the international negotiations with no other choice than to approve an agreement as it emerges from the negotiations.

B. Hierarchy of norms

1. Primacy over the law of the Member States

In the landmark *Costa v. ENEL* case, the ECJ famously stated that "the law stemming from the [TEC], an independent source of law, could not, because of its special and original nature, be overridden by domestic legal provisions, however framed, without being deprived of its character as Community law and without the legal basis of the Community itself being called into question".[178] Hereby, the primacy of (primary and secondary) Community law over national law was established.[179] International agreements that are concluded on the basis of the TEC become, upon their conclusion by the EC, part of the Community legal order.[180] These agreements are binding upon the Member States.[181] Moreover, since they are part of the Community legal order, the principle of primacy applies to them and their provisions will prevail over national provisions of the Member States. In addition, to the extent that the nature and structure of the international agreement allows this[182] and the provisions of the international agreement are sufficiently clear, precise and unconditional,[183] they will have direct effect within the Community legal order, and thus also within the legal order of the Member States. Under these circumstances, citizens are able to challenge national law before their national courts due to incompatibility with the international agreement at hand.[184]

The principle of primacy was proclaimed by the ECJ without any legal basis in (what was at that time) the EEC Treaty. The ECJ only referred to the 'special and original nature' of the Community legal order. In contrast, the Constitution included an explicit provision recognising the primacy of the Constitution and of the Union law in Article I-6:

"The Constitution and law adopted by the institutions of the Union in exercising competences conferred on it shall have primacy over the law of the Member States".

---

178 ECJ, Case 6/64, *Costa v E.N.E.L*, [1964] ECR 1199, p. 1219.

179 See also ECJ, Case 11/70, *Internationale Handelsgesellschaft mbH v EVGF*, [1970] ECR 1125; ECJ, Case 106/77, *Simmenthal* [1978] ECR 629 and ECJ, Case C-213/89, *R v Secretary of State for Transport ex parte Factortame* [1990] ECR I-2433. For a critical view, see *Bono* (2006), 369-375 and *Hartley* (2001).

180 See *inter alia* ECJ, Case 12/86 *Demirel* [1987] ECR 3719, para 7.

181 See Article 300(7) TEC.

182 See ECJ, Case 104/81 *Kupferberg* [1982] ECR 3641, para 22. and ECJ, Case 21-24/72 *International Fruit Company* [1972] ECR 1219, para 20.

183 See ECJ, Case 12/86 *Demirel* [1987], ECR 3719, para 14.

184 See, for a further discussion of this process of "europeanisation" of international law, *Wouters / Nollkaemper / de Wet* (2008).

This provision did not exclude the area of CFSP from this stated principle of primacy. Neither did any other provision in the Constitution affirm that primacy did not apply to CFSP. Nonetheless, several authors argued that it could not have been intended that the principle of primacy applied to CFSP. *Dashwood* advanced two arguments in this respect. First, he noted that national courts that would be called upon to disapply national law because of incompatibility would be left without guidance of the ECJ, whose jurisdiction, as we have seen above, has indeed been almost totally excluded in the CFSP field. In his view, it would not be acceptable that national courts could apply primacy to EU acts in the field of CFSP.[185] Secondly, he noted that the Constitution clearly treated CFSP "as having its own specific character",[186] which would be an argument for excluding primacy in this area.[187] *Cremona*[188] and *Cramér*[189] have argued in a similar fashion. Arguably, these assertions were based on the object and purpose as well as on the context of Article I-6 of the Constitution rather than on its literal wording. While the ordinary meaning of the text of Article I-6 would seem to leave no ambiguity as to the applicability of the principle of primacy, the context of the provision[190] in the Constitution would

---

185 This "could lead to an uncontrolled proliferation of conflicting interpretations". See Common Market Law Review (2005), 327.

186 It is listed in a separate paragraph 4 in Article I-12 of the Constitution, which article lists the categories of competence. Hence, the formal categories of competence (exclusive, shared, complementary) do not seem to be applicable to CFSP. See Common Market Law Review (2005), 327.

187 See *Dashwood* (2005), 37-38.

188 *Cremona* (2007), 1196.

189 *Cramér* (2005), 72-73.

190 See Article 31(1) Vienna Convention on the Law of Treaties, done in Vienna on 23 May 1969. It is stated that a treaty "shall be interpreted in good faith in accordance with the ordinary meaning to be given to the terms of the treaty in their context and in the light of its object and purpose." Article 31(2) clarifies that the "context for the purpose of the interpretation of a treaty shall comprise, in addition to the text, including its preamble and annexes [...]." Hence, other provisions in the Constitution, like those on the CFSP (especially those confirming its intergovernmental nature), as well as the Annex with declarations, are part of the context of the treaty.

make this far from evident. Indeed, as *Dashwood* stated, an analysis of the relevant provisions shows that the Constitution reserved a special status for CFSP.

The Intergovernmental Conference added a declaration to the Constitution in which it noted that "Article I-6 reflects existing case law of the Court of Justice of the European Communities and of the Court of First Instance".[191] *Corthaut* has derived from this declaration that primacy extends to the three former pillars and therefore also to CFSP.[192] However, since the Declaration only refers to *existing* case law and no case-law on primacy for CFSP is available yet, it seems difficult to derive from this that primacy extends to this area. Still, it must be admitted that the existing case-law does not state that primacy does *not* extend to CFSP either.[193] On the other hand, the fact that the Constitution explicitly included a provision confirming primacy, led the UK to push for the attachment of a declaration. It would have made no sense to confirm in a declaration what is already said in an explicit provision. Therefore, the negotiation history of the Constitution provided an indication that the declaration was meant to *limit* the application of primacy to what was stated in the case-law *at that moment*.

Contrary to the Constitution, the Lisbon Treaty does not include a provision that explicitly states that Union law prevails over Member State law.[194] Hence, it could be argued that the existence of this principle of primacy remains dependent upon the case-law of the ECJ. Since the ECJ has until now not pronounced itself on the primacy of CFSP measures, it cannot be stated that primacy extends to CFSP, though once again this does not mean that the case-law on the basis of the Treaties could evolve. However, the previously-mentioned arguments on the 'specificity' of CFSP matters apply

---

191 Declaration on Article I-6, Annex to the Final Act of the Conference of the Representatives of the Member States, convened in Brussels on 30 September 2003, OJ 2004 C 310/420.

192 See *Corthaut* (2008). *Corthaut* argues that "the – probably unintended – side-effect of this Declaration was to confirm that the primacy of EU law extends to the three pillars of EU law, irrespective of the Constitutional Treaty." See also *Corthaut* (2005), note 21.

193 Common Market Law Review (2005), 327.

194 The primacy clause that figured in Article I-6 of the Constitution was removed in the Lisbon Treaty at the request of Austria, Greece and the Netherlands. See *de Búrca* (2008), 20.

even more strongly under the Lisbon Treaty. CFSP is formally separated in a Chapter in the TEU-L, whereas other Union Competences are elaborated in the TFEU. There is still a Declaration concerning primacy at the end of the Final Act of the Intergovernmental Conference. Declaration 17 reads:

"In accordance with well settled case law of the Court of Justice of the European Union, the Treaties and the law adopted by the Union on the basis of the Treaties have primacy over the law of Member States, under the conditions laid down by the said case law".[195]

The Declaration refers to the *well-settled* case-law of the ECJ to confirm primacy. Since the case-law does not include any confirmation of primacy for CFSP matters yet, it cannot be part of the well-settled case law. The purpose of the declaration is therefore apparently only to confirm the existence of primacy for the areas in which the case-law of the ECJ has already accepted this.[196] The importance of the principle of primacy is further reinforced through the Declaration's reference to the opinion of the Council Legal Service of 22 June 2007. The latter reads:

---

195 Declaration Concerning Primacy, Annex to the Final Act of the Conference of the Representatives of the Member States, convened in Brussels on 23 July 2007, OJ 2007 C 306/256.

196 One can argue about the legal value and use of this declaration. It is difficult to use it as context for interpreting the TEU-L or TFEU since, as stated above, there is no provision on primacy in these Treaties anymore. However, the declaration is made by *all* Member States (contrary to some other declarations made in Annex C to the Final Act of the Intergovernmental Conference). The Vienna Convention on the Law of Treaties defines a 'treaty' as "an international agreement concluded between States in written form and governed by international law, whether embodied in a single instrument or in two or more related instruments and *whatever its particular designation*." (Article 2(1) (a) Vienna Convention on the Law of Treaties, supra n 190 (emphasis added)). It is thus not important what the instrument is called, from the perspective of international law. (See *Corten / Klein* (2006), 52-53). This declaration is attached to the Final Act of the Intergovernmental Conference and once it is approved by all the Member States, it could be argued that it is binding upon all the Member States. On this interpretation, national constitutional courts would have no other choice than to accept primacy for non-CFSP matters, since this would be stated in a binding international instrument.

"It results from the case-law of the Court of Justice that primacy of EC law is a cornerstone principle of Community law. According to the Court, this principle is inherent to the specific nature of the European Community. At the time of the first judgment of this established case-law (Costa/ENEL, 15 July 1964, Case 6/641) there was no mention of primacy in the treaty. It is still the case today. The fact that the principle of primacy will not be included in the future treaty shall not in any way change the existence of the principle and the existing case-law of the Court of Justice".[197]

The fact that an opinion that only refers to Community law is explicitly included may be a further confirmation that primacy is not meant to extend to CFSP. But this is, again, not very decisive either. In sum, while Declaration 17 on primacy seems to be a confirmation that the principle of primacy is part of Union law, considerable ambiguity remains as to whether this principle extends to CFSP.[198]

2. Relationship to primary and secondary Union law

The hierarchical position of the international agreements concluded by the Union is *below* the provisions of the Treaties[199] but *above* the

---

197 See Opinion of the Council Legal Service of 22 June 2007, JUR 260, 11197/07.

198 Note that for the former 'third pillar' (Police and Judicial Cooperation in Criminal Matters), the ECJ has confirmed in *Pupino* that "the principle of conforming interpretation is binding in relation to framework decisions adopted in the context of Title VI of the Treaty on the European Union. When applying national law, the national court that is called upon to interpret it must do so as far as possible in the light of the wording and purpose of the framework decision [...]". See ECJ, Case C-105/03, *Pupino*, [2005] ECR I-5285, para 43. Hence, with regard to police and judicial cooperation in criminal matters, primacy seems to have been confirmed. However, this case law does not extend to CFSP.

199 This can be derived from the fact that it is possible for the Member States, the Parliament, the European Council or the Commission to ask for an Opinion from the ECJ as to whether an agreement envisaged is compatible with the provisions of the EC Treaty. See Article 218(11) TFEU.

law adopted by the Union on the basis of the Treaties.[200] Hence, international agreements that are concluded by the Union prevail over the law adopted by the Union on the basis of the Treaties. It should be noted, however, that the Court of First Instance ('CFI') in the *Yusuf* and *Kadi* cases stated that the UN Charter as well as Security Council Resolutions prevail over secondary *as well as* primary Community law.[201]

VI. Restrictive measures

Restrictive measures are measures adopted by the Union to impose sanctions against governments or (natural or legal) persons in third countries. International sanctions often involve the interruption of economic relations. EU sanctions are often adopted as an implementation of United Nations Security Council sanctions. Before the Lisbon Treaty, such sanctions required a combination of an action under the EC pillar and an action under the CFSP pillar.[202] The Maastricht Treaty introduced Article 301 in the TEC. This provision made a link between the TEC and the TEU to allow for the interruption or reduction of economic relations with third countries,

---

200 See Article 216(2) TFEU.

201 The Court derived this from international law, namely Article 103 of the Charter of the United Nations, which states that in case of incompatibility of the UN Charter with other international obligations of the Members of the UN, the obligations under the UN Charter prevail. (See CFI, Case T-306/01, *Ahmed Ali Yusuf et al. v Council and Commission*, [2005] ECR II-3533, para 233.) Furthermore, the Court derived this also from Community law, referring to 307 TEC (new Article 351 TFEU) which provides that the application of the TEC does not affect the duty of the Member States to respect the rights of third countries under a prior agreement and to perform its obligations thereunder. The Court noted that all Members of the EC were already Members of the UN before their accession to the EC. Hence, at the moment of the conclusion of the TEC, the Member States could not transfer to the Community more powers than they had at that moment. These powers were already constrained by the UN Charter. (*Ibidem*, paras 235-236.) The Court concluded from this that the TEC was subject to the obligations under the UN Charter. See also CFI, Case T-315/01, *Kadi v Council and Commission*, [2005] ECR II-3649, paras 221 and 225-226 and CFI, Case T-253/02, *Ayadi v Council*, [2006] ECR II-2139, para 116.

202 See *Paasivirta / Rosas* (2002), 216-218.

where it was provided in a common position or a joint action adopted under the TEU. In a similar fashion, Article 60 TEC provided for sanctions that restrict the movement of capital or payments.

Two problems emerged with regard to restrictive measures. The first problem concerned sanctions targeting individuals ('smart sanctions'). To avoid affecting the whole population of a country through sanctions (the consequence being the suffering of innocent citizens), it is nowadays preferred to adopt sanctions that specifically target persons or entities that are controlled by the government or persons or entities that are closely associated with the government. However, the existing Articles 60 and 301 TEC only provided for interruption or reduction of economic relations with *States*. As long as the entities or individuals could be linked to the regime that is sanctioned, it could be accepted that Articles 60 and 301 TEC provided a legal basis for 'smart sanctions'. However, for sanctions affecting individuals or entities that are not linked to a government, but rather to terrorist organisations, Articles 60 and 301 TEC were not sufficient as a legal basis. In the *Yusuf* case, the Court of First Instance accepted that such sanctions could be adopted on the basis of Articles 60 or 301 TEC *in combination with* Article 308 TEC.[203]

The Lisbon Treaty solves this problem by replacing Article 301 TEC with a new Article 215 TFEU. A decision adopted under Chapter 2 of Title V of the TEU-L (CFSP) can provide for a partial or complete interruption or reduction of economic and financial relations with third countries. The Council will then adopt the necessary measures by QMV upon a joint proposal of the High Representative and the Commission.[204] There is no provision for involvement of the European Parliament. Smart sanctions now have an explicit legal basis in Article 215(2) TFEU: the Council may adopt restrictive measures "against natural or legal persons and groups or non-State entities", by following the aforementioned procedure.

A second problem that emerged with regard to restrictive measures is that of the judicial protection for those affected by sanctions. Indeed, 'smart sanctions' in particular may have grave consequences for entities and individuals. They may lead to freez-

---

203 See CFI, Case T-306/01, supra n 201, para 164 and CFI, Case T-315/01, supra n 201, para 135.

204 Under Article 301 TEC, the initiative was only with the Commission.

ing of assets and deprive individuals of their means of existence. Entities and individuals may need to challenge the restrictive measure. However, the fact that sanctions are often the result of a political decision (especially when taken on the basis of a UN Security Council Resolution) has led governments to argue that the judiciary should show deference when being asked to assess the sanction.[205] The CFI in *Yusuf* indeed decided that it could not rule on the compatibility with primary EC law of a Council regulation that gave effect to Security Council Resolutions, since that "would therefore imply that the Court is to consider, indirectly, the lawfulness of those resolutions".[206] Nonetheless, the CFI accepted that it was empowered to check the lawfulness of these resolutions (indirectly through the assessment of the regulation implementing them) with regard to *jus cogens* (peremptory rules of international law).[207] The CFI then examined the Resolution in the light of the right to property, right to a fair hearing and right to an effective judicial remedy.[208] Yet, the CFI did not accept a violation of any of these rights. Hence, it seems that the CFI only paid lip-service to providing judicial protection to the individuals affected by sanctions.[209]

The Lisbon Treaty remedies this situation. Article 275, para 2, TFEU provides an exception to the exclusion of ECJ jurisdiction regarding CFSP matters (*supra*). The Court can review "the legality of decisions providing for restrictive measures against natural or legal persons adopted by the Council on the basis of Chapter 2 of

---

205 This was argued by the Council, the Commission and the United Kingdom in response to the appeal to the decision of the CFI in *Yusuf*. See the arguments mentioned in the Opinion of Advocate General *Poiares Maduro* delivered on 23 January 2008, Case C-415/05 P, *Al Barakaat International Foundation v Council and Commission*, para 33.

206 See CFI, Case T-306/01, *loc. cit.*, supra n. 201, para 266.

207 *Ibidem*, para 277.

208 One may have serious doubts as to whether these rights are part of *jus cogens*. There seems only to be consensus that *jus cogens* includes the prohibition of the use of force, genocide, racial discrimination, crimes against humanity, slavery, piracy as well as the principle of permanent sovereignty over natural resources and the principle of self-determination. See *Brownlie* (2003), 488-489.

209 For comments, see *inter alia Eeckhout* (2005), 37, and *Lavranos*, (2007), 1-17.

Title V of the Treaty on European Union." Hence, a natural or legal person can challenge a restrictive measure if it is of direct or individual concern to him or her.[210] As far as such measures are taken under Title IV (Area of freedom, security and justice), the jurisdiction of the ECJ applies fully.[211] However, if such measures would be based on CFSP provisions, it is now possible to bring an action for annulment.[212]

---

210 Article 275, para 2, *juncto* Article 263, para 4, TFEU.

211 Compare to the situation before the Lisbon Treaty. In the *Segi* case, the Court of First Instance ruled that it did not have jurisdiction to address an action for damages against a Common Position that included *Segi* on a list of terrorist organisations. Even though the Common Position was taken on the basis of *ex* Article 15 TEU (CFSP) as well as *ex* Article 34 TEU (police and judicial cooperation in criminal matters), according to the CFI, the specific provision affecting the claimants was taken on the basis of Article 34. See CFI, Case T-338/02, *Segi et al.* v *Council*, Order of 7 June 2004, [2004] ECR II-1647, para 40. The CFI hereby recognised that this meant that there was no effective remedy available for Segi. Ibid, para 38. The ECJ confirmed this upon appeal. See ECJ, Case C-355/04, *Segi et al.* v *Council*, [2007] ECR I-1657, para 46. See *Peers* (2007).

212 Note that still no preliminary rulings can be asked on the CFSP Decision. However, it seems possible to request a ruling on the Regulation or Decision that implements the CFSP Decision. As mentioned in the main text, a natural or legal person can only bring an action for annulment against the CFSP Decision if this Decision is of *direct* and *individual concern* to the person. One may wonder whether the CFSP Decision itself may be of *direct* concern to the person. The CFSP Decision requires further implementation through a Regulation or Decision imposing the restrictive measures on the basis of Article 215 TFEU and thus produces not immediately legal effects on the person. On the other hand, the mere fact of being included in the list of persons being sanctioned may arguably already create direct concern because the person is stigmatised as being dangerous, affecting the legal position of the person as it interferes with the person's right to his good name. Proving *individual concern* will often not be a problem since the names of the persons who are subject to the sanction are indicated in a 'smart sanction'. Moreover, even if the name is not indicated, it is arguable that the CFSP Decision is a 'regulatory act' in the sense of the fourth paragraph of Article 263 TFEU. (It is certainly not a 'legislative act' in the sense of Article 289(3) TFEU since it is not adopted by legislative procedure.) If the CFSP Decision is a

If the CFI or the ECJ were to rule that a restrictive measure is incompatible with Union law (because for example no effective legal remedy is foreseen), the implementation of Security Council Resolutions by the EU may run into difficulties. Article 215(3) TFEU aims to prevent such a situation by providing that the restrictive measures "shall include necessary provisions on legal safeguards". The Union thus has a constitutional obligation to guarantee judicial protection of the individuals and entities affected by the measures, even if the Security Council Resolutions that are being implemented do not provide for this.[213]

VII. Conclusion

The Lisbon Treaty "will bring increased consistency to our external action." This contribution has shown that this rather modest appreciation by the European leaders – though perhaps inspired by political rather than analytical reasons – seems to be well-founded. Indeed, the ratification of the Lisbon Treaty will increase the consistency of external Union action given that it formally abolishes, for example, the pillar structure, bundles the objectives of the Union and creates a new 'bridging' function for the High Representative.

The explicitation of the external competences of the Union in the Lisbon Treaty is also a welcome development from the perspective of improving the Union's external action. In combination with the ECJ's case-law on external competences, the legal basis for external action by the Union seems to be firmly established. Also the reformed procedures for the conclusion of international agreements, with QMV voting as the basic rule (save for a number of exceptions, especially for CFSP), will affirm the external role of

---

'regulatory act', no *individual concern* needs to be proven. However, it is then still necessary to show that no implementing measures are necessary As indicated, this is problematic in case of the CFSP Decision at stake.

213 Note that the CFI in the *Ayadi* case referred to Guidelines of the Sanctions Committee that contain procedures on how affected persons should address their State to apply to the Sanctions Committee for a re-examination of the sanction. The CFI derived from this a "right guaranteed not only by those Guidelines but also by the Community legal order". Case T-253/02, *Ayadi v Council*, [2006] ECR II-2139, para 145. Whether this reasoning is correct or not, this remedy is now secured by Article 215(3) TFEU.

the Union. This is complemented by an increased role for the European Parliament (save for CFSP). The confirmation in a Declaration of the existing case-law on primacy is a further element in support of consistency. If an international agreement concluded by the Union prevails over the national law of the Member States, this avoids non-uniform application of this agreement throughout the Union. Finally, also the revision of the article on restrictive measures, with guarantees for judicial protection, is to be applauded. The Union will be able to fulfill its international obligations without compromising on the rule of law.

At the same time, some doubts can be raised as to whether consistency will be fully achieved. The institutional and decision-making duality in the external action field is still too deep seated in the Lisbon Treaty. The specific character of foreign policy might justify a different set of rules in this domain, but the Lisbon Treaty arguably does not sufficiently limit its intergovernmental nature. It therefore remains an open question whether the High Representative will be able to bridge such a large gap between the CFSP and the other aspects of the Union's external action (as well as among these other aspects *inter se*, e.g. within the Commission). Much of his / her leverage will depend on the creation of the EEAS, the detailed features of which remain, for the time being, unknown. The secrecy of the preparatory work concerning the EEAS shows the sensitivity, but also the importance, of the setting up of this new service. A skilful High Representative backed by a well-functioning EEAS might be able to effectively use his 'indirect' tool to unlock the principle of unanimity and open the gate for decisions by QMV in the Council on CFSP matters.

To be sure, the wide gap between CFSP and the other fields was essentially the same in the Constitution because the Lisbon Treaty incorporates all substantive modifications envisaged by the Constitution on the Union's external action. But the emphasis in the Lisbon Treaty on this gap (e.g. formal separation of CFSP and Declarations 13 and 14) as well as the title change from Minister to High Representative, reveal the unwillingness of some Member States, which are still in the driving seat of the CFSP, to be co-piloted by the High Representative in the CFSP area. Therefore, from a political rather than a legal viewpoint, the Lisbon Treaty might offer less hope (or is just more realistic) than the Constitution that coherence in the Union's external action will soon be reached.

What is more, political tensions and differences in points of view during the negotiation of the Lisbon Treaty have resulted in provisions that still leave much open to interpretation. The drafters of the Lisbon Treaty missed the opportunity to clarify issues that were already ambiguous in the Constitution. For example, the legal basis for the conclusion of international agreements may be read as going beyond what is currently stated in the case-law and allowing external action to achieve one of the objectives of the Union even without any internal competence. Furthermore, even if we argue that primacy does not extend to CFSP matters, the phrasing of the Declaration on primacy remains ambiguous. Such uncertainties are obviously not conducive to effective external action by the Union. Apparently, the Member States could only find 'unity within obscurity'.

References

David Allen (2004), So who will speak for Europe? The Constitutional Treaty and coherence in the EU external relations, in: CFSP Forum 2 (2004), No. 5, 1-7.

Sven Biscop (2008), *Permanent Structured Cooperation and the future of ESDP* (= Egmont Paper 20), Brussels (Academia Press) 2008 (available at: http://www.irri-kiib.be/paperegm/ep20.pdf).

Ricardo Gosalbo Bono (2006), Some Reflections on the CFSP Legal Order, in: Common Market Law Review 43 (2006), 337-394.

Barbara Brandtner / Alan Rosas (1998), Human Rights and the External Relations of the European Community: An Analysis of Doctrine and Practice, in: European Journal of International Law 9 (1998), 468-490.

Ian Brownlie (2003), Principles of Public International Law, Oxford (Oxford University Press) [6]2003.

Gráinne de Búrca (2008), Reflections on the path from the Constitutional Treaty to the Lisbon Treaty, (= Jean Monnet Working Paper 03/08), New York / NY 2008 (available at http://www.jeanmonnetprogram.org/papers/08/080301.html).

Enzo Cannizzaro (2002), The Scope of EU Foreign Power: Is the EC Competent to Conclude Agreements with Third States including Human Rights Clauses?, in: *Enzo Cannizzaro* (ed.), The European Union as an Actor in International Relations, The Hague (Kluwer) 2002, 297-319.

CEPS, EGMONT and EPC (2007), Joint Study, The Treaty of Lisbon: Implementing the institutional innovations, Brussels, November 2007 (available at: http://shop.ceps.be/downfree.php? item_id=1554).

Olivier Corten / Pierre Klein (eds.) (2006), Les conventions de Vienne sur le droit des traités, Brussels (Bruylant) 2006.

Common Market Law Review (2005), Editorial Comments: The CFSP under the EU Constitutional Treaty – Issues of depillarization', in: Common Market Law Review 42 (2005), No. 2, 325-329.

Tim Corthaut (2005), An Effective Remedy for All? Paradoxes and Controversies in Respect of Judicial Protection in the Field of CFSP under the European Constitution, in: Tilburg Foreign Law Review 12 (2005), 110-144.

Tim Corthaut (2008), Plus ça change, plus c'est la même chose? A comparison with the Constitutional Treaty, in: Maastricht Journal of European and Comparative Law 15 (2008), 21-34.

Per Cramér (2005), Does the Codification of the Principle of Supremacy Matter?, in: *Giulia Amato / Hervé Bribosia / Bruno de Witte* (eds.), Cambridge Yearbook of European Legal Studies (Cambridge University Press) 2005, 57-79.

Marise Cremona (1996), Human Rights and Democracy Clauses in the EC's Trade Agreements, in: *David O'Keeffe / Nicholas Emiliou* (eds.), The European Union and World Trade Law: After the Uruguay Round, Chichester (Wiley) 1996, 62-77.

Marise Cremona (2001), A Policy of Bits and Pieces? The Common Commercial Policy after Nice, in: Cambridge Yearbook of European Legal Studies, Cambridge (Cambridge University Press) 2001, 61-91.

Marise Cremona (2003), The Draft Constitutional Treaty: External Relations and External Action, in: Common Market Law Review 40 (2003), 1347-1366.

Marise Cremona (2004), The Union as a global actor: roles, models and identity, in: Common Market Law Review 41 (2004), 553-573.

Marise Cremona (2007), *The Union's External Action: Constitutional Perspectives,* in: *Giulio Amato / Hervé Bribosia / Bruno de Witte* (eds.), Genesis and Destiny of the European Constitution, Brussels (Bruylant) 2007, 1173-1218.

Sophie Dagand (2008), The impact of the Lisbon Treaty on CFSP and ESDP, (= European Security Review 37), Brussels, March 2008 (available at: http://www.isis-europe.org/pdf/2008 _artrel _150_esr37tol-mar08.pdf).

Alan Dashwood (2005), The EU Constitution – What Will Really Change?, in: Cambridge Yearbook of European Legal Studies, Cambridge (Cambridge University Press) 2005, 33-56.

Udo Diedrichs (2003), The Provisions on ESDP in the Constitutional Treaty: No revolution in Military Affairs, in: CFSP Forum 1 (2003), No. 1, 4-5.

Udo Diedrichs (2004), Flexibility in ESDP: From the Convention to the IGC and Beyond, in: CFSP Forum 2 (2004), No. 5, 1-5.

Simon Duke (2004), The European External Action Service: a Diplomatic Service in the Making?, in: CFSP Forum 2 (2004), No. 4, 4-7.

Martin R. Eaton (1994), Common Foreign and Security Policy, in: *David O'Keeffe / Patrick M. Twomey* (eds.), Legal issues of the Maastricht Treaty, London (Chancery) 1994, 215-225.

Piet Eeckhout (2004), External Relations of the European Union – Legal and Constitutional Foundations, Oxford (Oxford University Press) 2004.

Piet Eeckhout (2005), Does Europe's Constitution Stop at the Water's Edge? Law and Policy of the EU's External Relations, Groningen (Europa Law Publishing) 2005.

European Policy Centre (ed.) (2007), The EU Foreign Service: how to build a more effective common policy (= EPC Working Paper No. 28), Brussels, November 2007 (available at http://www.epc.eu/).

Giorgio Gaja (1983), The European Community's Rights and Obligations under Mixed Agreements, in: *David O'Keeffe / Henry*

G. *Schermers* (eds.), Mixed Agreements, Deventer (Kluwer) 1983, 133-140.

Angelika Hable (2005), The European Constitution: Changes in the Reform of Competences with a Particular Focus on the External Dimension (= Europainstitut Wirtschaftsuniversität Wien Working Paper No 67), Vienna, March 2005.

Trevor Hartley (2001), International Law and the Law of the European Union – A Reassessment, in: British Yearbook of International Law 72 (2001), 1-35.

Christopher Hill (2003), A Foreign Minister without a Foreign Ministry – or with too many?, in: CFSP Forum 1 (2003), No. 1, 1-2.

Mustafa T. Karayigit (2006), Why and to What Extent a Common Interpretative Position for Mixed Agreements?, in: European Foreign Affairs Review 11 (2006), 445-469.

Markus Krajewski (2005), External Trade Law and the Constitution Treaty: Towards a Federal and More Democratic Common Commercial Policy?, in: Common Market Law Review 42 (2005), 91-127.

Sebastian Kurpas (2007), The Treaty of Lisbon – How much 'Constitution' is left? – an overview of the main challenges (= CEPS Policy Brief 147), Brussels, December 2007.

Nikolaos Lavranos (2007), UN Sanctions and Judicial Review, in: Nordic Journal of International Law 76 (2007), 1-17.

Koen Lenaerts (2004), Structuurelementen van de Unie volgens de Grondwet voor Europa, in: Sociaal-Economische Wetgeving (2004), 400-411.

Koen Lenaerts / Piet van Nuffel, Constitutional Law of the European Union, London (Sweet & Maxwell), ²2005.

James Mackie / Heather Baser / Jonas Frederikson / Oliver Hasse (2003), Ensuring that Development Cooperation Matters in the New Europe, Brussels (European Centre for Development Policy Management) 2003.

Antonio Missiroli (2007), Introduction: A tale of two pillars – and an arch, in: 'The EU Foreign Service: how to build a more effective common policy (= EPC Working Paper 28), Brussels, November 2007, 9-27.

Esa Paasivirta / Alan Rosas (2002), Sanctions, Countermeasures and Related Actions in the External Relations of the EU: A Search for Legal Framework, in: *Enzo Cannizzaro* (ed.), The European Union as an Actor in International Relations, The Hague (Kluwer) 2002, 207-218.

Ricardo Passos / Stephan Marquardt (2007), International Agreements – Competences, Procedures and Judicial Control, in: *Giulio Amato / Hervé Bribosia / Bruno de Witte* (eds.), Genesis and Destiny of the European Constitution, Brussels (Bruylant) 2007, 875-918.

Steve Peers (2007), Salvation Outside the Church: Judicial Protection in the Third Pillar after the *Pupino* and *Segi* Judgements, in: Common Market Law Review 44 (2007), 894-902.

Gerrard Quille (2008), The Lisbon Treaty and its implications for CFSP / ESDP (= Briefing Paper Directorate General External Policies of the Union), Brussels, February 2008.

Laura Rayner (2005), The EU Foreign Ministry and Union Embassies, London (The Foreign Policy Centre) June 2005 (available at: http://fpc.org.uk/fsblob/499.pdf).

Jean de Ruyt (2005), A Minister for a European Foreign Policy (= Robert Schuman Centre, Policy Paper No. 05/03), San Domenico 2005.

Eva Steinberger (2006), The WTO Treaty as a Mixed Agreement: Problems with the EC's and the EC Member States' Membership of the WTO, in: European Journal of International Law 17 (2006), 837-862.

United Kingdom (2008a), House of Commons, Foreign Affairs Committee, Foreign Policy Aspects of the Lisbon Treaty (Third Report of Session 2007-08) London, January 2008.

United Kingdom (2008b), House of Commons, Defence Committee, The Future of NATO and European Defence (Ninth Report of Session 2007-08) London, March 2008.

Wolfgang Wessels (2004), A saut constitutionnel out of an intergovernmental trap? The provisions of the Constitutional Treaty for the Common Foreign, Security and Defence policy, in: *Joseph H. H. Weiler / Christopher L. Eisgruber* (eds.), Altneuland: The EU Constitution in a Contextual Perspective (= Jean Monnet Working Paper 5/04), New York, November

2004 (available at: http:// www.jeanmonnetprogram.org/ papers/04/040501-17.html).

Jan Wouters (2002), De Europese Unie als internationale actor na het Verdrag van Nice, in: Nederlands Tijdschrift voor Europees Recht 2002, 62-70.

Jan Wouters (2004), The Union Minister for Foreign Affairs: Europe's Single Voice or Trojan Horse?, in: *Jaap W. de Zwaan / Jan H. Jans / Frans A. Nelissen* (eds.), The European Union. An Ongoing Process of Integration. Liber Amicorum Alfred E. Kellermann, The Hague (T.M.C. Asser Press) 2004, 77-86.

Jan Wouters / André Nollkaemper / Erika de Wet (eds.) (2008), The Europeanisation of International Law. The Status of International Law in the EU and Member States, The Hague (T.M.C. Asser Press) 2008.

Christine Kaddous

Role and position of the High Representative of the Union for Foreign Affairs and Security Policy under the Lisbon Treaty

The creation of the function of the "High Representative of the Union for Foreign Affairs and Security Policy" (the "High Representative") in Article 18 TEU-L appears to be one of the newest aspects introduced by the Lisbon Treaty.[1] This new position com-

---

1   Article 18 of the consolidated version of the Treaty on European Union, as it will result from the amendments introduced by the Treaty of Lisbon, signed on 13 December 2007 in Lisbon. The consolidated versions of the Treaty on European Union and of the Treaty on the Functioning of the European Union, together with the annexes and protocols thereto are published in [2008] OJ C 115/1.

bines the competences of the present High Representative for the Common Foreign and Security Policy and of the Commissioner for External Relations. In fact the Lisbon Treaty includes practically the same provisions regarding the Common Foreign and Security policy (CFSP) and the European Security and Defence Policy (ESDP) as the Treaty establishing a Constitution for Europe, with only minor changes. The "Union Minister for Foreign Affairs" is renamed "High Representative". The change in the title is purely cosmetic or purely symbolic in the sense that it aims to dispel the fears related to the terms evoking the image of a 'constitution' or of a 'state' that led in part to the objections raised in France and in the Netherlands to the Constitutional Treaty.

Apart from the change in the title of the High Representative, two new declarations on CFSP are attached to the Lisbon Treaty (13 and 14).[2] They underline that the new provisions on CFSP, on the creation of the function of High Representative and on the European External Action Service "do not affect the responsibilities of the Member States, as they currently exist, for the formulation and conduct of their foreign policy nor of their national representation in third countries and international organisations". It also recalls that the provisions on CSDP do not "prejudice the specific character of the security and defence policy of the Member States" and confirm "the primary responsibility of the Security Council and of its Members for the maintenance of international peace and security". Declaration No. 14 stresses that the new provisions will not affect the "existing legal basis, responsibilities, and powers of each Member State in relation to the formulation and conduct of its foreign policy, its national diplomatic service, relations with third countries and participation in international organisations, including a Member State's membership of the Security Council of the United Nations". It also reiterates that no new powers in this domain are given to either the Commission or the European Parliament.

The content of these two declarations is restrictive. Even if they only state the existing norms, they do however reflect the political will of the Member States to retain the existing differences

---

2   Declarations No. 13 and 14 concerning the common foreign and security policy, annexed to the Final Act of the Intergovernmental Conference which adopted the Treaty of Lisbon signed on 13 December 2007.

between the EU pillars and to prevent the reforms from resulting in a 'communitarisation' of the CFSP, which could in theory be a consequence of the dual role of the High Representative.

As for the rest, the Lisbon Treaty reiterates the main changes already provided for in the Constitutional Treaty in the field of foreign policy.[3]

The aim of this contribution is to examine the role and position of the High Representative in the external action of the Union in order to ascertain whether the expectations for improvement have been met in respect of this area of the Lisbon Treaty. At the outset of the work of the European Convention on the Future of Europe, three primary needs were clearly expressed in relation to foreign policy: first, the need for greater coherence between different EU and EC external policies, second the need for greater co-ordination between EU / EC and Member States' external policies and finally, the need for a stronger projection of unity abroad. After an analysis of the appointment procedure of the High Representative and of his or her functions we will then (I.) examine his or her relations with the main EU institutions as well as with the Member States (II.) before giving a general appraisal of what is considered to be one of the most striking amendments to the existing framework made by the Lisbon Treaty (III.).

I. Appointment and Functions of the High Representative

The appointment procedure of the High representative involves the participation of different organs active in the field of EU external action. Examining this procedure helps us to better understand the role and position of the High Representative as they result from the Lisbon Treaty as well as the solutions that had to be found in order to respect the institutional balance established by the Treaties in the CFSP and in the other fields of external relations.

---

3   On the Union Minister for Foreign Affairs, see comments on the corresponding provision in the Constitutional Treaty (Article I-28), notably *Sobrino* (2007); *Cremer* (2006); *Maddalon* (2005); *Delcourt et al.* (2005); *Ponzano* (2007); *Cremona* (2003); *Thym* (2004). For an appraisal of the European Union's external action after the Lisbon Treaty, see *Kaddous* (2008).

A. The Beginning and End of the High Representative's mandate

Due to his or her 'double hat', the appointment procedure is complex. The High Representative shall be appointed by the European Council, acting by a qualified majority, with the agreement of the President of the Commission. The European Parliament also has a part in the appointment procedure. The High Representative, in being one of the Vice-Presidents of the Commission, is subject to a vote of consent by the European Parliament.[4]

There is no indication in the Treaty as regards the High Representative's term of office. It would however make sense to assume that he or she shall have a term of five years like the other members of the European Commission considering that the High Representative will be a member of the College.

According to Article 18 TEU-L, the High Representative's mandate may be brought to an end by a decision of the European Council taken on the basis of a qualified majority vote. At the same time, the President of the Commission may request that the High Representative resign in accordance with Article 17, paragraph 6, TEU-L. In this case, the procedure laid down in Article 18 is applicable and the decision is taken by the European Council. Furthermore, the European Parliament may vote on a motion of censure. If such a motion is carried, the members of the Commission shall resign as a body according to Article 17, paragraph 8, TEU-L and the High Representative shall then resign from the duties that he or she carries out in the Commission. Does this mean that the High Representative nonetheless retains his or her position as chairperson of the Foreign Affairs Council? The Lisbon Treaty makes no mention of this. In principle, the answer should be positive. He or she should retain the position in the Council until the appointment of the new Commission.

It appears that the involvement of different actors in the appointment procedure may explain the possible allegiance of the High Representative to different institutions. This conclusion will follow from the analysis concerning the different functions that he or she will have to fulfil.

---

4   Article 17 (7) TEU-L.

B. Double Hat and Multiple Functions

The High Representative shall conduct the Union's common foreign and security policy under the Council's mandate[5] and preside over the Foreign Affairs Council.[6] He or she shall contribute by the making of proposals to develop the policy areas, which he or she shall carry out as mandated by the Council. The same shall apply to the common security and defence policy.[7] The High Representative will then combine powers of initiative, management and implementation in CFSP matters.

The Foreign Affairs Council is separate from the General Affairs Council. The presidency of the latter and COREPER will be subject to the rotating system and will change every six months.[8] Difficulties may occur in the field of CFSP and CSDP as the General Affairs Council will deal with a number of administrative issues, including budgetary matters relevant for CFSP and CSDP.

At the same time, he or she will be one of the Vice-presidents of the Commission.[9] In this capacity, he or she will ensure the consistency of the Union's external action and be responsible for handling external relations and for co-ordinating other aspects of external action.

According to the formula of 'double hat', the High Representative will combine the responsibilities currently falling to the High representative '*Javier Solana's* current role' and to the Commissioner for External Relations (*Benita Ferrero-Waldner's* current role). However, his or her actions shall be coherent and "co-ordinated". He or she shall be responsible for the co-ordination of the entirety of the Union's external action. He or she shall represent the Union in matters relating to the common foreign and security policy, without prejudice to the powers of the President of the European Council and to those attributed to the Commission in other fields of external action. In fulfilling his or her mandate, the High Representative shall be assisted by a European External Action Service.[10] This service shall work in co-operation with the diplo-

---

5   Article 18 (2) TEU-L.

6   Article 18 (3) TEU-L.

7   Article 18 (2) TEU-L.

8   Article 16 (9) TEU-L.

9   Article 18 (4) TEU-L.

10   Article 27 (3) TEU-L.

matic services of the Member States and shall comprise officials from relevant departments of the General Secretariat of the Council and of the Commission as well as staff seconded from national diplomatic services of the Member States.

In the general procedure provided for the conclusion of international agreements, the High Representative shall submit, where the agreement envisaged relates exclusively or principally to the CFSP, recommendations to the Council, which shall adopt a decision authorising the opening of negotiations and nominating the Union's negotiator or the head of the Union's negotiating team.[11] Furthermore, the High Representative may jointly with the Commission propose to the Council the adoption of restrictive measures against one or more third States as well as against natural or legal persons and groups or non-State entities.[12]

It follows from the above comments that the institutional simplification based on the merging of the two different responsibilities of the current High Representative and of the Commissioner for External Relations does not seem to be accompanied by a simplification in the procedures and methods applicable to external action. The field is still governed by strong intergovernmental mechanisms and there is little room for the Community method. It is as though the pillars had survived the reform brought by the Lisbon Treaty.

II. The Relationship between the High Representative and the European Union's Institutions and with the Member States

According to Article 13 TEU-L, the institutional framework of the Union will comprise seven institutions: the European Parliament, the European Council, the Council, the European Commission and the Court of justice of the European Union. In this section we address the relationship between the High Representative and different institutions as well as with the Member States.

A. Relations with the European Council

The European Council plays a very important role in relation to the High Representative simply as a result of the appointment procedure whereby his or her appointment requires a decision adopted on

---

11   Article 218 (3) TFEU.
12   Article 215 (1 and 2) TFEU.

the basis of qualified majority with the agreement of the President of the Commission.[13]

The very tight link between the European Council and the High Representative may also be explained by the fact that during his or her mandate, the latter shall take part in the work of the European Council. He or she will sit beside the Heads of State or Government of the Member States, together with the President and the President of the Commission.[14]

Under the Lisbon Treaty, the relations between the High Representative and the President of the European Council are not clear. According to Article 27, paragraph 1, TEU-L, the High Representative shall contribute through the making of proposals addressing the preparation of the CFSP and shall at the same time ensure implementation of the decisions adopted by the European Council and the Council. How will these two powers of initiative on one hand, and of implementation on the other be combined concretely on a day-to-day basis? No precise answers are given by the texts.

Furthermore as chairperson of the Foreign Affairs Council, the High Representative shall elaborate the Union's external action on the basis of strategic guidelines laid down by the European Council and ensure that the Union's action is consistent.[15]

According to the EU Treaty, the President of the European Council shall, at his or her level and in that capacity, ensure the external representation of the Union on issues concerning the common foreign and security policy, without prejudice to the powers of the High Representative.[16] What is the exact meaning of this? Does it mean that the President of the European Council will represent the Union in CFSP and CSDP summits, in which the Heads of third States participate and the High Representative will represent the Union in other meetings which take place at a lower level? The question remains open and only practice will give us an answer.

B. Relationship with the Commission

The appointment of the High Representative requires the agreement of the President of the Commission.[17] At the same time, he or she

---

13   Article 18 (1) TEU-L.
14   Article 15 (2) TEU-L.
15   Article 16 (6) TEU-L.
16   Article 15 (6) TEU-L.
17   Article 18 (1) TEU-L.

may be requested by the President of the Commission to resign in accordance with Article 17, paragraph 6, TEU-L. In this case, the procedure laid down in Article 18 is applicable and a decision of the European Council is required, acting by a qualified majority. Furthermore, on application by the Commission, the High Representative, as a member of this body, may be retired by the Court of justice if he or she no longer fulfils the conditions required for the performance of his or her duties or if he or she has been guilty of serious misconduct as is provided for in Article 247 TFEU.

It is also provided that the High Representative shall be one of the Vice-Presidents of the Commission.[18] As such, he or she will be responsible for handling external relations and for co-ordinating other aspects of the Union's external action. The High Representative shall, and only in relation to these responsibilities, be bound by Commission procedures to the extent that this is consistent with Article 18, paragraphs 2 and 3, TEU-L.

The High Representative also shares with the Commission the task of external representation of the Union in matters other than CFSP. Indeed, the task of external representation is shared by three entities: the President of the European Council, the Commission and the High Representative. As to the idea of improving EU external representation in the world and to the question of *Henry Kissinger* joke "Europe … what telephone number?", the Union will go from a situation with no phone number to one with at least three phone numbers. Should the new situation be considered better in terms of the projection of unity abroad?

In the field of CFSP, the High Representative, or the High Representative with the Commission's support, may refer any question relating to the CFSP to the Council and may submit to it initiatives or proposals as appropriate.[19] This is fundamental. As we know, the right of initiative is essential because it gives its holder a tremendous power in the definition of policy and in this way it rests mainly with the High Representative.

In the economic aspects of the external action, according to Article 215 TFEU which deals with restrictive measures that may be adopted to interrupt or reduce, in part or completely, economic or financial relations with one or more third states, the Council acts by a qualified majority on a joint proposal from the High Repre-

---

18   Articles 18 (4) and 17 (4 and 5) TEU-L.

19   Article 30 (1) TEU-L.

sentative and the Commission to adopt the necessary measures. Here again, the right of proposal is attributed to the High Representative, but is systematically shared with the Commission.

In the procedure for concluding international agreements, the Commission or the High Representative where the agreement envisaged relates exclusively or principally to the CFSP shall submit recommendations to the Council which shall adopt the decision authorising the opening of the negotiations and the nominating of the Unions' negotiator or the head of the Union's negotiating team.[20] In the same way, it is on a proposal of the Commission or the High Representative that the Council shall adopt a decision suspending the application of an agreement and establishing the positions to be adopted on the Union's behalf in a body set up by an agreement. This occurs when that body is called upon to adopt acts having legal effects with the exception of acts supplementing or amending the institutional framework of the agreement.[21]

Finally, the High Representative and the Commission together are responsible for the implementation of the Union's relations with international organisations, such as the organs of the United Nations and its specialised agencies, the Council of Europe, the Organisation for Security and Co-operation in Europe and the Organisation for Economic Co-operation and Development.[22]

C. Relationship with the European Parliament

The role of the European Parliament in the appointment procedure of the High Representative and of the other Commissioners is important. They are subject as a body to a vote of consent by the Parliament.[23] Furthermore, this institution has the right to pass a motion of censure on the activities of the Commission. If such a motion is carried, the members of the Commission shall resign as a body according to Article 17, paragraph 8, TEU-L and the High Representative shall resign from the duties that he or she carries out in the Commission.

The High Representative shall regularly consult the European Parliament on the main aspects and the basic choices of the CFSP and inform it of how those policies are evolving. He or she shall

---

20   Article 218 (3) TEU-L.

21   Article 218 (9) TFEU.

22   Article 220 (2) TFEU.

23   Article 17 (7) TEU-L.

ensure that the views of the Parliament are duly taken into consideration.[24] At the same time, the Parliament may ask questions to the Council or make recommendations to it and to the High Representative. Twice a year the Parliament shall hold a debate on progress in implementing the CFSP as well as the CSDP.

Furthermore, the European Parliament may exercise political control through its budgetary authority with regard to the CFSP issues where an action of the Union is charged to the EU budget.[25] The importance of such a power should not be underestimated.

D. Relationship with the Council

Although the Council is not involved in the appointment procedure of the High Representative, it is interesting to note that according to Article 247 TFEU and on application by this institution acting by a simple majority, the High Representative, as a member of the Commission, may be retired by the Court of justice if he or she no longer fulfils the conditions required for the performance of his or her duties or if he or she has been guilty of serious misconduct.

Otherwise, the High Representative will preside over the Council for Foreign Affairs. He or she will participate in the elaboration of the Union's external action in that respect. The Council will work on the basis of strategic guidelines laid down by the European Council and ensure that the Union's action is consistent.

According to Article 21, paragraph 3, the Union shall ensure consistency between the different areas of its external action and between these and its other policies. The Council and the Commission, assisted by the High Representative, shall ensure consistency and shall co-operate to that effect. The Council and the High Representative shall ensure compliance with the spirit of loyalty and mutual solidarity in the field of CFSP.[26] In the same manner, both shall ensure the unity, consistency and effectiveness of Union action.[27]

The High Representative, chairing the Foreign Affairs Council, shall contribute through his or her proposals towards the prepara-

---

24   Article 36 (1) TEU-L.

25   Article 14 (1) TEU-L.

26   Article 24 (3) TEU-L.

27   Article 26 (2) TEU-L.

tion of the CFSP and shall ensure implementation of the decisions adopted by the European Council and the Council.[28]

According to Article 31, paragraph 2, in the case of a declaration by a member of the Council to the effect that, for vital and stated reasons of national policy, it intends to oppose the adoption of a decision to be taken by qualified majority, a vote shall not be taken. Here, the High Representative will, in close consultation with the Member State involved, search for a solution acceptable to it. This is clearly a mediation role given to the High Representative. If he or she does not succeed, the Council may, acting by a qualified majority, request that the matter be referred to the European Council for decision by unanimity.

Under the Lisbon Treaty there is the possibility, on proposal by the High Representative, for the Council to appoint a special representative with a mandate in relation to particular issues. The special representative shall carry out his or her mandate under the authority of the High Representative.[29]

In the field of CFSP, a Political and Security Committee shall monitor the international situation and contribute to the definition of policies by delivering opinions to the Council at the request of the Council, the High Representative or on its own initiative. This Committee shall also monitor the implementation of agreed policies, without prejudice to the powers of the High Representative. It also exercises, under the responsibility of the Council and of the High Representative, the political control and strategic direction of crisis management operations referred to in Article 43.[30]

The Council shall adopt a decision establishing the specific procedures for guaranteeing rapid access to appropriations in the Union budget for urgent financing of initiatives in the framework of the CFSP, and in particular for preparatory activities for the tasks referred to Articles 42, paragraph 1 and Article 43 related to missions outside the European Union for peace-keeping, conflict prevention and strengthening international security. The preparatory activities which are not charged to the budget of the Union shall be financed by a start-up fund made up of Member States' contributions. The decisions establishing the procedures for setting up and financing the start up fund, for administering the start-up fund and

---

28   Article 27 (1) TEU-L.

29   Article 33 TEU-L.

30   Article 38 TEU-L.

the financial control procedures are adopted by the Council on a proposal from the High Representative.[31]

Decisions relating to CSDP, including those initiating a mission as referred to in Article 42, shall be adopted by the Council acting unanimously on a proposal from the High Representative on an initiative from a Member State.[32]

When the European Union is to make use of civilian and military means in the tasks referred to in Article 42, paragraph 1, the Council shall adopt the relevant decisions as regards the definition of the objectives, scope and general conditions of the implementation. In that respect, the High Representative, acting under the authority of the Council and in close and constant contact with the Political and Security Committee, shall ensure co-ordination of the civilian and military aspects of the tasks.[33] The High Representative will then play a coordinating role in that respect.

The Member States wishing to participate in the permanent structured co-operation and which fulfil the criteria and have made the commitments on military capabilities set out in the Protocol on permanent structured co-operation, shall notify their intention to the Council as well as to the High Representative.[34]

E. Relationship with the Court of Justice of the European Union

The CFSP is subject to specific rules and procedures.[35] The Court of justice shall have no jurisdiction with respect to these provisions, with the exception of its jurisdiction to monitor compliance with Article 40 TEU-L and to review the legality of certain decisions as provided for by Article 275, paragraph 2, TFEU. So the reduced role of the Court of justice is maintained under the new Treaties.

As far as Article 40 TEU-L is concerned, the Court shall ensure that the implementation of CFSP does not affect the applica-

---

31   Article 41(3) TEU-L.

32   Article 42 (4) TEU-L.

33   See Article 43 TEU-L.

34   Articles 42 (6) and 46 (1) TEU-L. See also the Protocol on the permanent structured co-operation established by Article 42 of the Treaty on European Union.

35   On the decision making rules in CFSP matters, see Article 31 TEU-L. For comments on the corresponding provision in the Constitutional Treaty (Article I-40), see e.g. *Auvret-Finck* (2007); *Cremer* (2006).

tion of the procedures and the extent of the powers of the institutions laid down by the Treaties for the exercise of the Union competences referred to in Articles 3 to 6 TFEU.[36]

According to Article 263, the Court shall review the legality of legislative acts, of acts of the Council, of the Commission and of the European Central Bank, other than recommendations and opinions, and of acts of the European Parliament and of the European Council intended to produce legal effects vis-à-vis third parties. At the same time, any natural or legal persons will be entitled to institute proceedings against a regulatory act which is of direct concern to them and does not entail implementing measures. This last mentioned possibility is important in relation to the cases of restrictive measures that may be adopted against natural or legal persons on the basis of Article 215, paragraph 2, TFEU.[37]

Furthermore, as provided for by Article 247 TFEU the Court of justice is the authority that may be referred to in order to retire the High Representative as a member of the Commission, on application of this institution or on application by the Council, if he or she no longer fulfils the conditions required for the performance of his or her duties or if he or she has been guilty of serious misconduct.

F. Relationship with the Member States

The Member States of the European Union do not intervene strictly speaking in the appointment procedure of the High Representative, but exert influence through their Head of State or Government sitting in the European Council. Therefore the links between these two 'entities' are very tight. The CFSP shall be put into effect by the

---

36   The Court held that "[i]t is the task of the Court to ensure that acts which, according to the Council, fall within the scope of Title VI of the Treaty on European Union do not encroach upon the powers conferred by the EC Treaty on the Community" and it also referred to its previous case-law. See Case 176/03 *Commission v Council* [2005] ECR I-7879, para 39 as well as Case C-170/96 *Commission v Council* [1998] ECR I-2763. This case law may be applicable by analogy in the field of CFSP and in relation to the new Article 40.

37   See, eg, Case T-228/02 *Organisation des Modjahedines du peuple d'Iran v Conseil* [2006] ECR II-4665 ; Case T-306/01 *Yusuf* [2005] ECR II-3533 ; Case T-315/01 *Kadi* [2005] ECR II-3649. An appeal is pending in the last mentioned case in which the opinion of the Advocate General was rendered on 18 January 2008.

High Representative and by the Member States in accordance with the Treaties.

A Member State, the High Representative or the High Representative with the support of the Commission may refer any question relating to the CFSP to the Council and may submit to it initiatives or proposals as appropriate.[38] This means that the right of proposal belongs to the Member States as well as to the High Representative or to the High Representative and the Commission depending on the circumstances.

Before undertaking any action on the international scene or entering into any commitment which could affect the Union's interests, each Member State shall consult the others within the European Council or the Council. Member States shall ensure that the Union is able to assert its interests and values on the international scene. Member States shall show mutual solidarity. When the European Council or the Council has defined a common approach of the Union within the above meaning, the High Representative and the Ministers of Foreign Affairs of the Member States shall co-ordinate their activities within the Council.[39]

According to Article 34 TEU-L, the Member States shall co-ordinate their action in international organisations and at international conferences. They shall uphold the Union's positions in such forums. The High Representative shall organise this co-ordination. In international organisations and at international conferences where not all the Member States participate, those which do take part shall uphold the Union's positions.

Member States represented in international organisations or international conferences where not all the Member States participate shall keep the other Member States and the High Representative informed of any matter of common interest.

Member States which are also members of the United Nations Security Council will consult and keep the other Member States and the High Representative fully informed. Member States which are members of the Security Council will, in the execution of their functions, defend the positions and the interests of the Union, without prejudice to their responsibilities under the provisions of the United Nations Charter.

---

38   Article 30 TEU-L.

39   Article 32 (1 and 2) TEU-L.

When the Union has defined a position on a subject which is on the United Nations Security Council agenda, those Member States which sit on the Security Council shall request that the High Representative be invited to present the Union's position.[40]

Finally, the Treaty provides for co-operation between the diplomatic and consular missions of the Member States and the Union's delegations in third countries and international conferences and their representations in international organisations in ensuring that the decisions defining Union's positions and actions adopted in the CFSP are complied with and implemented.[41]

According to Article 221 TFEU, Union delegations, which are placed under the authority of the High Representative, shall act in close co-operation with Member States' diplomatic and consular missions.

III. Concluding Remarks

It is very difficult to give a general appraisal of the amendments brought about by the Lisbon Treaty in the field of CFSP and specifically in relation to the creation of the new High Representative due to the fact that it is not possible to make accurate predictions on the basis of the texts. It is practice that will determine and develop the rules and procedures. Therefore, the following comments consist of observations and questions which attempt to assess whether the felt needs for improvement in the creation of the function of High Representative have been satisfied.

First, it remains uncertain whether greater unity and coherence will be projected on the international scene. The task of external representation is shared by the High Representative, the President of the European Council and the Commission. Three entities! This comes out at least three phone numbers. Much will depend on the personality of the High Representative as well as on the personalities of the President of the European Council and of the President of the Commission and on the 'chemistry' between them. This will determine whether or not they work well together. In our view, it is preferable that the question of 'unity and coherence' of external representation should be examined in terms of the credibility of the

---

40   Article 34 (2), subparagraph 3, TEU-L.

41   Article 35 TEU-L.

Union on the international scene rather than on the basis of the internal allocation of powers between the entities involved.

Second, it is true that the High Representative with his or her double hat and dual role in the Council and in the Commission makes him or her answerable to both institutions. However, the legitimacy of the High Representative seems to be more closely linked to the Council than to the Commission as we have seen. The main question that follows from this situation is whether the High Representative will be able to play his or her role as 'bridge builder' in a field where the Member States are reluctant to diminish their influence as this results from the declarations Nos. 13 and 14.

Third, there are no major changes in the use of procedures in CFSP and CSDP fields in comparison with the present legal situation. This area of EU law is still governed by a strongly intergovernmental decision-making process. In relation to this, there are strong doubts about the influence or the extension of the Community method in these fields of external action. In that respect, the Lisbon Treaty does not bring much simplification in its maintenance of a similar situation as that prevailing today under the second pillar of the TEU-L. Clearly the merging of different functions in the High Representative does not necessarily lead to a merging of the policies. Therefore, a great deal of pragmatism will be needed in order to ensure co-ordination and coherence in external action.

References

Josiane Auvret-Finck (2007), Article I-40, in: *Laurence Burgorgue-Larsen / Anne Levade / Fabrice Picod* (eds.), Traité établissant une Constitution pour l'Europe – Commentaire article par article, Vol. 1, Brussels (Bruylant) 2007, 517-528.

Hans Joachim Cremer (2006), Artikel I-40, in: *Christian Calliess / Matthias Ruffert* (eds.), Verfassung der Europäischen Union, Munich (Beck) 2006.

Marise Cremona (2003), The Draft Constitutional Treaty: External Relations and External Action, in: Common Market Law Review 40 (2003), 1347-1366.

Barbara Delcourt / Eric Remacle / Catherine Smits / Gaëlle Dusepulchre / Inge Govaere / Rodolphe Munoz (2005),

L'action extérieure de l'Union, in: *Marianne Dony / Emmanuelle Bribosia* (eds.), Commentaire de la Constitution de l'Union européenne, Brussels (Editions de l'Université) 2005, 355-430.

Christine Kaddous (2008), L'action extérieure de l'Union européenne après Lisbonne: adaptations ou novations majeures?, in: Annuaire de droit européen, Vol. IV, Brussels (Bruylant) 2008 (forthcoming).

Philippe Maddalon (2005), L'action extérieure de l'Union européenne, in: Revue Trimestrielle de Droit Européen 40 2005, No. 2, 493-532.

Paolo Ponzano (2007), Le traité de Lisbonne: l'Europe sort de sa crise institutionnelle, in: Revue de Droit de l'Union Européenne 2007, No. 3, 569-584.

José Manuel Sobrino (2007), Article I-28, in: *Laurence Burgorgue-Larsen / Anne Levade / Fabrice Picod* (eds.), Traité établissant une Constitution pour l'Europe – Commentaire article par article, Vol. 1, Brussels (Bruylant) 2007, 365-383.

Daniel Thym (2004), Reforming Europe's Common Foreign and Security Policy, in: European Law Journal 10 (2004), 5-22.

Marcel Kau

Justice and Home Affairs in the European Constitutional Process – Keeping the Faith and Substance of the Constitution

The failure of the Constitutional Treaty (CT) in 2005 could very well have been the end of the European constitutional process for a long time.[1] Too harsh was the impression of the declining votes in France and the Netherlands and too opaque the motives of those who voted against the Treaty. Even today it appears surprising that the project of a European Constitution was resumed so quickly after the Constitutional Treaty failed. There is surely a host of reasons why this became possible. However, among the most important ones, two are very striking: first of all, the project was favoured by the skilful and able approach of the German Presidency, which recovered as much as possible from the Constitutional Treaty of 2004 and abandoned most of the disturbing provisions which ulti-

---

1   Cf. on the European Constitutional Process: *Oppermann* (2007); *Oppermann* (2006); *Fischer* (2006); *Geiger* (2006); *Einem* (2006); *Stark* (2007), *Ziller* (2005); *Amato / Ziller* (2007).

mately led to its rejection among European citizens.[2] The second even more important aspect was the alluring political success which would be bestowed upon those governments finalising the long-lasting and prestigious endeavour of a European constitution. The goal of a consolidated and further developed European constitutional framework was too tempting for the current political leaders in Europe (especially those who were not involved in the constitutional process of 2004) to resist the opportunities related to this project. This is also the reason why the setback caused by the negative Irish referendum of 12 June 2008 will presumably not bury the project of the Lisbon Treaty. However, there is the need of negotiations between the Member States which ultimately will result in some delay of the procedure. Hence, the Treaty will not enter into force on 1 January 2009, but probably later.

For the field of Justice and Home Affairs it has to be added that the possibilities conferred by the current set of intergovernmentalist rules have almost been exhausted within recent years. Therefore, the transfer of additional competencies and a supranational mode of decision-making, as specified under the Lisbon Treaty, are needed in order to further develop the existing legal framework and to enhance its shortcomings.[3] The scope of the analysis at hand will mainly be confined to the changes made after the failure of the 2004 Constitutional Treaty and incorporated into the Lisbon Treaty of 2007. The analysis begins with some short introductory remarks (I.) and then - in the second part – it addresses the general structure of the provisions in this field of law (II.). Subsequently, the analysis will focus on the major changes, supplemental modifications and deletions made during the drafting of the Lisbon Treaty (III.). Finally, the conclusions to be drawn from the identified changes and supplementary provisions will be outlined (IV.).

I. Introductory Remarks

The expanded and more detailed rules in the field of Justice and Home Affairs – as laid down in Articles III-257 through III-277 of the Constitutional Treaty – were not in the centre of the controversial discussion on the 'ill-fated' project of European Constitution-

---

2   Cf. *Häberle* (2008), 523.

3   See *Amato / Ziller* (2007), 220.

alism in France and the Netherlands three years ago.[4] The same applies to the Irish referendum in 2008. Although there are, from time to time, issues in the realm of Justice and Home Affairs that reach the public's attention in at least some Member States – like the Commission's Blue Card initiative of September 2007[5] – this field of law lives mostly in the shadows when it comes to public debates on the scope of European constitutional change.[6]

One reason for this is that the provisions on immigration, visa policy and asylum are in many cases assessed as being chiefly of a technical nature, and not worth further analysis. While this is, on the merits, not entirely false, this attitude contrasts strongly with the true impact of the new provisions in Justice and Home Affairs on the Member States' sovereignty and on the everyday life of many third-country nationals and EU-citizens within or beyond the borders of the European Union.

It may be that debates on these issues are the domain of the academic community insofar as it gives room for a more thorough analysis than public discussions would offer. Bearing this in mind, an interesting question arises as to whether the European heads-of-state have even used this remarkable gap between the impact and meaning of provisions on the one hand and the almost complete lack of public attention on the other to expand or supplement the provisions of the 2004 Constitutional Treaty while drafting the Lisbon Treaty of 2007.

One would not lift the veil prematurely in stating that the provisions of the two treaties in the field of Justice and Home Affairs strongly resemble each other in structure and contents. This result is neither very striking nor surprising: considering the fact that the public debate on the 2004 Constitutional Treaty almost entirely ignored subjects of Justice and Home Affairs, there was no real need to question the fundamental rules of this chapter. However, even marginal and slight changes, supplementary provisions and deletions can cast light on the dominant intentions and purposes

---

4   Cf. on the historical background *Mayer* (2007), 1142; *Weber* (2008a), 7; *Weber* (2008b), 55.

5   COM (2007) 637 final.

6   Also intimating this: *Amato / Ziller* (2007), 220 *et seq.* ("...where the European response has not met significant opposition from the citizens, there has been a continuous change").

during the drafting of the Lisbon Treaty and the conclusions drawn from the failure of the 2004 Constitutional Treaty.

In order to focus on the most important modifications introduced by the Lisbon Treaty as compared with the Constitutional Treaty, the specific contents of the provisions on Justice and Home Affairs will not be addressed and outlined in depth. However, it should be noted that the basic change contained in the Constitutional Treaty, which merged the former Title VI of the Treaty on European Union (Arts. 29 to 42 TEU) together with the provisions of Title IV of the Treaty establishing the European Community (Arts. 61 to 69 TEC) under the heading of an 'Area of Freedom, Security and Justice', endures in the Lisbon Treaty.[7] The second most important change relates to the decision-making process in Justice and Home Affairs, as all measures concerning border controls, immigration and asylum are shifted to a qualified majority vote in the Council while the European Parliament is given joint decision-making powers with the introduction of the co-decision procedure.[8] In addition, some very pertinent and important provisions with regard to the relationship between the Constitutional Treaty and the Lisbon Treaty and the changes carried out in the meantime will be also mentioned.

II. General Structure of the Treaties in Comparison

In the Constitutional Treaty, the provisions on Justice and Home Affairs were enshrined in Chapter IV, ranging from Art. III-257 to Art. III-277, with altogether 21 provisions distributed among 5 sections. Similarly, the Lisbon Treaty's provisions on Justice and Home Affairs are located in Title IV, which is separated into 5 chapters of a total of 23 provisions ranging from Art. 67 to Art. 89 of the Treaty on the Functioning of the European Union (TFEU).

This means that, instead of the term "Chapter", the term "Title" is now used, and instead of 5 "sections" there are 5 "chapters" in the TFEU. So there are only minor terminological changes so far, while the mere number of provisions on Justice and Home Affairs remained almost the same: originally 21, now 23. However, the two new provisions deserve a closer look; they will be discussed below in part III.

---

7   Cf. *Weber* (2008a), 55; *Weber* (2008b), 13; *Peers* (2006), 90.

8   Cf. *Peers* (2006), 86.

Additionally, with respect to the general structure of the provisions, a comparison of the headings of the Sections (respectively Chapters) shows that they are identical. The headings are correspondingly the following:

- Section 1 / Chapter 1: *'General Provisions'* with 8 (respectively 10) provisions (Arts. III-256 to III-264 CT, resp. Arts. 67 to 76 TFEU);
- Section 2 / Chapter 2: *'Policies and Border Checks, Asylum and Immigration'* with correspondingly 4 provisions (Arts. III-265 to III-268 CT, respectively Arts. 77 to 80 TFEU);
- Section 3 / Chapter 3: *'Judicial Cooperation in Civil Matters'* with 1 provision in each text (Art. III-269 CT, respectively Art. 81 TFEU);
- Section 4 / Chapter 4: *'Judicial Cooperation in Criminal Matters'* with 5 provisions in each text (Arts. III-270 to III-274 CT, respectively Arts. 82 to 86 TFEU); and
- Section 5 / Chapter 5: *'Police Cooperation'* with 3 provisions in each text (Arts. III-275 to III-277 CT, respectively Arts. 87 to 89 TFEU).

Prima facie, the result of the structural comparison is not very exciting as it shows many corresponding details between the 2004 Constitutional Treaty and the Lisbon Treaty. Yet this result is quite astonishing because it means that the sweeping changes the field of Justice and Home Affairs has undergone in the Constitutional Treaty have almost entirely been maintained. Therefore, the changes between the Constitutional Treaty and the Lisbon Treaty might not be very remarkable, but the changes between the current legal situation in the field of Justice and Home Affairs and the prospective framework of the Lisbon Treaty will be extensive.

III. Major supplemental modifications and changes

Compared with the Constitutional Treaty of 2004, the Lisbon Treaty provides for four major changes and supplemental modifications on the merits and some minor, mostly terminological changes. The analysis below will focus on the more important elements.

A. Return to the original legislative procedure

The first change to mention is the return to the previous legislative forms and procedures, which are laid down in today's Arts. 249 to 256 TEC. As is well known, one of the major obstacles for the ratification of the 2004 Constitutional Treaty, and an important reason for its ultimate failure, were the provisions and concepts indicating the state-like quality of the new European Union (e.g., the flag, anthem, and symbols[9]). These symbolic elements alienated several Member States, and the supposed impending foundation of a European Super-State also put off many EU citizens, especially in France and in the Netherlands. As a result, in drafting the Lisbon Treaty the Member States refrained from any references to the state-like quality of the EU.

The Lisbon Treaty thus entirely abandons those of the Constitutional Treaty's legislative concepts that indicated a state-like legislative branch, replacing the terms 'European laws' or 'framework laws' with the traditional legislative forms of regulations, directives and decisions.[10] Whereas, in Chapter IV of the Constitutional Treaty, there were frequent references to 'European laws' 'framework laws', or to 'European regulations and measures', the Lisbon Treaty now regularly contains the phrase "The European Parliament and the Council, acting in accordance with the ordinary legislative procedure", or it simply refers to 'measures'. These terminological and procedural alterations necessitated a total of 33 changes in the new Title IV to avoid creating the impression that the Lisbon Treaty would also eventually lead to a European state. In this context, it appears less important that this change engendered only minor alterations with respect to the contents of the applicable rules.

In sum, these changes are predominantly an expression of a general intention of the Member States to initiate a new European constitutional process by abandoning any indication of the state-like quality of the new European Union; they are not specifically related to issues of the "area of freedom, security and justice". By contrast, the three major changes between the Constitutional Treaty and the Lisbon Treaty which are described in the following paragraphs are more closely connected with the peculiarities of the field of Justice and Home Affairs.

B. National Security Concerns (Art. 73 TFEU)

The second major change relates to an entirely new provision introduced by the Lisbon Treaty: the new Art. 73 TFEU. This new pro-

---

9   *Häberle* (2008), 537, laments the removal of these symbols, referring to "major losses" ("*Die schwersten inhaltlichen Abstriche*").

10   See *Mayer* (2007), 1172.

vision stipulates the right of the Member States to enter "between themselves" into "such forms of cooperation and coordination as they deem appropriate "in order to safeguard "national security".[11] Obviously, the Member States found it necessary to supplement the statutory framework of the Constitutional Treaty which guaranteed the states' own "exercise of the responsibilities" in Art. 72 TFEU (former Art. III-262 CT) and, in Art. 74 TFEU (former Art. III-263 CT), measures to be adopted by "the Council" to "ensure adminis-trative cooperation" between the Member States.

Indeed the issue of 'national security', which is addressed by the new Art. 73 TFEU, appears to be too important for the Member States to be addressed either by themselves alone or in the rigid organisational scheme of the Council. Furthermore, decisions of the Council with respect to administrative co-operation require a pro-posal of the Commission and the consultation of the European Par-liament. Such decisions thus entail a rather time-consuming proce-dure which, in case of an emergency, might not be fast enough to safeguard the Member States' national security interests. At any rate, it seems that the Member States sought to shift the compe-tencies in the field of Justice and Home Affairs slightly to their side by allowing co-operation or co-ordination outside the organisational framework of the EU, and hence without the involvement of the Council.

At first glance, when seen in the context of Chapter 1, Art. 73 TFEU appears to be a technical addition for reasons of clarification. However, where national security interests are at stake, most Mem-ber States would take all necessary steps which appear to them to be necessary and effective, regardless of what the other Member States or bodies of the EU would advise. Therefore, the opportunity offered by Art. 73 TFEU provides for a procedure which would be self-evident in the case of an emergency. Hence, by insisting on adopting the right to enter into co-operation or co-ordination meas-ures, this supplemental addition to the Constitutional Treaty does not enhance the Member States' sovereignty but rather emphasises their dependence on the explicit authorisation in the European Treaties. The newly adopted Art. 73 CT therefore proves the oppo-site of what was intended by its introduction.

---

11   See *ibid.*, 1170.

C. Combating the financial basis of terrorism (Art. 75 TFEU)

The newly inserted Art. 75 TFEU is a provision authorising the EU to combat terrorism and related activities by taking measures with respect to capital movements and payments. In the Constitutional Treaty, a similar provision was already part of the section on the free movement of capital and payments.[12] By transferring it to the new Title IV, it has become subject to possible British opt-outs, which was ultimately the purpose of the transfer.

Among the examples mentioned in Art. 75 TFEU, there are the freezing of funds, of financial assets and of economic gains, irrespective of the person, group or organisation in question.[13] After all, Art. 75 TFEU in its new context supplements Art. 83 para. 1 subpara. 1 TFEU, which refers in more neutral terms to criminal offences "in the areas of particularly serious crime with a cross-border dimension", including, *inter alia,* "terrorism" (subpara. 2). However, in Art. 83 TFEU, which is one key element of the "judicial cooperation in criminal matters" (Chapter 4), only minimum rules concerning the definition of criminal offences and sanctions are allowed. Therefore, the more palpable measures with respect to capital movements and payments required a more precise competence for the EU, which is now provided by Art. 75 TFEU.

In this context, the provision appears predominantly to be a technical provision when it comes to adopting specific measures against terrorism which now appears appropriately located in Title IV. Notably, this specific rule addresses the financial aspects of terrorism, which are considered to be both very important and vulnerable. Therefore, measures with respect to capital movements and payments are deemed to be very effective for combating terrorism. Furthermore, Art. 75 TFEU conveys the impression of a highly political provision, in that it declares a strong commitment against international terrorism. In this regard, Art. 75 TFEU might address some security concerns of the Member States, and it can also be interpreted as an accommodation directed to the United States, which is of course also actively combating international terrorism.

---

12   Cf. Art. III-160 Constitutional Treaty.

13   Cf. *Weber* (2008a), 55; *Mayer* (2007), 1169.

D. The 'fundamental aspects' exception
and enhanced cooperation

Besides the return to the original legislative forms (under 1.), the two new provisions of Art. 73 TFEU (under 2.) and the transfer of Art. 75 TFEU to Title IV (under 3.), the most crucial change under the Lisbon Treaty has been made simultaneously in three distinct provisions of chapter 4 on 'judicial cooperation in criminal matters', namely in Art. 82 para. 3, Art. 83 para. 3 subpara. 3 and – with slight changes – in Art. 86 para. 1 subparas. 2 and 3 TFEU.

Pursuant to each of these three provisions, when the EU adopts harmonisation measures by establishing minimum rules, or when it is supposed to act unanimously, any Member State can request that a draft be referred to the European Council if it "would affect fundamental aspects of its criminal justice system". In this case, the legislative procedure is suspended. If the Member States find a compromise the rules of the Lisbon Treaty are quite similar to the ones of the 2004 Constitutional Treaty. However, if a compromise is not entered into within four months, there is the chance to save the legislation when "at least nine Member States" wish to establish enhanced co-operation pursuant to Art. 20(2) of the Treaty on European Union, which is currently stipulated in Arts. 11 and 11a of the EC Treaty.

This loophole of 'enhanced co-operation' for a group of at least nine Member States is supposed to reduce the bargaining power and obstructive potential of individual Member States which might feel inclined to invoke the 'fundamental aspects' exception too often if there was no danger of becoming isolated over time. Even though the 'enhanced co-operation' has not been a success lasting recent years, the behaviour of several Member States in the accession process and during the drafting of the Constitutional Treaty (2004) and the Lisbon Treaty (2007) has amply shown the necessity of some kind of a pressurising medium. Otherwise, a union of now 27 Member States runs the risk of becoming inflexible and vulnerable to the obstructive tactics of individual Member States.

IV. Conclusion

The changes and supplementary additions to the Constitutional Treaty brought about by the Lisbon Treaty are indeed of marginal nature. Therefore, the most striking conclusion of the analysis at hand is that the far reaching and sweeping changes between the current statutory framework of the TEU and the EC Treaty on the one hand and the 2004 Constitutional Treaty on the other have almost entirely been maintained. In particular, the Lisbon Treaty reaffirms the merging of Title VI of the TEU and Title IV of the EC Treaty, as well as the changes made to the decision-making process by shifting several measures to a qualified majority vote in the Council and by giving the European Parliament joint decision-making powers by introducing co-decision.

This has to be ascribed – as already pointed out in the introductory remarks – to the fact that the field of Justice and Home Affairs does not attract very much attention from the public because of its rather technical nature. In any case, this should not lead to the conclusion that the Lisbon Treaty does not bring along extensive changes compared to the current legal situation – on the contrary. By maintaining most of the provisions provided for in the failed 2004 Constitutional Treaty, the Lisbon Treaty administers a difficult task which is typical for the whole constitutional process of 2007. One could reduce this approach to the dictum: "How to avoid all harmful references to the foundation of a state-like organisation while keeping as much substance as possible of the Constitution".[14]

In conclusion, the rules now at hand in the Lisbon Treaty constitute a further step in the ongoing development in the field of Justice and Home Affairs. While this area only two decades ago was assessed to be the sole and sovereign domain of the Member States,[15] it has become more and more harmonised over the years. At their heart, the provisions of Title IV of the Lisbon Treaty appear to be an adequate basis for the current challenges with which the European Union is confronted in the realm of Justice and Home Affairs. Their shortcomings will soon be put to the test of experience and emerging practical requirements. Nevertheless, the Lisbon Treaty's provisions on Justice and Home Affairs are more than one could hope for after the failure of the 2004 Constitutional Treaty. Therefore, in order to obtain additional competencies which can be filled within the next years, the Member States have to find a solu-

---

14   In fact, this was almost the motto of the German Presidency in 2007, cf. *Häberle* (2008), 524.

15   Cf. *Hailbronner* (2000), 35 f. ("*domaine réservé*"); *Amato / Ziller* (2007), 220.

tion to overcome the negative result of the Irish referendum of June 2008.

References

Giulio Amato / Jacques Ziller (2007), The European Constitution – Cases and Materials, Cheltenham / Northampton (Elgar) 2007.

Caspar Einem (2006), Die Konventsmethode – Schlussfolgerungen nach zwei Erfahrungen, in: *Hans-Jörg Derra* (ed.), Freiheit, Sicherheit und Recht. Festschrift für Jürgen Meyer zum 70. Geburtstag, Baden-Baden (Nomos) 2006, 27-48.

Joseph Fischer, Grundrechtsschutz – Demokratie – Transparenz – Zur neuen Dimension des Europäischen Verfassungsvertrags, in: *Hans-Jörg Derra* (ed.) Freiheit, Sicherheit und Recht. Festschrift für Jürgen Meyer zum 70. Geburtstag, Baden-Baden (Nomos) 2006, 263-270.

Hansjörg Geiger (2006), Die Justizpolitik im EU-Verfassungsvertrag und die künftige Rechtspolitik, in: *Hans-Jörg Derra* (ed.), Freiheit, Sicherheit und Recht. Festschrift für Jürgen Meyer zum 70. Geburtstag, Baden-Baden (Nomos) 2006, 339-357.

Peter Häberle (2008), Die deutsche EU-Ratspräsidentschaft (1. Januar 2007 bis 30. Juni 2007), in: Jahrbuch für öffentliches Recht NF 56, Tübingen (Mohr Siebeck) 2008, 523-541.

Kay Hailbronner (2000), Immigration and Asylum Law and Policy of the European Union, The Hague/London/Boston (Kluwer) 2000.

Franz C. Mayer (2007), Die Rückkehr der Europäischen Verfassung? Ein Leitfaden zum Vertrag von Lissabon, in: Zeitschrift für ausländisches öffentliches Recht und Völkerrecht 67 (2007), No. 4, 1141-1191.

Thomas Oppermann (2006), Der Europäische Verfassungsvertrag – Legenden und Tatsachen, in: *Hans-Jörg Derra* (ed.), Freiheit, Sicherheit und Recht. Festschrift für Jürgen Meyer zum 70. Geburtstag, Baden-Baden (Nomos) 2006, 281-299.

Thomas Oppermann (2007), Von der Gründungsgemeinschaft zur Mega-Union – eine europäische Erfolgsgeschichte?, in: Deutsches Verwaltungsblatt 122 (2007), 329-336.

Steve Peers (2006), EU Justice and Home Affairs Law, Oxford (Oxford University Press) [2]2006.

Christian Starck (2007), Die europäischen Institutionen und die Nationalstaaten – Die Rechtskultur im Bau Europas, in: *Rainer Pitschas / Arnd Uhle* (eds.), Wege gelebter Verfassung in Recht und Politik: Festschrift für Rupert Scholz zum 70. Geburtstag, Berlin (Duncker & Humblot) 2007, 179-188.

Albrecht Weber (2008a), Migration im Vertrag von Lissabon, in: Zeitschrift für Ausländerrecht und Ausländerpolitik 28 (2008), 55-58.

Albrecht Weber (2008b), Vom Verfassungsvertrag zum Vertrag von Lissabon, in: Europäische Zeitschrift für Wirtschaftsrecht 19 (2008), 7-14.

Jacques Ziller (2005), The European Constitution, The Hague (Kluwer) 2005.

Ingolf Pernice[*]

The Treaty of Lisbon and Fundamental Rights

I. Introduction

When I commented on the Treaty establishing a Constitution for Europe,[1] some years ago, I welcomed it as a major achievement in the constitutional process of the EU not so much because of the substantial changes made with regard to the Treaty of Nice, but essentially due to the fact that the Constitutional Convention and the governments of the Member States had made great efforts to call their baby by its real name: Constitution. Laws were called laws, the person in charge of foreign relations was called Foreign minister, the primacy of European law was expressly recognised and it was agreed that fundamental rights were to be made visible and operational in a legally binding form. Nevertheless,

---

[*]   I would like to express my greatest thanks to my two research assistants, *Ariane Grieser* and *Michael von Landenberg*, for their critical review of the draft and helpful contributions to the present paper.

[1]   *Pernice* (2003); see also *Pernice* (2007).

it was quite clear to everybody that the EU continued to be a supranational organisation and was not developed into a beast which could be qualified as a 'super-state', or to which could be attributed any kind of statehood.

In 2004, however, after the French and Duch referenda, an amazing 'roll-back' campaign was initiated against this attempt at straightforwardness, transparency and simplicity. With enormous efforts, the substance of the reform agreed under the Constitutional Treaty has now been salvaged in the Treaty of Lisbon,[2] but the language returns to the somewhat placatory terminology of the original EU. There is one item, however, which survived the revision almost without any change: The Charter of Fundamental Rights.

This contribution will firstly indicate the reasons why, in my view, recognising the legally binding effect of the Charter is a cornerstone of the reform of the EU. Secondly, the conditions under which the Charter has been recognised as a binding instrument have in certain aspects positive effects as compared to the Constitutional Treaty, at least they are not a considerable regression. The Charter, thirdly, makes clear that the Union is specifically different in its kind from an international organisation or any other form of cooperation among states: It is a Union of citizens, and the Charter is an indication that the citizens are taking ownership of it.[3]

II. The Charter of Fundamental Rights in Context

Considering, in particular, the European Charter of Fundamental Rights, it seems to be important to evaluate it in its contextual framework; as part of the "internal affairs" of the European Union, as counterpart to the principle of primacy of European law, and as one of the "Three pillars" of the system for the protection of fundamental rights in the Union.

A. Fundamental Rights and "internal affairs"

Why are fundamental rights addressed in the part of this conference devoted to 'Internal affairs', together with 'Justice and Home Affairs'? The answer is obvious: It is the counterpart for new competencies of the Union regarding the "area of freedom, security and justice". The policies of the third pillar will be shifted from intergovernmental co-operation between Member States to the 'Community method'. All the matters

---

2   Full text with protocols and declarations in OJ 2007 C 306.

3   See below as follows.

and measures envisaged here: security, home affairs, and justice affect very closely the citizens' personal rights and freedoms. The Tampere-Program and Hague II on the "area of freedom, security and justice" and its implementation give clear indication of how important it is for the citizens to see that the action of the EU in this area is guided and limited by fundamental rights. The need for a Charter of Fundamental Rights became evident when these policies began to be developed in 1995, and the recognition of its binding effect turned out to be a condition for accepting such new competencies at the Union level – not to mention the fact that the switch to the Community method also means that more transparent and democratic procedures will apply to what has been dealt with, so far, in secret diplomatic negotiations, agreed between the ministers and implemented by the national institutions without competent democratic involvement.

Thus, two elements that had been the offspring of fundamental rights in history finally meet in the development of the EU: The first one being the moderation of an executive power or government as did for example the *Magna Carta Libertatum* (1215), addressing the individuals but as subjects submitted to that power, yet nevertheless limiting that submission with regard to their personal freedom and especially with regard to freedom from measures of security and justice.[4] In this (first) sense, fundamental rights are understood as a reaction and limitation to governing power while in another sense, (occurring much later in history) they constitute first of all the governing power treating individuals as free people by themselves establishing a political body or power to protect these freedoms, as is found in the *Virginia Bill of Rights* from 1776 or the *Déclaration des droits de l'homme et du citoyen* (1789), the latter explicitly stating in its Article 2:

"*Le but de toute association politique est la conservation des droits naturels et imprescriptibles de l'Homme. Ces droits sont la liberté, la propriété, la sûreté, et la résistance à l'oppression*".

and further Article 12:

"La garantie des droits de l'Homme et du Citoyen nécessite une force publique: cette force est donc instituée pour l'avantage de tous, et non pour l'utilité particulière de ceux auxquels elle est confiée".

---

4   See also the similar Charters in Spain (1188), Denmark (1282), Belgium (1316) and later also the *Habeas Corpus* Act of 1679.

Thus, government becomes a kind of trustee of the citizens.[5] As we know, this concept was extended by *James Madison* in the Federalist No. 46 explaining the federal division of powers:

> "The federal and state Governments are in fact but different agents and trustees of the people, instituted with different powers, and designated for different purposes".[6]

The question is, what might this mean for the recent developments of the EU? Both aspects, indeed, seem to be relevant with regard to the new reference to the Charter of Fundamental Rights as a legally binding instrument. First: Submitting pillar three to the Community method enlarges the powers at the Union level (especially the crucial ones regarding freedom and security) and reduces – at the same time - the direct control and legitimisation of such policies by the national governments and parliaments. Consequently there is a need for fundamental rights facing and limiting these enlarged powers at the Union level, thus for fundamental rights in the first sense mentioned above. But fundamental rights also work in the second sense: As long as the protection of freedom and security was primarily the responsibility of the Member States, their constitutions (including fundamental rights) permitted the use of measures of security and justice only for the sake of and with regard to the liberty of their citizens. At the Union level such a guarantee is yet to be established. Therefore, the new reference to the Charter of Fundamental Rights as a legally binding instrument means far more than carrying coals to Newcastle. Even conceding that – in its contents – it might state nothing very different from what has already been or could in future be developed by the case law of the ECJ, with an independent validity these fundamental rights are not only re-born but actually newborn and serve to underline the constitutional character of the new Treaties. By addressing the citizens of the EU directly as individuals especially concerning their personal freedom and security they merge (at least within the reach of the Union powers) the national societies into a European society of free people and thus hold the political powers on the Union level directly responsible for their rights and freedoms. The Charter of Fundamental Rights, consequently, not only underlines and clarifies the legal status and freedoms of the Union's citizens facing the institutions of the Union, but also gives the Union

---

5   For further information and references concerning the development of fundamental rights see e.g. *Pound* (1957) and *Jellinek* (1919).

6   *Hamilton / Madison / Jay* (1787/88).

and, in particular, the policies regarding the "area of freedom, security and justice" a new explicit normative foundation.

B. Counterpart to the Principle of Primacy

Yet, the Charter should also be regarded in relation to a further issue too: The multilevel construction of the Union. It can be seen as a counterpart to the unconditional acceptance of the primacy of European law over national law, which is now confirmed in the Declaration (17) concerning primacy. There is no express provision on primacy in the Treaty any more, as was envisaged by Article I-6 of the Constitutional Treaty. But more clearly even than the Declaration (1) "concerning provisions of the Constitution", attached to the Constitutional Treaty, the new Declaration to the Lisbon Treaty on primacy refers to the case law of the ECJ, wherein[7] the principle of primacy was already established since 1964[8] as "*a cornerstone principle of Community law*". These are the words of the Legal Services' opinion of 22 June 2007 expressly referred to in the Declaration to the Lisbon Treaty. This reference is made without any reservation whatsoever. The Declaration recognises the principle of primacy "under the conditions laid down by the said case law". This means that provisions of the national constitutions, even those regarding fundamental rights, cannot be invoked against "the Treaties and the law adopted by the Union".[9]

In return, it will be crucial for the citizens to see the EU as being subject to a common catalogue of fundamental rights, providing for effective protection of their individual rights and freedoms at the

---

7   See the settled case law of the ECJ e.g. : Case 6/64, *Flaminio Costa v. ENEL* [1964] ECR 585, 593; Case 11/70, *Internationale Handelsgesellschaft mbH v. Einfuhr- und Vorratsstelle für Getreide und Futtermittel*, [1970] ECR 1125; Case 106/77, *Amministrazione delle Finanze dello Stato v. Simmenthal SpA*, [1978] ECR 629. For details see *Pernice* (2006), 22-27, 53-56.

8   Case 6/64, *Flaminio Costa v. ENEL* [1964] ECR 585, 593.

9   Case 11/70, *Internationale Handelsgesellschaft* [1970] ECR 1125. For the reluctance of national (Constitutional) Courts in this respect see: Pernice, Ingolf, *Verhältnis* (note 7), p. 21-43; see also for the recent case law of the French Conseil d'Etat, in particular Decision of February 8, 2008, case No. 287110, Arcelor, available at: http://www.conseil-etat.fr/ce/jurispd/index_ac_ld0706.shtml, German version published with comments by *Mayer / Lenski / Wendel* (2008), 63 *et seq.*

European level – that means, against threats originating from the
European Union.

C. Three pillars of the EU system of Fundamental Rights

Like the Constitutional Treaty in its Article I-9, the Treaty of Lisbon
retains in Article 6 the "three pillars" of Fundamental rights: The
Charter, the recognition of the rights "as guaranteed by the European
Convention for the Protection of Human Rights and Fundamental
Freedoms" and the rights "as they result from the constitutional
traditions common to the Member States", the latter two groups of rights
constituting "general principles of the Union's law". While these general
principles have been – and will continue to be – established by the case-
law of the ECJ,[10] Article 6, para. 2 TEU-L in addition provides for the
formal accession to the European Convention, by which the EU will be
integrated in the Strasbourg control system, including the jurisdiction of
the European Court of Human Rights.

Given the difficulties any desired revision of the Charter will face
in a Union of 27 Member States, the necessary openness and dynamic
development of the European system for the protection of fundamental
rights will be ensured, in particular, by the reference to the general
principles of law and, consequently, the existing and future case-law of
the ECJ as well as of the European Court of Human Rights.

III. Constitutional and Lisbon Treaty compared

Comparing the Constitutional Treaty to the Treaty of Lisbon with
particular regard to the Charter of Fundamental Rights, there are a
number of changes regarding the general approach, the contents and
even the reach and validity of the Charter.

A. A new approach: Reference to Charter and explanations

First of all, the Mandate of June 2007[11] and the Lisbon Treaty do not
follow the approach of the Constitutional Treaty. The Charter is not

---

10   Case 29/69, *Stauder v. City of Ulm* [1969] ECR 419; Case 11/70,
     Internationale Handelsgesellschaft [1970] ECR 1125; Case 4/73,
     Nold v. Commission [1974] ECR 491; Opinion 2/94 on *Accession by
     the Community to the ECHR* [1996] ECR I-1759, para. 33; Case C-
     299/95 *Kremzow v. Austria* [1997] ECR I-2629. Para.14.

11   IGC Mandate of June 26, 2007, attached to the Conclusions of the
     European Council, see: http://register.consilium.europa.eu/pdf/en/
     07/st11/st11218.en07.pdf.

incorporated into the new EU Treaty. With some minor amendments, instead, the Charter was solemnly proclaimed and formally signed in Strasbourg the 12th December 2007 by the Presidents of the European Parliament, the Council and the Commission, and was published later in the Official Journal.[12] It was the day before the Treaty of Lisbon was signed in Lisbon. Para. 1, clause 1 of Article 6 of the new EU-Treaty reads:

> "The Union recognises the rights, freedoms and principles set out in the Charter of Fundamental Rights of the European Union of 7 December 2001, as adapted at Strasbourg, on 12 December 2007, which shall have the same legal value as the Treaties".

This new approach deliberately avoids the appearance of a Constitution. But above all, it avoids the very odd situation of including two preambles in one Treaty, one at the top and another in the middle of the text. Instead, the reference in the TEU-L to the Charter as a separate constitutional document gives the Charter an independent existence and may even allow other Organisations or States to refer to it as a binding instrument. As Article 6, para. 1, clause 1 TEU-L expressly gives the Charter "the same legal value as the Treaties", all its merits as a Constitutional document for the EU, thus, are preserved, and its independent existence even allows it to be used as a more general reference for fundamental rights.

Thanks to permanent British pressure there is another peculiar provision in the new EU Treaty: Article 6, para. 1, clause 3 TEU-L reads:

> "The rights, freedoms and principles in the Charter shall be interpreted in accordance with the general provisions in Title VII of the Charter governing its interpretation and application and with due regard to the explanations referred to in the Charter, that set out the sources of those provisions".

Article I-9 of the Constitutional Treaty did not include a similar provision, while Clause 5, final sentence, of the preamble of the Charter in Part II as well as Article II-112, para. 7 of the Constitutional Treaty did so, and Declaration (12) to the Constitutional Treaty included the text of the explanations. The explanations now referred to in the general provision on fundamental rights of the EU-Treaty, and retained in the

---

12   OJ 2007 C 303/1.

preamble of the Charter as well as in its Article 52, para. 7, are attached to the text of the Charter as published in the same Official Journal as the Charter itself.[13]

Does it make a difference whether the reference to the explanations is in the Treaty, situated amongst the basic principles and objectives of the Union, or in the preamble and the text of the Charter only? In formal legal terms, the answer is no. Symbolically, however, the answer is yes, and this means for the practical application of the Charter in a given case that the explanations will have more weight.

Although the method of referring to such authoritative explanations seems to be questionable from a traditional legal point of view, it may prove to be very effective and useful regarding possible divergencies of the a priori understanding and construction of any specific rights in the different legal cultures and traditions of the 27 Member States. This is particularly important since the effective protection of the citizens' fundamental rights against acts of the European Union or, as Article 51, para. 1, TEU-L reads, of the Member States "when they are implementing Union law", will primarily be a matter for the national courts. As already envisaged under the Constitutional Treaty, the new EU-Treaty states in Article 19 EU (ex Article 220 EC), para. 1, clause 2:

"Member States shall provide remedies sufficient to ensure effective legal protection in the fields covered by Union law".

As long as, on this basis, there is no direct access to the ECJ for "constitutional complaints" against European measures, it seems to be important that national courts have some common idea of what each particular provision of the Charter really means.

B. Fundamental rights and the competences of the Union

There is another new provision in Article 6, para. 1, clause 2, TEU-L, which Article I-9 of the Constitutional Treaty did not contain:

"The provisions of the Charter shall not extend in any way the competences of the Union as defined in the Treaties".

As this was not considered to be clear enough, a special Declaration was already foreseen in the Brussels Mandate and is now included as Declaration (1) to the Treaty of Lisbon. It states that

"The Charter does not extend the field of application of Union law beyond the powers of the Union or establish

---

13   OJ 2007 C 303/17.

any new power or task for the Union, or modify powers and tasks as defined by the Treaties".

The Charter already includes such a clause in its Article 51, para. 2[14] and the authoritative explanations to this Article reiterate this limitation.[15] These provisions are the expression of a deep concern, almost a phobia of at least some Member States anxious to ensure a restrictive approach regarding the EU competences. Similar clauses can repeatedly be found in the new Treaties, e.g. in the provisions regarding the accession of the EU to the European Convention on Human Rights in Article 2 of the Protocol relating to Article 6(2) of the Treaty on European Union on the Accession of the Union to the European Convention on the Protection of Human Rights and Fundamental Freedoms, and in particular in the provisions on the competencies of the

---

14   Article 51, para 2, CHR reads: "This Charter does not establish any new power or task for the Community or the Union, or modify powers and tasks defined by the Treaties".

15   Explanation on Article 51 – field of application, paras. 3 and 4 read: "Paragraph 2, together with the second sentence of paragraph 1, confirms that the Charter may not have the effect of extending the competences and tasks which the Treaties confer on the Union. Explicit mention is made here of the logical consequences of the principle of subsidiarity and of the fact that the Union only has those powers which have been conferred upon it. The fundamental rights as guaranteed in the Union do not have any effect other than in the context of the powers determined by the Treaties. Consequently, an obligation, pursuant to the second sentence of paragraph 1, for the Union's institutions to promote principles laid down in the Charter may arise only within the limits of these same powers.

Paragraph 2 also confirms that the Charter may not have the effect of extending the field of application of Union law beyond the powers of the Union as established in the Treaties. The Court of Justice has already established this rule with respect to the fundamental rights recognised as part of Union law (judgment of 17 February 1998, C-249/96 Grant [1998] ECR I-621, paragraph 45 of the grounds). In accordance with this rule, it goes without saying that the reference to the Charter in Article 6 of the Treaty on European Union cannot be understood as extending by itself the range of Member State action considered to be 'implementation of Union law' (within the meaning of paragraph 1 and the above-mentioned case-law)".

EU, such as Articles 4, para. 1, Article 5 para. 2 TEU-L or Article 308 para. 2 TFEU, and in the related protocols and declarations.[16]

This concern, however, was already met by the principles of conferred competencies and subsidiarity and needs therefore no further reiteration.[17] One could be doubtful about the real meaning of these principles if the authors of the Treaty consider it necessary to repeat the limitation so abundantly. It is all the more surprising since fundamental rights are by their nature not conferring, but rather limiting the competences conferred to the institutions: Inasmuch as they deny the power to affect certain rights and liberties of the individual they have therefore rightly been constructed as 'negative competences' of the institutions concerned.[18]

C. 'Opt-out' for Britain and Poland

Regarding the Charter of Fundamental Rights representatives of the UK and Poland have not only made all efforts to avoid the Charter or at least to limit its impact, but have finally achieved what is called an opt out from the Charter.[19] In fact, the Protocol on the Application of the Charter of Fundamental Rights of the European Union to Poland and to the United Kingdom states:

"Article 1

1. The Charter does not extend the ability of the Court of Justice of the European Union, or any court or tribunal of Poland or of the United Kingdom, to find that the laws, regulations or administrative provisions, practices or ac-

---

16 See in particular Declaration (24) concerning the legal personality of the European Union: „The Conference confirms that the fact that the European Union has a legal personality will not in any way authorise the Union to legislate or to act beyond the competences conferred upon it by the Member States in the Treaties".

17 Apparently dissentig on this point *Weber* (2008), 8.

18 For the construction of fundamental rights as "*negative Kompetenznormen*" see *Hesse* (1999), 133; see also *Mayer* (2001), 583; *Pernice* (2001); for the possible effect of fundamental rights on the division of competencies between the European Union and the Member States see also *Pernice / Kanitz* (2004).

19 On this 'opt-out' see e.g. *Fischer* (2008), 34 *et seq* and also 44, 116 *et seq*; *Mayer* (2008), 88 *et seq*; for the link between 'opt-out' and the possible want of a referendum in the U.K. concerning the Lisbon treaty see *Donnelly* (2008), 207 *et seq.*

tion of Poland or of the United Kingdom are inconsistent with the fundamental rights, freedoms and principles that it reaffirms.

2. In particular, and for the avoidance of doubt, nothing in Title IV of the Charter creates justiciable rights applicable to Poland or the United Kingdom except in so far as Poland or the United Kingdom has provided for such rights in its national law.

Article 2

To the extent that a provision of the Charter refers to national law and practices, it shall only apply to Poland or the United Kingdom to the extent that the rights or principles that it contains are recognised in the law or practice of Poland or of the United Kingdom".

Is this really an 'opt-out'? I believe the answer must be no. If it is true, as the Preamble of the Charter specifies, that the Charter is meant to

"strengthen the protection of fundamental rights ... by making those rights more visible in a Charter";

if it is true, as the Declaration (1) concerning the Charter of Fundamental Rights of the European Union stresses in its first clause, that the Charter

"confirms the fundamental rights guaranteed by the European Convention for the Protection of Human Rights and Fundamental Freedoms and as they result from the constitutional traditions common to the Member States";

if it is true that, as the 'opt-out'-Protocol states in the Preamble, "The Charter reaffirms the rights, freedoms and principles recognised in the Union and makes those rights more visible, but does not create new rights or principles",

what then could reasonably be the meaning and effect of an opt-out to the Charter? All its provisions are already recognised as binding law. If the Charter, legally speaking, does not add anything further, how can the opt-out have a legal effect?[20]

---

20   For an enlightning impression concerning the discussion of this question in the United Kingdom see: 10th Report of Session 2007-08, The Treaty of Lisbon: an impact assessment, Volume I/II: Evidence, House of Lords, European Union Committee. In particular: Evidence provided by *Jo Shaw* on the 14th November 2007, Question 67-76,

But let us have a look at the substantial provisions of the protocol: The first question is to what extent, under European law, are the ECJ and national courts able to find that national law is inconsistent with European fundamental rights? An answer in general terms is that the ECJ has no power whatsoever to nullify national law, while national courts or tribunals may have such a power. More specifically, however, inconsistencies of national law or action with European law may be found by the ECJ in infringement cases (Article 258 TFEU, ex 226 EC) and also in reference procedures under Article 267 TFEU (ex 234 EC). The new powers of the ECJ under Article 269 TFEC to hear Member States' appeals against sanction-decisions under Article 7 TEU-L are limited to procedural matters. Regarding the area of freedom, security and justice a new Article 276 TEU-L excludes any competence of the ECJ to

> "review the validity or proportionality of operations carried out by the police or other law-enforcement services of a Member State or the exercise of the responsibilities incumbent upon Member States with regard to the maintenance of law and order and the safeguarding of internal security".

The question, however, of the extent to which European fundamental rights may be taken as criteria for the legal review not only of measures of the EU but also of national law must be answered in the light of the principles and case-law of the ECJ. This is exactly what Article 51, para. 1, of the Charter is meant to capture: The provisions of the Charter are addressed "to the Member States only when they are

---

where she stated with regard to the protocol: "... this is merely a clarification of the law as we understand it to be, so I might venture the view that this is a Declaration masquerading as a Protocol". And at Q74: "I am not saying it does not have legal effect but I would doubt what legal effect it would have". Similar the supplementary memorandum by *Martin Howe* to his oral evidence, stating that "the Protocol does no more than reiterate the provision of Art. 51(1) of the Charter [...], and has no substantive legal effect". Even more explicit the conclusion of the Committee: "The protocol is not an opt-out from the Charter. The Charter will apply in the U.K., even if its interpretation may be affected by the terms of the protocol" (para.5.87 at Volume I) and its summary concerning the legal effect of the protocol at para. 5.103. The report is available at: http://www.publications.parliament.uk/pa/ld/ldeucom.htm.

implementing Union law". The explanations on this provision reveal that this formula intends to meet the law as it stands. The explanation on Article 51 states in paragraph 2:

"As regards the Member States, it follows unambiguously from the case-law of the Court of Justice that the requirement to respect fundamental rights defined in the context of the Union is only binding on the Member States when they act in the scope of Union law (judgment of 13 July 1989, Case 5/88 Wachauf [1989] ECR 2609; judgment of 18 June 1991, Case C-260/89 ERT [1991] ECR I-2925; judgment of 18 December 1997, Case C-309/96 Annibaldi [1997] ECR I-7493). The Court of Justice confirmed this case-law in the following terms: 'In addition, it should be remembered that the requirements flowing from the protection of fundamental rights in the Community legal order are also binding on Member States when they implement Community rules ...' (judgment of 13 April 2000, Case C-292/97 [2000] ECR I-2737, paragraph 37 of the grounds). Of course this rule, as enshrined in this Charter, applies to the central authorities as well as to regional or local bodies, and to public organisations, when they are implementing Union law".

If this is so, a Protocol which confirms that the Charter will not extend the ability of the ECJ and the national courts in Britain and Poland to find that their national law or practices "are inconsistent with the fundamental rights that it reaffirms" can hardly be understood as a reservation or an opt-out.

The same applies to the part of the protocol which excludes that the provisions of chapter IV – on solidarity – of the Charter create justiciable rights for Britain and Poland. Could collective bargaining rights, as recognised in Article 28 of the Charter, be invoked against national measures restricting the freedom to provide services (Article 56 TFEU, ex Article 49 EC), in order to question whether mandatory requirements of public interest could justify the measures? This is the situation dealt with in the ERT-case, to which the explanations refer. It is clear for Britain and Poland that Article 28 of the Charter would not be applied, but instead the fundamental right which it reaffirms and which the ECJ recently recognised in its recent case-law.[21]

In case 438/05, *Viking*,[22] the Court mentioned, for the very first time, the Charter and its Article 28 by which the right to take collective action was "reaffirmed". I do not see the difference.

Finally, Article 2 of the Protocol limits references in the Charter to national law and practices in a provision of the Charter so as to apply only insofar as the rights and principles reaffirmed in that provision are also recognised in the law or practices of the two countries. Thus, again, the relevant provisions of the Charter are understood not as creating new rights but as principles confirming the existing social rights and protecting them against challenges by European legislation. They are 'standstill-rules' regarding the level of protection achieved so far. Article 52, para. 5, of the Charter clarifies what their normative content shall be:

> "The provisions of this Charter which contain principles may be implemented by legislative and executive acts taken by institutions, bodies, offices and agencies of the Union, and by acts of Member States when they are implementing Union law, in the exercise of their respective powers. They shall be judicially cognisable only in the interpretation of such acts and in the ruling on their legality".

Again, the Protocol contains clarifications but not, as I see it, any real reservation in respect of the Charter. The same applies, by the way,

---

21 Case C-341/05, *Laval* [2005] OJ C281/10, para. 91 et sequ.; for the freedom of establishment see case C-438/05, *International Transport Workers Federation v. Viking Line* [2006] OJ C60/16. para. 44: "Although the right to take collective action, including the right to strike, must therefore be recognised as a fundamental right which forms an integral part of the general principles of Community law the observance of which the Court ensures, the exercise of that right may none the less be subject to certain restrictions. As is reaffirmed by Article 28 of the Charter of Fundamental Rights of the European Union, those rights are to be protected in accordance with Community law and national law and practices. In addition, as is apparent from paragraph 5 of this judgment, under Finnish law the right to strike may not be relied on, in particular, where the strike is contra bonos mores or is prohibited under national law or Community law".

22 See note 21 above.

to the special Declarations of the Czech Republic and Poland.[23] They have no legal effect except for recalling the interpretation of certain provisions of the Charter by these countries.

D. The Charter and the Court of Justice

With regard to the 'three pillars' of the European system of fundamental rights, mentioned above, the role and powers of the ECJ are of particular importance to the question of the future developments of fundamental rights in the European Union. Though the three sources each have a separate basis and the accession of the Union to the European Convention on Human Rights will imply that the Strasbourg Court will supervise, as it does for all Member States individually, respect for human rights by the EU, including the ECJ, the Charter of Fundamental rights reflects and reaffirms both the guarantees included in the Convention[24] as well as the other general principles of law developed so far by the case-law of the ECJ. Since these principles are mentioned specifically and separately as one of the sources of fundamental rights to be protected, nothing excludes a further dynamic development of other, new fundamental rights by the ECJ, inspired, as it was so far, by the "constitutional traditions common to the Member States". This openness seems to be particularly important for the unity and coherence of the European multilevel constitutional system regarding the need for the ECJ to keep track with the national and Strasbourg developments concerning fundamental rights.

Is there any important change regarding the role and powers of the ECJ relevant to the protection of fundamental rights in the Treaty of Lisbon? It is clear that with the 'communitarisation' of the Third Pillar the general system of judicial review will also apply in this area. And regarding the Common Foreign and Security Policy, the new Article 275 TFEU gives the Court the competence to review

---

23   Declaration (53) by the Czech Republic on the Charter of Fundamental Rights in the European Union (p. 368); Declaration (61) by the Republic of Poland on the charter of Fundamental rights of the European Union (p. 270) – family law; Declaration (62) by the Republic of Poland on the Charter of Fundamental Rights of the European Union in relation to Poland and the United Kingdom (p. 270) – Solidarity.

24   For further consideration of the relationship between Charter and Convention see: *Grabenwarter* (2006); *Busse* (2001); *Goldsmith* (2001), 1211; *Thym* (2002).

"the legality of decisions providing for restrictive measures against natural or legal persons adopted by the Council on the basis of Chapter 2 of Title V of the Treaty on
European Union".

As soon as the ECJ gives its judgment in the cases *Yusuf & Kadi*,[25]
we will know the exact implications of this provision for the protection
of fundamental rights against measures implementing decisions of the
UN Security Council.

However, for the institutional and procedural law, the Brussels
Mandate did not include any specific amendments regarding the reform
of the ECJ as envisaged by the Constitutional Treaty. Thus, the
provisions of the Treaty of Lisbon regarding the ECJ take over what has
already been agreed.[26] It seems to be important to note, however, that the
general provisions of Articles 220 EC will not only be transferred to the
fundamental provisions of the new EU-Treaty, but they will also be
complemented by a provision reflecting requirements expressed by the
recent jurisprudence of the ECJ:[27] The new Article 19 TEU-L adds to
the former text of Article 220, para. 1, EC that

"Member States shall provide remedies sufficient to ensure effective legal protection in the fields covered by
Union law".

As already mentioned, this provision addresses the primary responsibility of the national courts for the judicial review also regarding
the protection of fundamental rights against legislative acts of the
European Union being implemented by national authorities. In
accordance with the principle of subsidiarity, this provision thus reflects
for the judiciary, the co-operative multilevel structure of the Union. This
obligation of the Member States implies that in all cases where a national
court of last instance is confronted with a case in which the validity of a

25   For CFI ruling see: Case T-315/01 *Yassin Abdullah Kadi v. Council
     and Commission* [2005] ECR II-3649; Case T-306/01 *Ahmed Ali Yu-
     suf and Al Barakaat Foundation v. Council and Commission* [2005]
     ECR II-3533. For the Opinion of Advocate General *Maduro* in *Kadi*,
     Case   C   402/05,   see   http://curia.europa.eu/jurisp/cgibin/
     form.pl?lang=EN&Submit=rechercher&numaff=C-402/05.

26   See, in particular, Article 1, clause 20, of the Treaty of Lisbon.

27   Case C-50/00 P *Unión de Pequeños Agricultores v. Council* [2002]
     ECR I-6677, para. 41; Case C-263/02 P *Commission v. Jégo-Quéré*
     [2004] ECR I-3425, paras. 29-39.

European legislative or regulatory act is challenged because of a violation of fundamental rights, the question has to be referred to the ECJ under Article 267 TFEU (ex 234 EC). As the German Federal Constitutional Court has rightly stated in its decision of 8 January 2001, such mandatory reference to the ECJ is the only way to achieve effective judicial protection of fundamental rights against European legislation in individual cases.[28] Attempts of the EC Court of First Instance and Advocate General *Jacobs* in the cases *Jégo-Quéré* and *UPA* to weaken the very restrictive conditions under the case-law of the ECJ for actions of individual against legislative acts of the Community[29] had been rejected by the Court.[30] The Court, indeed, has stressed the responsibility of the Member States as it is now retained in Article 19, para. 1, clause 2 TEU-L, and referred to the procedure for the revision of the Treaty as to any general reform, if necessary, regarding the individual's access to the Court. Under Article 2, clause 214 (d) of the Treaty of Lisbon, consequently, the conditions laid down under Article 263, para. 4, TFEU (ex 230 EC) are broadened insofar as any natural or legal person may institute proceedings also

"against a regulatory act which is of direct concern to them and does not entail implementing measures".

Regulatory acts, though, are distinguished under the new provisions of Articles 288 to 290 TFEU, and particularly in Article 289, para. 3, TFEU from "legislative acts", defined as "legal acts adopted by legislative procedure". Though there is no definition of "regulatory acts", the new Article 290 deals with "non-legislative acts of general application" which may be adopted by the Commission, if so empowered by a legislative act, to supplement or amend certain non-essential elements of the legislative act. As a result, the need for specific provisions at national level, ensuring judicial protection against European legislation violating directly or indirectly individual

---

28   German Federal Constitutional Court, ruling of 9 January 2001, Case 1 BvR 1036/99 – *Part Time*, para 24.

29   Case T-177/01, *Jégo-Quéré v. Commission*, [2002] ECR II-2365, para. 51; advocate general *Francis Jacobs*, opinion on case C-50/00 P, *Unión de Pequeños Agricultores*, para. 102.

30   Case C-50/00 P, *Unión e Pequeños Agricultores*, paras. 36-45; Case C-263/02 P, *Jégo-Quéré*, paras. 30-36.

fundamental rights, through references to the ECJ, as required by the ECJ in its case-law[31] remains relevant.

IV. A Charter for the citizens of the Union

To conclude, let me summarise the results of my short and very provisional analysis with three remarks:

1. The difference between the Constitutional Treaty and the Treaty of Lisbon regarding fundamental rights are of minor importance compared to the great impact of the development from the existing Article 6 TEU to the three pillars of fundamental rights referred to in Article 6 TEU-L. Taken seriously, all three pillars: the Charter as a binding instrument, the accession to the European Convention of Human Rights and the reference to the general principles of law as established by the ECJ, together will change the face of the Union fundamentally. The Charter, in particular, explains what the common values referred to in Article 2 TEU-L as the foundation of the Union may really mean. It gives a clear wording and number to each of the rights to be invoked both in the political process and individual actions for judicial review, and with its balance found between liberal rights and solidarity it may even serve as a model for modern instruments designed to protect fundamental rights worldwide.

2. The Mandate and Lisbon have expressly abandoned the 'constitutional concept' as well as all references to the word 'Constitution' and related symbolism of the Constitutional Treaty. But in retaining a reference to the Charter of Fundamental Rights as a legally binding instrument for the European institutions and policies, the Treaty of Lisbon confirms and makes visible the real status and normativity of the European Primary law, as qualified by the case-law of the ECJ:[32] Could there exist a more compelling argument for the constitutional character of a treaty than the guarantee of fundamental rights protecting the citizens against the institutions and their actions based on that treaty? The new reference in Article 6, para. 1 TEU-L underlines that the Treaty establishes a direct legal relationship between the citizens and those

---

31   See the cases referred to above, notes 29 and 30.

32   Case 294/83 *Parti Ecologist les Verts v. European Parliament* [1986] ECR I-1368; Opinion 1/92, *Agreement onb the Creation of the European Economie Area II* [1992] ECR I-2821.

who are exercising power on their behalf and upon them. I am not aware of any other treaty or international instrument with this specific feature. It does constitute, I submit, the basis of what we call in French terms the *contrat social*.[33]

3.   Indeed, fundamental rights and their effective protection are, in some respect, the conditions under which people may agree to entrust institutions with legislative, executive and judicial powers to be exercised upon them in the public interest of the community of which they are the citizens. They are guidelines[34] for the policies to be implemented by the institutions established under the Constitution, and they limit their respective powers in order to ensure that the citizen remains a free and autonomous individual, member of his / her community. In a multilevel system where the Union powers are established as supranational devices, complementary to the national institutions, to meet challenges which may not be met by their national States individually, the need for commonly agreed, visible and clearly defined fundamental rights is even more important. The common values they express also serve as general guidance for the policies implemented by the national and European institutions at the EU level.[35] The European Union Agency for

---

33   Finding an english equivalent for example in *John Locke's* "Two Treatises of Government", esp. II § 95 (ch. 8) reading as follows: "Men being, as has been said, by nature, all free, equal and independent, no one can be put out of this estate, and subjected to the political power of another, without his own consent. The only way whereby anyone divests himself of his natural liberty, and puts on the bonds of civil society is by agreeing with other men to join and unite into a community, for their comfortable, safe and peacable living one amongst another, in a secure enjoyment of their properties". For the history of the term *"contrat social"* see *Bastid* (1985). For the application to the EU see already: *Pernice / Mayer / Wernicke* (2001) with further references. And for the use of the term "European social contract" see *Weiler* (1995), 439; *Pernice / Kanitz* (2004), 6.

34   For a guideline-function of the french Déclaration des droits (1789) see *Grimm* (2005).

35   For this objective dimension of fundamental rights see: *Pache* (2006); *Pernice* (2000). For the provisions of the EMRK as objective principles see: *Michelman* (2005), 167 *et seq*; referring to the German origin of this view: *Schlink* (1994), and further: *Dreier* (2004).

Fundamental Rights, created in 2007,[36] could monitor their implementation. They are a common fundament of the composed national and European system of governance, and the guarantees they contain are preserving for each citizen the inalienable rights and liberties which allow the individual to lead a decent life and actively participate in the processes at different levels, which frame European policies.

References

Paul Bastid (1985), L'Idée de Constitution, Paris (Economica) 1985.

Christian Busse (2001), Das Projekt der Europäischen Grundrechtecharta vor dem Hintergrund der EMRK, in: Thüringer Verwaltungsblätter 10 (2001), 73-80.

Brendan Donnelly (2008), A British Referendum on the Treaty?, in: Der Vertrag von Lissabon: Reform der EU ohne Verfassung?, Kolloquium zum 10. Geburtstag des WHI, Baden-Baden (Nomos) 2008, 207-212 (available at http://www.whi-berlin.de).

Horst Dreier (2004), Vorbemerkung zu Paragraph 94 in: *Horst Dreier* (ed.), Grundgesetz-Kommentar, Tübingen (Mohr Siebeck) ²2004.

Alexander Hamilton / James Madison / John Jay (1787/88), The Federalist Papers, The Federalist No. 46.

Peter Henry Lord Goldsmith Q.C. (2001), A Charter of Rights, Freedoms and Principles, in: Common Market Law Review 38 (2001), 1201-1216.

Christoph Grabenwarter (2006), Die Grundrechte-Charta als Schritt auf dem Weg in die Grundrechtsgemeinschaft, in: *Peter J. Tettinger / Klaus Stern* (eds.), Kölner Gemeinschaftskommentar zur Europäischen Grundrechte-Charta, München (C. H. Beck) 2006, 205-213.

---

36 See Council Regulation (EC) No. 168/2007 of 15 February 2007, OJ 2007 L 53/1.

Dieter Grimm (2005), The Protective Function of the State, in: *Georg Nolte* (ed.), European and US Constitutionalism, Cambridge (Cambridge University Press) 2005, 137-155.

Konrad Hesse (1999), Grundzüge des Verfassungsrechtes der Bundesrepublik Deutschland, Heidelberg (Müller) [20]1999.

Georg Jellinek (1919), Die Erklärung der Menschen- und Bürgerrechte, Munich / Leipzig (Duncker & Humblot) [3]1919.

Franz Mayer (2001), Die drei Dimensionen der Europäischen Kompetenzdebatte, in: Zeitschrift für ausländisches öffentliches Recht und Völkerrecht 61 (2001), 577-640.

Franz Mayer (2008), Schutz vor der Grundrechtecharta oder durch die Grundrechtecharta? Anmerkungen zum europäischen Grundrechtsschutz nach Lissabon, in: Der Vertrag von Lissabon: Reform der EU ohne Verfassung?, Kolloquium zum 10. Geburtstag des WHI, Baden-Baden (Nomos) 2008, 81-91 (available at http://www.whi-berlin.de).

Franz Mayer / Edgar Lenski / Mattias Wendel (2008), Der Vorrang des Europarechts in Frankreich – zugleich Anmerkung zur Entscheidung des französischen *Conseil d'Etat* vom 8. Februar 2007 (*Arcelor* u.a.), in: Europarecht 43 (2008), No. 1, 63-87.

Frank Michelman (2005), The Protective Funktion of the State in the United States and Europe: the Constitutional Question, in: *Georg Nolte* (ed.), European and US Constitutionalism, Cambridge (Cambridge University Press) 2005, 156-180.

Eckhard Pache (2006), § 4. Begriff, Geltungsgrund und Rang der Grundrechte der EU, in: *Sebastian Heselhaus / Carsten Nowak* (eds.), Handbuch der europäischen Grundrechte, Munich (C. H. Beck) 2006, 142-186.

Ingolf Pernice (2000), Eine Grundrechte-Charta für die Europäische Union, in: Deutsche Verwaltungsblätter 115 (2000), 847-859 (also available as WHI-Paper 1/00 para. 31, http://whi-berlin.de/papers/2000.dhtml).

Ingolf Pernice (2001), Europäische Grundrechte-Charta und Abgrenzung der Kompetenzen, in: Europäische Zeitschrift für Wirtschaftsrecht 12 (2001), 673.

Ingolf Pernice (2003), Die neue Verfassung der Europäischen Union – Ein historischer Fortschritt zu einem europäischem Bundesstaat? (= Forum Constitutinis Europae 8/03), Berlin 2003 (available at http://whi-berlin.de/fce/2003.dhtml).

Ingolf Pernice (2006), Das Verhältnis europäischer zu nationalen Gerichten im europäischen Verfassungsverbund, Berlin (de Gruyter) 2006.

Ingolf Pernice (2007), Salvaging the Constitution for Europe – A Reform Treaty for the EU (= WHI-Paper 4/07), Berlin 2007 (available at http://www.whi-berlin.de).

Ingolf Pernice / Ralf Kanitz (2004), Fundamental Rights and Multilevel Constitutionalism in Europe (= WHI Paper 7/04), Berlin 2004 (available at http://www.whi-berlin.de/documents/ whipaper0704.pdf).

Ingolf Pernice / Franz Mayer / Stephan Wernicke (2001), Renewing the European Social Contract: The Challenge of Institutional Reform and Enlargement in the Light of Multilevel Constitutionalism, in: King's College Law Journal 12 (2001), 61-74.

Roscoe Pound (1957), The Development of Constitutional Guarantees of Liberty, New Haven / CT (Yale University Press) 1957.

Bernhard Schlink (1994), German Constitutional Culture in Transition, in: *Michel Rosenfeld* (ed.), Constitutionalism, Identity, Difference and Legitimacy. Theoretical Perspectives, Durham (Duke University Press) 1994, 197-222.

Daniel Thym (2002), Charter of Fundamental Rights: Competition or Consistency of Human Rights Protection in Europe?, in: Finish Yearbook of International Law 11 (2002), 11-36.

Albrecht Weber (2008), Vom Verfassungsvertrag zum Vertrag von Lissabon, in: Europäische Zeitschrift für Wirtschaftsrecht 19 (2008), 7-14.

Joseph Weiler (1995), We will do: And hearken. Reflections on a Common Constitutional Law of the European Union, in: *Roland Bieber / Pierre Widmer* (eds.), The European Constitutional Area, Zurich (Schulthess) 1995, 413.

Catherine Barnard[*]

The 'Opt-Out' for the UK and Poland from the Charter of Fundamental Rights: Triumph of Rhetoric over Reality?

I. Introduction

When negotiating the IGC mandate for the Lisbon Treaty, one of the UK government's much vaunted 'red lines' was to protect the UK from the consequences in the change of status of the Charter of

---

[*] I am grateful to the conference participants for their very useful comments and to *Michael Dougan* and *Eleanor Spaventa* for subsequent discussion and observations.

Fundamental Rights.[1] The principal and most public demonstration
of this desire was the adoption of what became Protocol 7 on the
application of the Charter of Fundamental Rights of the European
Union to Poland and to the United Kingdom. Under Article 51
TEU-L, the Protocol will have the same legal value as the Treaties.

The status of the UK / Poland Protocol is much contested. I
will argue that, for Eurosceptic audiences, the UK government has
been willing to let it be referred to as an opt-out. Yet for more informed audiences the UK government insists that it is not an opt-
out but merely a clarification. I will consider the force of these arguments and suggest that the reality may lie somewhere in between.
However, I begin by placing the Protocol into the broader context
of the incorporation of the Charter into the Treaty, before examining the content of the Protocol.

II. The Lisbon Treaty and the Charter

A. Incorporation of the Charter into the Treaty

The Charter,[2] first solemnly proclaimed in December 2000, was
intended to make existing fundamental rights more visible[3] rather

---

1   *Tony Blair* MP, then British Prime Minster, described these red lines
    to the Liaison Committee of the 18 June 2007 (reported in the House
    of Commons' European Scrutiny Committee's 35th Report, para. 52)
    in the following terms: "First we will not accept a treaty that allows
    the charter of fundamental rights to change UK law in any way. Sec-
    ondly, we will not agree to something which displaces the role of
    British foreign policy and our foreign minister. Thirdly, we will not
    agree to give up our ability to control our common law and judicial
    and police system. Fourthly, we will not agree to anything that moves
    to qualified-majority voting, something that can have a big say in our
    own tax and benefits system".

2   OJ [2007] C303/1. On the background to the Charter, see *de Búrca*,
    (2001); *Lenaerts / de Smijter* (2001).

3   The Cologne Presidency conclusions of June 1999 said (http://ue.eu.
    int/ueDocs/cms_Data/docs/pressData/en/ec/57886.pdf, para. 44)
    "The European Council takes the view that, at the present stage of
    development of the European Union, the fundamental rights applica-
    ble at Union level should be consolidated in a Charter and thereby
    made more evident.' Annex IV adds "Protection of fundamental
    rights is a founding principle of the Union and an indispensable pre-
    requisite for her legitimacy. The obligation of the Union to respect
    fundamental rights has been confirmed and defined by the jurispru-

than to create new rights.[4] A large number of the rights are derived from the European Convention on Human Rights, the Community Social Charter 1989 and the Council of Europe's Social Charter 1961.[5] Others are derived from the constitutional traditions common to the Member States, as general principles of Community law. The Charter is therefore intended to codify existing rights[6] – to act as a showcase for those rights. As *Dashwood* puts it, the Charter is not, in itself, a source of rights but simply a record of rights that receive protection within the Union, from one source or another.[7]

Article 6(1) TEU-L gives legal effect to the Charter of Fundamental Rights 2000 as amended during the Constitutional Treaty negotiations.[8] The first paragraph of Article 6(1) provides:

"The Union recognises the rights, freedoms and principles set out in the Charter of Fundamental Rights of the European Union of 7 December 2000, as adapted at Strasbourg, on 12 December 2007, which shall have the same legal value as the Treaties".

Thus, instead of the Charter being incorporated as a whole into the text of the Lisbon Treaty, as it had been in the Constitutional

---

dence of the European Court of Justice. There appears to be a need, at the present stage of the Union's development, to establish a Charter of fundamental rights in order to make their overriding importance and relevance more visible to the Union's citizens".

4   See, e.g. the Preamble to the Protocol "WHEREAS the Charter reaffirms the rights, freedoms and principles recognised in the Union and makes those rights more visible, but does not create new rights or principles".

5   5th Recital to the Charter 2007 Preamble. Art. 6(2) TEU-L gives the EU the power to accede to the ECHR. It adds "Such accession shall not affect the Union's competences as defined in the Treaties".

6   See also the Preamble to the Protocol "WHEREAS the Charter reaffirms the rights, freedoms and principles recognised in the Union and makes those rights more visible, but does not create new rights or principles".

7   'The paper tiger that is no threat to Britain's fundamental rights' *Parliamentary Brief*, 10 March 2008. http://www.thepolitician.org/articles/the-paper-tiger-646.html.

8   Amendments were made to the horizontal provisions, notably the addition of Arts 52(4) and (5). The revised Charter can be found in OJ [2007] C 303/1.

Treaty, it is incorporated by reference. Nevertheless, it has the "same legal value as the Treaties". In other words, it will form part of the primary law of the EU. The consequence of this is that its provisions are potentially enforceable (i.e. directly effective) in the national courts, when Community law issues are at stake, as well as before the European Court of Justice. This has given rise to a number of worries, especially in the UK.

The UK was particularly concerned that social and economic rights were included in the same document as civil and political rights,[9] reasoning that while civil and political rights are essentially negative and do not require state resources, economic and social rights are positive and do. The UK has therefore been most reluctant to talk about economic and social *rights*, preferring instead the word 'principles' which the UK considers not to be directly effective.

The crude dichotomy between civil and political rights on the one hand, and economic and social rights on the other, has been challenged.[10] It did, nevertheless, influence the drafting of the Charter. While traditional civil and political rights tend to be drafted in the language of rights (e.g. Article 2 "Everyone has the *right* to life", Article 11 "Everyone has the *right* to freedom of expression"), economic and social rights, found predominantly in the Solidarity Title, tend to be drafted in the language of principles (e.g. Article 25 "The Union *recognises and respects* the rights of the elderly to lead a life of dignity and independence and to participate in social and cultural life").[11] As we have seen, principles are not intended to be directly effective. Rather, they are "factors to be taken

---

9   See Cologne Presidency Conclusions 1999, Annex IV (http://ue.eu. int/ueDocs/cms_Data/docs/pressData/en/ec/kolnen.htm) "In drawing up such a Charter account should furthermore be taken of economic and social rights as contained in the European Social Charter and the Community Charter of the Fundamental Social Rights of Workers (Article 136 TEC), insofar as they do not merely establish objectives for action by the Union".' For discussion of the difficulty of equating the two groups of rights, see *Goldsmith* (2001), 1212.

10   For a discussion of the distinction between the two groups of rights, see *Kenner* (2003).

11   For a full discussion, see *Hepple* (2005), 35.

into account by courts when interpreting legislation but which do not in and of themselves create enforceable rights".[12]

To make this point abundantly clear, the UK was behind the move to amend the horizontal provisions of the Charter at the time of the Constitutional Treaty and these changes were maintained at Lisbon. A new Article 52(5) was introduced which says that the provisions of the Charter containing principles "may be implemented by legislative and executive acts" of the Union and the Member States when implementing Union law. Such provisions "shall be judicially cognisable only in the interpretation of such acts and in the ruling on their legality". In other words principles will not be directly effective in the national courts.

However, the stumbling block remains that the Charter does not identify which provisions contain rights and which principles.[13] The revised explanations[14] were intended to address this problem. They were "drawn up as a way of providing guidance in the interpretation of this Charter" and must be "given due regard by the courts of the Union and of the Member States".[15] The explanations give examples of principles, including Article 25 on the rights of the elderly, Article 26 on the integration of persons with disabilities and Article 37 on environmental protection. The explanations also state that some articles may contain elements of rights and principles, such as Article 23 on equality between men and women, Article 33 on family and professional life and Article 34 on social security and social assistance. Therefore, some social and economic rights will

---

12   House of Lords Constitution Committee, *European Union (Amendment) Bill and the Lisbon Treaty: Implications for the UK Constitution*, 6th Report, 2007-8, HL Paper 84, paras. 60-61. See also *Goldsmith* (2001), 1212.

13   See also House of Lords EU Select Committee, *The Treaty of Lisbon: An Impact Assessment*, 10th Report, 2007-8, HL Paper 62, paras. 5.15, 5.18-5.20.

14   Explanations relating to the Charter of Fundamental Rights OJ [2007] C303/17.

15   Art. 52(7) of the Charter. See also Art. 6(1), third para TEU-L "The rights, freedoms and principles in the Charter shall be interpreted in accordance with the general provisions in Title VII of the Charter governing its interpretation and application and with due regard to the explanations referred to in the Charter, that set out the sources of those provisions".

not be mere principles but may give rise to directly effective rights.[16] Unfortunately for the UK government, two of the provisions in the Solidarity Title which cause British business most concern, Article 28 on collective agreements and collective action and Article 30 on unfair dismissal (which are considered in detail below), appear to be drafted in terms of rights, not principles, and so are potentially directly effective.[17] As we shall see, the need to address this perceived problem influenced the drafting of the Protocol. However, first we need to consider the scope of application of the Charter.

B. To whom / what does the Charter Apply?

Article 51(1) of the Charter says the Charter applies to (1) to the institutions, bodies, offices and agencies of the Union, with due regard for the principle of subsidiarity; and (2) to the Member States but only when they are implementing Union law, a point emphasized by the Czech Republic in its Declaration in the Charter. This says "The Czech Republic stresses that [the Charter's] provisions are addressed to the Member States only when they are implementing Union law, and not when they are adopting and implementing national law independently from Union law".[18] In other words, purely national issues will not be affected by the Charter.

The meaning of Article 51(1) is clarified in the explanations. These make clear that Article 51 "seeks to establish clearly that the Charter applies *primarily* to the institutions and bodies of the Union, in compliance with the principle of subsidiarity".[19] The institutions include the European Court of Justice.

---

16   See, e.g. Article 31 "Every worker has the right to working conditions which respect his or her health, safety and dignity".

17   See,. Case C-438/05 *International Transport Workers' Federation* v. *Viking Line ABP* [2007] ECR I-000, para. 44.

18   Declaration 53, first paragraph. See also Art. 4(1) TEU-L and Art. 5(2) second sentence.

19   Emphasis added. The institutions already consider themselves bound by the Charter: Commission Communication, *Compliance with the Charter of Fundamental Rights in Commission Legislative Proposals*, COM(2005) 172. See also House of Lords EU Select Committee: *Human Rights Proofing EU Legislation*, 16th Report of Session 2005-06, HL Paper 67.

However, the explanations add "As regards the Member States,[20] it follows unambiguously from the case-law of the Court of Justice that the requirement to respect fundamental rights defined in the context of the Union is only binding on the Member States when they act in the scope of Union law" (citing *Wachauf*,[21] *ERT*[22] and *Annibaldi*[23]). Thus, at first sight the explanations seem wider than the Charter due to the reference to "the scope of Union law" which would include situations of Member States derogating from Community law as well implementing it. However, the remaining text of the explanations talks of the application of the Charter to states only when *implementing* Union law. Even if the explanations are wider, it is unlikely that they will be used to contradict the express wording of the Charter since the explanations are merely guidance on the interpretation of the Charter.

The Charter will therefore apply to states only when implementing Community law (*quaere* as to the meaning of implementing) and not when they are derogating from it. Does this, in fact, matter? Probably not as much as would first appear, due to the role of general principles of European Community law. General principles of law, recognised by the European Court of Justice as binding on the Community institutions and the Member States when acting in the field of Community law, are derived from the Constitutional traditions of the Member States and international treaties.[24] It has long been established that fundamental rights are one of the general principles of law.[25] This point has been confirmed by Article 6(3) TEU-L:

"Fundamental rights, as guaranteed by the European Convention for the Protection of Human Rights and Funda-

---

20   The explanation adds "Of course this rule, as enshrined in this Charter, applies to the central authorities as well as to regional or local bodies, and to public organisations, when they are implementing Union law".

21   Case 5/88 *Wachauf* [1989] ECR 2609.

22   Case C-260/89 *ERT* [1991] ECR I-2925.

23   Case C-309/96 *Annibaldi* [1997] ECR I-7493.

24   See generally, *Tridimas* (2006).

25   See eg Case 29/69 *Stauder* [1969] ECR 419; Case 11/70 *Internationale Handelsgesellschaft mbH* v *Einfuhr und Vorratsstelle für Getreide und Futtermittel* [1970] ECR 1125, para. 4.

mental Freedoms and as they result from the constitutional traditions common to the Member States, shall constitute general principles of the Union's law".

Traditionally, general principles of law have been used to
challenge European Community legislative acts. When that challenge is based on fundamental rights, the challenge is usually un-
successful on the facts.[26] However, the European Court of Justice is
more willing to strike down Community *administrative* measures
on the basis that they breach fundamental human rights.[27]

Increasingly, fundamental rights, as general principles of law,
have also been used to limit Member State action[28] or to allow
Member States to restrict free movement.[29] Therefore, due to the
existence of the general principles of law, when acting in the sphere
of Community law (otherwise than when implementing Community
law to which the Charter will apply), Member States will still be
required to respect – not the Charter – but the general principles of
law which include human rights, many of which, like the Charter
itself, will be derived from international treaties, including the
European Convention of Human Rights.[30] So much for visibility
and clarification.

C. Competence

During its original drafting, a number of states were concerned that
the Charter might be used as a Trojan horse to expand the EC's

---

26 Case C-377/98 *Netherlands* v. *Council* (Biotechnology Directive)
[2001] ECR I-7079.

27 Case C-404/92P *X v Commission* [1994] ECR I-4737.

28 E.g. Case C-60/00 *Carpenter* [2002] ECR I-6279; Case C-109/01
Akrich [2003] ECR I-9607.

29 E.g. Case C-36/02 *Omega Spielhallen* [2004] ECR I-9609; Case C-
112/00 *Eugen Schmidberger, Internationale Transporte und Plan-
züge v. Republic of Austria* [2003] ECR I-5659.

30 Art. 6(2) TEU-L gives the EU the power to accede to the ECHR.
Declaration 2 adds: "The Conference agrees that the Union's accession to the European Convention for the Protection of Human Rights
and Fundamental Freedoms should be arranged in such a way as to
preserve the specific features of Union law. In this connection, the
Conference notes the existence of a regular dialogue between the
Court of Justice of the European Union and the European Court of
Human Rights; such dialogue could be reinforced when the Union
accedes to that Convention".

competence to legislate. The horizontal provisions found in Title VII of the Charter try to reassure the Member States. The second sentence of Article 51(1) provides:

> "They [the Unions institutions, bodies, offices and agencies as well as the Member Sates] shall therefore respect the rights, observe the principles and promote the application thereof in accordance with their respective powers and respecting the limits of the powers of the Union as conferred on it in the Treaties".

In addition, Article 51(2) provides:

> "The Charter does not extend the field of application of Union law beyond the powers of the Union or establish any new power or task for the Union, or modify powers and tasks as defined in the Treaties".

This is reinforced by the second paragraph of Article 6(1) TEU-L which says:[31]

> "The provisions of the Charter shall not extend in any way the competences of the Union as defined in the Treaties".

The accompanying explanations to the Charter add that Article 51(2) and the second sentence of Article 51(1) confirm that "the Charter may not have the effect of extending the competences and tasks which the Treaties confer on the Union".[32]

---

31   See also Declaration 1 of the Final Act of the Treaty of Lisbon: "The Charter of Fundamental Rights of the European Union, which has legally binding force, confirms the fundamental rights guaranteed by the European Convention for the Protection of Human Rights and Fundamental Freedoms and as they result from the constitutional traditions common to the Member States.

The Charter does not extend the field of application of Union law beyond the powers of the Union or establish any new power or task for the Union, or modify powers and tasks as defined by the Treaties".

32   The explanations add: "Explicit mention is made here of the logical consequences of the principle of subsidiarity and of the fact that the Union only has those powers which have been conferred upon it. The fundamental rights as guaranteed in the Union do not have any effect other than in the context of the powers determined by the Treaties. Consequently, an obligation, pursuant to the second sentence of paragraph 1, for the Union's institutions to promote principles laid

Clearly, this careful ring-fencing of competence in Title VII of the Charter had satisfied the UK since there is no reference to it in Protocol No. 7. The Czech Republic and Poland were less certain. In its Declaration on the Charter, the Czech Republic emphasises:

"... that the Charter does not extend the field of application of Union law and does not establish any new power for the Union. It does not diminish the field of application of national law and does not restrain any current powers of the national authorities in this field".[33]

Poland is also keen to ensure that the Charter does not curtail its right to legislate. Its Declaration says:

"The Charter does not affect in any way the right of Member States to legislate in the sphere of public morality, family law, as well as the protection of human dignity and respect for human physical and moral integrity".

Given these Declarations, what is the nature and function of the UK / Poland Protocol? In order to make an assessment, we begin by examining the provisions of the Protocol.

III. The UK / Poland Protocol

A. Article 1(1): Compatibility

The Protocol offers protection to Poland and the UK in three ways. First, it addresses the question of litigants raising the Charter before national courts or the ECJ to challenge the compatibility of national law with Charter rights. According to Article 1(1):

---

down in the Charter may arise only within the limits of these same powers".

Paragraph 2 also confirms that the Charter may not have the effect of extending the field of application of Union law beyond the powers of the Union as established in the Treaties. The Court of Justice has already established this rule with respect to the fundamental rights recognised as part of Union law (... C-249/96 *Grant* [1998] ECR I-621, paragraph 45 ...). In accordance with this rule, it goes without saying that the reference to the Charter in Art. 6 of the TEU-L cannot be understood as extending by itself the range of Member State action considered to be "implementation of Union law" (within the meaning of para. 1 and the above-mentioned case-law).

33   Declaration 53, second paragraph.

"The Charter does not extend the ability of the Court of
Justice of the European Union, or any court or tribunal of
Poland or of the United Kingdom, to find that the laws,
regulations or administrative provisions, practices or action of Poland or of the United Kingdom are inconsistent
with the fundamental rights, freedoms and principles that
it reaffirms".

There are three possible readings of this provision. The first,
and most natural, focuses on the phrase "The Charter does not *extend the ability* of the ECJ or any Polish or British court ...". This
suggests that the Charter does not give these courts greater powers
than they already have under Community law when national law is
implementing Community law. So, at a minimum, where the Charter incorporates a right that has already been recognised by the ECJ
– for example, the right to freedom of expression[34] – British and
Polish courts, and the ECJ when acting in the course of Article 226
proceedings, can rely on the Charter to declare national law inconsistent with that right where national law is implementing Community law. However, the British and Polish courts cannot apply the
Charter to situations governed purely by national law.

Therefore, if this first reading is correct then Article 1(1)
merely confirms Article 51(1) and (2) of the Charter and emphasises that the Charter is not a universal bill of rights. It therefore
serves as a reminder to national courts that they should apply the
Charter only to national law when implementing Community law
and not to issues of purely internal law. This helped to address UK
concerns about so-called "competence creep" where national judges
might decide to apply the Charter to situations governed purely by
national law.

A second possible reading of Article 1(1) is that if the Charter
goes further than the fundamental rights already recognised as general principles of law – a question which itself is highly contested[35]

---

34   Case C-260/89 *ERT* [1991] ECR I-2925, Case C-368/95 *Vereinigte
Familiapress Zeitungsverlags- und vertriebs GmbH ('Familiapress')*
v. *Heinrich Bauer Verlag* [1997] ECR I-3689.

35   See the discussion in EU Select Committee, *The Treaty of Lisbon: An
Impact Assessment*, 10th Report, 2007-8, HL Paper 62, para. 5.37ff
which considers whether Article 8 on protection of personal data and
Article 13 on freedom of the arts and sciences go further than the pre-
existing general principles of law.

– then these "new" provisions cannot be used by the British and Polish courts and the ECJ to review UK and Polish legislation.

The third, and least likely, reading of Article 1(1) is that it is intended to prevent the Charter from being used to challenge national law implementing Community law. If this is the case then the UK and Poland are in fact derogating from the Charter and it becomes a true opt-out. However, the UK government does not claim the Protocol is a full opt-out (see below) and the recitals to the Protocol appear to indicate that there is no change intended to the *status quo*. And, even if the third reading is correct, there would be nothing to prevent the ECJ / national courts avoiding the Protocol's limitations by relying on general principles of law, instead of the Charter, to challenge national rules in the scope of EC Law.

Whatever the ultimate interpretation of Article 1(1), nothing in the Protocol will prevent British courts from continuing to refer to the Charter in identifying the scope of fundamental rights,[36] drawing on the Charter in the same way as they draw on many international human rights instruments, when interpreting the content of fundamental rights.[37]

B. Article 1(2): No Justiciable Rights in Title IV

1. The Content of Article 1(2)

The second way that Poland and the UK are protected by the Protocol can be found in Article 1(2). It provides:

"In particular, and for the avoidance of doubt, nothing in Title IV of the Charter creates justiciable rights applicable to Poland or the United Kingdom except in so far as Po-

---

36 See for example *R v East Sussex County Council and the Disability Rights Commission ex parte A, B, X & Y* [2003] EHC 167 (Admin) per Munby J at paragraph 73: "the Charter is not at present legally binding in our domestic law and is therefore not a source of law in the strict sense. But it can, in my judgment, properly be consulted insofar as it proclaims, reaffirms or elucidates the content of those human rights that are generally recognised throughout the European family of nations, in particular the nature and scope of those fundamental rights that are guaranteed by the Convention".

37 Conclusions of House of Lords EU Select Committee, *The Treaty of Lisbon: An Impact Assessment*, 10th Report, 2007-8, HL Paper 62, para. 5.111.

land or the United Kingdom has provided for such rights in its national law".[38]

Title IV is the Solidarity Title of the Charter. As we have seen, the UK thought that the content of this Title related to *principles*, not rights, and so the question of their direct effectiveness would not arise. However, as we have also seen, some of the provisions in the Solidarity Title, in particular Articles 28 and 30 appear to be drafted in terms of rights, or at least a mixture of right and principles. Article 1(2) therefore does a belt and braces job, making sure ("for the avoidance of doubt") that if any of the provisions of Title IV are in fact classed as rights they are not directly effective in the UK and Poland. In this respect the Protocol does appear to contain a genuine opt-out for the UK and Poland. This opt-out is, however, subject to the (rather obvious) caveat that Title IV rights are not justiciable except in so far as Poland or the UK has provided for such rights in its national law. Presumably this means that national rules on strike action and dismissal will continue to apply but could be interpreted, *Marleasing*-style, in the light of the Charter.

We turn now to consider the two Articles in Title IV of the Charter most likely to be affected by this Protocol, Articles 28 and 30, both sensitive provisions in the UK.

2. Article 28 of the Charter

a. Article 28 and the Protocol

Article 28 provides:

"Workers and employers, or their respective organisations, have, *in accordance with Union law and national laws and practices*, the right to negotiate and conclude collective agreements at the appropriate levels and, in cases of conflicts of interest, to take collective action to defend their interests, *including strike action*".[39]

---

38 See also the Preamble to the Protocol "REAFFIRMING that references in this Protocol to the operation of specific provisions of the Charter are strictly without prejudice to the operation of other provisions of the Charter".

39 The Explanations add: "This Article is based on Article 6 of the European Social Charter and on the Community Charter of the Fundamental Social Rights of Workers (points 12 to 14). The right of collective action was recognised by the European Court of Human Rights as one of the elements of trade union rights laid down by Arti-

The UK, with its absence of a written constitution, has no *'right* to strike'. Instead, trade unions enjoy only an *immunity* from being sued in tort where certain conditions are satisfied (see below). From a trade union perspective, a right-based system, as typically found on the Continent, is more favourable because strikes are presumed *lawful* and so the state has to justify limiting the 'right'. By contrast, in an immunity based system, strikes are presumed *unlawful* and trade unions have to justify why they are going on strike by fitting themselves into the immunity provided by the statute. Given the structural differences in approach between the common law and Continental systems, the UK government was concerned about the EU introducing a 'right' to strike in the UK via the backdoor of the Charter. Further, successive Conservative governments in the UK have, since 1979, significantly curtailed the trade unions' ability to call their members out on strike. The Labour government has maintained this stance,[40] thereby helping to ensure a flexible labour market in the UK.[41] This background helps to explain why the UK wanted an opt-out from Article 28 if Article 28 does indeed enshrine a *right* to strike (as opposed to a principle on collective action). Article 1(2) appears to deliver this.

Yet, Article 1(2) might be less significant in practice than would first appear. This can be demonstrated by examining the following examples. First, consider the situation of the police in the UK who are prohibited, by statute, from taking industrial action. They might try to rely on Article 28 to argue that they should be able to strike. Such a claim will fail because the matter falls outside the scope of the Charter since the UK is not implementing Community law, as required by Article 51(1).

---

cle 11 of the ECHR. ... The modalities and limits for the exercise of collective action, including strike action, come under national laws and practices, including the question of whether it may be carried out in parallel in several Member States".

40   See e.g. the Prime Minister's Foreword to the *Fairness at Work White Paper*, Cm3968 (1997): "There will be no going back. The days of strikes without ballots, mass picketing, closed shops and secondary action are over".

41   CBI's evidence to House of Lords EU Select Committee, *The Treaty of Lisbon: An Impact Assessment*, 10th Report, 2007-8, HL Paper 62, para.5.32.

Second, consider the situation of a dock workers' trade union calling its members out on strike to protest at the health and safety implications of dangerous waste being imported into a British dock from another Member State. As a result, the waste cannot enter the UK and the importers allege a breach of Article 28 EC by the trade unions. The trade union wishes to invoke Article 28 of the Charter in its defence. It cannot do so because, as the discussion in heading II.B above indicates, the Charter does not apply where states/trade unions are derogating from EC Law. Article 1(2) of the Protocol is thus not relevant in this situation.

Third, consider a Directive that bans strike action in sensitive sectors, such as energy, which is duly implemented in the UK. The trade unions might wish to challenge the implementing measure in the UK as contravening Article 28. Here the Protocol would have some effect by denying the trade unions a claim in the national courts. However, assuming they had *locus standi*, the trade unions could have challenged the original Directive directly before the ECJ under Article 230, relying on the right to strike as a general principle of law as the ground of challenge. They could also argue that the Community had no power to adopt such a measure in the first place, due to the exclusion of competence under Article 137(5).

So it would only be in the most exceptional situations that the UK government would need to invoke Article 1(2). Furthermore, Article 28 of the Charter may be less significant to trade unions than they had first anticipated due to the Court of Justice's ruling in *Viking*.

b. *Viking* and the UK

The Charter tried to limit the scope of the right in Article 28 by referring to taking collective action in accordance with (1) Union law and (2) national laws and practices.[42] At first it was thought that the reference to national law and practices would be the greatest limit on the right to strike. In the UK, national law grants trade unions immunity from liability in tort if the so-called 'golden formula' is satisfied i.e. the collective action is taken "in contemplation or furtherance of a trade dispute".[43] A 'trade dispute' is defined in s.244(1) Trade Union Labour Relations (Consolidation) Act 1992 as a dispute be-

---

42   See also Art. 52(6) of the Charter: "Full account shall be taken of national laws and practices as specified in this Charter".

43   S.219 TULR(C)A 1992.

tween "workers and their employer which relates wholly or mainly"
to one or more of the following:

a. Terms and conditions of employment, or physical working
    conditions
b. Engagement or non-engagement of workers, termination or
    suspension of employment or duties of one or more workers
c. Allocation of work or job duties between workers or groups of
    workers
d. Matters of discipline
e. A worker's membership / non-membership of a trade union
f. Facilities for officials of a trade union
g. Trade union recognition, negotiation and consultation agree-
    ments or machinery.

Further, courts will check whether the immunity has been lost
because the strike is for a prohibited reason (e.g. secondary industrial action) or because the relevant procedures have not been complied with (e.g. failure to ballot the relevant workers, failure to give
employers the correct notice).

While national law, in the UK at least, imposes significant restrictions on strike action, the *Viking* case[44] suggests that *Union* law
might provide the greatest limit on the right to take collective action
in the future. *Viking* concerned a Finnish company that wanted to
reflag its vessel, the *Rosella* which traded the loss-making route
between Helsinki and Tallinn in Estonia, under the Estonian flag so
that Viking could man the ship with an Estonian crew to be paid
considerably less than the existing Finnish crew. The International
Transport Workers' Federation (ITF) had been running a Flag of
Convenience (FOC) campaign trying to stop ship owners from
taking just such action. It therefore told its affiliates to boycott the
Rosella and to take other solidarity industrial action against both the
Rosella and other Viking vessels. The Finnish Seaman's Union
(FSU) also threatened strike action. Viking therefore sought an in-
junction in the English High Court,[45] restraining the ITF and the
FSU from breaching, *inter alia*, Article 43 EC.

The first question was whether Community law applied at all.
For the ECJ the answer was clear: collective action falls in principle

---

44 Case C-438/05 *International Transport Workers' Federation* v.
    Viking Line ABP [2007] ECR I-000.

45 ITF had its base in London and so jurisdiction was established pursu-
    ant to the Brussels Regulation 44/2001 OJ [2001] L12/1.

"within the scope of Article 43".[46] The Court dismissed the argument that just because Article 137(5) excluded Community competence in respect of, *inter alia*, the right to strike, strike action as a whole fell outside the scope of Community law.[47] The Court also rejected the argument that fundamental rights fell outside Community law.[48] It then appeared to make a significant concession: it recognised the right to strike as a fundamental principle of Community law for the first time. It said the right to take collective action, including the right to strike, was recognised both by various international instruments which the Member States have signed or co-operated in,[49] and the Charter of Fundamental Rights 2000.[50] It then said:

"... the right to take collective action, including the right to strike, must therefore be recognised as a fundamental right which forms an integral part of the general principles of Community law the observance of which the Court ensures".[51]

However, this observation came with a sting in its tail: the right to take industrial action is not absolute but subject to "certain restrictions" under Community law and national law and practices.[52] *Viking* lays down the Community restrictions: collective action would be justified only if it were established that the jobs or conditions of employment at issue were jeopardised or under serious threat[53] and the action was proportionate. Proportionality meant

---

46   Para. 37.

47   Paras. 39-41.

48   Citing C-112/00 *Schmidberger* [2003] ECR I-5659, para. 77, Case C-36/02 *Omega* [2004] ECR I-9609, para. 36.

49   Citing the European Social Charter 1961 – to which express reference is made in Article 136 EC – and ILO Convention No 87 concerning Freedom of Association and Protection of the Right to Organise and by instruments developed by those Member States at Community level or in the context of the EU, such as the Community Charter of the Fundamental Social Rights of Workers 1989.

50   Para. 43.

51   Para. 44. Case C–341/05 *Laval un Partneri Ltd v Svenska Byggnadsarbetareförbundet and others* [2007] ECR I-000, paras. 90-92.

52   Para. 44.

53   Para. 81.

in this context whether FSU had other means at its disposal which
were "less restrictive of freedom of establishment in order to bring
to a successful conclusion the collective negotiations entered into
with Viking, and, on the other, whether that trade union had exhausted those means before initiating such action".[54] Thus, the
Court of Justice appears to suggest that industrial action should be
the last resort; and the British courts would have to verify whether
the FSU had exhausted all other avenues under Finnish law before
going on strike. Since the case has now been settled we shall never
have the opportunity of hearing what the Court of Appeal thought
on these matters.

It could be argued that the effect of the *Viking* judgment is to
narrow still further the immunity granted to trade unions by UK
law. As we have seen, according to *Viking,* trade unions can call
their members out on strike only if the jobs of their members or the
terms and conditions of employment are seriously jeopardised.
While this might cover headings (a) and (b) of s.244 TULR(C)A,
headings (c)-(g) appear to fall outside the ECJ's definition. Moreover, the proportionality test in these cases may well mean that
trade unions have to carry on negotiating longer than before, especially when a well-advised employer holds out the prospect that
there might be a settlement just round the corner. How will trade
unions know if they have "exhausted those means"?

If this analysis is correct, it may well mean that the reference
in Article 28 of the Charter to limits laid down by *Union* law is, in
the context of transnational disputes, a more powerful constraint on
the right to strike than the limits laid down by national law. As the
House of Lords Select Committee noted, the Charter "seemed to be
employed by the Court more as a brake than an accelerator in these
cases".[55] Little did the UK government expect that it would have
the ECJ as an ally not a foe in its desire to draw the teeth of Article
28 of the Charter. The *Viking* litigation has thus significantly reduced the need for Article 1(2) of the Protocol.

---

54   Para. 87.

55   House of Lords Constitution Committee, *European Union (Amend-
     ment) Bill and the Lisbon Treaty: Implications for the UK Constitu-
     tion*, 6th Report, 2007-8, HL Paper 84, para.5.35.

3. Article 30

The other provision which caused the UK concern was Article 30. This provides:

"Every worker has the right to protection against unjustified dismissal, in accordance with Union law and national laws and practices".

UK business was concerned that this gave individuals the right to protection against unfair dismissal, a right that had not previously been recognised by the Court of Justice. To an extent the UK's concerns appear unfounded: the UK already has legislation governing dismissal, extensive case law (which, through the application of the 'band of reasonable responses' test,[56] tends to favour employers) and important guidance offered by the Advisory, Conciliation and Arbitration Service (ACAS) Code of Practice. Article 2, the third limb of protection for Poland and the UK in the Protocol, was included to ensure that such rules and practices would continue to govern Article 30 of the Charter as well as the other rights in the Charter which refer to national laws and practices.[57] It provides:

"To the extent that a provision of the Charter refers to national laws and practices, it shall only apply to Poland or the United Kingdom to the extent that the rights or principles that it contains are recognised in the law or practices of Poland or of the United Kingdom".

This suggests that the Charter goes no further than pre-existing national law. British and Polish employers can breathe a sigh of relief.

---

56   *Iceland Frozen Foods v. Jones* [1982] IRLR 439, 442 (EAT) "in judging the reasonableness of the employer's conduct an industrial tribunal must not substitute its decision as to what the right course to adopt for that of the employer ... in many, though not all, cases there is a band of reasonable responses to the employee's conduct within which one employer might reasonably take one view, another might quite easily take another; .. the function of an industrial tribunal, as an industrial jury, is to determine whether in the particular circumstances of each case the decision to dismiss the employee fell within the band of reasonable responses which a reasonable employer might have adopted". Confirmed in *Post Office* v. *Foley*; *Midland Bank plc* v. *Madden* [2000] IRLR 827 (Court of Appeal).

57   See also Article 52(6) of the Charter.

4. Conclusion

There is a perplexing irony about the UK and Polish position under
Article 1(2) of the Charter in particular. The UK has a labour government. The Labour party's origins lie in the workers' movement.
Yet it is a Labour government which has highlighted the Solidarity
Title as problematic. This irony is more acute in Poland where the
Solidarity movement was so influential in challenging the Commu-
nist regime. This point was admitted by the (new) Polish government elected between the conclusion of the IGC in October 2007
and finalising the Treaty of Lisbon in December 2007. Its Declaration on the Protocol says:[58]

> "Poland declares that, having regard to the tradition of so-
> cial movement of 'Solidarity' and its significant contribu-
> tion to the struggle for social and labour rights, it fully re-
> spects social and labour rights, as established by European
> Union law, and in particular those reaffirmed in Title IV
> of the Charter of Fundamental Rights of the European
> Union".

This Declaration appears to undermine significantly any potential use of the Article 1(2) 'opt-out' in respect of Poland. In
truth, as this Declaration shows, Poland's concerns are not with social and labour rights. Poland's real fears lie with subjects such as
gay marriage and abortion but the Protocol (and the Charter) do not
touch on these.

IV. Is the Protocol an Opt-out?

In the previous section we considered the content of the Protocol.
Depending on the reading of Article 1 of the Protocol, it may
contain elements of opt-out for the UK and Poland, particularly in
respect of Title IV of the Charter, although most of the Protocol is
merely clarification. The Preamble to the Protocol makes this point
clear. It says the purpose of the Protocol is to "*clarify* certain aspects of the application of the Charter" (emphasis added). Therefore, outside the rights in Title IV, the Charter will apply to the UK
and Poland. They will continue to have to respect Charter rights
under Article 6(1) TEU-L when they are implementing EC law, a
point noted by the Preamble to Protocol:

58　Declaration 62. See *Dougan* (2008), 669.

"WHEREAS the Charter is to be applied in strict accordance with the provisions of the aforementioned Article 6
and Title VII of the Charter itself;
WHEREAS the aforementioned Article 6 requires the
Charter to be applied and interpreted by the courts of Poland and of the United Kingdom strictly in accordance
with the explanations referred to in that Article".

However, there is a remarkable feature of the public discourse
in the UK about this Protocol. On the one hand there is a general
perception that the Protocol contains a full opt-out for the UK (and
Poland) from the Charter *as a whole*. On the other, the British government, in its public pronouncements to official *fora* (e.g. Select
Committees), suggests the opposite.

In fact, there appears to be a rather complex political game at
play. To a predominantly Eurosceptic audience, the more UK opt-
outs there were to the Lisbon Treaty the better (although this does
not answer the question why, if an 'opt-out' to the Charter was necessary at Lisbon, an opt-out had not been negotiated from the Constitutional Treaty[59]). The perception of an opt-out, and certainly the
existence of the Protocol, helped the UK government make the case
that the Lisbon Treaty was different to the Constitutional Treaty
and so there was no need to have a referendum on the Lisbon
Treaty (*Tony Blair* had made a manifesto commitment in 2005 for a
referendum on the Constitutional Treaty, a referendum which was
highly likely to result in a "no" vote).

So, it was very helpful to the UK government that the Eurosceptic press in the UK, at least initially, was willing to accept the
line that there was now an opt-out to the Charter of Fundamental
Rights. For example, in June 2007 the DAILY MAIL said: "Mr
Blair's final appearance on the European stage produced a clear
negotiating success as Britain won a legally-binding opt-out from
the controversial charter".[60] The NEWS OF THE WORLD said "EU
chiefs have agreed to give Britain an opt-out on the Charter of Fundamental Rights which could bring in new laws which would de-
stroy jobs".[61] The DAILY EXPRESS also repeated *Tony Blair's* views
that he has "already signed up to the charter in principle, but insists

---

59   *Craig* (2008) 163.

60   B. *Brogan*, Deal but at What price?, DAILY MAIL, 23 June 2007.

61   J. *Lyons*, EU Traitor, THE NEWS OF THE WORLD, 24 June 2007.

he has secured an opt-out that means it won't apply here".[62] The
SUNDAY EXPRESS echoed similar sentiments: "Under the treaty, the
charter will be legally binding on all EU states, but the UK has an
opt-out designed to limit its effect on our own national laws". It did,
however, add that "Judges at the ECJ insisted that the so-called
'safeguards' will not prevent the charter from altering national law
and it will be the ECJ's judges who would ultimately decide on
how to interpret the charter".[63]

The SUNDAY EXPRESS' story, only a couple of days after the
Brussels European Council in June 2007, shows just how quickly
the mood began to change. By mid-July 2007 THE SUN was already
saying "Opt-out a 'sham'".[64] As the Treaty was coming up to be
signed, THE SUN said:[65] "Mr *Brown* insists Britain has won an opt-
out [from the Charter]. But Labour MPs have warned the opt-out is
meaningless". The SUNDAY EXPRESS also noted that "Critics claim
Government opt-outs will not work and that this charter of 50 rights
will be imposed by the European Court of Justice through the 'back
door', affecting policies on abortion, immigration and public services and force an end to the ban on secondary picketing in industrial disputes".[66]

While, on the one hand, the UK government was trying to pla-
cate Eurosceptics in the UK, on the other the UK did not want to
upset its partners, particularly other Member States to whom the
Protocol was presented by the UK very late in the day. It also did
not want to upset the trade unions who threatened to throw their
weight behind a campaign for a referendum on the treaty.[67] So the

---

62   Q&A, SUNDAY EXPRESS, 24 June 2007

63   *Julia Hartley-Brewer* and *Jason Groves*, EU Deal Unravels within
     Hours, SUNDAY EXPRESS, 24 June 2007.

64   13 July 2007 and 29 August 2007

65   *George Pascoe-Watson*, Two words that could change the shape of
     Britain forever, THE SUN, 12 December 2007.

66   How Brussels will get its way, SUNDAY EXPRESS, 21 October 2007.

67   "In the face of the prospect that they [trade unions] will throw their
     weight behind the campaign for a referendum on the treaty, Mr
     Brown has now said that there was no 'opt-out' after all. Instead his
     Government will insist that the charter will create no new rights
     anywhere across the EU": *S. Cable*, Brown olive branch to unions
     over EU treaty, DAILY MAIL, 7 September 2007. See also *J. Goves*

government offered reassurances to 'informed' audiences that the Protocol was merely clarificatory and not an opt-out.[68] For example, in evidence to the House of Lords Select Committee, the Department of Work and Pensions (DWP) said categorically, "The UK Protocol does not constitute an 'opt-out'. It puts beyond doubt the legal position that nothing in the Charter creates any new rights, or extends the ability of any court to strike down UK law".[69] *Jack Straw*, Secretary of State for Justice, was even more robust. He said the Protocol was intended to reflect the terms of the Charter's horizontal articles themselves and puts beyond doubt what should have been obvious from other provisions.[70]

Alan Dashwood, who has advised the UK government extensively on the Constitutional Treaty, shares *Jack Straw*'s view. He

---

Now the unions call for EU referendum; Fury at PM's bid to sign away the right to strike, SUNDAY EXPRESS, 9 Sept. 2007.

68   The British government also does not describe the protocol as an opt-out, using instead its official title of Protocol. Its formal title is "Protocol on the application of the charter of fundamental rights of the European Union to Poland and to the United Kingdom". See e.g. the Foreign Office's website on the Charter although its presentation of the successful achievement of the UK's four 'red lines' might cause confusion if not read carefully:

"We have also secured a UK-specific deal different to that in the other 26 Member States – and different from the Constitutional Treaty – because we have secured extra safeguards for the UK (the four 'red lines')":

- The UK has a right to opt-in to JHA, thus protecting our common law system and criminal and judicial processes.
- *The UK has a legally-binding Protocol on the Charter, thus protecting our social and labour legislation.*
- There is clarification on the role of the High Representative including a Declaration confirming that foreign policy will remain in the hands of the Member States.
- There are stronger safeguards for protecting our social security system.

http://www.fco.gov.uk/resources/en/pdf/pdf19/fco_beu_pdf_reformtr eaty10myths (emphasis added).

69   House of Lords EU Select Committee, *The Treaty of Lisbon: An Impact Assessment*, 10th Report, 2007-8, HL Paper 62, para.5.86.

70   House of Lords EU Select Committee, *The Treaty of Lisbon: An Impact Assessment*, 10th Report, 2007-8, HL Paper 62, paras. 5.96.

wrote that the function of the Protocol was "interpretative – to state unequivocally, and with the force of primary law, what ought to be obvious from a reading of the Charter in the light of the horizontal provisions and of the official explanations".[71]

It is, however, surprising that these reassurances emphasise Article 1(1) of the Charter and the question of competence – and the fact that the Charter does not extend it – rather than the question of enforceability in Article 1(2)..

The extent of the government's political game was revealed when *Jim Murphy MP*, Minister for Europe, wrote to the House of Commons' European scrutiny committee:[72]

> "The UK-specific Protocol which the Government se-cured is not an 'opt-out' from the Charter. Rather, the Protocol clarifies the effect the Charter will have in the UK".

The right wing press responded angrily. For example, the DAILY MAIL said "As the Scrutiny Committee forcibly pointed out, the Government's opt-outs do not stand up to even cursory scrutiny".[73] THE SUN said "When Tony Blair agreed the outline EU Treaty last June, he boasted Britain had an 'opt-out' from the Charter of Fundamental Rights – which includes the right to strike. But the Commons European Scrutiny Committee report publishes a letter from Labour's Europe Minister Jim Murphy in which he concedes we do NOT".[74]

> So, is Protocol No.7 an opt-out, in the same way as, say, the Social Policy Protocol and Social Policy Agreement which gave the UK a real opt-out from the Social Chapter of the Maastricht Treaty? Or is the function of Protocol No.7 merely to "clarify certain aspects of the application of the Charter" and is thus not an opt-out at all? The EU House of Lords' Select Committee said "The Protocol is not an opt-out from the Charter. The Charter will apply in

71   The paper tiger that is no threat to Britain's fundamental rights, *Parliamentary Brief*, 10 March 2008. http://www.thepolitician.org/articles/the-paper-tiger-646.html.

72   European Scrutiny, 35th report, 2006-7.

73   *E. Heathcoat*, Blatant deception and a betrayal of trust, DAILY MAIL, 17 October 2007.

74   *G. Wilson*, 10 days to save Britain, THE SUN, 9 October 2007.

the UK, even if its interpretation may be affected by the terms of the Protocol".[75] I would generally share this view, except in respect of the points outlined in section C above where there is evidence of an opt-out from the rights outlined in Title IV.

V. Conclusions

The Protocol to the Charter is an exercise in smoke and mirrors. It was introduced largely for presentational reasons to help convince the British public that the Lisbon Treaty was different to the Constitutional Treaty. This presentational ploy has come unravelled but the government has nevertheless achieved its objective: the European Union (Amendment) Bill 2007, and now Act of 2008, ratifying the Lisbon Treaty has passed through the UK Parliament relatively unscathed, albeit subject to a judicial review brought by spread-betting millionaire Stuart Wheeler, on the government's decision not to hold a referendum.[76]

Will the Charter have a particular impact? Many think that the position pre- and post- the Lisbon Treaty will not be as different as might at first appear.[77] The Court of Justice has finally come off the fence and started to refer to the Charter[78] but the reference to the

---

75   House of Lords EU Select Committee, *The Treaty of Lisbon: An Impact Assessment*, 10th Report, 2007-8, HL Paper 62, paras. 5.87.

76   http://news.bbc.co.uk/1/hi/uk_politics/7442980.stm.

77   House of Lords Constitution Committee, *European Union (Amendment) Bill and the Lisbon Treaty: Implications for the UK Constitution*, 6th Report, 2007-8, HL Paper 84, para. 67.

78   Case C-540/03 *EP v EU Council (Family Reunification Directive)* [2007] ECR I-000, para. 38, Case C-432/05 *Unibet* v. *Justitiekanslern* [2007] ECR I-000, para. 37, Case C-244/06 *Dynamic Medien Vertriebs GmbH* v. *Avides Media AG* [2008] ECR I-000, para. 41. Prior to this the Charter has been referred to by a number of Advocates General (see, e.g. AG *Jacobs'* Opinion in Case C-50/00 *Unión de Pequeños Agricultores v. Council of the European Union* [2002] ECR I-6677; AG *Geelhoed*'s Opinion in Case C-224/98 *D'Hoop v. Office National d'Emploi* [2002] ECR I-000), as has the Court of First Instance (see, e.g. Case T-177/01 *Jégo Quéré et Cie SA v. European Commission* [2002] ECR II-000), the European Court of Human Rights (see eg *Godwin v UK* [2002] 35 EHRR 18) and national courts (see, e.g. *R (on the application of Robertson) v. Wakefield MDC* [2002] QB 1052, 170)).

Charter is merely to buttress or confirm the interpretation of a Community measure.[79] And, as we saw in *Viking*, the reference to the Charter might not necessarily be good news for individuals actually invoking the Charter in support. On the other hand, others suggest that, in time, reference to the Charter will become the norm and that it will wholly transform certain types of litigation. This has been the experience in the UK when the European Convention of Human Rights was incorporated into national law by the Human Rights Act 1998. If this is the case then the Protocol may become more significant than first appeared.

References

Brian Bercusson (2007), The Trade Union Movement and the European Union: Judgment Day, in: European Law Journal 13 (2007), 279-308.

Paul Craig (2008), The Treaty of Lisbon, process, architecture and substance, in: European Law Review 33 (2008), 137-166.

Gráinne de Búrca (2001), The drafting of the European Charter of Fundamental Rights, in: European Law Review 26 (2001), 126-137.

Michael Dougan (2008), The Treaty of Lisbon 2007: Winning Minds, Not Hearts, in: Common Market Law Review 45 (2008), 617-703

Peter Henry Lord Goldsmith Q.C. (2001), A Charter of Rights, Freedoms and Principles, in: Common Market Law Review 38 (2001), 1201-1216.

Bob Hepple (2005), Rights at Work: Global, European and British Perspectives, London (Sweet & Maxwell) 2005.

Jeff Kenner (2003), Economic and Social Rights in the EU Legal order: the Mirage of Indivisibility, in: *Tamara Hervey / Jeff Kenner* (eds.), Economic and Social Rights under the EU Charter of Fundamental Rights, Oxford (Hart) 2003, 1-26.

---

79 See e.g. *Viking* "As is reaffirmed by Article 28 of the Charter of Fundamental Rights of the European Union, those rights are to be protected in accordance with Community law and national law and practices" (para. 44).

Koen Lenaerts / Eddy de Smijter (2001), A "Bill of Rights" for the European Union, in: Common Market Law Review 38 (2001), 273-300.

Takis Tridimas (2006), The General Principles of Law, Oxford (Oxford University Press) 2006.

Jean-Victor Louis

Economic Policy under the Lisbon Treaty

This contribution should be read in parallel to the report presented by *Antonio Saínz de Vicuña* on the ECB and monetary union in the Lisbon Treaty. We have mostly preserved the form of the oral presentation made at the conference. We will first offer some elements of comparison between the Constitutional Treaty and the Lisbon Treaty and then we will proceed with an analysis of the reform of the provisions on economic policy and on provisions specific to the euro area. Finally, we will conclude by evoking some perspectives.

I. From Rome 2004 to Lisbon 2007

1. The Lisbon Treaty differs on very few points from the Treaty establishing a Constitution for Europe (the Constitutional Treaty) in the field of economic policy, as in many others. But, on the one hand, the analysis has to bear on the changes in respect of the existing Treaties and on the other, we have to take into account the fact that the provisions of the Constitutional Treaty (CT) have already been broadly commented on,[1] in particular, at the conference organised by the EUI two years ago on the CT. For this reason we have

---

[1] See in particular, *Louis* (2004); *Smits* (2005); *Servais / Ruggeri* (2005); *Dony / Louis* (2005); *Bribosia* (2007).

limited the exposé to the main elements, without entering into many details.

2.   The Lisbon Treaty, like the Constitutional Treaty, does not change the allocation of powers in economic policy between the Member States and the Union. Article 5 of the TFEU, concerning economic and employment policy, has the same wording as Article I-15 of the Constitutional Treaty. Paragraph 1 was one of the most discussed texts at the European Convention and within the IGC 2003-2004. Its wording looks very restrictive as far as the competences of the Union are concerned. The intention is clear: Member States maintain primary responsibility as regards their economic policies. But there is no impact of this wording on the competences of the Union in this field, as they are provided in Part III of the Constitutional Treaty and in the related chapters of the TFEU. Nothing has substantially changed in comparison with the existing Treaties.

3.   Nevertheless, the place reserved to EMU, and more generally its meaning in the evolution of European integration, are viewed in a different way by the Constitutional Treaty and the Lisbon Treaty. The EMU was not listed among the objectives of the Union in Article I-3 of the CT, but it has reappeared in Article 3 of the TEU-L. One can discuss the importance of the list of objectives: are they purely symbolic or do they offer useful help for the interpretation – or perhaps something of both? But politically,[2] the suppression of EMU in Article I-3 CT appeared to be a concession to the UK; the explicit motivation given during the Convention – that EMU is not an objective any more because it has already been realised – is not to be taken seriously. EMU, like the internal market, is work in progress. But there is something more in the way both the CT and the Lisbon Treaty envisage the EMU: it is the kind of, if not assimilation, at least approximation of EMU to an enhanced co-operation, that is conceived under the general clause

---

2   The insertion of EMU in the list of the general objectives of the Union should help if one intends to use Article 352 TFEU, that replaces Article 308 in the present EC Treaty but we are of the opinion that this provision can also be used in order to implement specfic objectives of the Treaties not included in Article 3 TEU-L. As everybody does not share our view, it is surely better to be able to have EMU inserted in article 3 TEU-L.

of Article I-44 of the CT. The careful analysis conducted by *Hervé Bribosia*[3] reveals that the idea of streamlining the respective processes was present in the minds of the drafters. It was more than just symbolic that it was made to appear that for a State to have adopted the euro was an exceptional situation and not the rule. Seen more positively, perhaps we should think that the idea was also to single out the growing identity[4] and the specific needs of the euro area. In any case, it was clear from Part III of the CT that participation in EMU remained an objective for all the Member States and that the regime provided for the 'Outs' was a transitory one. But the provisions of Part III were not necessarily read with the same attention as Part I of the CT. The Lisbon Treaty restored the EMU in its original nature. It places EMU as an objective equal in importance to the single market and reminds us that it is the supreme stage of economic integration, as the *Delors* Report called it, conditioning the evolution of sectoral policies, such as fiscal, social, employment and trade policies. It is important to note that the euro is also mentioned in Article 3(4) of the TEU-L, where the 'symbols' have been omitted.

4. Also symbolically politically, and perhaps legally important, are the insertion in the Lisbon Treaty of the concept of solidarity and the mention of the area of energy in relation with severe difficulties arising in the supply of certain products in Article 122 TFEU. Considering the text of Article 100 TEC and its use in one decision in the past for the supply in crude oil,[5] nobody could have doubted the fact that the products concerned could be energy sources, and it was also clear that this Article was inspired by solidarity in a chapter that by contrast includes a rigorous 'no bailouts' clause. But these additions demonstrate the concern of the authors of the Treaty for this priority of the Union. The potential of Article 100 TEC (122 TFEU) was never realised, as observed by *René Smits*.

---

3   See *Bribosia* (2007); and above all, his EUI PhD thesis on enhanced co-operation (to be published).

4   The consolidation of the UK 'opt out' is one of the elements to take into account, as is the progress towards financial integration realised in the euro area.

5   See *Smits* (2007), 8, note 11.

One can qualify with the same words the insertion of the fight against climate change in the Environment chapter.

II. The amendments to chapter 1 on 'Economic Policy' of Title VIII on 'Economic and Monetary Policy'.

1.   As we have observed above, there is no meaningful innovation in the Lisbon Treaty in comparison with the Constitutional Treaty. The amendments to the EC Treaty are limited to three categories: a) a modest increase in the powers of the Commission; b) the suppression of the voting powers of the State concerned by a procedure or of the 'Outs' when 'Ins' are concerned; and c) the adaptation of procedures to the modification of the decision-making process in the TEU-L.

2.   The Commission gains a 'warning power' under Article 121, paragraph 4, as a preliminary step[6] before the recommendation of the Council addressed to a Member State in the process of economic surveillance. Article 126, paragraph 5 grants the Commission the right to send, on its own initiative, an 'opinion' to those Member States it considers as having an excessive budget deficit, and Article 126, paragraph 6 gives the Commission competence to make a 'proposal' (and not a simple 'recommendation') to the Council for a decision on the existence of such excessive deficit.

3.   The Member State concerned will not have a voting right under Article 121, paragraph 4, subparagraph 2 (economic policy surveillance) or under Article 126, paragraph 13, subparagraph

---

6   One should observe at this regard, that the Ecofin report of 20 March 2005 to the European Council on "Improving the implementation of the Stability and Growth Pact", endorsed by the European Concil in its conclusions of 22 March 2005, provides that "the Commission will issue policy advice to encourage Member States to stick to their adjustment path [towards the medium term budgetary objective (MTO)]". The Code of conduct endorsed by the Ecofin Council of 11 October 2005 specifies that this policy advice could be given in the form of a recommendation under Article 211, second indent of the ECT and made public. The Commission addressed to France in May 2008, a recommendation "providing a policy advice on [its] economic and budgetary policy", see SEC(2008) 1942/3. Article 211, second indent of the ECT provides that the Commission may adopt a recommendation when it considers it necessary.

2 for decisions under paragraphs 6 to 9 and 11 / 12 (in the fight against excessive deficits). Only the Ins vote for decisions under Article 121, paragraph 4 (economic policy surveillance) when euro area members are the addressees. Likewise, only the Ins vote under Article 126, paragraphs 6 to 8 and 11, when euro area members are concerned by a procedure against excessive deficits.

4.   The procedures are adapted to the modifications of the rules applicable to the decision-making process, and especially to the suppression of the so-called co-operation procedure: this procedure is changed to the ordinary legislative procedure in Article 121, paragraph 6 for adopting the modalities of the surveillance procedure, in an *ad hoc* procedure in Article 125, paragraph 2 for specifying the definitions for the application of Article 123 (prohibition of monetary financing) or 124 (prohibition of privileged access of the public sector to credit institutions), and to a special legislative procedure in Article 126, paragraph 14, subparagraph 2 for the adoption of appropriate provisions in order to replace the protocol on excessive deficits. New QMV will be introduced in accordance with Article 238, paragraph 3, *litt.* a, beginning 1 November 2014 in Article 121, paragraph 4, last subparagraph and in Article 126, paragraph 13, last subparagraph.

Conclusion on points II, 2 to 4: changes are limited, as the content remains substantially as it was before. Peer review will still be the rule; although the Commission receives somewhat more powers, its intervention is still restricted to a power of recommendation for a number of decisions. The consolidation of the Employment Guidelines[7] (Article 148 TFEU, initially known as the 'Luxembourg process'), and the Broad Economic Policy Guidelines (BEPG) in Integrated Guidelines realised in 2005 were not included in the Treaty and, consequently, the procedures for the adoption of both guidelines have not been harmonised.[8] Declaration 30 on the Stability and Growth Pact reproduces the text that was joined to the Final Act of the Constitutional Treaty. It confirms the objectives of the Pact, but the Treaty does not integrate its content, which

---

7   See, on this point as more generally for the whole report, *Begg* (2008), 7.

8   Comp. Article 121, paragraph 3 (BEPG) and Article 148, paragraph 2 (Employment Guidelines).

remains a combination of European Council political resolutions (1997 and 2005) and regulations as well as a code of conduct.[9] In sum, the new Treaty effectuates a revision *a minima,* in line with the poor content of the report of the Group on economic governance for the Convention.

III. The provisions specific to Member States whose currency is the euro in chapter 4 of Title VIII on Economic and Monetary Policy of the TFEU and the Protocol on the Eurogroup

Chapter 4 implements Article 5, paragraph 1 of the TFEU providing for 'specific provisions'. Three points are to be mentioned: a) enhanced co-operation in the euro area; b) the recognition of the Eurogroup and the creation of the function of a stable presidency; and c) the international projection of the euro.

1. Enhanced co-operation in the field of economic policy co-ordination and surveillance is organised under Article 136, paragraph 1. The measures have to be in accordance with the Treaty and must also be taken in accordance with Articles 121 and 126 (with the exception of paragraph 14: there is no possible review by the euro area members of the Protocol on excessive deficits). Economic policy guidelines could be adopted for the euro area members. Those guidelines must be compatible with guidelines for the Outs. Only the Ins will have a voting right. But, in our opinion, notwithstanding the silence of these provisions on this point, the Outs will be allowed to participate in the deliberation, although this proposition is controversial.

2. Article 137 and a protocol confirm the existence of the Eurogroup as an informal gathering without the right to take legally binding decisions. The main modification on the existing situation consists of the creation of the post of a stable president (elected by his peers for two and a half years), a novelty that has been anticipated by appointing (and renewing) a president for two years. The Eurogroup does not acquire a secretariat on its own. But the protocol provides for the preparation of the meetings by representatives of the Finance Ministers, which corresponds to the practice. Also remarkable is the reference in the preamble of the Protocol on the Eurogroup to the development of "ever closer coordination of economic policies

---

9   See *Louis* (2005); and *Louis* (2007a).

within the euro area". It is the only allusion in the Treaty to the necessity of an "ever closer coordination of economic policy" in the euro area; it is also the only place where the expression "euro area" is used in the new Treaties.

3.   The Lisbon Treaty replaces Article 111, paragraph 4 of the EC Treaty, a provision which remains a dead letter,[10] with Article 138, paragraph 1 on common positions and paragraph 2 on the unified representation of the euro area within international financial institutions and conferences. The wording is more specific than the broad reference to the "international level" in Article 111, paragraph 4 of the EC Treaty. Decisions are to be taken by QMV on proposals from the Commission and after consulting the ECB; priority seems to be given to common positions (a 'shall' provision) over unified representation (a 'may' provision), but the latter does not only depend on the euro area. As is the case pursuant to Article 111, paragraph 4, of the TEC, only the Ins will have a voting right for these decisions.

Conclusion on III, points 1 to 3: BEPG, specific for the Ins, can already be adopted by Ecofin, and considering the role of the Euro-group in their preparation, Article 136, paragraph 1 only formalises this possibility. The preoccupation of the Outs about having a say in the general framework of EMU (convergence criteria) is manifest in the restrictions imposed on the adoption of 'specific measures' for the Ins. There will be no Euro-Ecofin, contrary to what both France and the Commission requested during the Convention, in addition to the informal Eurogroup. The proposal was too divisive for most Ins and Outs. With the necessary political will, Article 138 could be helpful 'in order to secure the euro's place in the international monetary system'.

IV. General conclusions and perspectives

1.   Notwithstanding the mandate given by the Laeken Declaration (adopted by the European Council in December 2001) in order to strengthen economic policy co-ordination, the Convention and the IGC 2003 / 2004 seemed to have wasted too much time in expressing a minimalist view of the role of the Union

---

10   See *Louis* (2007b). See also the report of *A. Sainz de Vicuña* in this volume.

in this matter, not to mention the sterile discussions within the *Hänsch* Group[11] on the objectives of monetary policy[12] and the independence of the ECB.

Various factors explain this result. There is a visible resistance on the part of national administrations to significantly strengthening the powers of the Commission. Only an independent arbitrator could exercise an effective control, and that is precisely what is not wanted by the Member States. For this reason, one should think carefully before unifying in a further reform the positions of the Commissioner in charge of the EMU and the president of the Eurogroup, on the model of the High Representative of the Union for Foreign Affairs and Security Policy, who will also act as a vice president of the Commission. Often, those Governments who are more in favour of an improvement of economic governance or of an economic government[13] are the less prompt to obey the rules and to respect their commitments.

Control by peers seems for some to be a guarantee against too vigilant an application of the rules-based system. The Court of Justice[14] has recognised the margin of discretion left to the Council under the Treaty in the application of the excessive deficit prohibition. The SGP could not eliminate this discretion, in spite of the will of his promoters to favour automatism in the application of the rules.

There are divergent views on the usefulness of economic policy co-ordination. As *Iain Begg* observes, "the virtues of coordination are hotly disputed".[15] But one can easily follow

---

11   See CONV 76/02, 30 May 2002.

12   The discussion on this point is not closed. Prime Minister *Silvio Berlusconi* has not waited long, following his victory in the Italian elections, to call for a more general mandate for the ECB. See www.WSJ.com, 17 April 2008.

13   See *Lettre de mission de M.* Nicolas Sarkozy, *Président de la République, adressée à Mme* Christine Lagarde, *Ministre de l'Economie, des Finances et de l'Emploi*, 11 July 2007, 7, http://www.elysee.fr/elysee/root/bank/print/79066.htm.

14   See judgment of the Court, 13 July 2004, C-27/04, *Commission / Council*, ECR I-6649.

15   See *Begg* (2008), 7. *Giavazzi / Alesina* (2006) evoke the "Rhetoric of dirigism and coordination" (chapter 11). See the Italian edition

his recommendation to "rethink co-ordination in the perspective [of] an enlarged and more diverse Europe".[16]

2.   By stressing the need for measures specific to the Member States that have adopted the euro, the Treaty also opens the way to the development of enhanced co-operation of the euro area members through the general enhanced co-operation clause of Article 20 of the TEU-L and Articles 326 to 334 of the TFEU. The limitation of the co-operation to these members is now possible, taking into consideration the possible conditionality in the authorisation of participation in such co-operation under the Lisbon Treaty. But as is well known, such co-operation has inherent limits: it is not to be regarded as being comparable to Treaty revisions and, in particular, it cannot modify the institutional framework.[17] No Euro-Ecofin can be created under these schemes. Many fields are possible for such co-operation, and it would be a priority to look at the ideas that have been formulated in the past in various fields, such as, for example, management of the debt that handicaps public finances especially in some Member States.

3.   A number of small steps can also be made under Article 136 TFEU in order to strengthen economic policy co-ordination and surveillance, in particular among euro area members. It has up to now been impossible to have national budgets built on uniform economic forecasts; the calculations of the Commission, which would be a legitimate reference, are not trusted by all the Member States, so it has been proposed without success up to now to rely upon independent forecasts.[18] Furthermore, budget policy co-ordination would suppose a parallelism

---

"Goodbye Europa. Chronache de un declino economico e politico", BUR Saggi, 2006, 167 *et seq*. The officials of Brussels would encourage co-ordination in order to justify their existence. At the opposite of the spectrum, *Stefan Collignon* pleads for "The European Republic: reflections on the political economy of a future constitution*".*

16   *Begg* (2008), 22.

17   Member States engaged in an enhanced co-operation "may make use of [the] institutions" (Article 20 TEU-L), but they may not create new ones.

18   See *Begg* (2008), 15. As noted by *Begg*, some have proposed to "depoliticise" the management of fiscal policies, by delegating it to independent institutions.

of national calendars for the adoption of the different stages of the procedure, and Member States remain reluctant to speak with their partners about draft budgets that have not been presented to their parliaments. *Marco Buti* has advocated a split in the fiscal year into a euro area semester and a domestic semester.[19] Furthermore, the revised SGP tends to promote national ownership of budgetary discipline (as required by the March 2005 revision of the SGP), by associating, for example, finance committees of national parliaments with the process of co-ordination[20]. The reality is that the integrated guidelines (whose contents are often too general, not to say cryptic) and the commitments assumed by Member States for the reduction of budget deficits are not at the centre of the preoccupations of national parliaments. And very few are done in order to change things.

4. The Eurogroup has mainly worked, up to now, on budgetary discipline. It should have a more important role in the reform of structural policies. Therefore, the idea of joint meetings of ministers responsible for other sectors could help to make progress in this direction. The usefulness of informal gatherings like the Eurogroup has also raised the question of extending this format that is considered as the most important factor of the success of the Group (one minister per country plus a direct collaborator) to other sectors that have a link with EMU, such as employment or social affairs.[21] Others, like former Prime Minister *Verhofstadt* and President *Sarkozy*, have called for (informal) meetings of Euro European Councils, an idea that surely will meet with the opposition from the UK and other Out countries. The proposals for a core Europe, based on the

---

19 *Buti* (2005), quoted by *Begg* (2008), 14.

20 See European Commission (2008), 290.

21 *Iain Begg* mentions ministers responsible for labour market and employment policies, enterprise, social protection and technology. But he observes that such joint meetings under the Eurogroup format would lose the advantage of the relatively small number of participants in the finance ministers meetings within the Group (*Begg* (2008), 11).

euro, included in *Guy Verhofstadt's* pamphlet on "The United States of Europe" are well known.[22]

As such, the Eurogroup can obviously add a useful complement to the mechanisms in place through its informality. But it is precisely the Eurogroup's informality that also marks its limits, despite its undeniable usefulness, and appears to make it impossible to base the future economic government of the EU on it. The price of the informality is also its lack of transparency (despite efforts made for better communication) and a lack of accountability. The European Parliament has invited the president of the Eurogroup to attend a meeting every semester (half as frequently as the ECB president).[23]

5.   As far as the international projection of the euro area is concerned, some progress has been made in the practice, thanks in particular to the appointment, in anticipation of the Treaty, of a president with a two-year mandate, renewable, for the Eurogroup. A troika consisting of the president of the Eurogroup, the member of the Commission in charge of EMU and the president of the ECB participated in the multilateral consultation process on global imbalances organised by the IMF in 2006 and in the bilateral dialogue with Chinese authorities on the exchange rate of the Yuan in 2007. But the troika representation formula has not been generalised. It is the rotating EU Ecofin presidency that participates with the president of the ECB at the G20 meetings. On the other hand, the informal feature of the Eurogroup is an obstacle to the recognition of its president as the formal titular of external powers. Representation in informal caucuses and groups is one thing; representation in international institutions, such as the IMF, is another. A

---

22   *Verhofstadt* (2006). In the view of *Verhofstadt*, the construction of a core Europe, based on the euro, within the EU would allow for the further enlargement of the EU without impeding progress towards a political Europe. New Member States would not be obliged to accept a level of commitments equal to the one accepted by the members of the core, and that would permit the core to progress towards a more political union. The negative referendum on the Lisbon Treaty in Ireland has prompted a resurrection of the idea of a core Europe. The paradox is that Ireland as member of the euro area should be a natural member of such a core.

23   See *Begg* (2008), 11.

meaningful reform of this organisation,[24] which would have to
take place simultaneously with better representation for the
euro area, seems to face important obstacles. We would like to
end these remarks with a quotation of two economists: "The
time has come for [the euro area] to adopt a more responsible
global leadership position."[25]

References

Alan Ahearne / Barry Eichengreen (2007), External Monetary and
Financial Policy: a Review and Proposal, in: *André Sapir* (ed),
Fragmented Power: Europe and the Global Economy, Brussels
(Bruegel) 2007, 128-155.

Iain Begg (2008), Economic governance in an enlarged euro area,
(= European Economy. Economic Papers 311), European
Commission, Directorate-General for Economic and Financial
Affairs, Brussels, March 2008 (available at: http://ec.europa.
eu/economy_finance/publications/publication12319_en.pdf).

Lorenzo Bini-Smaghi (2006), Powerless Europe: Why is the Euro
Area still a Political Dwarf?, in: International Finance 9
(2006), No. 2, 261-279.

Hervé Bribosia (2007), La politique économique et monétaire, in:
in: *Giulio Amato / Hervé Bribosia / Bruno de Witte* (eds.),
Genesis and Destiny of the European Constitution, Brussels
(Bruylant) 2007, 2007, 663-685.

---

24 The reform that is contemplated by the IMF (see the Communiqué of
the International and Financial Committee of the Board of Governors
of the IMF of 12 April 2008, Press Release N°. 08/78), whatever its
merits, does not deserve this qualification. The IMF did a good job in
adopting a new definition for the quotas, in adjusting the quotas of
some of its members and recommending further realignments of
members' quota shares in the context of future general quota reviews
but the composition of the Executive Board, and *a fortiori* the
representation of the EU or the euro area, were not at the agenda. EU
institutions and national   authorities seem to adopt a defensive
attitude in response of the pressure coming, in particular, from the
US.

25 *Lombardi / O'Neill* (2008). See on the international projection of the
euro, *Bini-Smaghi* (2006); *Ahearne / Eichengreen* (2007).

Marco Buti (2005), Monetary and Fiscal Policies in EMU, Cambridge / UK (Cambridge University Press) 2005.

Stefan Collignon (2003), The European Republic: reflections on the political economy of a future constitution, London (Kogan Page) 2003.

Marianne Dony / Jean-Victor Louis (2005), L'Union économique et monétaire et la gouvernance économique, in: *Marianne Dony / Hervé Bribosia* (eds.), Commentaire de la Constitution de l'Union européenne, Brussels (Editions de l'Université de Bruxelles) 2005, 261-277.

European Commission (2008), Successes and Challenges after 10 Years of EMU (= European Economy, No. 2 (provisional edition)), Brussels, May 2008.

Alberto Giavazzi / Francesco Alesina (2006), The Future of Europe: Reform or Decline, Cambridge / MA (MIT-Press), 2006.

Domenico Lombardi / Jim O'Neill (2008), How Europe can shape the Fund, FT.com, 9 April 2008.

Jean-Victor Louis (2004), L'Union économique et monétaire dans la Constitution, in: Les dynamiques du droit européen en début de siècle, Etudes en l'honneur de Jean-Claude Gautron, Paris (Pédone) 2004, 421-441.

Jean-Victor Louis (2005), The Review of the Stability and Growth Pact, in: Common Market Law Review 42 (2005), 85-106.

Jean-Victor Louis (2007a), The Legal Foundations of the SGP in Primary and Secondary Law, in: *Fritz Breuss* (ed.), The Stability and Growth Pact. Experiences and Future Aspects, Vienna / NewYork (Springer) 2007, 3-31.

Jean-Victor Louis (2007b), L'Espace euro, l'Union européenne et le FMI, in: Revue d'Economie financière No. 88 (April 2007), 123-139.

Dominique Servais / Rodolphe Ruggeri (2005), The EU Constitution: Its Impact on Economic and Monetary Union and Economic Governance, in: ECB (ed.), Legal Aspects of the European System of Central Banks. Liber Amicorum Paolo Zamboni Garavelli, Frankfurt (ECB) 2005, 43-71 (available at: http://www.ecb.int/pub/pdf/other/ legalaspectsescben.pdf).

René Smits (2005), The European Constitution and EMU: An Appraisal, in: Common Market Law Review 42 (2005), 425-468.

René Smits (2007), Some Reflections on Economic Policy, in: Legal Issues of Economic Integration, 34 (2007), No. 1, 5-25.

Guy Verhofstadt (2006), The United States of Europe. Manifesto for a New Europe, London (The Federal Trust) 2006.

Antonio Sáinz de Vicuña[*]

The Status of the ECB

The ECB was not invited to take part in the European Convention on the Future of Europe, neither as a participant nor as observer. The justification given by the Convention Secretariat in 2002 was that the existing provisions on EMU would be left untouched: the introduction of the euro was still a recent event, the existing framework was working well and the Convention would address issues of more pressing importance.

Similarly, the ECB was not invited to attend the subsequent IGC. After the conclusion of the Convention and before the IGC, the ECB was invited to give its Opinion on the draft Constitution under Art. 48 of the Treaty on European Union (TEU) because the draft Constitution had foreseen some changes for the institutional framework in the monetary area. In its 2003 Opinion,[1] the ECB stated its understanding that the Constitution "*will not entail any changes to the substance, and the tasks, mandate, status and legal regime of the ECB and of the ESCB remain substantially unchanged*". Moreover, it understood that "*the substance of the [ESCB] Statute ... will not be subject to changes*", and as a consequence "*this Opinion is based on the premise that the substance of the Statute will not be changed*". Finally, it stated that in the event of changes to the Statute "*the ECB would wish to be associated with the preparatory activity for any such revision of the Statute*".

The ECB observed in its 2003 Opinion that the draft Constitution had characterised it as an "Other institution" within the new Treaty Title IV named "The Union's Institutions". The Opinion explained that, contrary to the hitherto concept of "Institution" in the Community, the ECB had separate legal personality, its own and independent finances, and a narrow mandate. As a consequence, it was suggested that the name of Title IV be changed to "The Institutional framework of the Union", a name that would al-

---

[*] The views expressed in this paper are personal and cannot be deemed to express the view of the ECB.

[1] ECB Opinion of 19.9.2003 on the draft Treaty establishing a Constitution for Europe, CON/2003/20, OJ C229 25.9.2003.

low for the accommodation of the ECB in that Title of the Constitution without its being assimilated to the other EU institutions.

This suggestion was not accepted.

The ECB 2003 Opinion contained a number of other suggestions to improve the draft Constitution, most of which were not accepted, in spite of the fact that the Governing Council of the ECB
had decided to be minimalist and concentrate on a few very selec-
tive items. For example, it asked that the new provision on voluntary withdrawal from the union should foresee also an ECB role in
the procedure, should the withdrawing country belong to the euro
area.

In 2007 the ECB was asked to provide an Opinion under Art.
48 of the TEU on the Reform Treaty. This time the ECB gave a
short statement based on the understanding that "*as regards the
status, mandate, tasks and legal regime of the ECB, the Eurosystem
and the ESCB, the changes to the current Treaties to be introduced
by the IGC will be limited to and will comprise all the innovations
agreed at the 2004 IGC*"; a footnote to the Opinion recalled the
ECB's advice given in 2004.[2] The ECB was not invited to attend
the IGC. The justification this time was that the very narrow mandate for the IGC, limited to preparing a Reform Treaty that would
be based on the provisions of the failed draft Constitution, was
without novelties in the substance. As a result, the ECB refrained in
its Opinion from suggesting amendments.[3] However, the IGC did

---

2   ECB Opinion of 5 July 2007 on an IGC to draw up a Treaty amend-
     ing the existing Treaties. OJ C160 of 13.7.2007.

3   The only additional request of the ECB concerned the name of the
     single currency in the Cyrillic alphabet: the ECB asked confirmation
     in primary law of the hitherto practice in the EU's monetary *acquis*,
     carried out in accordance with the Madrid European Council Conclu-
     sions of 1995 and with existing international standards on translitera-
     tion between Latin and Cyrillic alphabets, whereby euro becomes
     ЕУРО. Such practice had been contested by Bulgaria, which rather
     than transliterating the Latin spelling of the single currency wished to
     use the first four letters of the Cyrillic name for "Europe": ЕВРО
     (evro); the ECB being in the process of preparing a new series of
     euro banknotes needed legal certainty on this question; this additional
     ECB request for confirmation of a single name for the single
     currency throughout the EU was not satisfied, and the Lisbon Treaty
     uses the slightly different name for the single currency requested by
     Bulgaria in the Cyrillic alphabet.

introduce an innovation in the institutional framework for EMU: the ECB had been 'upgraded' from its previous constitutional classification as 'Other institution' into an 'Institution', explicitly preserving its separate legal personality and independent finances.[4]

The classification of the ECB as an 'Institution' deviates from pre-existing concepts but has no material effects, since the separate legal personality and finances are explicitly preserved. It begs the question of why the other European public banking institution, the European Investment Bank (EIB)[5] is not also listed as such since, like the ECB, it also has separate legal personality and finances. The usual preferred application of the *lex specialis* over the general law entails that the Statute and the Treaty provisions on the ECB, which remain substantially unchanged, continue to apply as before. Even the principle of 'loyal co-operation' among institutions was already applied by the ECB by way of constant and close interaction with the European Commission, within the *Lamfalussy* committees, and with the several EU organs and bodies with whom the ECB regularly, even daily, co-operates. Such a principle applies, of course, without prejudice to the statutory objectives, tasks and independence of the ECB. Quoting *Shakespeare*, "*Much ado about nothing*". Possibly the reasons behind the Treaty drafters' idea of classifying the ECB as an EU institution were: (i) to bring to the forefront the central institution of the euro, to enhance the profile of the EMU as the most remarkable achievement of the EU; (ii) to respond to the question of 'Of What is the ECB the Central Bank?'[6], and anchor clearly the ECB in the constellation of the EU institutional framework; (iii) give a positive law interpretation of the

---

4   Now also including the ECB's separate tort liability: Art. 340, modifying the current Art. 288.

5   The EIB is another European success story: it is today the most important public development bank of the world, with a balance sheet larger than the one of the IBRD, EBRD, ADB, or other regional development banks, and with financial operations in the five continents (e.g. ACP countries).

6   A former lawyer of the Legal Services of the European Council, Dr. *Ramón Torrent*, had published in 1999 an article under the title "Whom is the European Central Bank the Central Bank of?" in an influential legal magazine (*Torrent* (1999)), arguing that the ambiguity as to the institutional status of the ECB within the Community and as a central bank should be clarified.

OLAF Judgement by understanding one of its conclusions[7] as implying the need to 'institutionalise' the ECB.

One of the difficulties in classifying the ECB as an EU institution lies in the fact that the central bank of the euro is not the ECB but the Eurosystem, which is composed of the ECB and the NCBs of the euro area. Indeed, the tasks, the single policies that result from monetary unification in Europe are statutorily attributed to the *"ECB and the NCBs"* together. Although the ECB is a fully-fledged central bank, able to undertake all the tasks listed in the Statute, the NCBs are at the same time fully-fledged central banks, now operating under a single Eurosystem decision-making structure placed in the ECB, namely, the Governing Council and the Executive Board. Since central bank interaction with credit institutions is subject to legal, linguistic, market practices and other national peculiarities, most central bank operations of the Eurosystem are carried out by NCBs, under a common framework and decisions adopted by the Eurosystem decision-making bodies. Because of this, the Treaty requires NCBs to be independent. This is another basic difference between the ECB and the other EU institutions: whilst the monetary exclusive competence is attributed to both the ECB and the NCBs, the other EU institutions have exclusive competences attributed only to them (and not jointly to the Member States, for which there are also other 'shared' competences).

Perhaps on the occasion of the characterisation of the ECB as an EU institution, it might have been important to recall that in many important jurisdictions central banks are neither mentioned in national constitutions nor considered a constitutional body[8] and that

---

7   The ECB "falls squarely within the Community framework". However, nowhere in the OLAF Judgement is it suggested that the ECB is, or should be, an EU institution (ECJ Judgement 31.7.2003 Case C-11/00 [2003] ECR I-7147).

8   States whose Constitution does n o t refer to their central bank: Austria, Belgium, Denmark, Germany, Greece, Finland, France, Ireland, Italy, Latvia, Luxembourg, Malta, The Netherlands, Romania, Spain, United Kingdom. Also, the United States of America, Canada and Japan.

     States whose central bank is somehow mentioned in their respective Constitution are: Bulgaria, Cyprus, Czech Republic, Estonia, Hungary, Lithuania, Poland, Portugal, Slovakia, Slovenia, Sweden, Switzerland.

many central banks are not even owned today by their respective State.[9] Also, older central banks did not have monopoly of currency issuance until well into the 20th century[10] and older central banks were created with private shareholding and were nationalised only during the 20th century,[11] either as a consequence of socialist ideologies or of *Keynes*ian economics demanding a managed "policy mix" of fiscal and monetary policies to achieve full employment. That European central bank co-operation has existed since well before the establishment of the European Communities in 1957. It remained outside the European Communities framework until the establishment of the European Monetary Institute in 1994,[12] and still today a great part of international central bank co-operation is carried out in an international context rather than within the

---

9   Some examples: the US Federal Reserve District Banks are owned by their respective local banks; 100% of the capital of the Bank of Italy is owned by a series of institutions and organisations; some 70% of the capital of the Bank of Greece, a company by shares, is floated in the Athens stock exchange; the capital of the National Bank of Belgium, a company by shares, is 50% floated in the Brussels stock exchange; some 30 % of the capital of the Austrian central bank, a company by shares, is owned by trade unions and organisations.

10 Still today in the United Kingdom the Bank of England does not have the monopoly of banknote issuance: five commercial banks in Scotland and Northern Ireland have the privilege of British Pound banknote issuance. Outside Europe, it is to be noted that banknote issuance is carried out by three commercial banks in the SAR of Hong Kong, and not by the central bank.

11 Some examples are the Banque de France, nationalised in 1936; the Bank of England, nationalised in 1946; De Nederlandsche Bank was nationalised in 1948; the Bank of Spain, nationalised in 1962; the Banco de Portugal was nationalised in 1974.

12 The Committee of Governors of the European Economic Community, established in 1964, was based in Basel (Switzerland), outside the EEC, and its secretariat was hosted by the Bank of International Settlements (BIS). Several EEC Commissioners responsible for monetary affairs (e.g. *Robert Marjolin* in the 1960s, *Raymond Barre* in the 1970s) attempted to participate regularly in the EEC Governors Committee meetings with very limited success, and to bring the seat of the Committee to a EEC Brussels structure, without success. It remained in Basel until the IME moved to Frankfurt in late 1994.

boundaries of Europe.[13] The monetary arrangements derived from
the monetary turbulences that followed the demise of the Bretton
Woods system in the 1970s and the 1980s were discussed and decided in *fora* outside the EEC framework, like Basel[14] or New
York, and organised by way of agreements between central banks,
including the implementation of the political decision to establish
the European Monetary System (EMS) in 1978.[15] The issuance and
clearing of ECUs was mostly done by the BIS. All these facts
somehow support the idea that the ECB, as a central bank of EU
central banks, has a *sui generis* nature when compared with the
other EU institutions, and justifies the lack of enthusiasm of the EU
governors in being characterised as such. However, as stated above,
from a purely technical perspective, the characterisation of the ECB
as an EU institution does not have any material legal effect: the
primary law containing its *lex specialis* remains intact after the
Treaty of Lisbon.

Would something have been different should the ECB have
been invited to the Convention or to the IGCs? Perhaps not, but at
least the ECB could have participated in the discussions about its
institutional status, and given some arguments supporting the recommendations contained in its two Opinions of 2003 and 2007.
Furthermore, in the context of the Convention discussions on Economic Governance of the EU might have been richer if the ECB
had been invited. To give some examples of possible topics that
may have been improved in the final text:

---

13 For example: the several G10 groupings hosted by the BIS (banking
    supervisors, payment systems, etc.); the IMF, where European cen-
    tral banks maintain different IMF constituencies instead of acting to-
    gether within a single constituency; etc. International monetary coop-
    eration among central banks did not stop even during the 2nd World
    War, namely to settle international trade debts, as a recent history
    book on the BIS has proven (*Toniolo* (2005)).

14 E.g. Plaza Accord, agreed in New York in 1985; the Bâle-Nyborg
    Agreements of 1987; etc.

15 The EMS consists of a Resolution of the European Council
    (5.12.1978) and of an Agreement between the NCBs of the EEC
    dated 13.3.1979. In retrospect, the scarcity of proper EEC legal acts
    regarding the EMS is notable. Until the Treaty of Maastricht, most of
    the EEC "monetary legislation" refers to budgetary mechanisms to
    cope with the volatility of European currencies (e.g. "monetary com-
    pensatory amounts", "green exchange rates", etc.).

a) Convergence towards the "three best performing Member
    States" or towards "the euro area"? Article 121(1) of the
    Treaty clearly refers to "three best performing Member States"
    for inflation. And Art. 4 of the Protocol on the Convergence
    Criteria extend this reference to the long-term interest rate cri-
    terion. The application of the Treaty and Protocol was foreseen
    for a situation where there was not yet a formal and clear defi-
    nition of "price stability", and as a substitute the reference to
    the "three best performing Member States" was adopted. Not
    to be forgotten is the fact that the Treaty was negotiated within
    a Community of 12 and not of 27 Member States.[16] The Proto-
    col stated in its Preamble that its aim was to "*guide the Com-
    munity in taking decisions on the passage to the third stage*" of
    EMU. And its Art. 6 foresaw thereafter revised convergence
    criteria "*which shall then replace this Protocol*". The applica-
    tion of the unchanged provisions of the Treaty and Protocol in
    the enlarged EU led to the fact that the "three best performing
    Member States" were two non-euro-area countries and one
    euro-area country in the ECB's and Commission's Conver-
    gence Reports of 2004, 2006 and 2007.[17] The European Parlia-
    ment suggested in 2006[18] changing the benchmark and intro-
    ducing instead the definition of "price stability" adopted by the
    ECB under Art. 105(2) of the Treaty. Such or alternative con-
    siderations could have been considered in a discussion – in the
    context of the economic governance of EMU – by our consti-
    tutional drafters.

b) The recognition of the Eurogroup. Whilst the Lisbon Treaty
    retains the officialisation of the Eurogroup and introduces a
    new Protocol thereto, it does not draw the logical consequence
    of considering its President as being the participant in the ECB

---

16 The Community in 1992 was enlarged by 12 Member States. It
    enlarged to 27 Member States in 1995, 2004 and 2007.

17 In 2004: Denmark, Finland and Sweden. In 2006: Finland, Poland
    and Sweden. In 2007: Finland, Poland and Sweden. In 2004 use was
    made of the (non-Treaty) notion of "outlier" to exclude Lithuania
    from the best-performing reference list, since its downside inflation
    rate was considered as distorted due to exceptional factors.

18 Resolution of 1 June 2006 on the Enlargement of the euro zone
    (2006/2103/INI). It also regretted the disqualification of Lithuania
    because of the current benchmark.

Governing Council meetings. According to Art. 113(1) of the Treaty, it is the President of the Ecofin who is entitled to attend Governing Council meetings. The Lisbon Treaty could have recognised that the President of the Eurogroup is the relevant attendant.

c)   The name "Eurosystem". One of the few suggestions of the ECB in its 2003 Opinion that was taken on board by the Convention was to officialise the term "Eurosystem", used since 1999 to refer to the ECB and the NCBs of the euro area Member States. The approach taken by the Treaty drafters is less than satisfactory. On the one hand, the term appears only in Art. 282(2) of the new Treaty, and later on in Art. 1 of the revised Statute. This means that the whole Title VIII on Economic and Monetary Policy still refers to the "ESCB" without any distinction with or reference to the "Eurosystem", who is the important player in this part of the Treaty. The reader would first read the monetary chapter, only to learn later on that its main player is named "Eurosystem". Furthermore, good drafting techniques would have recommended changing "ESCB" to "Eurosystem" where relevant, which would have permitted the deletion of the ugly articles that contain the legal distinction between one legal concept and the other.[19]

d)   The new Art. 50 of the Treaty of Lisbon contemplates the withdrawal from the EU of a Member State, and imposes a negotiation and signature of a Withdrawal Treaty. The possibility that such withdrawing Member State be of the euro area should have been contemplated, since the withdrawing from the monetary institutional set up and the market consequences would be of great importance. Regrettably, the drafters did not follow ECB's recommendation in its 2003 Opinion to foresee an ECB role in such an unlikely event.

e)   Art. 127(6) of the new Treaty contains the enabling clause to entrust the ECB with some supervisory capacity. The sweeping trend of the two IGCs towards QMV did not reach this provision, which is kept at unanimity. Such an enabling clause is unlikely to be used in the foreseeable future, namely because all 27 Member States would be –if exercised- subject to the ECB's Governing Council for the given supervisory powers, in spite of not being part of the euro area and thus not having a

---

19   Art. 139(2)(3)(4) of the Treaty and Art. 42 of the Statute.

governor in the ECB's Governing Council. The current market turbulences have renewed the old discussions about the shortcomings of today's EU supervisory arrangements, still national and with national mandates in spite of the Level 3 "*Lamfalussy committees*". There is a growing number of doctrine and official papers advocating some sound pan-European supervisory arrangements.[20] Some capacity to look into the future would have led to a recommendation to the constitutionalists in the Convention to establish another enabling clause in the Treaty to permit some kind of EU-wide supervisory arrangements outside the ECB. This is a missed opportunity.

f)   Resolve the contradiction between the scopes of Art. 105(1) of the Treaty and Art. 2 of the Statute. A mistake of the Maastricht IGC is being perpetuated by not addressing it this question. Under Art. 139(2)(c), the NCBs of non-euro-area countries do not have the objectives of the ESCB, namely, price stability and the support of Community policies. To the contrary, under Art. 42 of the Statute, the NCBs of non-euro-area countries have the objectives of the ESCB as defined in Art. 2 of the Statute.

The only discussion on the ECB was about its being classified as an Institution. One benefit for the ECB ensuing from its now being qualified as an Institution is that, like other EU institutions, it will be invited to future Conventions or IGCs.

References

Charles A. E. Goodhart / Dirk Schoenmaker (2006), Burden sharing in a banking crisis in Europe (= LSE Financial Markets Group, Special Paper Series No. 164), London, March 2006.

Karel Lannoo (2008), European Financial System Governance, CEPS. Financial Stability Report of 11.4.2008, Brussels (CEPS) 2008.

---

20   Some examples: *Goodhart / Schoenmaker* (2006); *Schoenmaker / Oosterloo* (2006); *Lannoo* (2008), chapter on "Arrangements for Crisis Management". Ecofin 'Roadmap', October 2007, chapter on Improving Information and Co-operation Among Authorities.

Dirk Schoenmaker / Sander Oosterloo (2006) Financial supervision in Europe: do we need a new Architecture? (= Cahier Comte Boël No. 12), Brussels (ELEC / LECE) February 2006 (available at: http://staff.feweb.vu.nl/dschoenmaker/ELEC_Financial_Architecture.pdf).

Gianni Toniolo (2005), Central Bank Cooperation at the BIS, Cambridge (Cambridge University Press) 2005.

Ramón Torrent (1999), Whom is the European Central Bank the Central Bank of? Reaction to Zilioli and Selmayr, in: Common Market Law Review 36 (1999), 1229-1241.

Jacques Ziller

The Law and Politics of the
Ratification of the Lisbon Treaty

I. The state of ratifications

At the moment of writing the final draft of this paper,[1] according to
the official Internet page dedicated to the ratification of the Lisbon
Treaty,[2] the Treaty "had been approved" by ten Member States out
of 27, i.e., Austria, Bulgaria, Denmark, France, Hungary, Poland,

---

1   End of April 2008. NB the paper has been updated on proofs at the
    end of June 2008 in order to comment upon the referendum in
    Ireland.

2   http://europa.eu/lisbon_treaty/countries/index_en.htm, visited 28
    April 2008. A certain number of 'private' tables of the ratification
    processes were published, e.g. by the *Fondation Robert Schuman* in
    the French language. See http://www.robert-schuman.org.

Portugal, Romania, Slovakia and Slovenia. Interestingly, while the legend to the map that appeared on this page stated: "In your country The Treaty of Lisbon, officially signed by the Heads of the Member States on 13 December 2007, will have to be ratified by each Member State in order for it to come into force", the indications which appeared for each country made a difference between the cases where the Treaty had been "ratified" and those where it had been "approved", stating the relevant date, e.g. 14 February for the ratification by France, 24 April for the approval by Denmark and 21 January for the approval by Slovenia.

This sophisticated distinction, which corresponds to important legal differences, compensated for the scarce information given for each country. Although the legend stated further that "The procedure by which this is done varies from country to country, depending on each Member State's constitutional system. Find out what is going on in your country by clicking on the map!", the information for each country only contained an indication of the "ratification procedure" (by parliament or by referendum, as in the case of Ireland), an indication about the "status of ratification" (i.e. approved, ratified or in progress), and links to the Representation of the European Commission and to the European Parliament information office. Contrary to the tables which had been published for the Nice Treaty of 2001 and the Constitutional Treaty of 2004, there was no further indication about the referenda which had taken place in some countries, nor were there details about the date on which the parliaments or their different houses had voted. The reason for this scarcity of information is rather easy to guess ...

With the negative referendum in Ireland on the Nice Treaty in 2001, and clearly even more so with the two negative referenda in France and the Netherlands in 2005, the attention politicians and academia gave to the importance of the ratification phase dramatically increased. However, commentaries on the Treaty on European Union (TEU) are still limited to a few sentences when it comes to the national phase of entry into force of amendments to the TEU and the EC Treaty, and to my knowledge there is no comprehensive comparative study of the constitutional mechanisms which are applicable in the 27 Member States, let alone about their application over time.[3]

Commenting on the state of ratification make little sense as long as the entire process remains unfinished for all of the 27 Member States, including the required registration of each instrument of ratification with the Ministry of Foreign Affairs of the Italian Republic, which has been the depository of the EC / EU Treaties and their amending Treaties since 1957. At best, the picture would be incomplete, and at worst there would be a great risk of making wrong assumptions or erroneous predictions: since the negotiation of the Single European Act in 1985, none of the deadlines which had been set for the entry into force of amending Treaties has been met: there was no statement of a precise date in the Amsterdam and Nice Treaties, but they both entered into force quite some time after the date that had been unofficially put forward. The reason for the late entry into force of the Nice Treaty is well-known: the referendum in Ireland. As far as the Amsterdam Treaty is concerned, only a few specialists know that the ratification by Belgium had been delayed for quite a long time by the Flemish section of the Brussels parliament, which refused to give its authorisation for the ratification of international treaties as long as there was no agreement with the federal government on the recruitment of firemen in Brussels.

This paper only tries to present partial answers to a few questions. These questions have been pushed to the forefront due to the circumstances which led to the drafting and signature of the Lisbon Treaty in order to get out of the stalemate which resulted from the negative referenda in France[4] and in the Netherlands[5] and from the decision of the United Kingdom government to postpone *sine die* the ratification procedure of the Constitutional Treaty on 6 June 2005.[6] The questions are as follows. Do Article 48 TEU and Article 6 Lisbon Treaty matter? Does it matter that the 'constitutional concept' has been dropped? Does the content of the Lisbon Treaty re-

---

3   So far as I am aware, the closest to such a comprehensive study is in *Albi / Ziller* (2007). See also *Amato / Ziller* (2007), chapters 1 and 2; *Claes* (2005); *De Witte* (2004); *Ziller* (2007a).

4   See *Ziller* (2007b).

5   See *Besselink* (2007).

6   See *Church* (2007).

quire specific forms for the authorisation of ratification? Are opt-ins, opt-outs and derogations a legal necessity, or are they a political pretext? Is it possible to identify possible sources of delay and surprises? And last but not least: is involving the citizens in ratification wishful thinking or is it a realistic endeavour? These questions might also help having a more comprehensive view of the problems raised by the negative referendum in Ireland on 12 June 2008 and of the possible responses to this referendum.

II. Do Article 48 TEU and Article 6 Lisbon Treaty matter? Answers for today and for tomorrow

The revision procedure for the TEU and the EC Treaty is set out in Article 48 TEU. The number of this Article will remain unchanged after the entry into force of the Lisbon Treaty. However, the Lisbon Treaty introduces a series of additions to Article 48: the Parliament will have the right of initiative; the simplified revision procedures will be added; and the provision will also contain the indication that "If, two years after the signature of a treaty amending the Treaties, four fifths of the Member States have ratified it and one or more Member States have encountered difficulties in proceeding with ratification, the matter shall be referred to the European Council". Such an indication was already present in the ECSC Treaty of 1951, and it was reinvented by the Constitutional Treaty of 2004. One indication will remain unchanged, namely that "The amendments shall enter into force after being ratified by all the Member States in accordance with their respective constitutional requirements" (Article 48, 3rd indent in the present version of the TEU; Article 48 § 4, 2nd indent in the post-Lisbon version).

In line with Article 48 TEU, Article 6 of the Lisbon Treaty says:

"1. This Treaty shall be ratified by the High Contracting Parties in accordance with their respective constitutional requirements. The instruments of ratification shall be deposited with the Government of the Italian Republic.

2. This Treaty shall enter into force on 1 January 2009, provided that all the instruments of ratification have been deposited, or, failing that, on the first day of the month following the deposit of the instrument of ratification by the last signatory State to take this step."

The reference to the "respective constitutional requirements" of the signatory States is superfluous from a strictly legal perspective, and does not give any clue as to the type of authorisation needed in Member States, whether it is by a vote of parliament or by a referendum. According to the Law of Treaties, the forms required for the authorisation to ratify a treaty are strictly a matter of internal law, and the EC / EU treaties are no exception in that respect. In theory, there could even be room for the Lisbon treaty to be considered, from the standpoint of national law, as an 'executive agreement', i.e. an agreement that does not require previous authorisation either by the legislative branch or by referendum for entry into force in a specific country.

As a matter of fact, it would be useful to start thinking about the consequences at national level of the new simplified revision procedures that will be introduced in Article 48.

As far as the simplified revision of Part III (internal policies) of the Treaty on the Functioning of the European Union (TFEU) is concerned, Art. 48 § 6 states explicitly that "The decision referred to in the second subparagraph shall not increase the competences conferred on the Union in the Treaties". This seems a good argument in support of the thesis that these amendments would be of a technical nature corresponding to the notion of executive agreement in most constitutions of the EU Member States.

As for the 'passerelle clause' of Art. 48 § 7, the right of a single national parliament to oppose a Council decision to apply the ordinary legislative procedure to a case where the Treaties foresee a special procedure may be read in the same light. Although it was probably not the initial intention of the proponents of this veto right for national parliaments during the 2003-2004 IGC, their power makes sense if it serves to avoid ratification by a simple decision of the executive in a situation where according to national law the authorisation of parliament would not be required. It may be argued that a change to an internal procedure in an international organisation would typically be an executive agreement. As consistently stated by the French Constitutional Council when it has had to scrutinise EC / EU Treaty amendments, changing from unanimity to qualified majority voting in the Council amounts to a transfer of decision-making power to the EU, even though it does not in itself change the distribution of competences between the Union and its Member States.

However, these reflections on executive agreements are only meant for the future. Such possibilities did not apply with respect to the negotiation of the Lisbon Treaty, as no simplified revision procedure yet existed.

The parallel clauses in Article 48 TEU and Article 6 Lisbon Treaty which foresee entry into force once all instruments of ratification have been deposited is not a legal necessity. From the perspective of the Law of Treaties a Treaty amending the EC/EU treaty could enter into force after a certain number of ratifications (with legal effect as between the ratifying countries), as happens with most multilateral treaties. Indeed, it would be conceivable to limit the requirement of unanimity to those amendments which either change the distribution of competences between the EU and its Member States or deprive any single State of a power that enables it to play a significant role within the EU institutions, such as the requirement of unanimity in the Council. From a legal point of view, in order to reach such a solution, a revision of Article 48 EU treaty would first be required, in order to change the conditions of entry into force from unanimous ratification to a certain number of ratifications. However, the requirement of unanimous ratification as a pre-condition for entry into force is politically unavoidable for the time being, and certainly after the statements which have been made by so many governments and politicians during the so-called 'reflection period'. The fate of the Lisbon Treaty is therefore in the hands of each single country, as has been the case for all previous Treaty amendments. Even those country which are usually indicated as "having ratified" can block the process as long as their instrument of ratification has not been deposited with the Italian Ministry of Foreing affairs.

The date of 1 January 2009, which is indicated in Article 6 Lisbon Treaty, is obviously not binding, as clearly indicated in the last part of § 2. Apart from an indication of a political / psychological nature, this has nevertheless an important technical function for the preparatory undertakings of the institutions, to which it gives a legal basis. With the election of the EU Parliament coming in June 2009, the deadline of January 2009 is particularly important. As a matter of principle it does not matter whether the last instrument of ratification is deposited before 31 December 2008 or before 31 May 2009. However, it would clearly be a quite difficult problem to resolve if it occurred later than end of March or April 2009, as the number of Members of the European Parliament to be elected in most Member States differs according to whether the pre-Lisbon or post-Lisbon version of the Treaties applies. The members of the European Council were fully aware of this when they decided on 20 June 2008 to ask Ireland to report on possible solutions for the European Council meeting of October.

III. Dropping the 'constitutional concept': does it matter? A Dutch answer to a European question

According to the Conclusions of the European Council of 21-22 June 2007, the 'constitutional concept' has been abandoned. The reason for this unanimous decision of Heads of State and Government was clearly to avoid referenda on the Lisbon Treaty. At first sight, however, abandoning the 'constitutional concept', whatever this means, was totally meaningless from a constitutional law perspective. There is no single constitutional provision in any of the Member States that refers explicitly or implicitly to the 'constitutional nature' of a treaty (be it European or international), let alone as a requirement for a referendum in order to authorise ratification. What matters for a referendum, in a small number of countries such as Ireland,[7] Denmark[8] and perhaps Slovakia,[9] is the content of the treaty – i.e. the fields it touches upon – and not its form or its 'constitutional nature'.

The question of whether the rules that apply to the amendment of the national Constitution should apply to the Treaty of 29 October 2004 establishing a Constitution for Europe has been raised in academia, and it was given a negative answer by the French Constitutional Council in its decision of 19 November 2004[10] and by the Spanish Constitutional Court in its "*declaration*" (binding opinion) of 13 December 2004.[11] These two constitutional courts mainly based their decision on the formal nature of the 2004 Treaty and the procedure for its approval and amendment; they did not spend much time discussing the implications of the word 'Constitution' in the Treaty's title. But the first to face the question was the Dutch State Council, in its Advisory Opinion of 14 July 2003.

---

7   See *Hogan* (2007).

8   See *Rasmussen* (2007).

9   See *Kühn* (2007).

10   See *Ziller*, (2007b); *Amato / Ziller* (2007), 48, 102.

11   See *Tremps / Saiz Arnaiz* (2007); *Amato / Ziller* (2007), 97.

The 'Advisory Opinion on the European Constitution (Consultative Referendum Bill)', which has only been published by the State Council in the original Dutch language version,[12] addressed the question of the possible constitutional nature of the draft Treaty that had been prepared by the European Convention, in order to indicate whether a referendum would be admissible in the Netherlands. According to the State Council, as the Dutch Constitution does not foresee the possibility of a referendum, it only allows for consultative, non-binding referenda. Furthermore, as the procedure for constitutional amendments is regulated in detail by the Constitution, and as it involves the dissolution of both houses of Parliament and a parliamentary election which has to take place on the basis of draft amendments, the Constitution does not allow for a referendum on constitutional matters. In this context, the State Council examined both the form and content of the draft Constitutional Treaty, and although it concluded that the text was different from the usual amendments to EU/EC treaties, the State Council stated that it did not have the nature of a constitution because it did not create a State-like organisation that would be fundamentally different from the existing EU and EC. Furthermore, the State Council stated, in a paragraph (9.) on the 'Consequences of referendums', that "The Council is of the opinion that it is of the utmost importance that the Constitution for Europe be ratified in the different Member States and that it come into force as quickly as possible. As the Council already stated in its opinion on the Nice Treaty, with the present institutional structure of the treaties, the limits of this institutional setting have been reached. Without the institutional changes which are foreseen in the Constitution for Europe, there is a risk that the functioning of the Union will be severely impeded" (author's own translation).

It is quite remarkable that scarce attention was given to this Advisory Opinion of the Dutch State Council, both outside the Netherlands and inside, amongst both politicians and academics. This lack of attention probably explains why references to the position of the State Council on the Constitutional Treaty of 2004 often seemed to imply that it had been in favour of such a referendum, whereas the truth is that it reluctantly admitted that there was no constitutional impediment to a mere consultation. This lack of

---

12   Available on the database of the Dutch State Council the *Raad van State*: http://www.raadvanstate.nl.

knowledge in public opinion and amongst experts enabled the Dutch Government to 'economise on truth', when it announced in early 2007 that it would submit the question of a referendum on a new Treaty to the State Council. Outside of the Netherlands, this was often interpreted as the Dutch Government announcing that it would abide by the decision of its constitutional court. But the Dutch State Council is far from being a constitutional court.

In the Netherlands, judicial review of the constitutionality of acts of Parliament are in fact forbidden by the Dutch Constitution. Like the model on which it is based, i.e. the French *Conseil d'Etat*, the Dutch *Raad van State* functions *both* as a superior administrative court and as a counsel to the Government. In the latter capacity, it only hands down non-binding advisory opinions, which examine the legal and political implications of a draft statute, decree or other instrument. Furthermore, these non-binding opinions are not necessarily published. It is therefore interesting to see that, unlike other relevant opinions, the State Council's opinion on the "Request for advice on the mandate of the Intergovernmental Conference to revise the Treaty on the European Union and the Treaty establishing the European Community"[13] has been published both in the original Dutch-language version and in an English-language translation prepared under the State Council's authority.

The formulation of the Advisory Opinion gives the clear impression to the reader that the State Council was determined to say the truth, nothing but the truth, but also the *whole* truth about the issue of the referendum. This is in contrast with the Dutch Government's position: the latter certainly said the truth in that it never indicated that it was for the State Council to decide whether a referendum should be held or not; but it never denied the interpretations given to the public which went in that direction. The Government also stated that, according to the State Council, a referendum was not necessary for the Lisbon Treaty. This was true, but could obviously be foreseen. As a matter of fact, the question that the State Council had to answer was not whether a referendum on the future Lisbon Treaty would be *necessary*, but whether it would be *admissible* under the Dutch Constitution.

---

13   Case   number   W02.07.0254/II/E,   available   at   http://www.raadvanstate.nl/adviezen/.

That is a totally different question. In a paragraph (under 1. Introduction) entitled "Assessment framework", the State Council explains:

"The government has asked the Council of State for its views on the nature of a treaty as referred to in the conclusions of the European Council ('the proposed Reform Treaty'). Should this lead to findings regarding the approval of the treaty, the government has asked the Council of State to give these also. It assumes that the Council of State will make use of its previous advisory opinions dated 13 June 2003 (Advisory opinion on the European Convention), 14 July 2003 (Advisory opinion on the European Constitution (Consultative Referendum) Bill), 10 December 2004 (Advisory opinion on the approval of the Treaty establishing a Constitution for Europe) and 15 September 2005 (Advisory opinion on the consequences of the European Union's institutional structures for national institutions). The latter opinion, on the consequences of the EU's institutional structures for the role and operation of the national institutions and their mutual relations, was published after the 2005 referendum. In the government's view, it provides an accurate analysis of the legitimacy of European policy."

Further on, when analysing "The Netherlands and Europe" (point 2.), the State Council adds:

"The initiators of the referendum of 1 June 2005 on the Treaty establishing a Constitution for Europe wanted to provoke a political and public debate which would shed more light on the issues. However, this did not happen. Two factors played a part here: (1) the implication that people were being asked to express their views about a present or future state and its constitution, and (2) the misconception that the content of the Treaty was entirely new, whereas most of it had already become part of the European legal order through earlier treaties. The referendum certainly mobilised public interest in the EU, but the political debate remained limited.

"What the referendum has made clear is that the Dutch do not feel a real sense of connection with the EU. Dutch citizens apparently do not have as much confidence in European cooperation as was assumed in the past. In

many people's minds, the EU is associated with techno-
cratic decision-making and over-regulation, which are
problems they also encounter at home.

"This scepticism on the part of the public is due not
only to the way the EU functions, but also to the way the
Dutch government handles EU affairs."

The Council then recalls that:

"In its advisory opinion on the proposal by MPs *Karimi*,
Dubbelboer and *Van der Ham* on the holding of a consultative referendum on the constitutional treaty for the
European Union, the Council of State gave its views on
the nature of the Treaty establishing a Constitution for
Europe with respect to its approval. The Council did not
comment on the desirability of holding a referendum, but
made its remarks in the light of the proposers' wish to enable a consultative referendum on the Treaty to be held. It
gave its views on the reasons that the proposers put forward for their proposal. In making this assessment of the
possibility and desirability of holding a referendum, the
Council of State concluded that approval of the Treaty
establishing a Constitution for Europe, in which the fundamental rights were enshrined and the pillar structure
was abandoned, was to some extent comparable to approval of a national constitutional amendment. However,
its opinion also expressly pointed out the differences between a national constitution and the Treaty establishing a
Constitution for Europe. The latter, it said, could not be
equated with a national constitution, for the EU could not
be considered a state. This is also apparent from the proposed Reform Treaty, which merely amends the existing
treaties and is thus in line with the constitutional development of the Union as described above."

Subsequently, the State Council even answers a question
which no other legal body has yet answered in any Member State,
namely the question of the possible effect of a referendum that has
been held or promised on the Constitutional Treaty. In other words,
it addresses the issue of whether a referendum is to be treated as a
legal precedent. In the Dutch context, the answer is very clearly
negative, as can be seen in the *Summary* of the Advisory Opinion:

"The Council of State also believes that, in assessing the possibility and desirability of holding a consultative referendum on the approval of the proposed Reform Treaty, account must first be taken of the restrictions laid down in the Constitution. This currently makes no provision for a binding referendum. The legislator can decide to hold a non-binding referendum on an ad hoc basis, but this must be based on a special justification. Mere precedent will not suffice. That would create a substantive basis for the referendum as a structural instrument (in this case, for use when approving treaties) that is not in keeping with the self-contained arrangements in the Constitution."

The Summary then proceeds with a very clear statement of the conditions which should be met for a referendum to be admissible under the Dutch Constitution (emphasis by the author):

"In determining *what may be* deemed *a* special *justification for holding* a non-binding *referendum when approving treaties*, the Council of State believes that the following factors must in any case be taken into account.

"(1) It is important to examine whether the content, methodology and goals of the treaty, taken together, are so far-reaching as to justify holding a consultative referendum in addition to the normal constitutional approval procedure.

"(2) When deciding whether to hold a referendum on the approval of a treaty, it is important to take account of the difference between bilateral and multilateral treaties.

"(3) It is important to consider whether an ad hoc referendum is a suitable instrument for involving citizens in the decision-making process. Referendums should not become a means of legitimisation that politicians and members of parliament can use at will to promote their own views.

"(4) Of crucial importance in all referendums is whether a clear, unequivocal choice can be formulated.

"(5) It is important to *know whether, after a non-binding referendum, the legislator will take a separate decision on the act of approval concerned and whether it will then have genuine latitude to disregard the re-sult of the referendum. If the government or parliamentary parties indicate that they will in any case abide by the result of the referendum, it can no longer be deemed non-binding.*

"These are the factors that the government should weigh up when determining whether it is possible or desirable to hold a non-binding referendum on the approval of the proposed Reform Treaty. *Another relevant issue in this case is whether the government believes that the questions raised by the referendum on the Treaty establishing a Constitution for Europe have been answered. If so, what special justification can there be to consult citizens once more by means of a non-binding referen-dum?*"

The Advisory Opinion of 2007 thus in no way says that a referendum is not necessary from a legal perspective. It says that a referendum might be admissible according to the Dutch Constitution, but only under certain conditions. Clearly these conditions were not met with the 2005 referendum, as parliamentary parties had indicated that they would in any case abide by the result of the referendum. However, the absence of constitutional review of acts of Parliament deprived this unconstitutional behaviour of any consequences.

The State Council then gives an indication of a political nature: if the Government deems that the answer has been given to questions raised by the 2005 referendum – albeit not admissible in legal terms – then a referendum no longer makes any sense. As a matter of fact, during the negotiations that led to the mandate of the 2007 IGC, the Dutch Government had indicated what its "red lines" were. As it received a positive answer to its demands, the Government could claim that the questions raised by the referendum of 2005 had been answered by the Lisbon Treaty. The Advisory Opinion makes it perfectly clear that it is not the State Council, but the Government, that has to decide on the advisability of holding a referendum on the Lisbon Treaty.

To my knowledge, there has been no enquiry in the Netherlands about the "questions raised by the referendum of 2005". Hence the importance of the reference by the State Council to the "opinion on the consequences of the EU's institutional structures for the role and operation of the national institutions and their mutual relations, [which] was published after the 2005 referendum. In the government's view, it provides an accurate analysis of the legitimacy of European policy". This Opinion of 2005[14] further developed an idea which was already present in the 2003 Opinion: though it did not have, as such, a constitutional nature, the Treaty of 2004 was different from the usual variety of Treaty amendments. In the 2007 Opinion this argument is further developed by a subsection on 'Symbols', which is worth quoting in its entirety (emphasis by the author):

> "The *name of the Treaty establishing a Constitution for Europe reflected a particular vision of European co-operation.* The existing treaties were to be repealed and replaced by a treaty which, as a single, binding constitutional document embracing the entire constitutional order, was unprecedented in the Union's political history. The new document no longer pursues such a goal. It does not repeal the existing treaties. The state symbols of European unification that were included in the Constitution for Europe, such as the flag, the anthem and the motto, and the renaming of items of European legislation as 'laws' and 'framework laws', are no longer to be found in the proposed Reform Treaty. Furthermore, it no longer explicitly codifies the supremacy of EU law.
>
> "The significance of these changes should not be underestimated. *EU terminology and symbols are apt to create expectations among citizens, and form potential points of reference for the further development of both EU policy, whose dynamics are inherent in the integration process, and EU case law, with its characteristic emphasis on teleological interpretation. In the past, treaty terminology_and symbolism have played an important part in the development of the EU. There is no reason to assume that things will be any different in the future.*

---

14   Available only in the Dutch language on the database of the Dutch State Council (the *Raad van State*). See http://www.raadvanstate.nl.

"In this respect, *the proposed Reform Treaty* is perfectly clear. Unlike the Treaty establishing a Constitution for Europe, it *provides no arguments for a gradual expansion of the EU towards a more explicit state or federation.*"

At the moment of writing, the Dutch State Council is the only institution in a Member State that has given in-depth attention to the legal and political consequences of the 'constitutional concept' embedded in the Treaty of 2004, and it is the only national institution that has developed reasons why this concept would indeed no longer be present in the Lisbon Treaty.

IV. Does the content of the Lisbon Treaty lead to specific requirements for the authorisation of ratification? A classical French answer to a classical question

The French *Conseil Constitutionnel* did not at all touch upon the question of the French referendum in its 'Decision no. 2007-560 of December 20th 2007 – Treaty amending the Treaty on European Union and the Treaty establishing the European Community'.[15] As authorised by Article 54 of the French Constitution, the President of the Republic, had asked the Constitutional Council, by letter of 13 December, whether the authorisation to ratify the Treaty of Lisbon had to be preceded by a revision of the Constitution. This has been a classical move of the Executive since the 1980s, when *François Mitterand* started using this procedure for the ratification of protocol no. 6 to the European Convention of Human Rights on the abolition of death penalty. It avoids the possibility of an unpleasant surprise after the vote of Parliament, as 60 members of the National Assembly or of the Senate may ask the Constitutional Council to judge upon the constitutionality of the statute authorising the ratification of such treaties and protocols.

The answer of the Constitutional Council was yes: under the same conditions as for the Treaties of Maastricht, Amsterdam, Nice and the Constitutional Treaty, the French Constitution should be revised as a precondition for ratification. This is stated in points 7 to 9 of the Council's decision:

---

15   Available in English (translation under the authority of the Constitutional Council) at http://www.conseil-constitutionnel.fr/langues/anglais/a2007560dc.pdf.

"7.   The conditions in which the French Republic partici-
      pates in the European Communities and the European
      Union are specified by the provisions of Title XV of
      the Constitution currently in force, with the exception
      of those of paragraph 2 of Article 88-1 pertaining to
      the Treaty establishing a Constitution for Europe
      which has not been ratified. Under paragraph 1 of
      Article 88-1 of the Constitution 'The Republic shall
      participate in the European Communities and in the
      European Union constituted by States which have
      freely chosen, by virtue of the treaties that estab-
      lished them, to exercise some of their powers in
      common'. The constituent power thus recognised the
      existence of a Community legal order integrated into
      domestic law and distinct from international law;

"8.   While confirming the place of the Constitution at the
      summit of the domestic legal order, these constitu-
      tional provisions enable France to participate in the
      creation and development of a permanent European
      organisation vested with a separate legal personality
      and decision-taking powers by reason of the transfer
      of powers agreed to by the Member States;

"9.   When however undertakings entered into for this pur-
      pose contain a clause running counter to the Consti-
      tution, call into question constitutionally guaranteed
      rights and freedoms or adversely affect the funda-
      mental conditions of the exercising of national sover-
      eignty, authorisation to ratify such measures requires
      prior revision of the Constitution".

French constitutional lawyers will spend due time explaining
whether and to what extent point 9 goes further than the usual jurisprudence of the Constitutional Council by its reference to "constitutionally guaranteed rights and freedoms", which recalls the classical positions of the German and Italian Constitutional courts. What
is specific to the issue of the Lisbon Treaty is that the Constitutional
Council repeatedly refers to its previous Decision no. 2004-505 DC
of November 19th 2004 pertaining to the "Treaty establishing a
Constitution for Europe".[16] It even quotes the numbers of the arti-

---

16   Also available in English (translation under the authority of the Con-
     stitutional Council) at http://www.conseil-constitutionnel.fr.

cles of the Constitutional Treaty that correspond to those articles of the Lisbon Treaty which have taken them up, when examining whether they necessitate a revision of the French Constitution. It also refers to that earlier decision in relation to the grounds for which there is such a need.

On the whole, reading the French Constitutional Council's 2007 decision, it is clear that the content of the Lisbon Treaty is the same as that of the Constitutional Treaty of 2004, as far as its relevance to the French Constitution is concerned. In theory, the Constitutional Council might have discussed whether the referendum of 2005 had consequences with respect to the procedure needed for ratification. The question had obviously not been asked as such by the President of the Republic. *Nicolas Sarkozy* had clearly announced that he would not submit the possible new 'simplified' or 'functional' treaty to a referendum, and his entourage had further argued that, having been elected, he had a mandate of the French people that would at any rate supersede the previously negative referendum. Nor was the Constitutional Council asked whether to confirm that the Lisbon Treaty was indeed 'simplified' or 'functional'.

The classical style of the decisions of French Supreme Courts has clearly been of help to the Council in its endeavour to touch upon the politically hot issue of the referendum. It is also easy to argue that it was up to those Members of the French Parliament who favoured a referendum to try and ask the Council to decide upon the issue on the basis of an action against the act that authorised the President to ratify; but they chose not to do so, probably due mainly to the fact that they felt that this was not the right way to try and destabilise President *Sarkozy* – unlike President *Chirac*'s opponents in 2004-2005.

As in France, a legal approach to the content of the Treaty of Lisbon leads to the conclusion that the Irish Constitution needs to be amended if the Treaty is to be ratified in Ireland – thus necessitating a referendum there.[17] For the same reason, reinforced majorities are needed in Austria, Germany[18] and Poland.[19] The only countries for which the differences in content between the Constitutional

---

17   See *Hogan* (2007), n. 7. The referendum is scheduled for 12 June 2008.

18   See *Arnold* (2007).

19   See *Lazowski* (2007).

Treaty and the Lisbon Treaty have been cited as reasons for *not* having a referendum are Denmark and the United Kingdom.

V. Opt-ins, opt-outs and other derogations: a legal necessity or a political pretext? Different answers in the countries of Hamlet and Shakespeare

Since the IGC of 1991, the governments of Denmark and of the United Kingdom have negotiated exceptions for their respective countries in the framework of Treaty revisions, allegedly in order to maintain their sovereignty intact with regard to matters close to the heart of their population, without preventing other Member States from taking steps forward as they wished. With the Constitutional Treaty and the Treaty of Lisbon, the differences between the two countries' strategies are more apparent than ever, and they are probably due to their difference in political and economic weight and power in Europe, but not also due to cultural differences.

The Danish Government's strategy could be called 'Derogations first, referendum later'. The provisions of the Danish Constitution matter in this respect, as Article 20 of the Constitution states that, if an international treaty implies a transfer of sovereignty from Denmark to 'international authorities', it needs to be approved by a majority of 5/6ths of the Members of Parliament, and that if such a majority is not met but a simple majority of MPs do vote in favour, a referendum needs to be held in order to authorise ratification. This explains only to a certain extent why there have been referendums on the Single European Act (before its signature, in fact), on the Treaties of Maastricht and Amsterdam, and why a referendum was envisaged for the Constitutional Treaty. In most cases (though not for Maastricht), the necessary 5/6ths majority would probably have been met, and lawyers debate whether, in such a case, a referendum is still admissible.[20] In the case of the Treaty of Nice there was no referendum, and the Government deemed that the Treaty did not entail a transfer of sovereignty.

In the case of the Lisbon Treaty, the Danish Government was extremely cautious during the negotiations that led to the mandate for the IGC of 2007, and during the IGC itself. It gave special attention to the clauses that maintain Denmark's opt-ins and opt-outs, and to new dimensions of the same type of derogations. This en-

---

20   See *Rasmussen* (2007), n. 8.

abled the Government's lawyers to state that there was no new transfer of sovereignty for Denmark under the Lisbon Treaty. The Danish Parliament approved its ratification on 24 April 2008 by a vote of 90 in favour, 25 against, and no abstentions, although 64 MPs, including Prime Minister *Anders Fogh Rasmussen*, were absent during the vote.[21] It is thus difficult to know whether there would have been a majority of 5/6ths if needed. Earlier, the Danish Government had announced its intention to hold a referendum after the summer in order to ask the Danish people whether they wanted to retain its specific positions in different sectors. This was clearly a strategy to allow the other Member States to go on with the reforms aimed at by the Constitutional Treaty and the Lisbon Treaty, while enabling Denmark to join the policies in which it did not participate later on.

By comparison, the British strategy is anything but clear, as demonstrated by the succession of events in connection with the Constitutional Treaty in 2004-2005[22] and, even more blatantly, by the protocol on the EU Charter of Fundamental Rights[23] and by the protocol on transitional provisions. One of the differences as compared with Denmark is that, in the UK, there is no constitutional provision of any kind that would indicate criteria about the necessity of a referendum. Strictly speaking, the decision to ratify a treaty is in the realm of the royal prerogative and therefore does not even necessitate a parliamentary authorisation. In the case of the amendments to EC / EU Treaties, however, they always necessitate corresponding amendments to the 1972 European Communities Act, by which the EC Treaties and secondary law were given effect in the UK legal order. A vote of Parliament is therefore obligatory. Whether a referendum should be held or not is not a matter of legal discussion but only of political decision. Strikingly, it took six hours of debate in the House of Commons to decide on (and reject) a motion that such a referendum was necessary, before the Commons could complete the three required readings of the European Union (Amendment) Bill. At the time of writing, the House of Lords still has to complete its own third reading.

---

21   According to a notice on http://www.euractiv.com/en, published on 25 April 2008.

22   See *Church* (2007), n. 6

23   See the contribution of *Catherine Barnard* to this volume.

Interestingly, holding a referendum was not an issue in the process of ratification of the Lisbon Treaty in Poland, contrary to the case of the Constitutional Treaty, where President *Alexander Kwacsnievski* had envisaged holding a referendum in order to by-pass the lack of a majority in Parliament. For the Treaty of Lisbon, it has been the need of reinforced majorities in Parliament for treaties involving a transfer of competences to international organisations that served as a blackmail tool for the party of the brothers *Kaczynski*. This explains why Poland maintained its participation in the protocol on the EU Charter of Fundamental Rights and did not insist on reopening discussions after the elections of October 2007.

After the negative result of the referendum of 12 June 2008 in Ireland, one of the possible solutions that will certainly be looked at would be to follow the Danish strategy. It is however a legally delicate option to handle, as Ireland already benefits of a series of opt-ins and opt-outs under the Lisbon treaty and its protocols. A careful study of the possibility of further options for Ireland might reveal some margin of manoeuvre for a specific new protocol that would enable Ireland to be in the same position as Denmark. There are precedents in this respect: such protocols were adopted in 1972 and 1994 following the negative referendum in Norway in order to adapt the relevant accession treaties, and in 1994 in order to adapt the Treaty on the European Economic Area after the negative referendum in Switzerland. The most delicate question however is that of the institutional changes provided by the Lisbon Treaty. Nobody knows whether the Supreme Court of Ireland – which would certainly be asked to rule on the question – would consider that the impact on Irelands' sovereignty of majority voting, of the number of members of the European Parliament, or of the number of Commissioners, would be such as to require a previous revision of the Irish constitution, and thus a referendum: back to square one.

VI. Nothing will be done until all has been done: possible sources of delays and surprises: beyond the Irish referendum

As stated in sections 1 and 2, the Lisbon Treaty will only enter into force once all Member States have ratified it. While it is impossible to make predictions about the final outcome, it is possible to identify conceivable sources of surprises that could lead to at least a delay in ratification, postponing entry into force beyond the foreseen date of 1 January 2009. The point which needs to be made is that referenda are not the only source of uncertainty.

As far as referenda are concerned, Ireland held it on 12 June, as it seemed legally necessary, and as it would have been be politically unwise to bet on the non-application of the *Crotty* jurisprudence of the Irish Supreme Court. The outcome of such a referendum is never easy to predict, as demonstrated by a number of precedents in Ireland, which are not limited to the Nice Treaty. Unlike President *Chirac*, who chose to announce that he would stay in power whatever the results of the 2005 referendum in France, and unlike Prime Minister *Jean-Claude Juncker*, who on the contrary announced that he would resign if the referendum of July 2005 in Luxembourg had a negative outcome, Irish Prime Minister *Bertie Ahern* announced in April 2008 that he would resign in order to be able to face the charges of corruption that had been voiced against him. This move has not been sufficient to avoid some parts of the electorate of using the June referendum for a purpose very different from approving or rejecting the content of the Lisbon Treaty. The first polls after the referendum anyway indicated that most of the no voters believed in the "Vote no for a better yes" argument, which was Sinn Fein's slogan during the referendum campaign. In the same way, an important part of the French electorate seems to have believed in the possibility of a "Plan B" when voting to the Constitutional treaty three years earlier.

The length of authorisation procedures is another source of delays. This problem already prevented Italy from being the first country to ratify the Treaty signed in Rome on 29 October 2004 even though Prime Minister *Berlusconi* immediately started the procedure for ratification once the text had been signed. The multiplicity of involved assemblies is a further possible source of delays, particularly important since the constitutional reform of 1993 in the case of Belgium. The King needs the authorisation of both houses of the Federal Parliament, and of five further parliaments (those of the regions and the 'linguistic' communities), and surprises are not excluded in the light of the precedent of the Treaty of Amsterdam.

A further source of possible delays or surprise would be court proceedings, as demonstrated by cases related to the Single European Act in Ireland and to the Maastricht Treaty in Germany. Two issues need to be taken into account. The first is the availability of court proceedings against the ratification of a treaty such as the Lisbon Treaty. At first sight, taking into consideration the relevant constitutional provisions, such a proceeding is possible in at least Belgium, the Czech Republic, Germany and Slovakia. As of this writing, the Czech Parliament has already asked for a decision from its country's constitutional court. Meanwhile, a German MP, Mr *Gauweiler*, who initiated a constitutional review of Germany's ratification of the 2004 Constitutional Treaty, still opposes the Treaty of Lisbon. However, it should be noted that in 1997 the German Constitutional Court rejected an application on the constitutionality of the Treaty of Amsterdam, although many commentators had concluded from its decision on the Maastricht Treaty that the court would be particularly strict in future cases of scrutiny. As the application was rejected by a panel of three judges as being without any possibility of success '*aussichtslos*', it is impossible to know the Court's position, because these types of decisions are neither reasoned nor published. In 2008 again, four court proceedings have been initiated on the Treaty of Lisbon, amongst which one by Mr Gauweiler. The most striking innovation was an application for judicial review against the decision not to hold a referendum in the United Kingdom, which impeded the immediate ratification of the Lisbon treaty after both Houses of Parliament had adopted the Act amending the UK legislation on the EU, which is needed for its entry into force in UK law.

Ex ante review is not the only cause of court proceedings, as demonstrated in Poland by Judgment K 18/04 of the Constitutional Court of 10 June 2004 on Poland's Membership in the European Union.[24]

The arguments that might be discussed in court proceedings include: the content of the Treaty, in order to state whether it is compatible with the national constitution – as happens in France – and the appropriateness of the mode of ratification. The latter was at stake with the application for constitutional review that had been made in Slovakia on the Constitutional Treaty,[25] on which the Constitutional Court ultimately did not take a decision, as the Treaty had been abandoned by June 2007. In 2008 again

A last source of delay is due to the fact that authorisation is separate from ratification: the role of the Head of State is often forgotten in discussions about ratification. Legal considerations may well prevent the Head of State from ratifying a treaty, even where

---

24   See *Amato / Ziller* (2007), 105.

25   See *Kühn* (2007), n. 9.

he or she is authorised to do so by Parliament. This is demonstrated by the precedent of Germany in 1992 and 2005, where the Federal President chose to wait for the decision of the Federal Constitutional Court on an application for review before perfecting the ratification procedure. Political considerations may also interfere: in Poland and in the Czech Republic, Presidents *Lech Kaczynski* and *Vaclav Klaus*, respectively, are renowned for their scepticism towards European integration. At the time of writing, both had announced – in different ways – that they would not oppose ratification. However, the way they formulated their decisions shows that they regard themselves as having discretion on the matter. After the referendum in Ireland, President *Vaclav Klaus* declared that according to him "the Lisbon Treaty was dead"; however, as the Czech Parliament was waiting for the outcome of the application for constitutional review – expected for September-October 2008, this remained a kind of private comment – after all, when the European Commission President Barroso declared during the summer 2005 that the Constitutional treaty "was dead", this had no impact on the ongoing ratification procedures in member states.

VII. Involving the Citizens?
Wishful thinking or realistic endeavour?

A last question, probably the most important in the light of the succession of events since the adoption of the draft Constitutional Treaty by the European Convention in June and July 2003 is whether it is possible to involve citizens in the ratification of a Treaty like the Constitutional Treaty or the Treaty of Lisbon. The fact that the words 'Reflecting the will of the citizens', which began Article 1 of the Constitutional Treaty have not been carried over in the Lisbon Treaty does not in my view change anything, either from a legal or from a political standpoint.

However, asking the question is certainly not answering it, and it goes far beyond the sole question of the legitimacy of separate referenda in different Member States.[26] Amongst the questions posed by the processes of 2005-2008, two are especially difficult to answer, and they will need to be taken up again if the process of ratification of the Lisbon Treaty is successful:

26   See *Auer* (2007), as well as *Tridimas / Tridimas* (2007).

1. Is it possible to have a real debate in a Member State – let alone in all Member States – out of the context of a referendum? Comparing the cases of France and Luxembourg with Spain and the Netherlands yields arguments in both directions. There were very serious debates in the first two countries, and very poor debates in the other two. This notwithstanding a big number of arguments which were not grounded by facts, flourished during both campaigns. It is a pity that no empirical work was done in 2005 – when memories were not yet distorted, in order to link the content or lack of content of the debates with the outcomes of the votes. The campaign in Ireland for the referendum of 12 June 2008 resembles more that of the Netherlands: in both countries, the number of people who voted no because they were not clear enough on the content of the Treaty was impressive. Furthermore, in both countries, information on the Treaty itself was supposed to be given by an independent Commission, in order to respect equality between the supporters of a positive answer and those of the no. Here again, serious field work by social scientist will be needed in order to understand what were really the reasons for voting yes, voting no or abstention.

2. Is it sufficient to believe that the real debate will or should start after the entry into force of the Lisbon Treaty? The ability of political classes to learn their lessons (as appears from the precedents of Denmark), or to forget them, is one of the issues that would also require empirical work. After the 1992 referendum on the Maastricht treaty, the French political class was unanimous in saying that the lesson would not be forgotten; it seems that twelve years later, only the Eurosceptic politicians were duly prepared... In 2008, until the end of the winter, it seemed that the Irish political class had also learnt the lesson of the referendums on the Nice treaty, as demonstrated by *Bertie Ahern*'s resignation. However, the way the campaign developed showed that this was not the case. The mere fact that on 12 June more than 10 other member states had not yet ratified was depriving the supporters of the Lisbon Treaty of an important argument: that Ireland would be blocking the reform of EU institutions which the other 26 member states were ready to implement.

An interesting contribution to these issues, referred to earlier, was given in the Netherlands by the State Council: the Advisory

opinion of 15 September 2005 (Advisory opinion on the consequences of the European Union's institutional structures for national institutions)[27] contains a very critical analysis of the attitudes
of the Dutch Government and Parliament, with a series of recommendations in order to enhance public communication and participation on European matters. The French State Council also tried to
tackle these issues in 2007, although it did so from the perspective
of the French Public Administration.[28] What is missing, as of this
writing is – amongst others – a serious analysis by the European
and national Parliaments. This will be one of the challenges to be
met by the newly elected MEPs in 2009, even if by that date the
Treaty of Lisbon eventually had entered into force, especially if
they want to make use of their new right of initiative for treaty
amendments, which is embedded in the Lisbon Treaty amendments
to Article 48 TEU.

What all the referendums on EC-EU treaty amendments have
amply demonstrated – especially, but not only – when their outcome has been negative, is the relevance of Andreas Auer's argu-
mentation that these kind of referendums are not legitimate, contrary to referendums on the entry of a country in the EU. A negative
referendum creates a problem whose solution is not in the hands of
the people who voted. In France, a first referendum in May 1946 on
the proposed new constitution had a negative result. The same voters had the possibility to approve – or not – the new version of the
draft constitution which was then submitted to a second referendum
in October. In 1992, 2001, 2005 and 2008 it was not in the hands of
the sole electorate who had first rejected a treaty amendment to
accept a modified version of the proposed amendments to the existing treaties. Furthermore, in the case of the Constitution of 1946,
the same electorate had indicated, in a previous referendum of October 1945 that they did not want to continue with the Constitutional laws of 1875. In 2005 in France and in the Netherlands, and
in 2008 in Ireland, a big number of no-voters clearly wanted to
demonstrate that they did not like the existing EU system; by voting
no, they were however blocking the reforms which were designed
to improve the system they disliked.

---

27   See supra note 12 and accompanying discussion. The Advisory Opin-
     ion is available (in Dutch only) on the database of the Dutch State
     Council the *Raad van State*: http://www.raadvanstate.nl.

28   Conseil d'Etat (2007).

References

Anneli Albi / Jacques Ziller (2007), The European Constitution and National Constitutions: Ratification and Beyond, The Hague (Kluwer) 2007.

Giuliano Amato / Jacques Ziller (2007), The European Constitution – Cases and Materials in EU and Member State's Law, Cheltenham (Edward Elgar Publishing) 2007.

Rainer Arnold (2007), Germany in the EU Constitutional Treaty, in: *Albi / Ziller* (2007), 57-65.

Andreas Auer (2007), National Referendums in the Process of European Integration: Time for Change, in: *Albi / Ziller*, (2007), 261-272.

Leonard Besselink (2007), The Dutch Constitution, the European Constitution and the Referendum in the Netherlands, in: *Albi / Ziller* (2007), 113-123.

Clive Church (2007), The United Kingdom: A Tragi-Comedy in Three Acts, in: *Albi / Ziller* (2007), 127-136.

Monica Claes (2005), Constitutionalising Europe at the Source. The 'European Clauses' in National Constitutions: Evolution and Typology, in: Yearbook of European Law 24 (2005), 81-125.

Conseil d'Etat (2007), Rapport public 2007: administration française et l'Union européenne: quelles influences? Quelles stratégies? (= Etudes et documents du Conseil d'Etat No. 58), Paris 2007 (available at: http://lesrapports.ladocumentationfrancaise.fr/BRP/074000224/0000.pdf).

Bruno De Witte (2004), The National Constitutional Dimension of European Treaty Revision – 2nd *Walter van Gerven* Lecture, Groningen (Europa Law Publishing) 2004.

Gerard Hogan (2007), Ratification of the European Constitution: Implications for Ireland, in: *Albi / Ziller* (2007), 137-147.

Zdenek Kühn (2007), Ratification Without Debate and Debate Without Ratification: the European Constitution in Slovakia and the Czech Republic', in: *Albi / Ziller* (2007), 157-170.

Adam Lazowski (2007), The Polish Constitution, the European Constitutional Treaty and the Principle of Supremacy, in: *Albi / Ziller* (2007), 171-181.

Hjalte Rasmussen (2007), Denmark's Waning Constitutionalism and Article 20 of the Constitution on the Transfer of Sovereignty, in: *Albi / Ziller* (2007), 149-156.

Pablo Perez Tremps / Alejandro Saiz Arnaiz (2007), Spain's Ratification of the Treaty Establishing a Constitution for Europe: Prior Constitutional Review, Referendum and Parliamentary approval, in: *Albi / Ziller* (2007), 45-55.

George Tridimas / Takis Tridimas (2007), Electorates v. Politicians: the 2005 French and Dutch Referendums on the EU Constitutional Treaty, in: *Albi / Ziller* (2007), 273-285.

Jacques Ziller (2007a), Le processus des ratifications et la période de réflexion, in: *Giulio Amato / Hervé Bribosia / Bruno de Witte* (eds.), Genesis and Destiny of the European Constitution, Brussels (Bruylant) 2007, 137-186.

Jacques Ziller (2007b), French Reactions to the Treaty Establishing a Constitution for Europe: from Constitutional Welcome to Popular Rejection, in: *Albi / Ziller* (2007), 103-112.

Ernst-Ulrich Petersmann[*]

The Reform Treaty and the Constitutional Finality of European Integration

Jean Monnet's method for realizing *Robert Schuman*'s objective of a 'European Federation' for the preservation of peace envisaged successive phases of economic, legal and political integration for "an ever closer Union". From the 1951 ECSC Treaty up to the 2007 Lisbon Treaty, European integration law evolved on the basis of international treaties reflecting intergovernmental compromises contingent on political support for functionally limited co-operation among European states as well as among their citizens. These multilateral European integration agreements differed fundamentally from European international law prior to World War II. Yet it was only since about the year 2000 – as illustrated by the speech of

---

[*] The author is grateful for research assistance by his doctoral researcher *Pedro Lomba*.

Germany's Minister of Foreign Affairs *Joschka Fischer* on *From Confederacy to Federation: Thoughts on the Finality of European Integration* in May 2000[1] and the approval of the *EU Charter of Fundamental Rights*[2] – that "the finality" of the European integration process became a widely discussed subject of public European reasoning, prompting even pragmatic British government ministers to deliver public speeches on "Europe 2030".[3] Most of these discussions focused on the (con)federal structures among Member States, their national peoples and EU citizens, based on market integration, policy integration and an "area of freedom, justice and security"; in view of the constitutional failures of nation states, even European 'federalists' no longer mention a European federal state as a desirable end-state of the "ever closer Union."

I. Multilevel Democratic Constitutionalism as Europe's Finality?

The European Council, in its mandate of June 2007 asking the Intergovernmental Conference to elaborate an alternative "Reform Treaty" in view of the *referenda* and political opposition against the 2004 Draft Treaty establishing a Constitution for Europe, stressed that the new Treaties "will not have a constitutional character": "The constitutional concept, which consisted in repealing all existing Treaties and replacing them by a single text called 'Constitution', is abandoned."[4] However, this politically motivated de-constitutionalisation strategy does not change the fact that – both in terms of a formal, positivist concept of constitution (e.g. as referring to the long-term, basic rules of a higher legal rank constituting the governance system for a political community) as well as in terms of a substantive concept of democratic constitutionalism (e.g. as referring to constitutional citizen rights and basic rules constituting legislative, executive and judicial self-governance) – EU law and the Lisbon Treaty remain based on European constitutional rules, as

---

1   Reproduced in *Joerges / Mény / Weiler* (2000), 19-30.
2   OJ C 364 of 18 December 2000.
3   Cf. the speech by British Foreign Secretary *David Miliband* on *Europe 2030: Model Power, not Superpower*, delivered at the College of Europe, Bruges, on 15 November 2007.
4   Presidency Conclusions of 21/22 June 2007, Annex I, at 15. For an analysis, see the contribution by *Stefan Griller* to this book.

explicitly acknowledged in Article 6 of the existing EU Treaty and Article 2 TEU-L. In contrast to the 1945 UN Charter – whose rules of a higher legal rank (cf. Article 103) for protecting human rights and sovereign equality of states already constituted a functionally limited, multilevel governance system with supranational governance powers (e.g. those of the UN Security Council and the International Court of Justice)[5] – and the constitutions (*sic*) establishing the International Labour Organization, the World Health Organization, the Food and Agricultural Organization or the UN Education and Scientific Cooperation Organization, EU law goes far beyond merely formal, positivist conceptions of constitutionalism. For example, the EU's comprehensive, multilevel guarantees of human rights and other fundamental freedoms, democratic governance and judicial protection of the rule of law directly protect ever more comprehensive citizen rights in all EU Member States. This constitutional *acquis communautaire* justifies the question discussed in this contribution: What is the finality of the EU's "common law constitution"? Will it never be replaced by a shorter treaty constitution that is readable and comprehensible for all EU citizens?

US President Ronald Reagan used to describe the North American Free Trade Agreement (NAFTA) as an international economic constitution protecting mutually beneficial free trade among constitutional democracies. Even though some NAFTA rules serve "constitutional functions" by providing for more effective legal and judicial guarantees of investor rights (cf. Chapter 11) and trading rights (cf. Chapter 19) than those in the respective national laws of NAFTA countries, the legal structures of NAFTA law remain dominated by rights and duties among sovereign states without multilevel, constitutional and judicial safeguards similar to those recognised in European law. The diverse constitutional structures of the European Convention on Human Rights (ECHR), of EU law and the European Economic Area (EEA law as interpreted by its EFTA Court) illustrate the diverse forms of multilevel constitutionalism in European integration. As institutions remain contingent on changing political contexts, it seems premature to speculate whether some of the European institutions may be "final." Yet, as long as the European courts continue to exist, their multilevel constitutional constraints make it almost inconceivable that the EU courts, the EFTA Court and the European Court of Human Rights (ECHR)

---

5   Cf. *Petersmann* (1997), 421-474.

could effectively abandon their constitutional self-commitment to judicial protection of inalienable human rights deriving from respect for human dignity and fundamental rights protected by EU law, EEA law and the ECHR. The historical experiences of European states – that national democratic constitutions (e.g. of the Weimar Republic) may fail to effectively protect human rights and constitutional rights of citizens – may repeat itself. Yet, even though European constitutional law does not prevent individual states from withdrawing from the European "treaty constitutions", the EU's multilevel constitutional law provides for far more comprehensive, legal and institutional "checks and balances" protecting EU citizens against abuses of national and European governance powers than any other regional integration agreement outside Europe. This constitutional premise – i.e. as long as European integration continues, it will continue to be founded on multilevel constitutional guarantees of freedoms and other fundamental rights – justifies the follow-up question discussed in this contribution: Which other principles of European constitutional law are likely to be irreversible, apart from multilevel constitutional guarantees of fundamental freedoms and other basic human rights?

Most reasonable people adopt a pragmatic 'wait-and-see attitude' *vis-à-vis* unpredictable future events, including the 'finality' of European integration. As explained by *John Rawls*, it is unreasonable for constitutions of modern democratic societies with a plurality of moral, religious and political conceptions of justice among free and equal citizens to prescribe comprehensive political doctrines of justice; democratic constitutionalism must limit itself to protecting an "overlapping consensus" of reasonably diverse moral, religious and political conceptions that are likely to endure over time in a democratic society.[6] Co-ordination in areas of common interests, with due respect for pervasive, reasonable disagreement among free citizens, is law's main function in well-ordered democracies. As illustrated by the imbalance between the over-ambitious "empowering constitution" of Germany's Weimar Republic (e.g. its comprehensive guarantees of economic and social rights) and its inadequate "limiting constitution" (which did not prevent the parliamentary delegation of governance powers to a dictator), finding the right balance between constitutional safeguards and constitutional limits of freedom and reasonable disagreement can also be

---

6   *Rawls* (1993), 154 *et seq.*

viewed as the main constitutional problem of European integration. Paradoxically, the success of European constitutionalism will depend on its limitation to essential constitutional principles and basic rules of a higher legal rank. Hence, it is reasonable to ask what European constitutional processes should not aim at; for example, it has turned out to have been politically unreasonable to ask European citizens to approve a "Constitution for Europe" including more than 470 pages with extremely complex, constitutional as well as legislative rules.[7]

The evolution of European constitutional law will continue to differ from the constitutionalisation of national legal systems.[8] Not only the pervasive distortions and "discourse failures" in "deliberative democracies" (as illustrated by the ownership of major Italian television channels by Italian Prime minister *S. Berlusconi*), but also constitutional liberalism itself make it unlikely that public reason will enable a comprehensive, constitutional agreement among European citizens with such diverse traditions and conceptions of justice and of a good life. Reasonable differences of opinion will especially continue in areas like economic and social policies with redistributive effects. The following chapters discuss "six finalities" and perennial "constitutional problems" of European constitutionalism that are likely to determine the future structures of European integration and its support or opposition by European citizens, without excluding the irreversible nature of other parts of Europe's constitutional *acquis*.

II. The Perennial Task of Limiting Abuses of Power Requires Multilevel Constitutionalism beyond the EU

Since antiquity, the *myth of Europe* has been described in terms of reconciling power with self-determination.[9] The European tragedies

---

7   Cf. Treaty Establishing a Constitution for Europe, OJ C 310 of 16 December 2004.

8   Cf. *Rawls* (1971), 195 *et seq*, who envisages a four-stage process of national constitutionalisation proceeding from (1) the choice of the principles of justice in the 'original position', (2) the framing of a just constitution, (3) the choice of legislation by representatives of the people, and (4) the application of constitutional and legislative rules by administration and judges to particular cases.

9   Cf. *Pagden* (2002).

of holocaust and totalitarian regimes leading to World War II illustrated not only the failures of international law as a "gentle civilizer of nations" (*Martti Koskenniemi*); national constitutionalism also turned out to be fragile in the face of *Machtpolitik* invoking emergency situations (*Carl Schmitt*'s *Ausnahmezustand*).[10] European integration law has successfully used diverse approaches (as illustrated by the EC Court, the EFTA Court and the ECHR) for progressively changing individual, national and international legal practices and beliefs – within, among and beyond the 27 EU Member States – by transforming national constitutionalism into a stronger, multilevel constitutionalism (following the plywood principle).[11] The Lisbon Treaty further strengthens the coherence of European law, for example by submitting also the EU's common foreign and security policy to more effective constitutional and judicial constraints, corresponding better to law's intrinsic claim to justice.[12] The self-conception of Europe and of EU law remains contested, however, as reflected in the Lisbon Treaty's Preamble beginning with "His Majesty the King of the Belgians" and committing European majesties, Presidents and government representatives "to enhancing the efficiency and democratic legitimacy of the Union". The decision to avoid publication – in the EU's Official Journal – of a consolidated text of the EU Treaties prior to ratification of the Lisbon Treaty confirmed not only the criticism (e.g. by *Giuliano Amato*) that the EU Reform Treaty was deliberately made unreadable for EU citizens so as to avoid calls for referendums; it also showed how *Machiavellian opportunism* often trumps Europe's legal ideals (e.g. of democratic self-governance) and political discourse (e.g. about Europe's borders *vis-à-vis* "others"). As tensions between rational egoism and limited social reasonableness are the *condicio humana*, the perennial task of limiting abuses of power through multilevel constitutionalism will remain Europe's finality. The more EU citizens exercise their freedoms in relations with third countries (e.g. by travelling abroad and consuming im-

---

10 Cf. *La Torre* (2007). On emergency legislation and jurisprudence relating to the "war on terror", see *Posner* (2006). On failures of international law, see *Koskenniemi* (2004).

11 On the emergence of a new "legal culture" in Europe, see *Gessner / Nelken* (2006).

12 On my long-standing criticism of the EC's foreign policy and security constitution, see *Petersmann* (1996).

ported goods), the more it will be necessary to "constitutionalise" also the external relations law of the EU (e.g. by means of judicial protection of human rights *vis-à-vis* UN Security Council decisions) as well as to "internationalise" domestic laws for the benefit of EU citizens (e.g. by enabling EU citizens to rely on rule of law also in the EU's external relations, including EU compliance with its WTO obligations).[13]

As stated in its Preamble, the consolidated Treaty on European Union "mark(s) a new stage in the process of European integration", whose final status remains unforeseeable. The reference, in the Preamble's second paragraph, to "the universal values of the inviolable and inalienable rights of the human person, freedom, democracy, equality and the rule of law" as having developed from "the cultural, religious and humanist inheritance of Europe" identifies the final sources of European values: according to Article 2 TEU-L, "(t)he Union is founded on the values of respect for human dignity, freedom, democracy, equality, the rule of law and respect for human rights". This "constitutional imperative" requires future

---

13   The interrelationships between these two tasks of citizen-oriented constitutionalism (in the sense of a legal method for protecting citizen rights at all levels of national and international governance) – i.e. the need for (1) not only justifying and interpreting international law rules in terms of their "constitutional functions" for protecting constitutional citizen rights, but also (2) for interpreting domestic laws in conformity with democratically ratified international treaties for the collective supply of international public goods – have long been, and continue to be, neglected, cf: *Petersmann* (1991a). Following the fall of the Berlin wall and the universal recognition of inalienable human rights as a constitutional foundation of European and international law, my publications focused especially on the need for multilevel "constitutional democracy" protecting human rights in the collective supply of international public goods, including judicial protection of citizens as legal subjects also of international law and of their mutually beneficial economic co-operation in and among civil societies, cf. *Petersmann* (1995). Most Europeans continue to argue not only for state-centred constitutionalism (based on "We the People") rather than for rights-based constitutionalism proceeding from normative individualism and civil society as foundational values for multilevel self-governance beyond the state; they also perceive international law as deriving its legitimacy from state consent, and rarely examine the collective action problems of the collective supply of international public goods beyond the EU from constitutional perspectives.

European integration to constantly review the state-centred international law rules from the perspective of human rights and constitutional safeguards of EU citizens *vis-à-vis* the ubiquitous abuses of private and public, national and international governance powers. The perennial constitutional question – what do human rights, democracy and rule of law mean in practical terms for constructing multilevel governance in Europe? – remains inevitably contested among EU citizens and their governments, even though the EU Charter of Fundamental Rights suggests a broader political consensus on rights-based democratic self-governance in the EU than, e.g., in the United States.[14] The third paragraph of the Preamble of the TEU-L recalls the dark sides of Europe's failures to protect citizen rights: Security ("the historic importance of the ending of the division of the European continent and the need to create firm bases for the construction of the future Europe") and peaceful "unity in diversity" remain the most important reasons for the European integration project. As illustrated by the jurisprudence of the European courts on judicial protection of human rights *vis-à-vis* UN Security Council measures against alleged terrorists, the EU's "overlapping consensus" on "inalienable" human rights, and the indeterminacy of Europe's multilevel constitutionalism, are likely to remain under constant challenge, notably in the EU's external relations and "foreign policy constitution".

III. European Constitutional Pluralism Entails Perennial Struggles by EU Citizens for their Self-Governance

All 27 EU Member States are constitutional democracies with diverse legal and political traditions (e.g. in terms of national peoples

---

14   On the pervasive disagreement among conservatives and democrats on human rights and democracy inside the US see *Dworkin* (2006), who argues for redefining the basis of American constitutionalism proceeding from two basic principles of human dignity, i.e. first, that each human life is intrinsically and equally valuable and, second, that each person has an inalienable personal responsibility for realizing her unique potential and human values in her own life. Arguably, rights-based, multilevel European constitutionalism protects equal citizen rights through more precise constitutional restraints (e.g. in terms of individual rights, corresponding public policy objectives, multilevel institutional and procedural constraints) than state-centred legal positivism and economic utilitarianism.

and citizenships). Legal and constitutional pluralism also charac-
terise the diverse European legal regimes (e.g. of EU law, EEA law,
the ECHR) and international legal systems (e.g. of lawmaking and
adjudication in worldwide organisations). The common foundation
of modern "constitutional pluralism" in inalienable human rights –
conceptualised as deriving from respect for human dignity (e.g. in
the sense of respect for human autonomy and equality as a source
of moral responsibility) rather than from state consent – appears to
be legally irreversible in European law, notwithstanding diverse
conceptions of human dignity (e.g. regarding its relationship to god
and freedom of religion). Yet the national and international legislative, administrative and judicial protection of individual freedoms
and other fundamental rights may legitimately differ depending on
the relevant legal and political contexts in diverse national and international jurisdictions. Democratic constitutionalism is founded
on human rights, but may legitimately differ among diverse national jurisdictions and international governance systems. The pervasive collective action problems in intergovernmental organisations, as well as the problems of co-ordinating competing private
and public, national and international legal regimes, confirm how
reliance on state consent – rather than on common constitutional
principles and citizen interests (e.g. in open markets and rule of law
promoting consumer welfare) – can impede international integration and effective protection of human rights.[15]

The EU Treaty (e.g. in Articles 1 and 2 as revised) describes
the EU as a union among Member States, "an ever closer union
among the peoples of Europe", a citizen-driven internal market and
an "area of freedom, security and justice... in which the free

---

15 Due to the diversity of national constitutional traditions, domestic
implementation of international rules is likely always to remain diverse. For example, should fundamental rights be interpreted and applied by way of balancing (as "optimization precepts" as proposed by
Alexy), or should they be considered as "trumps" (*Dworkin*) and de-
finitive rules which cannot be overruled in certain situations by public policies and public goods? Are "market freedoms" and other fundamental freedoms necessary consequences of respect for human liberty, or are they "Kitsch" (*Koskenniemi*) that should be replaced by
more flexible utilitarianism? On the diversity of domestic legislation
and adjudication implementing international economic rules, see *Hilf
/ Petersmann* (1993). On the diverse conceptions of constitutional
rights, see *Kumm* (2007).

movement of persons is ensured" by legal protection of individual freedoms and other fundamental rights. The legal relationships between these different value premises (e.g. state sovereignty, popular sovereignty, individual sovereignty) are likely always to remain contested. Depending on their respective values (e.g. normative individualism versus communitarian values) and self-interests (e.g. private self-regulation versus government intervention), EU citizens and their political representatives often legitimately disagree on how the diverse EU actors (e.g. state governments, EU institutions, EU citizens, their parliamentary representatives, non-governmental civil society institutions) should interpret and further develop the state-centred, intergovernmental, supranational and citizen-oriented dimensions of EU law and policies. The foundational "values of respect for human dignity, freedom, democracy, equality, the rule of law and respect for human rights" (Article 2 TEU-L), and recognition of EU citizens as democratic owners of EU law and institutions, justify not only struggles by EU citizens as "democratic principals" against abuses of power by national and international governance agents (in the sense of *R. Jhering's Kampf ums Recht*). National and international courts are also increasingly requested to act as "constitutional guardians" reconciling conflicts among competing constitutional rights (e.g. freedoms of trade versus human rights, freedom of services and establishment versus labour rights) so as to protect citizen rights against selfish power politics (e.g. including the frequent violations of the EC's WTO obligations for rules-based common commercial and agricultural policies maximizing consumer welfare).[16] The empowerment of EU citizens through multilevel, rights-based constitutionalism entails that such perennial conflicts among rational self-interests of citizens (e.g. in the rule of law) and the self-interests of their rulers (e.g. in limiting their judicial accountability) will remain part of the "finality" of the EU, calling for ever stronger "constitutional safeguards" protecting rule of law and the legitimacy of European integration.

IV. Integration through Law as Finality – Rule of Whose Law?

Post-war European integration has resulted from law rather than from culture. Law – as the most effective instrument for preventing conflicts of interests and settling disputes among individuals and

---

16   Cf. *Petersmann* (2008b).

governments with conflicting interests – is part of the "finality" of the EU. The more multilevel governance for the collective supply of international public goods leads to multilevel structures of competing legal orders, the more traditional concepts of the "rule of law" have become contested. EU law acknowledges not only that equal freedoms, human rights and democratic self-government require the "rule of law" (Article 2 TEU-L) and its judicial protection (Articles 251 ff TFEU); it also admits, and has long done so (e.g. in the existing Article 6 EU), that EU law derives its legitimacy from the protection of EU citizen rights and constitutional principles common to EU Member States rather than from "We the People", a European constitution approved by a constitutional assembly, or from state sovereignty and state consent. Since the 1970s, the EC courts have increasingly recognised this foundation of EU law in human rights, democracy and rule of law. Yet, the EC Court's characterisation of the EC as a community of law – in which "neither its Member States nor its institutions can avoid a review of the question whether the measures adopted by them are in conformity with the basic constitutional charter, the Treaty. In particular, … the Treaty established a complete system of legal remedies"[17] – is hardly consistent with reality. The ECJ's restrictive interpretation of EC provisions on individual access to the Court, the Court's political refusal to review EC trade restrictions on the basis of the EC's worldwide GATT and WTO obligations, and the case law of national courts on the constitutional limits of their judicial compliance with EU law illustrate the political limits of the rule of law inside the EU; rights-based democracy and rule of law remain contested in important areas of EU integration, to the detriment of EU citizens and their legal security.

The reality of constitutional pluralism is also illustrated by the fact that the relationships between national laws, European treaty regimes and international treaties can often no longer be explained by formal conflict rules (such as *lex specialis, lex posterior, lex superior*) and, arguably, challenge the state-centred "rules of recognition" of the Westphalian system of international law. The authority of EU law depends not only on the Reform Treaty's hidden claim (in Declaration 17) to legal primacy. National courts rightly insist on reviewing the legal, jurisdictional, democratic and substantive legitimacy of EC acts in terms of respect for fundamental rights and

---

17   Case 294/83, *Les Verts* v *Parliament* [1986] ECR 1339, para. 23.

democratic procedures.[18] The foundation of EU law on human
rights deriving from respect for human dignity, as explicitly recognised in the EU Charter of Fundamental Rights[19] as well as in Article 2 TEU-L, requires respect for this European reality of multilevel
constitutional pluralism, for example by interpreting private law,
state law, EU law and international law for the collective supply of
international public goods as complementary instruments for individual and democratic self-governance, with due respect for judicial
"balancing" of competing principles in concrete disputes and for
democratic "margins of appreciation" concerning domestic legislation implementing international law. The increasingly citizen-oriented conceptions of European and international law, the "balancing paradigms" applied by ever more national and international
courts, the internationalisation of "deliberative democracy", and the
changing "political equilibria" (as reflected in the numerous compromises leading to the 2007 Lisbon Treaty) entail that legal for-
malism often no longer offers legitimate criteria for defining the
'rule of law' in the interface between national, transnational and
international legal systems.[20]

For example, the presumption that legality requires applying
EU law may be rebutted by countervailing constitutional principles
of greater weight; as argued by national constitutional courts in

---

18   Cf. *Kumm* (2005).

19   On respect for human dignity and inalienable human rights as a con-
     stitutional foundation not only of European law, but also of modern
     international law, see *Petersmann* (2006). On the implications of the
     universal recognition of vaguely defined human rights, and of their
     diverse "constitutional concretisation" in national and regional legal
     systems (e.g. in the EC guarantees of fundamental freedoms), for
     "rules of recognition" and the judicial function, see *Petersmann*,
     (2008a).

20   Since human rights have become recognised as an integral part of EU
     law and international law, the debates between positivists (denying
     that moral values play any role in the determination of legal validity)
     and non-positivists (affirming the opposite thesis) are increasingly
     replaced by legal discourse on the 'constitutional principles' common
     to national laws, EU law and international law. On the insight that
     legal normativity cannot be something external to human thinking
     that can be studied "from the outside" as social facts, and that our
     knowledge of the law is the outcome of "reflexive" judging con-
     strained by reasons, see *Pavlakos* (2007).

some EU Member States, effective protection of fundamental rights of citizens against EU acts, respect for jurisdictional subsidiarity (Article 5 TEU-L) and procedural democratic legitimacy may justify constitutional review of EC acts by national courts, based on "balancing" of common, national as well as European constitutional principles and their public, deliberative explication. Even if the 'rule of law' remains a precondition of the legitimacy and success of European integration and part of the EU's *finalité*, its legal conception (e.g. as being founded in state consent, EU institutions, peoples, EU citizenship, human rights) will remain contextual and contested. It took European civilisation more than 3,000 years to "invent" the five major principles of national constitutionalism (legality, division of power, human rights, democratic governance, "checks and balances" among governance powers)[21] which finally enabled an increasing number of European citizens and states to co-operate in freedom and peace during the second half of the 20th century, albeit in the continuing shadow of unstable "balances of power". It remains uncertain whether EU citizens will ever learn how to realise the *Kant*ian dream of "perpetual peace" across Europe, which (according to *Kant*) depends on ever more precise, multilevel constitutional protection of equal freedoms *vis-à-vis* the perennial abuses of power in all human interactions at national, transnational and international levels. Re-conceiving the fragmented international legal system from a constitutional perspective as a necessary instrument for protecting human rights in transnational relations will challenge not only state-centred international law doctrines (e.g. perceiving international economic law as mere "global administrative law"), but also introverted, nationalist biases in constitutional law doctrines and resultant "constitutional failures" in nation states.[22] Europe's legal recognition and judicial empowerment of citizens as subjects of international law offer effective incentives for governments to restructure international law in con-

---

21 On the reality of "mixed constitutions" resulting from these five "political inventions", see *Riklin* (2006).

22 Cf. *Petersmann* (1991b). Most international lawyers continue to shy away from such "constitutional approaches" to international law as a necessary instrument for protecting human rights of citizens, just as most national constitutional lawyers continue to shy away from recognizing national constitutions as merely "partial constitutions" that cannot unilaterally protect human rights across national frontiers.

formity with the cosmopolitan ideal of mutually complementary national, transnational and international constitutional restraints promoting procedural as well as substantive justice in the transnational co-operation among citizens.

V. *Sisyphus* and the Perennial "Paradox of Liberty"

Similar to the existing Article 6 EU which names "liberty" as the first principle on which "the Union is founded", Article 2 TEU-L (following the entry into force of the Lisbon Treaty) lists "respect for human dignity" and "freedom" before other foundational principles of the EU. This "constitutional pre-commitment" to liberty subject to constitutional restraints – which is in conformity with modern theories of justice (from *Kant* to *Rawls*), prioritizing equal individual freedoms as a "first principle of justice" deriving from respect for human dignity (e.g. in the sense of individual autonomy, reasonableness and responsibility) – is likely to remain an irreversible part of constitutional law. However, the tensions between rational egoism, limited social reasonableness and "constitutional ignorance" (*Hayek*) of individuals, and their competition for scarce and arbitrarily distributed resources, entail inevitably conflicts of interests and related disputes (e.g. over the interpretation of EU rules) as a finality of European integration. Individual and collective freedoms are not only preconditions of human self-development and indispensable incentives for social progress (e.g. in terms of learning, development of human capacities and opportunities); they also risk destroying themselves through selfishness and abuses of power unless freedom of choice is constitutionally restrained. The myths of *Sisyphus* and *Ulysses* (whom some myths describe as the son of Sisyphus in view of the mythical cleverness of both) explain why constitutional self-restraints offer the only way out of this human and European dilemma.

The EU Treaties remain the only multilateral treaties regulating this "paradox of liberty" through comprehensive, multilevel constitutional guarantees and restraints of private and public freedoms at national, transnational and international levels. EU citizenship confers on citizens of EU Member States transnational freedoms and complementary rights (cf. Article 20 TFEU) which citizens never enjoyed before. By making the EU Charter of Fundamental Rights legally binding, providing for EU membership in the European Convention on Human Rights, and by broadening procedural and substantive EU citizen rights, the Lisbon Treaty will further strengthen legal and judicial protection of equal freedoms in the European integration process. Paradoxically, the effectiveness of these individual freedoms depends on the EU's constitutional and judicial restraints of abuses of private freedoms (e.g. market freedoms restrained by EU competition law, common market law, environmental and social law) as well as of collective public freedoms of Member States and EU institutions. This citizen-oriented, multilevel constitutionalism has transformed Europe into a unique "civilian power", whose civilizing effects on ever more neighbouring countries offer the most persuasive alternative to the state-centred, hegemonic policies prevailing outside Europe.[23] The recent EU measures against terrorist threats, illegal immigration, and against the failures in international financial market supervision (e.g. of lax lending standards, complex "credit products") illustrate that abuses of freedom, as well as of countervailing measures, will remain perennial, constitutional challenges for EU law and policies.

VI. *Janus* and the Perennial "Paradox of Equality"

The inherent tensions between equal human rights, unequal distribution of resources (including human capacities) and territorial fragmentation of constitutional systems are another perennial problem of European law. European integration is a response to centuries of welfare-reducing border discrimination and other discriminatory state regulations, for example defining citizen rights by exclusion and discrimination of "the others." Like the double-faced Roman god and guardian of doors *Janus*, the EU's requirements of non-discriminatory treatment of EU citizens (cf. Articles 18 ff TFEU), and the EU's positive obligations "to eliminate inequalities, and to promote equality, between men and women" (Article 8 TFEU) and "combat discrimination" (Article 10 TFEU), aim at reconciling the outside with the inside in mutually beneficial ways. The EC Court continues to progressively extend the scope of the general and specific EC prohibitions (e.g. in Article 12 EC) of "discrimination on grounds of nationality" to ever more areas of EC law, far beyond the single market paradigm.[24] The Lisbon Treaty, for example by transforming the "equality rights" of the Charter of Fundamental Rights (Articles 20 ff) into positive EU law, defines

---

23   Cf. *Joerges / Petersmann* (2006).

24   Cf. *Griller* (2006), 204.

the "European identity" in uniquely egalitarian, cosmopolitan and rights-based ways. In conformity with *Robert Schuman*'s famous Declaration of May 1950 that Europe "will be built through concrete achievements which first create a *de facto* solidarity", the progressive realisation of these egalitarian and redistributive dimensions of European integration must be accompanied by the development of a European civic identity, inducing citizens, governments and courts "to extend civic solidarity beyond their respective national borders with the goal of achieving mutual inclusion".[25]

The Lisbon Treaty's shelving of the "symbols of the Union" (as defined in Article I-8 of the 2004 Treaty establishing a Constitution for Europe), and its requirement to "respect the equality of Member States before the Treaties as well as their national identities" and "territorial integrity" (Article 4 TEU-L), underline that the EU project remains based on non-discriminatory competition (e.g. in the single market) among citizens wishing to preserve diverse EU Member States and distinct national peoples. The new legal, parliamentary and judicial safeguards to ensure that "the use of Union competences is governed by the principles of subsidiarity and proportionality" (Article 5 TEU-L), and the EC Court's future jurisdiction to secure respect of the Charter of Fundamental Rights in all acts of the EU, will reinforce not only the need for multilevel co-operation and judicial clarification of the constitutional principles common to European and national laws, but also the need to respect the often legitimately diverse normative conceptions among citizens as well as among their national and EU governance agents. Reconciling the cosmopolitan human rights principles of EU law with its exclusive, national and EU citizenship principles will remain a constant constitutional challenge (e.g. in the detention of illegal immigrants, constitutional tolerance *vis-à-vis* Muslim minorities inside EU Member States, recognition of non-territorial nationality claims by the Roma people and other minorities).

VII. Europe's 'Overlapping Consensus': 'United in Diversity'

According to *Rawls*, "in a constitutional regime with judicial review, public reason is the reason of its supreme court"; it is of constitutional importance for the "overlapping, constitutional consen-

---

25 On this need for developing a European identity, see *Habermas* (2006), chapter 6.

sus" necessary for a stable and just society among free, equal and rational citizens who tend to be deeply divided by conflicting moral, religious and philosophical doctrines.[26] The citizen-oriented interpretations of the intergovernmental European integration agreements, like other cosmopolitan and constitutional dimensions of European law, are largely due to the judicial protection of individual rights by European and national courts. The "public reason" (*J. Rawls*) of EU law and its interpretation by "(inter)governmental reasoning" are increasingly challenged by multilevel "judicial reasoning" and transnational "deliberative democracy". The legitimacy and persistence of widespread, reasonable disagreement among free citizens, as well as among their political representatives, about human rights, justice and law imply that multilevel judicial discourse and "balancing" of constitutional principles[27] will often remain the most legitimate means of clarifying indeterminate European legal rules and principles. Theories of justice, national constitutions, EU law and public international law offer no clear answers to many European and worldwide integration problems. International agreements among states with diverse constitutional traditions often depend on the use of "constructive ambiguity" and on delegation of the clarification of indeterminate rules to independent and impartial courts. The "common law approach" to European constitutional law, as illustrated by the judicial clarification and protection of "constitutional principles" common to the EU and its Member States, has proven not only more successful than over-ambitious codification of "treaty constitutions" that remain incomprehensible to most EU citizens. Pragmatic focus on the limited "overlapping consensus" among EU citizens with divergent moral, legal and political conceptions is also more respectful of citizens in the face of their reasonable disagreement on the constitution and finality of European integration.

---

26 *Rawls* (1993), 231 *et seq.*

27 Principles differ from the "if-then" structure of legal rules of conduct by their more general definition of essential legal values underlying rules of conduct.

VIII. Conclusion: Europe's Multilevel Democratic Self-Governance Depends on Respect for Reasonable Disagreement

International trade law is one of the oldest branches of international law because markets offer decentralised information, co-ordination and sanctioning mechanisms promoting mutually beneficial co-operation without requiring citizens and governments to relinquish their diverse conceptions of law and social justice. The progressive transformation of the EC's customs union into a common market and an economic and monetary union was rendered possible by pragmatic agreements on a constitutional framework that respected reasonable disagreement among EU governments and citizens. This paper has discussed six "constitutional finalities" emerging from European integration: the multilevel constitutionalism and inescapable limits of EU law in its attempt to limit power politics (chapters I-II); the perennial struggles for competing political conceptions and rights of EU citizens (chapter III); the need for multilevel judicial clarification and "balancing" of national and European constitutional principles necessary for the coherence and legitimacy of multilevel governance based on "rule of law" in Europe (chapter IV); the "constitutional paradox of liberty" requiring ever more constitutional limitations of liberty in the national, transnational and international co-operation among citizens and their multilevel self-governance (chapter V); the "constitutional paradox of equality" requiring a reduction of the pervasive inequalities among EU citizens and the exclusion of others (chapter VI); and the wisdom of limiting the "overlapping constitutional consensus" among EU citizens and their political agents on essential human rights and constitutional principles, with due respect for pervasive and persistent, reasonable disagreement about social and legal justice (chapter VII).[28] The future of European integration – as a treaty-based, constitutional project guided by public reasoning and democratic contestation – will depend on protecting human rights, including participatory and 'deliberative democracy', as the constitutional core of the European identity.

The limited purpose of this contribution was to argue that, rather than discrediting "finality" as another "F word" in favour of

---

28 On the creative forces of reasonable disagreement in law, see *Besson*, (2005).

pragmatic 'wait-and-see' attitudes,[29] reflections about "finality" may help identify the reasonable limits and perennial, constitutional problems of EU law. For example, discourse about a unitarian 'United States of Europe' and one 'European people' has, fortunately, become as rare as nationalist discourse ignoring the past "governance failures" of European nation states. Of course, there are other "finalities" of European integration than those discussed above, such as:

- the constitutional dependence of European integration on a division of powers;
- the ever more complex constitutional "checks and balances" in the EU;
- *demoi*-cratic participation of "the peoples of Europe" (Art. 1 TEU-L) in the exercise of EU governance;
- rights-based rather than communitarian forms of European citizenship (in the sense of "A Citizen's Europe" that "places the individual at the heart of its activities", as declared in the Preamble of the EU Charter of Fundamental Rights);
- the perennial need for market regulation in response to changing citizen demand for public goods (e.g. protecting 'sustainable development'); and
- the ever increasing importance of international law and international governance institutions as indispensable instruments for the collective supply of international public goods demanded by European citizens.

Just as past successes of European integration resulted from combining the pragmatic "Monnet method" and constitutional "common law approaches" with more ambitious, federalist conceptions of integration (e.g. on legal primacy, direct effect and direct applicability of EC Treaty provisions), so political and legal "trial and error" will remain a *finalité* of future European integration. The absence of dogmatic preconceptions has enabled European integration to develop into the most successful international legal framework for peaceful co-operation among citizens across state borders, offering a model also beyond Europe for reducing the pervasive

---

29 Cf. *Wallace* (2000), 139, 142: "The notion that, on some distant horizon, an 'end-state' of perfect integration exists simply carries little cogency in the British discussion. It seems too abstract, too speculative, and, hence, not a productive area of debate."

collective action problems in the international supply of public goods. Future European generations, in searching answers to the perennial question *'Quo vadis, Europa?'*, can no longer ignore – but have to build on – the constitutional structures that emerged from half a century of uniquely successful European integration, with due respect for reasonable disagreement on how European integration should further evolve. Even if future European integration should succeed in making some of its constitutional achievements an irreversible foundation of Europe's 'overlapping consensus', the 'future of European Constitutionalism' (i.e. the subject of this conference) remains unforeseeable and contested.

References

Samantha Besson (2005), The Morality of Conflict. Reasonable Disagreement and the Law, Oxford (Hart) 2005.

Ronald Dworkin (2006), Is Democracy Possible Here? Principles for a new political debate, Princeton/NJ (Princeton University Press) 2006.

Volkmar Gessner / David Nelken (eds.) (2006), European Ways of Law. Towards a European Sociology of Law, Oxford (Hart) 2006.

Stefan Griller (2006) Vom Diskriminierungsverbot zur Grundrechtsgemeinschaft? Oder: von der ungebrochenen Rechtsfortbildungskraft des EuGH, in: *Metin Akyürek et al.* (eds.), Staat und Recht in europäischer Perspektive, Festschrift Heinz Schäffer, Vienna 2006, 203-249.

Jürgen Habermas (2006), The Divided West, Cambridge (Polity Press) 2006.

Meinhard Hilf / Ernst-Ulrich Petersmann (eds.) (1993), National Constitutions and International Economic Law (= Studies in transnational economic law, Vol. 8), Deventer (Kluwer) 1993.

Christian Joerges / Yves Mény / Joseph H. Weiler (eds.) (2000), What Kind of Constitution for What Kind of Polity? Responses to Joschka Fischer, Florence (Robert Schuman Centre) 2000.

Christian Joerges / Ernst-Ulrich Petersmann (eds.) (2006), Constitutionalism, Multilevel Trade Governance and Social Regulation; Oxford (Hart) 2006.

Martti Koskenniemi (2004), The Gentle Civilizer of Nations. The Rise and Fall of International Law 1870-1960, Cambridge (Cambridge University Press) 2004.

Matthias Kumm (2005), The Jurisprudence of Constitutional Conflicts, in: European Law Journal 11 (2005), 262-307.

Matthias Kumm (2007), Political Liberalism and the Structures of Rights, in: *George Pavlakos* (ed.), Law, Rights and Discourse, Oxford (Hart) 2007, 131-165.

Massimo La Torre (2007), Constitutionalism and Legal Reasoning, Dordrecht (Springer) 2007.

Anthony Pagden (ed.) (2002), The Idea of Europe: From Antiquity to the European Union, Washington/DC (Woodrow Wilson Center Press) 2002.

George Pavlakos (2007), Our Knowledge of the Law. Objectivity and Practice in Legal Theory, Oxford (Hart) 2007.

Ernst-Ulrich Petersmann (1991a), Constitutionalism, Constitutional Law and European Integration, in: *Ernst-Ulrich Petersmann* (ed.), Constitutional Problems of European Integration: EC 92, the European Economic Area and Beyond (Special Issue of – Aussenwirtschaft, 1991), 247-280.

Ernst-Ulrich Petersmann (1991b), Constitutional Functions and Constitutional Problems of International Economic Law. International and domestic foreign trade law and foreign trade policy in the United States, the European Community and Switzerland, Fribourg (Fribourg University Press) 1991.

Ernst-Ulrich Petersmann (1995), Proposals for a New Constitution of the European Union: Building-Blocks for a Constitutional Theory and Constitutional Law of the European Union, in: Common Market Law Review 28 (1995), 1123-1175.

Ernst-Ulrich Petersmann (1996), The Foreign Policy Constitution of the European Union: A Kantian Perspective, in: *Ulrich Immenga* (ed.), Festschrift für Ernst-Joachim Mestmäcker, Baden-Baden (Nomos) 1996, 433-447.

Ernst-Ulrich Petersmann (1997), How to Reform the UN System? Constitutionalism, International Law and International Organizations, in: Leiden Journal of International Law 10 (1997), 421-474.

Ernst-Ulrich Petersmann (2006), Human Rights, Markets and Economic Welfare: Constitutional Functions of the Emerging UN Human Rights Constitution, in: *Christine Breining-Kaufmann / Thomas Cottier* (eds.), International Trade and Human Rights, Ann Arbor/MI (University of Michigan Press) 2006, 29-67.

Ernst-Ulrich Petersmann (2008a), Multilevel Constitutionalism and Judicial Protection of Freedom and Justice in the International Economic Law of the EC, in: *Anthony Arnull / Piet Eeckhout / Takis Tridimas* (eds.), Continuity and Change in EU Law. Liber amicorum Francis Jacobs, Oxford (Oxford University Press) 2008, 338-353.

Ernst-Ulrich Petersmann (2008b), Multilevel Judicial Governance as Guardian of the Constitutional Unity of International Law, in: Loyola International and Comparative Law Review 29 (2008) (forthcoming).

Richard A. Posner (2006), Not a Suicide Pact. The Constitution in a Time of National Emergency, Oxford (Oxford University Press) 2006.

John Rawls (1971), A Theory of Justice, Cambridge/MA (Harvard University Press) 1971.

John Rawls (1993), Political Liberalism, New York (Columbia University Press) 1993.

Alois Riklin (2006), Machtteilung. Geschichte der Mischverfassung., Darmstadt (Wissenschaftliche Buchgesellschaft) 2006.

Helen Wallace (2000), Possible Futures for the European Union: A British Reaction, in: *Christian Joerges / Yves Mény / Joseph H. Weiler* (eds.) (2000), What Kind of Constitution for What Kind of Polity? Responses to Joschka Fischer, Florence (Robert Schuman Centre) 2000, 139-149.

Index

About the Authors of this Volume

Catherine Barnard MA (Cantab), LLM (EUI), PhD (Cantab) is a Reader in EU Law at the University of Cambridge and a fellow of Trinity College. She also holds a *Jean Monnet* chair of European Law. She is co-director of the Centre for European Legal Studies at Cambridge.

José María Beneyto is Professor of International Law, European Law and International Relations at the *Universidad San Pablo* in Madrid. He is Director of the Institute for European Studies at that university and holds a *Jean Monnet* chair.

Hervé Bribosia is Head of research and scientific co-operation at the *Centre Virtuel de la Connaissance sur l'Europe* in Luxembourg, and Guest Professor at the University of Paris I (Panthéon-Sorbonne).

Dominic Coppens is Junior Member of the Leuven Centre for Global Governance Studies and Assistant at the Institute for International Law, Leuven University.

Paul Craig is Professor of English Law at the St. John's College of the University of Oxford.

Stefan Griller is *Jean Monnet*-Professor for European Law at the Europainstitut of *Wirtschaftsuniversität*, Vienna. He was founding President of ECSA Austria in 1996 and since 2002 serves as its Secretary General. His paper was prepared during his stay as a *Fernand Braudel* Scholar at the EUI in Florence.

Marcel Kau holds a Ph.D. from Konstanz University and an LL.M. from Georgetown University. Currently he works on his habilitation in public law and is assistant researcher at the chair of Prof. Dr. Dr. h.c. *Kay Hailbronner* at the University of Konstanz / Germany.

Christine Kaddous studied at Neuchâtel, Cambridge / UK and at the Free University of Brussels. She teaches EU Law at Geneva where she holds a *Jean Monnet* chair and is Director of the *Centre d'études juridiques européennes*. She publishes extensively on EU external relations.

Jean-Victor Louis, honorary professor of the Free University of Brussels, former president its Institute of European Studies, honorary general counsel of the Belgian National Bank, former professor at the EUI, editor of the *Cahiers de droit européen*, Dr. h.c. (Paris II (Panthéon-Assas)).

Bart Meesters is Junior Member of the Leuven Centre for Global Governance Studies and Researcher at the Fund for Scientific Research-Flanders (FWO) and at the Institute for International Law, Leuven University.

Ingolf Pernice Professor Dr. jur. Dr. h.c., holds a Chair for public, international and European Law of the Humbodt-University of Berlin. He is managing director of the *Walter Hallstein* Institute for European Constitutional Law (WHI) of the Humboldt-University of Berlin.

Ernst-Ulrich Petersmann is Professor of International and European Law at the European University Institute, Florence, and Head of its Law Department.

Paolo Ponzano, EU official since 1971. Before, he assisted *Ricardo Monaco* at the University of Rome and *Altiero Spinelli*. He was Director for Relations with the Council, Director of the Task Force on the future of the Union, alternate member of the European Convention, Director for Institutional Affairs and Better Regulation and Senior Fellow at the RSCAS. Currently, he is the Principal Adviser to the Secretary General for Institutional Issues.

Antonio Sáinz de Vicuña is General Counsel of the European Central Bank in Frankfurt and Director of the Bank's Legal Service.

Bruno de Witte is Professor of European Union law at the European University Institute in Florence.

Jan Wouters is Professor of International Law and International Organizations, Director, Leuven Centre for Global Governance Studies and Institute for International Law, Leuven University; *Of Counsel,* Linklaters, Brussels. His paper was prepared during his stay as a *Fernand Braudel* Scholar at the EUI in Florence.

Jacques Ziller is Professor of Comparative Public Law at the EUI in Florence, holds the joint chair at the RSCAS and is Professor for European Law at the University of Pavia. Previously at he taught at the University Paris I (Panthéon-Sorbonne).